The Transformation of Central Asia

States and Societies from Soviet Rule to Independence

The Transformation of Central Asia

States and Societies from Soviet Rule to Independence

Editor

Pauline Jones Luong

(Published in collaboration with Cornell University Press)

Manas Publications
New Delhi - 110 002 (India)

MANAS PUBLICATIONS
(Publishers, Distributors, Importers & Exporters)
4858, Prahlad Street,
24, Ansari Road, Darya Ganj,
New Delhi - 110 002 (INDIA)
Ph.: 23260783, 23265523 (O); 27131660(R)
Fax: 011- 23272766
E-mail: manaspublications@vsnl.com

Published in collaboration with Cornell University Press

2005

ISBN 81-7049-257-2
Rs. 695/-

Printed in India at
Nice Printing Press, Delhi
and Published by Mrs. Suman Lata for
Manas Publications, 4858, Prahlad Street,
24, Ansari Road, Daryaganj,
New Delhi 110002 (INDIA)

For my father

ROBERT W. JONES

CENTRAL ASIA
RUSSIAN FEDERATION
KAZAKHSTAN
UZBEKISTAN
TURKMENISTAN
KYRGYZSTAN
TAJIKISTAN
AFGHANISTAN
PAKISTAN
INDIA
CHINA
MONGOLIA
ISLAMIC REPUBLIC OF IRAN
GEORGIA
ARMENIA
AZERBAIJAN
UKRAINE
Caspian Sea
Aral Sea
Lake Balqash
Ysyk Köl
Kara Bogaz Gol
Astana
Almaty
Bishkek
Tashkent
Dushanbe
Ashgabat
Kabul
Tehrān
Baku
Tbilisi
Yerevan
Perm'
Izhevsk
Kazan'
Ufa
Samara
Togliatti
Penza
Saratov
Voronezh
Volgograd
Rostov na Donu
Astrakhan'
Orenburg
Orsk
Magnitogorsk
Chelyabinsk
Yekaterinburg
Tyumen'
Kurgan
Omsk
Novosibirsk
Tomsk
Krasnoyarsk
Novokuznetsk
Barnaul
Rubtsovsk
Oral
Aqtöbe
Atyraū
Aqtaū
Qostanay
Rūdnyy
Petropavl
Köshetau
Pavlodar
Semey
Öskemen
Temirtaū
Qaraghandy
Zaysan
Zhezqazghan
Taldyqorghan
Qyzylorda
Zhambyl
Shymkent
Nukus
Urganch
Dashhowuz
Türkmenbashi
Bukhoro
Samarqand
Qarshi
Chärjew
Mary
Chirchiq
Angren
Qūqon
Namangan
Osh
Farghona
Kashi
Ürümqi
Qondūz
Baghlān
Herāt
Mashhad
Rasht
Tabrīz
Volga
Oka
Sura
Don
Khoper
Vyatka
Ural
Tura
Tobol
Irtysh
Esil
Nura
Sarysu
Turgay
Irgiz
Zhayyq
Terek
Ob
Tom'
Katun
Biya
Chulym
Yenisey
Ertis
Ertix
Ili
Shu
Syr Darya
Amu Darya
Zeravshan
Karakumsk Canal
Murgab
Atrak
Tarim
Toxkan
Yarkant
Hotan
0 200 400 600 800 km
0 100 200 300 400 500 mi
The boundaries and names shown on this map do not imply official endorsement or acceptance by the United Nations.

Contents

Acknowledgments

I am grateful to all of those who have made this edited volume possible. It initially began as a lecture series, the Olin Critical Issues Lecture Series, that I co-organized with John Schoeberlein at Harvard University in the spring of 2001, with the financial and logistical support of the Olin Foundation and the Davis Center for Russian and Eurasian Studies at Harvard University, respectively. I am especially indebted to Timothy Colton (Morris and Anna Feldberg Professor of Government and Director, Davis Center for Russian and Eurasian Studies, Harvard University) and Lisbeth Tarlow (Associate Director, Davis Center for Russian and Eurasian Studies, Harvard University) for having invited John and me to co-organize the Olin series for 2000–2001 on a theme related to Central Asia. They, along with John, also supported my subsequent efforts to convert this lecture series into an edited volume. The administrative costs of editing a volume can be enormous, yet the efficiency, professionalism, and friendliness of the Davis Center staff, particularly Heidi Penix and Melissa Griggs, kept these to an absolute minimum. Roger Haydon at Cornell University Press and two anonymous reviewers were also instrumental in supporting and shaping the final version of this edited volume. Finally, I am thankful for having had the good fortune of choosing, with John's assistance, an outstanding collection of contributors, who made the editing of this volume educational, rewarding, and pleasurable. I am quite grateful for their scholarship, their collegiality, and their friendship.

For several years now, I have been wholly invested in furthering the empirical and theoretical basis of my profession's collective understanding of former Soviet Central Asia. With this edited volume, I hope to further these broader goals by advancing existing knowledge about the newly independent states and societies that constitute former Soviet Central Asia and demonstrating that the essays collected here significantly contribute to theories of the state and state-societal relations. As such, it is dedicated to my father, Robert W. Jones, who always taught me that whatever I chose to do in life, the truest measure of my achievements would be whether I had "left something better than it was when I had found it."

List of Acronyms

BONGO	Business-Oriented NGO
CASDIN	Central Asia Sustainable Development Information Network
DOTS	Directly Observed Treatment Short Course
ECOSAN	International Ecology and Health Foundation
GEF	Global Environment Facility
GONGO	Government-Organized NGO
HIVOS	International Humanist Institute for Cooperation with Developing Countries (a Dutch NGO)
ICAS	Interstate Council for Addressing the Aral Sea Crisis
IFAS	International Fund for the Aral Sea
INTRAC	International NGO Training and Research Centre
ISAR	Initiative for Social Action and Renewal in Eurasia
KPSS	Communist Party of the Soviet Union
KPUz	Communist Party of Uzbekistan
MVES	Ministry of Foreign Economic Relations
NBU	National Bank of Uzbekistan
NDPU	National Democratic Party of Uzbekistan (successor to the KPUz)
NEAP	National Environmental Action Plan
NGO	Nongovernmental Organization
NOVIB	Netherlands Organization for International Development Co-operation
OKIOC	Offshore Kazakhstan International Operating Company
OSI	Open Society Institute
SDC	Sustainable Development Commission
TACIS	Technical Assistance to the Commonwealth of Independent States
UNDP	United Nations Development Program
UNVP	United Nations Development Program/United Nations Volunteer Program

UNEP	United Nations Environmental Program
UNESCO	United Nations Educational, Scientific, and Cultural Organization
UNHCR	United Nations High Commissioner for Refugees
USAID	United States Agency for International Development
WTO	World Trade Organization
ZAGS	Zapisi Aktov Grazhdanskogo Sostayaniya (Soviet civil registry)

Introduction

POLITICS IN THE PERIPHERY: COMPETING VIEWS OF CENTRAL ASIAN STATES AND SOCIETIES

PAULINE JONES LUONG

The sudden shift of global attention toward Central Asia in the aftermath of the terrorist strikes against the United States on September 11, 2001, and the subsequent war in Afghanistan has revealed not only important factors affecting international security but also the enormous gap in our understanding of these factors. Until now, Central Asia has been treated as peripheral, both in the study of the Soviet Union and in the development of social science theory. With the fall of the Soviet Union in 1991, however, the opportunity arose for statesmen and scholars — both within and outside of Central Asia — to revisit this region's past, analyze its present, and shape its future.

Independent statehood came suddenly and unexpectedly to the five former Soviet Central Asian Republics (CARs) — Kazakhstan, Kyrgyzstan, Tajikistan, Turkmenistan, and Uzbekistan. The Communist Party leadership in most of these new countries simply took up the reins of power after independence, which they acquired without a fight and, indeed, without much desire.[1] Nevertheless, they were faced with the daunting task of creating new state institutions and building legitimacy in the wake of the Soviet Union's collapsing authority. The Soviet legacy both facilitated and complicated this task of building new states where they did not previously exist. On the one hand, these leaders benefited from the trap-

The author gratefully acknowledges the following individuals for their thoughtful commentary and useful suggestions: Laura Adams, Douglas Blum, Keith Darden, Bhavna Dave, Anna Grzymala-Busse, Stephen Hanson, Roger Haydon, Keith Jones, Marianne Kamp, Eric McGlinchey, Kelly McMann, Phillip Roeder, John Schoeberlein, Valerie Sperling, Erika Weinthal, and Cynthia Werner.

1. The CARs were the last to declare their sovereignty from the Soviet Union. In addition, with the exception of President Askar Akaev in Kyrgyzstan, the leaders of the CARs supported the coup against Mikhail Gorbachev in August 1991 and an overwhelming majority of the population in these republics voted to remain part of the Soviet Union thereafter. See, e.g., Bremmer and Taras 1997; Hale 1998.

pings of statehood bequeathed by the intricate Soviet administrative and economic infrastructure, as well as from an educated population from which to recruit and train new cadre. On the other hand, they had to confront other, less positive aspects of the Soviet institutional and ideological legacy as well as to cope with a very engaged set of international organizations.

The emerging relationship between new state actors and their respective multiethnic societies in Central Asia is not being built from scratch. Rather, these nascent states were already imbued with a well-developed set of formal and informal institutions that were created and reinforced by their common experience under Soviet rule. The Communist legacy across the former Soviet Union and East Central Europe included bloated bureaucracies, centralized economic planning, and a social contract in which society offered the state political quiescence in exchange for cradle-to-grave welfare (see, e.g., Hauslohner 1987; Jowitt 1992). Yet, it also included informal institutions, such as strong regionally based patronage networks that served as the basis for allocating scarce economic and political resources and for the development of robust political identities (Jones Luong 2002).[2] Central Asian state-builders could not move forward without confronting this vast institutional web — itself a legacy of the recombinance of Soviet structures and practices with pre-Soviet ones.

Furthermore, the Central Asian states — along with their counterparts across the former Soviet Union and East Central Europe — entered an international arena that is replete with other, more powerful states as well as international templates for statehood (Grzymala-Busse and Jones Luong 2002). This is not incidental, considering the fact that international actors have a much more direct and pervasive effect on the design of domestic political and economic institutions in the post-Cold War era (Weinthal 2002). As a result, the state-building process is often influenced as much from without as it is from within.[3]

Those now studying Central Asia are uniquely situated to reexamine the states emerging in place of Soviet republics and their "mutually transforming" interactions with society (Migdal, Kohli, and Shue 1994, 26). They have the opportunity to reassess the assumptions that guided previ-

2. Jowitt (1992) and Stark and Bruszt (1998), among others, also recognize the importance of informal social networks and patronage systems as a legacy of Soviet rule.

3. "State-building" is the process by which elites establish "the authority to create the structural framework through which policies are made and enforced" (Grzymala-Busse and Jones Luong 2002, 531).

ous studies of this region concerning state capacity,[4] patterns of societal resistance, and state-society relations. Moreover, the opportunity to conduct new empirical research that is informed by social science theory has enabled scholars to transport Central Asia from the margins of political, economic, and social analysis into the mainstream. Previous studies that heralded the theoretical contributions of developing countries (or the so-called Third World) to the comparative study of the state and its struggles with society were forced to omit Central Asia because of the dearth of empirical data (see, e.g., Kohli 1986; Migdal 1988; Migdal, Kohli, and Shue 1994). Yet, as this volume clearly demonstrates, systematic studies of Central Asia have a fundamental contribution to make to this rich body of literature. The authors' individual and collective findings in Central Asia both substantiate and transcend the key theoretical insights of these earlier seminal works.

Accordingly, the purpose of this edited volume is to bring the study of Central Asian politics out of the periphery — both empirically and theoretically. Each chapter contributes to this central goal by closely examining the emerging relationship between state actors and social forces in one or more of the five newly independent Central Asian states through the prism of a core political, economic, or social institution, and then using this vantage point to reassess both our understanding of Central Asia and of the state-building process more broadly. The scope and depth of this book's contribution is evident in the wide array of institutional actors under study in each chapter — ranging from regional governments (*hokimiats* or *akimats*) and neighborhood committees (*mahallas*) to transnational and nongovernmental organizations — as well as the original empirical research and theoretical insights that inform each author's analysis and conclusions.

The purpose of this chapter is to introduce readers to the competing views of previous and more recent scholarship concerning the development of states and societies in Central Asia — specifically, the degree to and form in which they have been altered under Soviet rule and in its aftermath. First, I provide an overview of the social, political, and historical depiction of Central Asia under Soviet rule. My intent is to reconstruct a coherent literature from the Sovietological approach to Central Asia, which was in fact quite fragmented. Under the influence of the totalitarian model, this literature unrealistically dichotomized "state" and "society"

4. In the literature on developing countries, state "strength" versus "weakness" is usually evaluated in terms of the state's capacity to effectively formulate and implement policy throughout the territory under its control (Grzymala-Busse and Jones Luong 2002, 532), which can be based on coercive or infrastructural means (Mann 1993).

and thus assumed either complete social control or an imminent rebellion of "traditional" society against Soviet dictatorship — and often, both at the same time. Second, based on recent empirical research contained in this volume and elsewhere, I argue that this widely accepted portrayal should be reconsidered. New evidence strongly suggests that the Soviet regime succeeded not only in profoundly transforming social and political organization in Central Asia but also in blurring the boundaries between state and society in distinctive ways.

View of Central Asia under Soviet Rule

Owing to severely limited access and linguistic barriers, the CARs received much less scholarly attention than other parts of the Soviet Union, particularly the Slavic republics to the north (e.g., Russia and Ukraine).[5] As a result, we knew far less about this particular group of former Soviet republics than any other when they were thrust into independent statehood in 1991.[6] What we did know, moreover, was based on several common assumptions about the nature of Soviet state institutions and policies in Central Asia and the response of Central Asian societies living under Soviet rule. The near inability to conduct research in the region led scholars to adopt analytical strategies that resulted in two polarized views. At one end of the spectrum, state institutions, policies, and societal responses in Central Asia were considered very similar to those in the rest of the former Soviet Union, and yet, at the other end, they were deemed wholly different. The combination of Soviet administrative-territorial divisions and a nationalities policy that elevated the status of titular nationalities in fifteen union republics, for example, was presumed to have engendered strong national identities in the five CARs just as they had in the other ten union republics (see, e.g., Beissinger 1992; Brubaker 1994; Carrere d'Encausse 1993; Naumkin 1994; Roeder 1991; Roy 2000; Slezkine 1994).[7] Yet, at the same time, Central Asian societies were often portrayed

5. The classic text on Soviet politics, for example, includes only four references to Central Asia. See Fainsod 1970.

6. Thanks to several pioneers, however, we did have a firm base from which to develop a broader study of these republics-turned-independent states, including the pathbreaking work of Martha Brill Olcott (1987) on Kazakhstan, William K. Fierman (1991a) and Nancy Lubin (1984) on Uzbekistan, and Muriel Atkin (1989) and Teresa Rakowska-Harmstone (1970) on Tajikistan.

7. The Soviet Union was divided administratively into fifteen national or union republics (SSRs), each of which were further subdivided into oblasts (regions), *raions* (districts), *gorods* (cities), and villages. Many union republics (SSRs) also contained autonomous

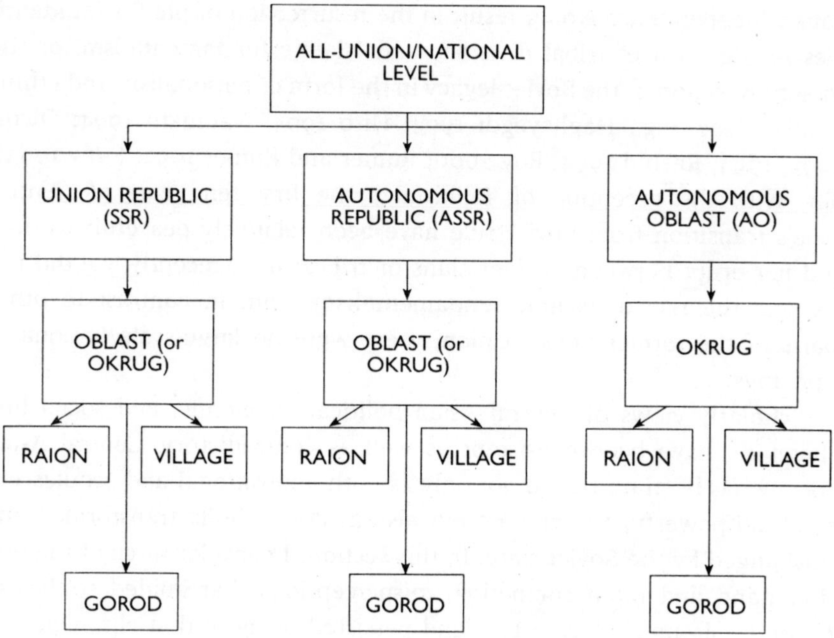

FIGURE I.I. *Soviet Administrative-Territorial Divisions*

as inherently more resistant to Soviet rule and thus their pre-Soviet identities, beliefs, and practices were virtually untransformed (see, e.g., Allworth 1989; Fierman 1991b).[8]

These largely unverified assumptions engendered a common set of misperceptions that pervaded the study of Central Asia, leading scholars to make a series of erroneous predictions both during Soviet rule and immediately following the Soviet Union's collapse. By the early 1980s, for example, predictions of violent ethnic, primarily religious, rebellion throughout Central Asia already dominated scholarly accounts of politics in this region (see, e.g., Bennigsen and Broxup 1983; Bennigsen and Wimbush 1985; Karpat 1983; Rywkin 1982). Such expectations were accelerated in the late 1980s as nationalist movements proliferated in other parts of the former Soviet Union and, ultimately, contributed to the country's demise in 1991. Thus, alongside Central Asia's so-called liberation from Soviet rule came a steady stream of predictions that this new-

---

republics (ASSRs), autonomous oblasts (AOs), and krais (territories), which were further subdivided into oblasts or *okrugs*, raions, cities, and villages. See figure 1.1.

8. These views also reflect the predominance of primordialist views of identity among Sovietologists more broadly.

found independence would result in the resurrection of pre-Soviet identities in the form of tribal divisions and Islamic fundamentalism, or the violent rejection of the Soviet legacy in the form of nationalism and ethnic conflict (see, e.g., Haghayegdi 1994; Hiro 1994; Naumkin 1994; Olcott 1993, 1994; Rashid 1994; Roy 2000; Rumer and Rumer 1992; Suny 1993). Yet, with the exception of Tajikistan,[9] the first ten years of Central Asia's transition from Soviet rule have been relatively peaceful: warfare did not erupt between ancient clans or tribes; until recently, we did not witness the rise of Islamic fundamentalism; and, in contrast to other parts of the former Soviet Union, there were no large-scale nationalist uprisings.

Scholarly views of Central Asian political, economic, and social life, therefore, have been consistent as well as contradictory. Central Asian society has been portrayed not only as both oppositional and acquiescent to an all-powerful Soviet state but also as both wholly transformed and unchanged by the Soviet state. In this section, I consider three of the predominant, and often competing, misperceptions that guided studies of Central Asia under Soviet rule and persisted in those that chronicled its first few years of independence.

The Strength and Pervasiveness of the Soviet State vis-à-vis Central Asian Society

According to the totalitarian paradigm (see, e.g., Brzezinski 1967; Friedrich and Brzezinski 1956; Shapiro 1972), the Soviet Union was ruled by a personalistic leadership that sought to dominate all levels of administrative, coercive, and legal control (in other words, the state) as well as every facet of individual and group activity (that is, society). The Soviet state was thus considered a strong and pervasive force vis-à-vis society with the unlimited capacity to control and, perhaps more important, to mold the population in its own image. Although this model was challenged by a variety of Sovietologists beginning in the 1950s (Breslauer 1992) and calls for a pluralist or corporatist view of Soviet politics emerged in the late 1970s and early 1980s (see, e.g., Hough 1977; Solomon 1983), it dominated scholarship on Central Asia for most of the Soviet Union's seventy-four-year life span. As a result, the indigenous population in Central Asia was often characterized as more submissive — and political domination was seen as more complete — than in other parts of the Soviet

9. In Tajikistan, violent civil war erupted soon after independence (1992) and lasted until a peace accord was signed in 1997.

Union (see, e.g., Carrere d'Encausse 1981; Rakowska-Harmstone 1970; Rywkin 1963).[10]

One of the areas in which scholars once deemed Soviet efforts at transforming Central Asia most successful was in the creation of nations where they previously did not exist. Unlike many of the other fifteen union republics, when the Bolsheviks seized power in 1917 there were neither clear territorial delineations based on ethnic groups nor a national form of identity corresponding to territory upon which republics could be readily established in Central Asia.[11] At the time of Russian expansion into this vast region, the peoples that lived there distinguished themselves according to clans and tribal lineages as well as by cultural and linguistic differences. According to the prevalent nomadic social organization, Kazakhs were divided into three "tribal confederations" (or Juzes), each containing several clans. The Kyrgyz were also organized according to tribes, but in the form of two "wings" — approximately twenty-one tribes on the right and eight tribes on the left. A complex tribal structure also characterized the Uzbeks. The most prominent distinction among peoples of the region was between two predominant lifestyles — nomadism and sedentarism; those groups later classified as Kazakhs, Kyrgyz, and Turkmen belonged to the first category, while Uzbeks and Tajiks belonged to the second (see, e.g., Porkhomovskii 1994, 17).[12]

Thus, to comply with their own conception of nationality and promise of self-determination, the Bolsheviks endeavored to draw entirely new boundaries between what they considered to be the region's primary ethnic groups for the purpose of constructing national identities (see Slezkine 1994; Hirsch 2000). In the end, five groups were identified as worthy of national republics based on their linguistic and tribal distinctiveness alone — the Kazakhs, Kyrgyz, Turkmen, Tajiks, and Uzbeks.[13]

10. As Gleason (1997, 37–39) notes, this has much to do with the characterization of Central Asian political culture as prone to authoritarianism. The fact that he concurs with this characterization as late as 1997 points to its salience. Rywkin, however, revised his own viewpoint somewhat in 1982 when he updated his 1963 book *Russia in Central Asia*, which he renamed *Moscow's Muslim Challenge*.

11. In those areas where nationalists had already staked their claims for territorial autonomy (e.g., Georgia, Armenia, Azerbaijan) or in which previous national administrative structures existed (e.g., Estonia, Latvia, and Lithuania), the national boundaries were more easily discernible. See Jones Luong 1998, chap. 3, for more detail.

12. Sedentary groups were referred to as "sarts," a rather generic term for urban dweller.

13. The Karakalpaks were also initially included among this group, but never constituted a union republic. Rather, in 1925, the Karakalpak AO was established within the Kazakh ASSR, and then in 1936 was transferred to the Uzbek SSR as the Karakalpak ASSR.

The difficulty in reaching a national "solution" for Central Asia is apparent in the length of time it took to establish the territorial boundaries for what today are known as the five CARs.[14] After Central Asia became part of the USSR in 1922, it was subdivided into the union republics of Uzbekistan (Uzbek SSR) and Turkmenistan (Turkmen SSR) in 1924, and then further subdivided into Kazakhstan (Kazakh ASSR), Kyrgyzstan (Kirghiz ASSR), and Tajikistan (Tajik SSR) in 1929.[15] The national delimitation was complete only in 1936, when Kyrgyzstan and Kazakhstan were elevated to the status of union republics.

Nonetheless, national identities were widely assumed to have taken hold across the CARs to the same degree that they had throughout the former Soviet Union (see, e.g., Akiner 1995b; Beissinger 1992; Carrere d'Encausse 1993; Naumkin 1994; Roeder 1991; Roy 2000; Slezkine 1994; Suny 1993). This became particularly evident when the Soviet Union's collapse invited predictions not only that nationalist conflict would erupt but also that it would cause the redrawing of state boundaries to incorporate those members of the titular nationalities left on the other side of the border when these boundaries were initially drawn (see, e.g., Akiner 1995b; Naumkin 1994; Olcott 1993). Yet, long before 1991, scholars had warned that the Soviet Union's very "success" at dominating and transforming Central Asia would ultimately contribute to its demise by strengthening nationalism and Muslim solidarity (see, e.g., Rywkin 1982; Carrere d'Encausse 1981).

Central Asian Society as Inherently Resistant to Soviet Rule

At the same time, Central Asian society was often portrayed as intrinsically more resistant to Soviet rule than other parts of the country. On a general level, this view reflected the primordialist sympathies of many Sovietologists toward identity and the nation (see, e.g., Conquest 1970). More concretely, it was often based on the mere persistence of what scholars considered to be indigenous traditions in Central Asia, including art forms, customs, and dress, as well as religious beliefs, despite the Soviet leadership's attempts to eradicate them (see, e.g., Allworth 1989;

14. No other area took so long except for the Transcaucasian Federation, which did not become separately recognized as the union republics of Armenia, Azerbaijan, and Georgia until 1936 yet had already been subdivided in 1922. See Jones Luong 1998, chap. 3, for more detail.

15. The Kazakh ASSR (first known as the Kirgiz Autonomous Oblast) was originally incorporated into the Russian Federation (RSFSR). Thus, although I refer to Kazakhstan as a part of Central Asia throughout, the Soviets used the category "Central Asia and Kazakhstan" to refer to this region.

Carrere d'Encausse 1981). Because these societies remained "traditional," they were considered unique in their ability not only to resist Soviet power but also to thwart one of the Soviet Union's primary goals — modernization. Yet, what appeared to be traditional was in fact "as much a response to and creation of the [Soviet] system itself as a feature of local communities" (Kandiyoti 1996, 529).

Moreover, according to numerous scholarly accounts, Central Asians expressed their resistance to Soviet transformation not only through the persistence of tradition but also by exercising "covert autonomy" (Akiner 1995b, 12) and practicing "unofficial Islam" (see, e.g., Bennigsen and Broxup 1983; Bennigsen and Wimbush 1985; Ro'i 2000). Both forms of resistance were described as parallel structures through which Central Asian elites and masses alike deliberately circumvented the Soviet system. Scholars interpreted pervasive corruption, therefore, as either a sign that pre-Soviet power structures had remained unchanged or a method for defying the Soviet regime, rather than as self-interested elite behavior or a rational response to a centrally planned economy (see, e.g., Akiner 1995b; Fierman 1991b; Gleason 1990b; Lubin 1984). The notorious falsification of cotton production figures under Sharaf Rashidov's reign as first secretary of Uzbekistan from 1959 to 1983, for example, has often been portrayed as a deliberate act of defiance against Moscow (see, e.g., Critchlow 1988; Fierman 1991b).

The role of Islam as a source of resistance to Soviet rule attracted even more scholarly attention. In short, it was commonly viewed as the dominant social force in Central Asia and, more important, as purely an oppositional one (see, e.g., Atkin 1989; Bennigsen and Broxup 1983; Bennigsen and Wimbush 1985; Karpat 1983; Rywkin 1982). More specifically, because modernization was equated with secularization, Islam was depicted as the primary weapon "against the forces of Soviet modernity" (Saroyan 1997, 17). Thus, Islam was considered a crowning symbol of both Central Asia's inherent ability to resist Soviet rule and the Soviet Union's failure to achieve modernization in this region.

Such views fostered two dominant kinds of predictions, both before and after the Soviet Union's collapse. First, after independence, some scholars expected to find that Central Asian society was essentially unchanged from pre-Soviet times. Clan and tribal identities, for example, had persisted during Soviet rule, and therefore, along with Islam, they would form the basis for building legitimacy and state authority after independence (see, e.g., Akbarzadeh 1996; Olcott 1994). They were also considered a likely source of interethnic conflict (see, e.g., Porkhomovskii 1994). Second, others predicted that Islamic fundamentalism would serve as the primary source of popular mobilization — both against the Soviet regime and following the Soviet Union's collapse. These expectations converged in the tendency for scholars to characterize the civil war in Tajikistan, which erupted in the spring of 1992, as either intertribal warfare or a battle between Islamic fundamentalists and the forces of secularism and stability (see, e.g., Olimova 2000; Djalili, Grare, and Akiner 1997). Another, less common prediction was that conflict would arise from the Central Asian peoples' rejection of the "false" nationalities and borders imposed on them by Soviet rule in order to unite under their *real* identity as Turkistanis (see, e.g., Hayit 1987).

Central Asian Republics as Colonies of the Soviet Union

The aforementioned perceptions coincided with the view that the CARs were colonies of the Soviet Union rather than an integral part of this multinational state (see, e.g., Carrere d'Encausse 1981; Gleason 1997; Kul'chik, Fadin, and Sergeev 1996; Rumer 1989). In contrast to other titular nationalities, Central Asians were denied the opportunity to govern themselves directly, either because Russians and other Slavs were overrepresented in their local Communist Party organs or were appointed to monitor the activities of indigenous elites (see, e.g., Allworth 1989).[16] With the exception of Kazakhstan, where significant industrialization occurred (Olcott 1987), their economies were also deliberately structured so that they remained primarily agricultural, produced raw materials (e.g., cotton and wheat) to be processed elsewhere, and exhausted their nonrenewable resources (e.g., oil, gas, and minerals), and thus were wholly dependent on the other Soviet republics (see, e.g., Rumer 1989; Pomfret 1995).[17] Uzbekistan, for example, was often referred to as a cotton colony because its economy was based almost exclusively on cotton production (see, e.g., Gleason 1990a). In essence, then, the CARs were viewed as political and economic appendages of the Soviet Union.

This view contributed to the pervasive assumption that a clear boundary existed between the Soviet "state" and Central Asian "society." Thus, it was not only possible but in fact necessary to describe and analyze them

16. Many have argued that Russians and other Slavs were appointed as second oblast party committee (*obkom*) secretaries in order to monitor the activities of indigenous elites who served as first obkom secretaries. On the division of labor between first and second party secretaries, see Hough 1969. Edward Allworth does note that opportunities for local self-rule increase in the 1970s, especially in Uzbekistan under Rashidov. See Allworth 1989, 550–51.

17. Although Kazakhstan's industrial sector was larger than that of Uzbekistan and Kyrgyzstan, as in these other republics it was primarily based on extraction rather than manufacturing. See Olcott 1987 for more detail.

as separate entities. This is perhaps most obvious in the case of Islam, for which scholarly distinctions between "official" and "unofficial" were analogous to "'things Soviet' refer[ring] to the party-state" and "'things Muslim'... [referring to] aspects of society" (Saroyan 1997, 18). Yet, it was also present in depictions of the Soviet state as unable to mold Central Asia as it had intended. State and society thus lived side-by-side, accommodated one another when necessary, and were perhaps even compatible, but did not transform one another. Ironically, this view was both consistent with and served to reinforce two competing conceptions of Soviet rule in Central Asia: the totalitarian model and the notion that Central Asia was inherently resistant. The former depends on the notion that a clear boundary exists between state and society such that the former can dominate the latter,[18] while the latter meant that, to survive, society had to carve out a separate space from the state.

When they emerged as independent states in 1991, then, most agreed that the CARs were profoundly unprepared for independence (see, e.g., Gleason 1997; McAuley 1995; Olcott 1996). These were countries that lacked viable economies as well as state structures and ideologies capable of linking indigenous leaders to their societies. Among other things, this view suggested that Central Asian leaders would reject the institutions imposed on them under Soviet rule, including their own borders, and build new states, either from scratch or based on their pre-Soviet heritage. It also fed suspicions that there was a real danger that the post-Soviet states in Central Asia would essentially be "recolonized" by one or more of their more powerful neighbors. The primary candidate, not surprisingly, was the Russian Federation, which some argued was the region's most natural economic ally (see, e.g., E. Rumer 1995; Rumer and Zhukov 1998). Others suggested instead that Russia sought military domination through the Soviet Union's so-called successor — the Commonwealth of Independent States (see, e.g., Odom and Dujarric 1995). Yet, on the basis of presumed cultural affinities, many also argued that the Central Asian states would be more attractive to, and attracted by a close affiliation with, their Muslim counterparts to the south — Turkey, Iran, and Pakistan (see, e.g., Clawson 1995; Hunter 2000).

Reconceptualizing Central Asia after Independence

As the chapters that comprise this book attest, the dissolution of the Soviet Union provided unprecedented opportunities for scholars to conduct

18. In other words, to view society as consumed by and encapsulated within the state, there must first have been a clear separation between the "state" and "society."

empirical research in Central Asia, including elite interviews, mass surveys, and original archival work. These findings are illuminating — not only because they have furthered our limited knowledge of this region but also because they shed light on the ways in which the predominant conceptualization of Central Asia based on previous scholarship is flawed. In sum, more recent research has revealed (1) that the Soviet transformation of Central Asian societies was more complete and pervasive than many expected, yet did not include the creation of strong nationalist sentiment; (2) that Islam was neither the dominant social force nor necessarily an oppositional one; and (3) that post-Soviet Central Asian leaders have not wholly rejected, but rather strategically incorporated, the Soviet institutional and policy legacies of which they were an integral part.

Central Asian Societies Profoundly Transformed

More recent empirical evidence — including patterns of party formation, elite attitudes and behavior, societal expectations, and the failure of either unbridled nationalism or Islamic fundamentalism to emerge — overwhelmingly supports the view that the Soviet regime profoundly transformed Central Asian societies, albeit not as expected. Contrasted with views of Central Asian societies as inherently resistant to Soviet rule, the scope of this transformation is striking. In sum, it fostered identities, beliefs, and practices at the elite as well as mass level. What is even more noteworthy is that it did not include the creation of either strong nationalist sentiments or ethnic animosity (see, e.g., Beissinger 2002; Kuru 2002; Schoeberlein 1994). None of the Central Asian Republics, for example, witnessed the emergence of a broad-based nationalist movement and all voted overwhelmingly to preserve the Soviet Union in 1991. Moreover, the manufacturing of national identities to correspond with newly independent states has been largely an elite affair that mimics the Soviet process of constructing nations (Adams, chap. 3) and retains the Soviet definition of the nation as tied to language (Dave, chap. 4) as well as Soviet understandings of nationalism (Olcott 2002).

On the one hand, Soviet policies and institutions in Central Asia reconfigured elite power relations and fostered new political identities based on regionalism that superseded (yet coexisted with) relations and identities based on tribe, clan, and nationality (Jones Luong 2002, chap. 3).[19] Scholars who have either predicted nationalist uprisings in the former Soviet Union or offered explanations for the rise of nationalism ex post facto have universally based their analysis on the hypothesized effects of three

19. On the persistence of clans and tribes as "subethnic identities" within regions in post-Soviet Kazakhstan, see Schatz 2000.

Soviet policies and institutions: (1) the federal structure, which created territorial units for some national groups and not others; (2) the failure of a command economy to satisfy the demands of social and economic modernization; and (3) the creation and expansion of a national cadre in each of these territorial units (see, e.g., Roeder 1991, Slezkine 1994, Suny 1993, Zaslavsky 1992). Yet, because of their distinctive nature and effects, the same three policies and institutions did not engender identities and capacities to incite nationalist sentiments in Central Asia. Rather, they fueled regionalism by fostering the development of interregional political competition and intraregional patronage networks (Jones Luong 2002, chap. 3).

Regionally based power relations and identities, moreover, continue to be both salient and dynamic in post-Soviet Central Asia. Although the balance of power between regions as well as between the center and the regions has shifted dramatically during the transition, regionalism continues to be the focal point of elite bargaining and the primary mechanism for distributing scarce political and economic resources to the broader population (Jones Luong 2002). Regional affiliation also serves as a salient predictor of citizens' satisfaction with governance — in contrast to either clan or nationality — thus suggesting that it is the primary basis for political and economic inclusion (McGlinchey 2002).[20] As chapters 5 and 6 demonstrate, power shifts between regional and central elites are directly related to the change in access to, ownership of, and control over material resources. Pauline Jones Luong (chap. 6) argues that state-led privatization and strategies to attract foreign investment have bolstered local control over the economy in Kazakhstan by providing a new source of income to oil, gas, and mineral-rich regions. Conversely, Alisher Ilkhamov (chap. 5) finds that the central government's efforts to concentrate the proceeds from cotton production and export have threatened regional elites' primary source of income and bargaining leverage vis-à-vis the center in Uzbekistan.

On the other hand, the politicization of regional cleavages coincided with the repression and depoliticization of Islam. The Soviet regime succeeded in transforming Islam, reducing it from a potential supranational ideology to a local and primarily cultural identity marker across Central Asia. Elites who desired career advancement in the state and party organs were instructed to separate their belief in Islam from their political ideology because Islam was associated with both cultural backwardness and disloy-

20. McGlinchey (2002) finds that the relationship between "rule of law" and satisfaction with governance, however, is even more robust than that between region and satisfaction with governance.

alty to the Soviet regime. Although the continuation of Islamic faith and rituals was allowed within local communities, the Soviet regime made it clear from the outset that atheism was the state's official ideology and that even at the local level Islam was subordinate to secular political institutions. This further weakened Islam as a political force by destroying the capacity for Islamic ties to form the basis of an organized mass movement. At the same time, more than seventy years of Soviet rule engendered the belief among Central Asian elites that Islam was more prone to instability and conflict — particularly in contrast to regionalism, which was, and remains, the preferred mechanism for resolving political disputes (Jones Luong 2002).

Soviet rule in Central Asia also had a profound effect on shaping both societal expectations and social relations. Chapters 1 (Marianne Kamp) and 2 (Cynthia Werner) document the role that cradle-to-grave welfare policies and efforts to elevate the status of women have played in creating expectations about the Soviet state's responsibilities toward its citizenry. Central Asian women in particular came to expect a more equal role in society, including access to educational and employment opportunities, more involvement in the decision about whom to marry,[21] and generous maternity leave and child subsidies (see also Constantine 2001).

Where the post-Soviet state has attempted to preserve its role as welfare provider, these expectations have persisted. Marianne Kamp (chap. 1) discovered through extensive in-country focus groups in post-Soviet Uzbekistan that, as a direct result of Soviet welfare policies, citizens still expect the government to provide for their basic social and economic needs — particularly those tied to motherhood. This is reinforced by the Uzbekistani state's concerted attempt to retain authority over defining the basis for social service provision, while still devolving the task of implementation to local authorities. Similarly, Kelly McMann argues in chapter 7 that nongovernmental organizations (NGOs) in post-Soviet Kyrgyzstan maintain the notion that the state must provide them with structural and material resources largely because these resources still remain under the control of regional and local governments.

Yet, this is not the case where the post-Soviet state has diminished its role in monitoring social relations. Cynthia Werner (chap. 2) finds that the Kazakhstani state's retreat from its predecessor's role in providing opportunities for women and regulating marriage has fostered the belief that such issues are the rightful purview of local communities and individual families. Thus, although nonconsensual bride kidnapping was made illegal

21. As Cynthia Werner explains in her contribution to this volume, in pre-Soviet Central Asia marriages were primarily prearranged by relatives without the bride's consent.

under the Soviet system, both its frequency and level of social acceptance have increased since independence.

Beyond social services, Laura Adams argues in chapter 3 that the Soviet legacy limited the "repertoires of resistance" available to Central Asian societies and the cultural elites who ostensibly represented their interests. Because cultural elites were produced by and closely integrated with the Soviet state, they were more inclined to accommodate the production of state ideology after independence. Both this ideology and the mode of cultural production that cultural elites chose to disseminate it to the broader society emulated rather than challenged the limited "nationalist discourse" and bureaucratic constraints that defined their profession under Soviet rule.

Islam Is Not the Primary Social Force

The first decade of independence has also revealed that other social forces in the post-Soviet Central Asian states have exercised greater influence than Islam. Despite severe obstacles, including political repression, protracted civil war, and limited access to resources, many NGOs color these states' respective social, political, and economic landscapes. As both chapters 7 (Kelly McMann) and 8 (Erika Weinthal) illustrate, the emergence of NGOs is not limited to certain "safe" spheres but includes a variety of issue areas in Kazakhstan, Kyrgyzstan, Tajikistan, and Uzbekistan, ranging from labor and the environment to law and human rights.[22] These chapters also provide compelling evidence that NGOs are having some impact on state policies and the lives of average citizens. Kelly McMann's research in particular disputes the notion that NGOs in Central Asia are entirely the product of Western encouragement and financial aid.

Religious and ethnically based organizations are noticeably absent from the array of NGOs listed above. This is somewhat misleading because such organizations, particularly the latter, have emerged. None, however, were either militant Islamic movements or broad-based nationalist movements on a par with those that developed in other former Soviet republics (see, e.g. Beissinger 2002). Rather, they were narrowly based, often existing only in the capital cities of the Central Asian states, and drew on local or regional support. Religious and ethnic organizations include Asaba and Erkin Kyrgyzstan in Kyrgyzstan; Azat, Zheltoksan, Lad, and Russkaia Obshina in Kazakhstan; and, in Uzbekistan, Erk, Birlik, and the group Adolat that

22. For more detail, see http://www.civilsoc.org/eurasia. As Weinthal (chap. 8) documents, Turkmenistan has an embarrassingly low number of NGOs in comparison to the other Central Asian states. The fact that the most politically repressive state has any functioning independent organizations, however, is quite striking.

several local imams formed in the late 1980s to fight corruption in the city of Namangan (see Jones Luong 2002, chap. 4, for more detail).

Moreover, several of these countries also experienced some popular mobilization in support of democracy. Although miniscule and short-lived compared to other parts of the former Soviet Union, groups promoting some degree of political liberalization and the democratic contestation of public office did emerge in the late 1980s and early 1990s in Kyrgyzstan, Kazakhstan, Uzbekistan, and Tajikistan (see, e.g., Dawisha and Parrott 1997).[23] Ironically, the highest level of democratic mobilization occurred in Tajikistan, which is often considered the most traditional state in terms of religion (Schoeberlein 1994). In the early 1990s, a coalition emerged among several parties — Rastakhiz (Rebirth), the Islamic Renaissance Party (IRP), and the Democratic Party — in support of changing the government through democratic means. This coalition was not, as many previous accounts have suggested, dominated by radical Islamists, but included a broad set of social forces and political interests, such as Gharmis from Leninabad Oblast and Kurgan-Tyube Oblast, Pamiris from the Gorno-Badakhshan Autonomous Oblast, the Maschois peoples who had been resettled in northern Tajikistan, and Tajik intellectuals from Dushanbe (see, e.g., Schoeberlein 1994; Rubin 1993).

Few of these nascent democratic movements managed to survive more than a year or two, either because of modest popular support, internal disputes, brutal government repression, or some combination of these factors.[24] Nonetheless, along with NGOs, they are a testament to the dynamic nature of identities in general and Central Asian societies in particular. Central Asian societies were both profoundly transformed under Soviet rule and greatly influenced by the events that precipitated the Soviet Union's collapse. In contrast, pre-Soviet traditions have had only a minor influence on both the formation and attitudes of social and political organizations. In Kyrgyzstan, for example, Kelly McMann (chap. 7) finds that Soviet economic legacies and financial hardship after independence have had a profound effect on NGO leaders' expectations and willingness to receive direct assistance from the state, whereas what are commonly described as pervasive local customs — for example, deference to authority and kinship-based allegiances — have had no effect on NGO

23. On social and political mobilization in the Soviet Union, see, e.g., Sedaitis and Butterfield 1991.

24. For details, see Jones Luong 1998, chap. 4. In Tajikistan, the government's refusal to honor its agreement to form a coalition government with the democratic opposition precipitated the civil war that lasted from 1992 until 1997. See Schoeberlein (1994) and Rubin (1993).

development. The emergence and endurance of NGOs across Central Asia should also lead us to rethink the prevalent notion among Western and Central Asian scholars that Central Asian culture could not accommodate the development of modern civil society (see, e.g., Huskey 1997; Polat 1999). Yet, this is not only the case at the mass level. As Laura Adams argues in chapter 3, for example, cultural elites in Uzbekistan are not directly contesting the Karimov regime's vision of the state in crafting a new ideology not because they are traditionalist or naturally submissive but because it is not in their professional interest to do so.

This directly challenges the primordialist view of Central Asian societies that dominated Sovietology and informed predictions of interethnic conflicts after the Soviet Union's collapse based on the resurgence of unadulterated clan, tribal, and religious identities from the pre-Soviet era. Militant Islamic groups have flexed their muscles by launching armed incursions into Kyrgyzstan's southern territory in August 1999 and into Uzbekistan's in August 2000 from northern Afghanistan through Tajikistan. They are also gaining some popular support — particularly in the Fergana Valley and the districts along the border with Afghanistan, where most of the illicit trade in drugs and weapons has taken place and armed insurgents have sought (and often received) refuge. Yet, their growing strength since the late 1990s is not evidence that pre-Soviet identities have resurged. Rather, militant Islamic groups have developed domestic roots primarily in response to post-Soviet political repression — particularly in Uzbekistan — and because of the region's porous border with war-torn Afghanistan (Jones Luong and Weinthal 2002; see also ICG March 2001). Repression has enabled these groups, such as the Islamic Movement of Uzbekistan (IMU) and Hizb-ut-Tahrir al-Islami (Party of Islamic Liberation), to tap into popular discontent while the porous border has facilitated their access to the resources (proceeds from the weapons and drugs trade) with which to win popular support.

Tradition Reinvented as a Source of State Legitimation

The wide array of social forces and their importance in Central Asia is also evident in the various legitimation strategies that state leaders across post-Soviet Central Asia have employed since independence. What might be considered traditional factors — such as Islam and the pre-Soviet cultural heritage — were indeed among these strategies. Scholars are right to point out that, at least initially, several newly elected Central Asian presidents made a concerted effort to demonstrate their support for Islam. President Islam Karimov of Uzbekistan, for example, swore his presidential oath on the Qur'an, made the hajj to Mecca, and approved a secular state constitution that explicitly maintains a special status for Islam and recognizes its importance in the nation's history. These leaders also deliberately appealed to ancient myths and symbols of "the nation" in an attempt to recover Central Asia's cultural heritage. As Cynthia Werner (chap. 2) argues, this has also coincided with a move toward the "re-traditionalization" of society, which has amounted to using Islam as a justification for reinstating patriarchal authority and limiting options for women outside the home (see also Kamp, chap. 1).

Yet, political leaders' use of Islam and "the nation" as a source of legitimation was extremely limited. Karimov's regime, for example, simultaneously suppressed all autonomous appeals to or manifestations of Islam — a state policy that began in the city of Namangan in 1992 and accelerated out of control in 1997 with the arrest, detention, and torture of thousands of Muslims throughout the Fergana Valley and in the capital city of Tashkent (see, e.g., Human Rights Watch, May 1998; International Crisis Management Group, March 2001). By 1998, Islam had clearly lost its special status in Uzbekistan. Central Asian leaders also discouraged the rise of "unsanctioned" nationalism by pledging their support for a multiethnic state and selectively cracking down on social movements and political parties formed on the basis of nationality (Jones Luong 2002, chap. 4).[25]

At the same time, the Central Asian experience since independence questions the degree to which these states rely on "tradition" or their pre-Soviet "cultural heritage" to build legitimacy and establish authority. Instead, they seem to be strategically reinventing Soviet institutions as "traditional" ones (see, e.g., Adams 1999a). Islam Karimov's government in Uzbekistan, for example, co-opted the old village soviets and merged them with neighborhood committees (mahallas) that performed an important social role in Central Asian communities (see, e.g., Abramson 1998). As Marianne Kamp argues in chapter 1, these remade mahallas perform many of the former soviets' functions as well as some new administrative ones linked to social control and service provision. Thus, although the mahalla leaders are chosen from among local elders (or *oq soqols*) in order to explicitly link them to "traditional" relationships and they often invoke "traditional values" when performing their duties, they are not in fact wholly traditional institutions. In addition, while all the Central Asian states have looked to historical figures to glorify their pasts, such as Manas in Kyrgyzstan,[26] Amir Timur in Uzbekistan, and Magtymguly in

25. For more detail, see Jones Luong 1998, chap. four.

26. Manas, a legendary batyr-khan who led his people in their struggle against foreign invaders, is the main hero of the Kyrgyz epic poem *Manas*, which is named for him. For more information, refer to: http://www.freenet.kg/kyrgyzstan/manas.html.

Turkmenistan, they have simultaneously sought to present themselves to their respective populations — and to the outside world — as modern nation-states. After the first few years of independence, for example, all the Central Asian governments relaxed their stance on requiring that the titular language replace Russian in all official documents and communication and on returning to Arabic script in the name of civility or modernity (see, e.g., Fierman 1995; Kuru 2002, 85).[27] Kazakhstan and Kyrgyzstan went so far as to subsequently confer the status of an "official language" on Russian (Dave, chap. 4). This did not, however, necessarily mean the retention of Cyrillic. In Uzbekistan and Turkmenistan, for example, the government has adopted the use of the Latin script, which, quite conveniently, was also used during the Soviet period (from the mid-1920s until 1939) but nonetheless represents the modern.[28]

Although the exact mix of tradition and modernity in their rhetoric and actions varies from case to case, the legitimation strategies of all five Central Asian leaders exploit tradition to mask more modern forms of authoritarian rule. President Saparmurad Niyazov of Turkmenistan, who insists that he be referred to as Turkmenbashi (leader of the Turkmen) and was named "president for life" at the end of 1999, is perhaps the most extreme version of this. He has fastidiously crafted a personality cult reminiscent of Stalinism, yet with a local cultural and historic resonance, because he justifies his preferred style of dictatorship as part of Turkmenistan's sultanic past. Toward this end, he has continued the Soviet practice of using the media to promulgate state propaganda and litter the streets with slogans such as "The 21st century will be the golden age of Turkmens" and "The word of the President is the law" (Kuru 2002, 75–76).[29] Such strategies, moreover, seem to be oriented more toward self-legitimation than attaining popular support (Schoeberlein 2001).

27. Russian was the lingua franca of the Soviet Union and, as such, was required for higher education and professional advancement. Stalinist language policies also included changing the scripts of local languages from Arabic and Persian (Tajik only) to Latin and then Cyrillic. In the heyday of glasnost in the late 1980s, many Central Asian scholars and cultural elites began to argue that the titular languages should be revived and become the official language of their respective republics. In Uzbekistan and Tajikistan, some also advocated returning to the Arabic or Persian script, respectively.

28. Since the mid-1990s, the Latin alphabet has increasingly been taught in schools, appeared on street signs, and been used in newspapers in Uzbekistan. President Niyazov of Turkmenistan has endorsed adopting the Latin alphabet as a way to facilitate learning English.

29. President Karimov (Uzbekistan) has also continued this practice. For example, one often sees the slogans "Uzbekistan is a future great state" and "Navroz — the holiday of labor and spring."

Finally, Central Asian leaders have also sought to legitimate both their states and their own rule through the international community (Weinthal 2002, chap. 8). All five states, albeit to different degrees, have created institutions (at least on paper) that are consistent with international conceptions of modern statehood. Electoral systems, for example, are an important first step toward establishing independent statehood as well as winning the approval of the international community. Accordingly, three of the five Central Asian states (Kazakhstan, Kyrgyzstan, and Uzbekistan) established a set of rules governing the election of national legislatures within the first few years of their newfound independence — both to gain internal recognition and to bolster external legitimacy (see Jones Luong 2002 for details). They have also adopted international standards for environmental protection, particularly in their oil and gas sector where foreign investors play the greatest role (Jones Luong and Weinthal 1999). Moreover, as Erika Weinthal argues in chapter 8, they have designed domestic and interstate agencies in order to link themselves to an "international environmental culture" rather than to address the demands of their own citizens. Her findings suggest that Central Asian leaders are more concerned with attaining legitimacy abroad than at home.

Thus, neither Islam nor "the nation" has provided the primary or exclusive basis for state legitimation, as earlier studies predicted. Rather, Central Asian state leaders have sought to strike a careful balance between these different identities, often recasting them in modern, more secular, terms, and have been more concerned with self-legitimation and preventing opposition to their rule. The result is a state ideology that is either unlikely or fails to have broad popular appeal (Adams, chap. 3; Schoeberlein 2001).

CARs Were an Integral Part of the Soviet System

The process of state-building in Central Asia also challenges the presumption that the CARs were merely colonies of the Soviet Union and would thus reject Soviet policies and institutions after independence. These states are neither being built from scratch nor being rebuilt based on pre-Soviet or traditional structures. Rather, the Central Asian leaders have consciously employed templates from their Soviet past as well as the international present and often vigorously pursue Soviet policies that counter Western political and economic prescriptions. Although the recombining of "old" Soviet and "new" Western policies and institutions is a common phenomenon across post-Communist states (Grzymala-Busse and Jones Luong 2002), Central Asian leaders have relied more heavily on Soviet policies and institutions than elsewhere. This alone suggests that, although it was initially "imported" into Central Asia through brutal force,[30] the Soviet system grew strong indigenous roots there.

Contrary to scholars' expectations, the forces against change in Central Asia were much stronger than the forces for change. Institutional change has indeed occurred to varying degrees across these states, yet the state structure and centers of power inherited from Soviet rule have remained largely intact. The Soviet legacy created multiple centers of authority in Central Asia based on access to and control over the distribution of scarce political and economic resources — including the republican Communist Party and its first secretary, regional (oblast-level) party secretaries, factory managers, and kolkhoz (state farm) chairmen — all of which have persisted in some form in the post-Soviet era. Shortly after independence, for example, both President Niyazov of Turkmenistan and President Karimov of Uzbekistan quickly seized the assets (e.g., bank accounts, office space, and equipment) of their respective republican Communist Parties, co-opted their organizational structure and ideological appeal, and renamed them the Democratic Party of Turkmenistan (Turkmenistan Demokratik Partiyasi) and the People's Democratic Party of Uzbekistan (Ozbekistan Halq Demokratik Partiyasi). A successor to the republican Communist Party was also created shortly after independence in Tajikistan, yet without even the pretense of a name change, and continued as the de facto ruling party until 1997. Regional party secretaries were also recast in the post-Soviet period as *akims* (Kazakhstan and Kyrgyzstan), *hokims* (Uzbekistan), *khukums* (Tajikistan), or *khyakims* (Turkmenistan). As chapter 5 (Ilkhamov) and 6 (Jones Luong) demonstrate, however, in both Uzbekistan and Kazakhstan they have retained an important role in decision-making and policy implementation de facto, which has been expanded de jure in Kazakhstan. Factory managers and kolkhoz chairman also continue to influence state policy, particularly regarding privatization and economic restructuring (see, e.g., Ilkhamov 1998; Weinthal 2002, chap. 5).

The degree of continuity with the Soviet system has undeniably been greater in Turkmenistan and Uzbekistan than in Kazakhstan, Kyrgyzstan, and Tajikistan. Indeed, the leaders of these two states often pursue Soviet policies more vigorously than did their former counterparts. Both autarkic states have reinvigorated central economic planning and resisted opening

30. The brutality with which the Soviet system was established and enforced in Central Asia, particularly under Stalinism, should not be overlooked or underestimated. The dramatic decline in Kazakh population in the 1930s, for example, was the result of the collectivization of agriculture under Stalin, which amounted to forced sedentarization of nomadic tribes. For details, see, Olcott 1987, chap. 8.

their economies to international trade — both within and outside the CIS — as a way to maintain equally closed political systems (see, e.g., Darden 2000; Ilkhamov, chap. 5; Pomfret 1996). President Karimov of Uzbekistan in particular has maintained Soviet attitudes toward religion and dissent. He has moved beyond the notion that the state should simply "manage" Islam by institutionalizing and depoliticizing it, however, to the conviction that it must be eliminated as an independent social force. Thus, while Karimov created his own Committee for Religious Affairs to perform essentially the same function as the Soviet Islamic Central Asian Directorate — to oversee the practice of Islam — he has also executed a widespread crackdown on nonmilitant Islamists, which includes practicing Muslims and imams in both officially recognized and unofficial mosques (see, e.g., Jones Luong 2001; International Crisis Management Group, August 2001).

Yet, even where some political and economic liberalization has taken place, Central Asian leaders deliberately continue to govern based on their experiences under Soviet rule. Neither Kyrgyzstan nor Kazakhstan, for example, anointed a clear successor to the Communist Party, and yet, in both countries the president has extended his term in office and increasingly ruled by decree (see, e.g., J. Anderson 1999; Bremmer and Welt 1996; Huskey 1997). Similarly, while both have also adopted more extensive market reforms than the other Central Asian states, including privatization, since 1995 they have maintained vigilant state control over the media and continued to harass journalists (see, e.g., Human Rights Watch, October 1999) or offer them bribes in exchange for their silence (see, e.g., Werner 2000b).

The reinvigoration and relaxation of Soviet institutions and policies, moreover, have had a profound effect on the balance of power in these states, and thus on their capacity to govern. Central-regional relations developed under Soviet rule continue to form the core of this power balance (Jones Luong 2002). Attempts to centralize the cotton trade in Uzbekistan have thus created mounting resentment and noncompliance strategies among regional elites who expect to have greater autonomy in the production and sale of cotton (Ilkhamov, chap. 5). Regional leaders' access to independent revenue sources and opportunities to make and implement economic policy autonomously in Kazakhstan have fostered de facto economic decentralization, which central leaders have been forced to accept de jure. Ironically, the lack of a centrally dictated successor to the Communist Party in Kyrgyzstan and Kazakhstan also shifted power toward regional leaders, who used this opportunity to usurp party assets for themselves and embolden their control over scarce resources (Jones Luong 2002, chap. 4). Efforts at market reform have also failed to create viable markets, leaving the state as the primary generator and distributor of resources. Kelly McMann (chap. 7) finds that regional leaders' continued monopoly on resources has strengthened their influence over the development and activities of independent social and political organizations in Kyrgyzstan. The relative autonomy of regional and local leaders vis-à-vis the center has also taken its toll on society by giving these leaders greater authority to determine the distribution of social services (Kamp, chap. 1) and allowing illegal but socially accepted practices such as bride kidnapping to continue unabated (Werner, chap. 2).

Central Asian state-building has also been heavily influenced by the international setting in which it emerged. At a general level, the international community has bolstered these states merely by recognizing their legal right to exist. Similar to the postcolonial experience in Africa, they have been granted juridical statehood regardless of their empirical ability to govern effectively or defend their own sovereignty (Jackson and Rosberg 1992). Yet, international actors have also played a more direct role in propping up the former CARs as legitimate independent states (Weinthal 2002). Both have had a direct effect on the development of state capacity in the region. On the one hand, the international community's active role helps explain why these states have not been "recolonized" as many expected. U.S. foreign policy toward Central Asia in the 1990s, for example, deliberately sought to prevent any of the larger states bordering this region — Russia, China, Turkey, and Iran — from gaining a strong political or economic foothold. On the other hand, it sheds light on why many state institutions are merely cosmetic. Erika Weinthal (chap. 8) finds, for example, that although the Central Asian states have created environmental ministries, joined international environmental organizations, and signed numerous interstate agreements for environmental protection, they are not endowed with the capacity to make and implement environmental policies. For these states, building linkages to international organizations and environmental regimes is much more about enhancing their external than their internal sovereignty.

Central Asian states, like the societies they govern, are dynamic. Although they remain heavily influenced by the Soviet legacy, this legacy is not all pervasive. Central Asian leaders have choices about the future direction of their development, which is evident in the divergent paths they have chosen to follow thus far. None are firmly under Russia's sphere of influence. Some have even rejected this possibility outright by pursuing World Trade Organization (WTO) membership (Kyrgyzstan) and refusing to join economic unions that include Russia (Uzbekistan and Turkmenistan).

Boundary between State and Society Purposefully Blurred

The Soviet system did not create a clear boundary between the state and society in Central Asia. Rather, as in the other parts of the Soviet Union, the boundary between state and society was purposefully blurred in accordance with the vision of creating a heroic-Leninist state (Grzymala-Busse and Jones Luong 2002). State institutions and societal expectations developed in tandem, each transforming the other, and no distinction was made between political and economic elites or public and private property. Among other things, this obfuscation presented serious obstacles to the development of independent societal organizations that could pressure the Soviet government and facilitated the spontaneous transfer of public property into private hands after the Soviet Union collapsed (Grzymala-Busse and Jones Luong 2002).

Several of the chapters in this book suggest that the boundary between state and society remains indistinct in Central Asia. This is particularly clear from the multidimensional role that elites play. Marianne Kamp describes members of mahalla committees, for example, as both independent social actors and as local leaders empowered by the Uzbekistani state. It is not apparent whether they are acting as agents of the state or of society, though they clearly believe they are entitled to represent both. According to Laura Adams, cultural elites in Uzbekistan are also conflicted in their role as "mediators" between state and society because they serve as representatives of both. It is this duality that enables them to believe that the symbolic messages they are creating serve the broader community when they merely serve the state's self-legitimation (Adams, chap. 3). Kelly McMann's research in Kyrgyzstan demonstrates the degree to which political and economic elites as well as public and private property have remained one and the same. Because control over scarce resources has remained in the hands of government officials, the ability of NGOs to develop independently from the state is severely constrained (McMann, chap. 7). This directly contrasts with Erika Weinthal's findings in chapter 8 that transnational actors are creating a boundary between state and society in Central Asia by supporting NGOs as "environmental watchdogs."

Roadmap

The book is divided into four parts — each of which touches on one of the major theoretical issues concerning the relationship between the state and society.

Part I, "The Retreat of the State: Women and the Social Sphere," examines the diminishing role of the state in two key aspects of social life that the Soviet state deeply penetrated — social service provision and marriage — and its impact on women's lives. Marianne Kamp (chap. 1) finds that societal expectations developed under Soviet rule concerning both the types and extent of social welfare persist in Uzbekistan. Nonetheless, the devolution of responsibility to "local organs of citizen self-government" has enabled a more "patriarchal policy" — which discriminates especially against divorcees and abandoned wives — to replace the "late-Soviet maternalist policy." Cynthia Werner (chap. 2) finds that pre-Soviet patriarchal practices are also returning to some degree in post-Soviet Kazakhstan in the form of nonconsensual bride kidnappings, which were banned under Soviet rule. In both cases, the retreat of the central government from managing social issues has resulted in the deterioration of women's status since independence.

Part 2, "Linking State and Society: Culture and Language," analyzes the role of culture, symbolism, and language in state leaders' attempts to forge a new ideology, build a nation-state, and reformulate links with their respective societies. Laura Adams (chap. 3) argues that Uzbekistan's cultural elites are purposefully manufacturing a new state ideology that excludes public debate, creating a perverse danger of replacing the Soviet "monolithic discourse of communism" with one based on circumscribed Uzbek nationalism. Bhavna Dave (chap. 4) accounts for Kazakhstan's success in adopting and implementing a coherent language policy relative to Kyrgyzstan in terms of the cultural elites' ability to present a unified front. By essentially declaring the language problem "solved," the Kazakhstani government was also able to depoliticize language policy earlier on, whereas it remains politically salient in Kyrgyzstan despite the adoption of a law in 2000 granting official status for Russian.

Part 3, "The State against Itself: Central-Regional Relations," elucidates how the Soviet legacy has affected the balance of power between central and regional leaders and documents their struggle to (re-)define their respective spheres of influence after independence. Alisher Ilkhamov (chap. 5) contends that although Uzbekistan has a highly centralized regime, it faces serious challenges from regional elites who are dissatisfied with Karimov's attempts to shift the balance of power decisively toward the center since independence. This growing disgruntlement cannot be ignored, moreover, because, as in the Soviet period, stability is contingent on the political and economic support of regional forces. Pauline Jones Luong (chap. 6) contends that the popular image of Kazakhstan as a centralized, authoritarian state is inconsistent with the reality that regional leaders exercise a great deal of autonomy over economic policy making and implementation. These chapters clearly demonstrate that the Soviet legacy of central-regional bargaining over resources is an inherent part of the state-building process in both countries.

Part 4, "Redefining the State: Internal and External Forces," illuminates the role of nonstate actors — both within and outside the state — in redefining the relationship between the state and society. Kelly McMann (chap. 7) finds that the civic sphere in Kyrgyzstan is primarily defined by Soviet economic legacies and, as a result, NGO leaders do not fear dependence on the state for resources. In highlighting the importance of state control over basic resources, she provides a more nuanced appraisal of state strength. Erika Weinthal (chap. 8) finds, conversely, that Central Asian states are too "weakly institutionalized and poor" to address the acute environmental and health-related problems that they accumulated under Soviet rule. As a result, these states have relied on a variety of transnational actors, who have inadvertently undermined their capacity to protect the environment by supporting the creation of institutions that are merely cosmetic and bolstered their capacity by promoting local NGOs.

In the "Conclusion," I explore how new insights into Central Asia generated by recent empirical work in this edited volume and elsewhere both contribute to and challenge existing theories of the state and state-societal relations.

1

THE RETREAT OF THE STATE

Women and the Social Sphere

I. Between Women and the State

MAHALLA COMMITTEES AND SOCIAL WELFARE IN UZBEKISTAN

MARIANNE KAMP

Representatives of various women's nongovernmental organizations (NGOs) often share horror stories that reveal the inadequacy of Uzbekistan's social welfare system: young women turning to prostitution to support destitute families, violence against women, lack of information about sexuality and birth control and its disastrous results.[1] A young woman told me her story: She was married and had a young daughter, but after several years of marital discord, her husband threw her out of his home. She was unemployed, and she wanted to file for divorce so that her husband would be forced to pay child support. Her husband saw no need to file for divorce. After all, polygyny, although illegal, is socially acceptable in Uzbekistan; if he wanted a new wife, he could marry in a religious ceremony, facing no social consequences, and could avoid the expense of divorcing his first wife and paying child support.[2] He did not need to divorce; only she needed to do so. However, Uzbekistan recently made divorce more difficult, in accordance with a policy of "saving the family."[3] In her district, this meant she would have to pay more than one

1. I heard such stories from NGO representatives in Uzbekistan in 2001 as well as learning of them from Matluba Anvar's unpublished sociological research. Many such accounts can be found on NGO Web sites, in the July 2001 Human Rights Watch report, and in the *Report on the Status of Women in Uzbekistan*, 1999.

2. There is a law against polygyny in Uzbekistan, but its lax enforcement has permitted the rise of unofficial polygyny through the 1990s.

3. Human Rights Watch, 2001. The section headed "Civil Remedies for Domestic Violence: Divorce" explains some of the strategies that Uzbekistan has used to decrease its divorce rate; this is done mainly through setting up obstacles to divorce rather than by creating programs to improve family life. This report includes discussion of society's condemnation of divorced women. David Abramson notes that mahallas are rewarded with recognition from the state for having low divorce rates (Abramson 1998, 190). Sievers (2002, 103, 138) observes that lack of respect for courts makes approval from the mahalla leadership for divorce necessary.

month's salary for a divorce, impossible for an unemployed woman from a poor family. She applied for help to the Village Committee (the local "citizens' self-government organization") and to the Women's Committee, a state-organized system for women's representation and aid, but was refused.[4] The Village Committee could not provide assistance to her as a single mother unless she was divorced; her husband was supposed to be supporting her. Without money, she could not divorce; without a divorce, she could not claim aid. Even with a divorce, she would face problems: the village committees face more demands than they can meet, as the government pressures them to show a reduction in poverty through a reduction in the number of families receiving aid;[5] and in a community that disapproves of divorce, a divorced woman's claim on welfare resources is likely to be judged as less legitimate than a married woman's claim.

This chapter examines a changing welfare system in Uzbekistan, and the expectations that women — and, in particular, mothers — have of the state, drawing on focus group research conducted in Uzbekistan in 1996, more recent reports from NGOs and international organizations, and my conversations with women in Uzbekistan in the summer of 2001.[6] Uzbekistan has increasingly placed welfare decision making in the hands of local organs of citizen self-government, namely *mahalla* (neighborhood) committees in the cities and village committees in rural communities. In moving toward a community-based interface with welfare recipients through the mahalla and village committees, Uzbekistan has taken a novel approach to meeting needs, but it runs the risk of marginalizing those mothers who are in the direst need, especially divorcees and abandoned wives. In explaining why divorcees and abandoned wives have become the population most at risk of exclusion from the social welfare network, I contrast recent developments with the Soviet past and with the

4. She was told by the representative, "We don't need women like you." It would be fallacious to assume that women have common interests, and that those who are secure will be concerned for those who are not. Rather, many married women in villages and mahallas are suspicious of divorced and widowed women, who are assumed to be looking for new husbands or sexual partners.

5. Informant from a village in the Uchkurgon region, June 2001.

6. The 1996 research project was titled "Social Problems and Identity Formation in the Transition: Estonia, Ukraine, Uzbekistan." This study, which included twelve focus groups and ten oral histories in Uzbekistan, was carried out by the Center for Russian and East European Studies at the University of Michigan as part of the International Institute's grant from the Ford Foundation for "Crossing Borders." Research support came from the Ford Foundation (grant no. 950–1163) and the National Council of Soviet and Eastern European Research (NCSEER) (contract 812–11). My research in Uzbekistan in 2001 was sponsored by a Basic Research Grant from the University of Wyoming.

welfare systems of other countries. I point out that changing state policies are connected to changes in ideology about women and family in Uzbekistan, and explore the role that women's nongovernmental organizations may play in challenging the implications of Uzbekistan's welfare practices.

This chapter highlights two core aspects of the state — as a "regime of re/distributive policies" and as a "local site of policy formation and implementation" (Haney 1998, 750). It examines independent Uzbekistan's changing policies on social transfers to women as mothers, exploring the Soviet background for current practices as well as the particularities of welfare in the context of Uzbekistani society. I find that the unique path Uzbekistan has taken by putting welfare in the hands of the volunteers on the mahalla and village committees is similar to Japan's use of commissioned welfare volunteers (Gould 1993; Takahashi and Hashimoto 1997). In addition, Uzbekistan's recent designation of mahalla committees as organs of local self-government turns a social formation into an administrative unit empowered to act in the lives of its residents, much as China's residential committees and village committees do (Read 2000). Although the World Bank sees empowering mahalla, village, or residential committees as devolution of central authority to local government (Kudat et al. 2000), this move also creates stronger government control and social control over the lives of individuals. Without competitive politics and open information flows, devolution can support authoritarianism rather than lead to democratization.[7] When power is devolved as it has been in Uzbekistan, or, as Cynthia Werner shows (chapter 2) regarding Kazakhstan, the central government loses the ability to enforce unpopular laws or social policies, and thus those who lack social capital may be left with little recourse to justice.

Uzbekistan's changing welfare system is premised on the idea that the state can and should redistribute wealth through generous social welfare policies; this includes giving subsidies to mothers to support families in raising children. The Soviet system evolved toward the model adopted in Sweden, Germany, and France, where all mothers are entitled to such payments, rather than toward the need-based subsidies provided in the United

7. In Uzbekistan, village committees provide local self-government in small rural communities, while mahalla committees are the local self-government bodies in urban areas and larger rural villages. Parallels with China's village and (urban) residential committees are many. On residential committee functions, see Read 2000. On issues in welfare reform in China, with emphasis on China's lack of civil society, see Yi Feng, Ismene Gizelis, and Jeili Li, 1999. On authoritarianism in Uzbekistan's mahalla committee system, see Sievers 2002.

States and Britain. In Uzbekistan, a country where monthly salaries of individuals run the equivalent of $10 to $25, many families desperately need state aid, but the nature of entitlement is changing.

While Uzbekistan struggles to provide its citizens with a basic level of social support, a move from a late-Soviet maternalist policy to a more patriarchal policy is underway. This chapter examines that shift first at the level of the state as a regime of redistributive policies, through a historical look at the development of social welfare and mother's subsidies in Uzbekistan and then, examines, as a "local site of policy formation and implementation," the role of mahalla and village committees and women's expectations of them. Finally, I will discuss the discourse about women's social roles in independent Uzbekistan, which seems geared toward limiting women's choices rather than giving women more choices (IWRAW 2001, section 5).

A Comparative Framework

There is a wealth of literature on women and the welfare state. Much feminist scholarship on women and the state focuses on the reproduction of patriarchal relations within welfare systems, reveals women's roles in the creation of welfare systems, or portrays women's strategies of resistance as they manipulate those systems (Skocpol 1992; Haney 1996). Comparative studies of welfare systems have typically focused on Europe and the United States, with a growing interest in Eastern Europe in the years of post-Communist transition (Orloff 1993; Koven and Michel 1993; Bock and Thane 1991). Rarely were comparisons made between the Soviet welfare system and Western European systems; researchers emphasized a nexus of capitalism and welfare that seemed to set Western states apart from the former Eastern Bloc countries. Analyses of welfare states define the state in various ways, "as a regime of re/distributive policies, a national site of political struggle, or a local site of policy formation and implementation" (Haney 1998, 750).

Welfare state provisions for and control of women have been analyzed along a number of axes, all of which have implications for gender equality. In liberal market-economy systems, such as the United States and Japan, state benefits for support of mothers of young children are individual and need based and carry a social stigma. In social-democratic states, such as Sweden and Denmark, state benefits to support mothers are universal, not need based, and carry no social stigma, but are also designed to encourage women's participation in the labor force through strong support for child care. In some systems, women receive social welfare through their husbands; in Italy, child subsidies have been added to a husband's paycheck rather than being paid directly to the mother. Some systems, such as those of the Netherlands and Switzerland, give the most benefits when the model of husband as breadwinner, wife as housewife, is followed, and make difficult or unattractive the participation of mothers of young children in the labor force (Sainsbury 1994, 1996, 1999). Welfare policies that emerged in the twentieth century were strongly influenced by women's activism in some nations, such as the United States and Britain, but were crafted by the government without similar pressure from women in others, such as France (Koven and Michel 1993).

In many countries, whether or not they participated directly in government decisions regarding welfare, women formed discourses that could be called "maternalist," which sought to "[transform] motherhood from women's primary *private* responsibility into *public* policy" (Koven and Michel 1993, 2). In the early twentieth century, women's organizations in the United States and Europe legitimated women's claims on public resources through a defense of women's domestic roles and through calls for state support of mothers and children through subsidies or pensions. Middle-class reformist women argued for subsidies so that working-class women would be able to afford to stay home with their children rather than work. Socialist women argued for insurance and laws that would give mothers maternity leave with support and for daycare provision. Later, more radical socialist women argued that reproduction should be paid work, just as production is. Arguments seeking support for mothers often met opposition from those arguing for a "family wage." Ultimately, state concerns about declining birthrates and potential depopulation drove the establishment of government subsidies for mothers in many European states (Koven and Michel 1993). In the United States, feminists now see maternalist discourses as inherently limiting, but in many European states feminists continue to advocate "equality in difference," arguing that "motherhood is a social function" and should be supported by the state (Bock and Thane 1991). Soviet policies, as will be shown, showed strains similar to those of a variety of other states, but shifted from a system somewhat responsive to women's voices in the 1920s to a top-down system that served the government's emphasis on population growth and labor support.

The state shapes society through the disciplines that it imposes, both by regulating and by providing services. Health care and sanitation are both discipline and service: when the state takes upon itself the role of health care provider, it creates the expectation that the state will meet health needs and shapes society's actions by providing services to those who comply with regulations and limits service to the noncompliant. Social welfare also has disciplinary aspects: the state establishes the categories of those to be served and the terms by which they will receive aid. It creates specific relationships of dependency and fosters expectations of support.[8] The Uzbekistan state is an inheritor of the Soviet welfare system, of which Stephen Koktin writes: "Soviet socialism institutionalized comprehensive social welfare . . . that endlessly extended a logic of responsibility for, and state regulation of, society and populations" (Kotkin 2001, 160). In devolving welfare to local citizen self-government organizations, Uzbekistan has not dismantled but strengthened the disciplinary aspect of welfare provision.

Developing Welfare in Soviet Uzbekistan: A History of Subsidies for Mothers

In the Central Asian political units that preceded the Russian conquest, social welfare was largely a family, community (mahalla), and mosque-based function. These political units, the Kokand Khanate, Bukhara Emirate, and Khiva Khanate, were by any definition premodern states. Their essential functions included the preservation of order, defense, taxation, and the perpetuation of the regime. The idea that the state should intervene in family life, or provide social welfare, came with Russian conquest, and even then to a very small degree.

The first modern institutions of social welfare appeared in Central Asia with the Russian colonial administration; both their example and their limited scope pushed local Muslim elites to establish their own philanthropic organizations. The Russian administration in Turkistan was miserly; taxes raised from the colony were supposed to offset the costs of military occupation and colonial administration. Thus, government gave little support to institutions of social welfare, and those that existed served primarily the Russian colonists rather than the local population. The colonial administration saw a limited role for public health, becoming actively involved in hygiene and sanitation in order to prevent epidemics (Cavanaugh 2001).

8. Social welfare policies and social work have been criticized by U.S. scholars for creating these kinds of dependency and control, as, for example, in Margolin 1997, Polsky 1991, and Kunzel 1993. However, in drawing attention to social welfare as discipline, I am not suggesting that the people of Uzbekistan or any other place would be better off without the state's provision of social welfare. I am simply pointing out a fundamental characteristic of the modern state: its seemingly ever-increasing intervention in the lives of citizens (Kotkin 2001).

In the early twentieth century, Central Asian reformist intellectuals, the Jadids, introduced new forms of education, sociability, and philanthropy (Khalid 1998, 132). Reformers also sought change in Central Asian women's roles, and the discourses that arose elsewhere in the Islamic world in the late nineteenth and early twentieth centuries began to emerge in Central Asia as well. Many books with titles like "*The Reform of Women*" — published in Arabic, Persian, Ottoman, Chagatay, and Tatar — called for women to improve the nation by becoming educated and thus becoming better mothers. Throughout the Islamic world, Muslim women used these demands for improvement of the "nation's mothers" to lay claim to modern education and to new social roles (Badran 1995; Abu-Lughod 1998). In Central Asian cities, the Muslim Women's Association advocated girls' education and preached women's self-improvement, through public lectures on hygiene and motherhood (Kamp 1998). This linkage of reform and improvement with motherhood was liberating in the early twentieth century, in Central Asia as well as elsewhere in the Islamic world, because it gave women a way to claim rights to education and to a role in public life. However, a discourse that was liberating at that time set up limitations for women of more recent generations (Najmabadi 1998).

Changing governmental structures and political forms expanded Uzbek women's dependence on the state. After the October 1917 Bolshevik Revolution, the new Communist government placed high priority on deliberate social transformation. In the 1920s, the Soviet government began to take up the roles of educator, health care provider, social welfare provider, provider of justice, and controller of the economy, roles that had previously been the domain of private or religious bodies. By targeting its services to Uzbek women through the Women's Division of the Communist Party, the state began to raise women's expectations that the state would educate their children, direct the divorced and needy to paid labor, provide low-cost goods and basic health care, and defend them from some kinds of abuse.

The Women's Division served as a channel for the Communist Party's increasing involvement in social welfare, although its main purpose was to bring women into the party and politicize them. In Turkistan, between 1919 and 1926, the Women's Division established women's literacy courses, mother and child health clinics, legal clinics for women, job training for women, and lectures and clubs for women. However, between 1926 and 1930, many of the Women's Division social work activities were moved to the ministries of health and of education. In Uzbekistan, the Women's Division, left to focus on unveiling women and politicizing them, no longer acted as an organization that addressed a wide spectrum of women's and social problems. Although the Women's Division acted as a pressure group in the 1920s to influence Soviet welfare policy, it was dissolved in 1934, when the "woman question" was declared to be resolved. After this no single organization advocated for women's interests. Policies on social welfare appear to have been planned and implemented by the state without pressure from organized women's groups (see, e.g., Aminova 1977; Massell 1974; Kamp 1998, chap. 3).[9] The state's concept of welfare for women, and for everyone, was reformulated: women's labor was wanted on the collective farms and in new urban enterprises, and the reward for work would be access to certain kinds of welfare.

Soviet welfare policy in the Russian Federation in the 1920s and 1930s emerged at a time when liberal and illiberal regimes developed welfare as a core component of modernization (Kotkin 2001). Although Soviet welfare was linked to ideology, specific policies were driven by crises, such as the rising number of homeless children, high unemployment, and later a plunging birthrate (Goldman, 1993). Welfare policies designed to address crises in the Russian Soviet Federal Socialist Republic (RSFSR) were applied equally to the other republics, including Uzbekistan.

The Soviet state's policy from the 1920s was that welfare should be an entitlement, not charity. Social transfers were minimal, not enough to sustain their recipients, but the number of recipients was large: pensioners, invalids, orphaned and impoverished children, single mothers, and mothers of many children. Although social transfers were small in the 1920s and early 1930s, they expanded throughout the Soviet period. Of particular significance to Uzbekistan were, and remain, child subsidies for mothers of many children. The policy of paying such subsidies emerged with the Soviet government's adoption of the 1936 Family Code, itself a response to plummeting birth rates in the provinces of the Russian Federation (Madison 1968). Similar plunges in birthrates had prompted state subsidies for mothers in both liberal and fascist states in Europe in the 1920s and 1930s (Bock and Thane 1991). The Soviet Family Code granted four months of maternity leave, small payments (10 rubles) to working mothers of infants, and, for mothers who gave birth to a seventh child, a payment of 2,000 rubles per year for the child's first five years, and the same for any additional children. An eleventh child gained for its mother a payment of 5,000 rubles for "one year and 3,000 rubles for the next four years"(Goldman 1993, 331–32).

9. Recent literature on the Women's Division of the Communist Party includes Woods 1997, Clements 1997, and Stites 1978, 1990. Although the Women's Division cannot be seen as a voluntary or civil society element, it did provide a forum for limited public debate over policies on divorce, abortion, day care, and women's and children's welfare (Goldman 1993).

In the effort to increase the birthrate, the Soviet Union adopted a maternalist ideology concerning women. The new assumption was that all women should become mothers; along with work, motherhood became a socialist duty. The decline in fertility that helped to push the Soviet state toward pronatalism was not seen in Uzbekistan, where birthrates remained high; Uzbekistan's challenge in the early Soviet period was not to combat a declining birth rate but to reduce the high rate of infant mortality. In implementing policies that subsidized mothers, the Soviet Union was part of a welfare trend that shaped state policies in many European countries, and this trend would grow and continue to shape the welfare policy of Soviet successor states such as Uzbekistan.

Mothers' Expectations of the State

With the 1936 code, the Soviet state established one of the primary expectations that women in Uzbekistan still have: that the state will pay mothers subsidies for their children. In the 1930s, the rewards were greatest for those with truly large families, and with the creation of the award "Hero Mother," a woman's role in reproduction could receive the same sort of recognition as her role in production. In 1947, the state broadened the subsidies to begin with the fourth child, to be paid until the child reached age five, and to increase with each additional child (Madison 1968, 43, 208–9). After 1974, in low-income regions of the USSR, such as Uzbekistan, child subsidies were paid for every child until age eight. In 1989, this age was raised to twelve (Chapman 1991, 39). Maternity leave also grew from a few paid weeks in the 1950s, when the labor market needed workers, to one year with partial pay plus six unpaid months in the 1980s. The growth in maternity leave emerged when the economy could not provide jobs for all; in the 1980s, some politicians and economists urged that women should stay home rather than work (Buckley 1989, 195–96). In 1989, new laws gave paid maternity leave for eighteen months and allowed a mother to take unpaid leave while maintaining her place of employment and getting the time counted toward her pension, until her child was three years old (Buckley 1989, 40). By the time Uzbekistan became independent in 1991, mothers there took for granted that the state should pay them child subsidies regardless of need.

In independent Uzbekistan, relations between women and the state continue to be shaped by Soviet political formations; as Kelly McMann argues in chapter 7, Soviet legacies continue to shape expectations. Some women's expectations of the state have not changed; in particular, mothers continue to regard child subsidies as an entitlement. Although child subsidies are quite small, in aggregate they comprise a large direct transfer of state resources to individuals, and they establish a norm in which the state is patron to all mothers and all mothers are dependents. The policy also places the government of Uzbekistan in a contradictory position: on one hand, the government's policy is to reduce the birthrate, while on the other its child subsidies encourage childbearing.[10]

Mahalla Committees: The Local Site of Policy Implementation

In most of the countries of Europe and the Middle East, social work is a profession, and the social worker is the welfare claimant's gateway to government aid. However, the Soviet Union did not have a social work profession per se; instead, much of this work was handled by locally based social welfare committees composed of Communist Party members, health care workers, trade union representatives, and teachers, who assessed need and provided an interface between the state and the entitled. In the post-Communist period, states in East Central Europe and, to a lesser extent, Russia and Ukraine have begun using professional social workers in their welfare systems. Uzbekistan has retained a late-Soviet welfare ideal but has replaced former workplace-related systems for welfare distribution with a volunteer, neighborhood-based system. Uzbekistan has taken an innovative direction, placing responsibility for welfare decisions in the hands of volunteers on the mahalla committee. The mahalla committee's composition, consisting primarily of retired, "respected" men in the community, and its status not only as the welfare agency but also the local organ of citizen self-government has disturbing implications for the social control of women in Uzbekistan.[11]

10. *Report on the Status of Women in Uzbekistan*, published by the Regional Programme in Support to Gender in Development of RBEC/UNDP, chapter 4, 2. The International Women's Rights Action Watch Uzbekistan report, section 12, notes that the government supports contraception through its Ministry of Health, and that contraceptive use has been rising; NGOs provide information about sexuality and contraception as well. Some rural doctors have also been accused of forced sterilization of women who have given birth to four or five children.

11. The mahalla committee is led by the *oq soqol*, according to Shukur Timurov, head of the mahalla Fond (a government sponsored charity); an oq soqol is a whitebeard (Abramson 1998, 189). Sievers (2002, 121) describes an officially appointed *rais* as the mahalla committee leaders, with a parallel, unofficial oq soqol also providing leadership. The term *oq soqol* is traditional, is very obviously gendered, and is one of respect for an elder man in the community. However, there are women leaders of some mahalla committees; in 2000, there were 483 women leaders among 10,133 village and mahalla committees. CER: National Human Development Report 2000, http://www.cer.uz/nhdr/2000/ch-3.htm, accessed Jan. 6, 2002.

In 1994, the government of Uzbekistan began to transfer responsibility for most aspects of social welfare, including child subsidies, to the mahalla committees. Mahalla means urban neighborhood; scholars analyzing mahallas have evaluated them primarily as sites of social interaction (Abramson 1998; Koroteyeva and Makarova 1998; Makarova 1999). The mahalla committee (and the village committee in rural areas) is also an administrative body; it is the organ of local self-government in Uzbekistan below the *hokimiyat*, or district administration (Sievers 2002). Scholars, policy makers, and politicians regard the mahalla committee as the inheritor of a prerevolutionary form of community leadership, although it is more recognizably the inheritor of the role of local soviet, or council. The mahalla committee is generally made up of respected older men who take responsibility for community order.[12] In the Soviet period, the mahalla committee provided support for life-cycle rituals, such as weddings and funerals, within the neighborhood. In the early 1990s, mahalla committees were explicitly connected with the neighborhood mosques, though this connection may have weakened under the government's antifundamentalist policies in the late 1990s. After independence, the government began to turn the mahalla committee into the organ of local "citizen self-government," entrusting it with functions that had been provided by soviets and by bureaucracies. In 1994, mahalla committees were entrusted with the distribution of welfare, and in 1995, the Uzbekistan Constitution, in Article 105, recognized them as governing bodies, the head of which should be elected. By 1999, the mahalla committees' official responsibilities included controlling a local budget for development of territory and sanitation; assisting in environmental matters; proposing changes to mahalla borders, names, streets; distributing land plots; providing aid to poor families; taking an active role in law and order by appointing "prevention inspectors" who act as local police and health inspectors; mediating domestic disputes; providing or withholding divorce papers; and registering residency and religious activities (CER: NHDP 2000; Gleason 2001; Human Rights Watch 2001; Sievers 2002). Mahalla committees still

12. Community leaders traditionally were those who had social and cultural capital — men who had wealth, specific knowledge, and standing in the community because of lineage or political connections. I am using "respected" as shorthand for the idea that mahallas include many people, some of whom uphold community norms and have social and cultural capital and are therefore "respected" and selected as leaders, and those who are marginalized for various reasons. Khamidov (1999) points to the social capital of mahalla committee leaders as one of the reasons for their effectiveness. On the mahalla committee as the inheritor of prerevolutionary forms, see, e.g., Khamidov 1999; Abramson 1998; Makarova 1999; and Saktanber and Özataş-Baykal 2000.

perform their previous roles, providing help with funerals and weddings, but now they also are empowered to grant business credit and turn in criminals. The mahalla committees thus look rather like China's residential committees, which provide services to those in their neighborhoods while also patrolling and compiling information about them (Read, 2000). Just as in China, state "responsibility for, and state regulation of, society," are provided directly and cheaply by the mahalla committee in Uzbekistan.

According to Shavkat Mirolimov, the Uzbek author of a book that describes mahalla as an element in state ideology, the mahalla committee members are elected, but usually competitive elections are held only for the mahalla committee chair, from a slate of candidates that is approved by the hokimiyat (Saktanber and Özataş-Baykal 2000, 232).[13] In effect, this means that elections are not truly open and competitive, as only candidates with government approval may run. The chair of the mahalla committee fills a paid position, and mahalla committees may also have another paid employee or two. The other members are volunteers, generally men of high reputation within the mahalla, recognized and seen as legitimate leaders but not elected, and not to be thrown out of office in an election. The government requires that one vice-chair of the mahalla committee be a woman; otherwise, women's influence on the committee is indirect. Village committees in small rural communities have the same structure and functions.

In 1996, the government assigned mahalla committees the task of assessing need among mahalla residents and determining eligibility for welfare. Bakhtiyor Khamidov, deputy prime minister of Uzbekistan, justified the devolution of control over welfare to these local bodies in terms of flexibility and cost effectiveness:

> The mahalla system is particularly unique in empowering local communities to decide upon the allocation of benefits, combining a rules-based approach with discretionary allocation, being responsive to changing family needs, and having good poverty-targeting outcomes. Costs of administration are very low, making it one of the most effective schemes for providing targeted social benefits. (Khamidov 1999)

Those who are charged with assessing need are not required to have any professional training in this area, and they are the same people who

13. In the summer of 2001, well-informed people in various locations in Uzbekistan, in response to questions about elections in mahallas, said that elections were held only for the chair, not for members.

are in charge of most aspects of neighborhood order and government. For the government, there are advantages to using community members as assessors of need: the mahalla committee members are generally familiar with the lives of people in the neighborhood, and most work without pay.

During the late-Soviet period, benefits to mothers increased to such an extent that, by continuing Soviet policy, Uzbekistan was paying benefits to nearly all mothers of children in the first years of independence. In 1996, the government of Uzbekistan passed new laws that extended the term of subsidy for children from fifteen to sixteen years, but tried to target these subsidies to low-income families. In 1997, this included 40 percent of all households in Uzbekistan and consumed 6.3 percent of the government's budget (*Report on the Status of Women in Uzbekistan*, chap. 6, p. 3). Because this program now targeted needy families, this figure represented a substantial reduction from the preceding period, when subsidies were paid to all regardless of need. Now the mahalla committee must assess the family's income and level of need, and set benefits accordingly (Falkingham 1999, 41). The basic level of assistance is set according to Article 39 of the Uzbekistan Constitution (1992), which states: "Pensions, allowances, and other kinds of welfare may not be lower than the officially fixed minimum subsistence wage." For a needy family with one child, the subsidy is 50 percent of a monthly minimum wage; for a family with two children, it is 100 percent of the monthly minimum wage, and it rises from there (*Report on the Status*, chap. 6, table A).

While long-term child subsidies have been limited to the needy, all mothers qualify for other subsidies: a onetime birth payment and monthly payments for each child under two years of age. The birth allowance, which is paid either by the workplace or the mahalla committee, equals twice a monthly minimum wage. The monthly payments, paid through the mahalla committee, equal 150 percent of the monthly minimum wage (*Report on the Status*, chap. 2). In addition, as in the Soviet period, time off for maternity leave, up to three years, still counts toward time worked when reckoning retirement and pension. The direct rewards given for each birth are more widespread than they were at any time in the Soviet period.[14] However, although subsidies for birth are widespread, their monetary value is far less than it was in the 1980s and provides very limited aid to a family budget.

14. Similar policies are followed in some other post-Soviet states; Russia, for example, is proposing raising the initial payment for any birth to 10,000 rubles, and Russia's partially paid maternity leaves extend to three years.

Most of the money that women in Uzbekistan expect to receive from the government in support of motherhood is now channeled through the mahalla committees. A recent World Bank report notes that "these local committees are one of the few institutions that has retained, and even increased its status among ordinary citizens," and urges that "the local mahalla/qishlaq committees should also be given more authority and responsibility for developing and implementing social welfare programs" (Kudat et al. 2000, p. 253). However, Mark Waite raises the possibility that "the Mahalla environment may be oppressive to those who do not wish to conform with the generally conservative moral codes it promotes" (Waite 1997, 227–28). When these transfers were distributed by social welfare committees, made up of social workers, trade union representatives, and health care workers, and when the state directed some of its aid to women through the women's committees, women were involved in the decision-making process. Now, women usually are involved only as recipients of aid.

Although in most welfare states the interface between a claimant and the state is the professional social worker, Japan's system uses a neighborhood-based "commissioned welfare volunteer," or *minsei i'in*, in this role. Most minsei i'in are older men, between fifty and seventy, who do not have other work but who are paid only a stipend for their welfare work. The minsei i'in is appointed "based on his/her 'reputation in the local community [as a responsible person]' rather than on any vocational certification or professional qualification," (Takahashi and Hashimoto 1997, 308). The minsei i'in are local investigators into the needs of the elderly, children, and low-income families, who direct community members to the social services that they need but do not make decisions about welfare allocation. Likewise, China's Residential Committees, although they intervene directly in many aspects of the lives of neighborhood dwellers, "[help] social welfare agencies to identity and assist some of the neediest residents"(Read 2000, 817). In both cases, the government uses these local volunteers to facilitate welfare. They investigate need but do not determine the level of support to which the claimant is entitled; they are seen as helpful go-betweens, not as dispensers of the state's resources. In addition, the Japanese minsei i'in are obliged to "keep confidential any information on the private life of citizens" (Takahashi and Hashimoto 1997, 309–10). In Japan, as in the United States, welfare has a social stigma attached, and there are no broad entitlements or child subsidies for mothers. The local volunteer provides confidential advice to the needy on how to obtain help. In China, the residential committees have considerable local control but are not seen as a substitute for welfare agencies.

By contrast, in Uzbekistan, the volunteer committee is in charge of investigating need and determining what amount of support should be given to families. Child subsidies are at the core of women's expectations of the government in Uzbekistan, even more so in the 1990s than during the Soviet period; placing the mahalla committees in charge of them makes overt the two sides of women's dependency — on the state and on patriarchal structures.

The World Bank report recommended giving mahalla committees even greater authority in developing and implementing welfare programs, but the members' volunteer status and lack of professional qualifications should give pause to those eager to hand state resources over to unaccountable bodies. In 2001, investigators from the Ministry of Finance found substantial fraud in welfare determinations and judged that the "organs of local self-government," or mahalla and village committees, "either do not know the appropriate procedures fully or else they are practicing leadership in their own interests."[15] In this case, as in some others in which the public good has been made subject to local control, local bodies may ignore central laws, as Cynthia Werner shows in chapter 2, and make decisions based on short-term interests or in the interests of specific local actors. In the literature on public goods and decentralization the dominant argument is that decentralization provides public goods more efficiently than centralized approaches. However, the social, political, and economic conditions that may make decentralization an effective strategy in many places and for many kinds of public goods do not exist in Uzbekistan. In particular, the absence of lobbying and advocacy organizations, the absence of free flows of information, and lack of real local democracy or competitive parties, all bring many of the assumptions of decentralizers into question. Without options, alternatives, and safeguards, an exchange of central control for local control may simply be an exchange of central authoritarianism for authoritarianism with a local face, or of centralized corruption for local corruption (Akin et al. 2001; Feng et al. 1999).

What incentives do mahalla committees have for providing welfare to their least popular constituents, single mothers? Welfare money comes from the central government, which pressures the committees to show a reduction in poverty by reducing the numbers of families receiving aid.

15. *"Adresnaia pomoshch' — ne po adresu?" Narodnoe Slovo* (Tashkent), 26 June 2001. Typically, workplaces help employees to qualify for family subsidies by providing documents to show a lower monthly income than they actually receive. Other examples of fraud include mahalla committees certifying subsidies for children who are not yet born and assigning benefits without any documentation concerning income.

Although care of the elderly is a matter of pride, many communities would choose not to provide for single mothers, hoping that instead they will leave the community. John Akin and others (2001, 9) argue that "if individuals undervalue the public good, and if local governments are more responsible to individual preferences than is the central government, then decentralization unambiguously offers a lower level of public good provision." Although the Uzbekistan Constitution guarantees support to poor mothers, welfare that is allocated by the mahalla committee can be channeled according to local prejudice or favoritism.

From Soviet Women's Committees to Uzbek Women's Committees

Literature on the state and women points to the state's actions in constituting women's identities and roles; welfare programs express state ideologies about motherhood, reproduction, and women's sexuality. Although women have been active in shaping state ideologies and welfare policies in many other societies, in Uzbekistan women's voices are formally represented through the state-appointed women's committees, but women have not organized autonomously to represent their own interests in shaping the welfare system.

In addition to the mahalla committees, the government of Uzbekistan operates a network of women's committees, which inherited their role from the Soviet-period women's councils. In the early 1960s, Khrushchev drew attention to the low level of Soviet women's political activity, and with his drive for greater mass participation and "democratization" of the Communist Party, he also called for reviving the women's councils, which in the 1930s had been weak successors to the Women's Division (Buckley 1989, 141–43). The women's councils of the 1960s through 1980s were supposed to be ad-hoc, spontaneous groups, but they were adjunct organizations to party or soviet bodies or trade unions, and their purpose was to draw women into political life and into the workforce. They organized lectures and interest circles for women, and had sections concerned with "daily life, culture, work among children, healthcare and the organization of public services" (Buckley 1989, 149–50). They were also made channels of some small amounts of aid to women.

From the time of their revival, the women's councils saw women's special needs as their reason for existing and promoted an ideology that based social roles on biological roles:

> The rather rigid orthodoxy was that women were a separate group of workers from men and a specific category of social labour due to the

> "inalienable and irreplaceable" functions of motherhood. . . . Traditional gender role stereotypes were reinforced by these arguments. . . . It was not suggested that casting woman as the main childrearer, cook, shopper, washer and cleaner might result in gender inequalities. Such a suggestion was regarded as typical of bourgeois feminism. (Buckley 1989, 175)

The immutability of gender roles, and the primacy of motherhood in women's lives, all supported by Soviet ideology, fit well with Uzbek cultural attitudes toward gender roles and did not challenge them at all. Soviet pronatalist policies supported Uzbek ideas about the importance of fertility, and child subsidies, while making no one wealthy, helped sustain a high birthrate. Emphasis on women's role in child rearing, combined with extended maternity leave and subsidies in the form of direct payments to most Uzbek mothers of young children, contributed to the already strong tendency not to question gender roles but to perpetuate women's dependency on men and on the state. In the late 1980s, the Uzbek press echoed the idea, mentioned above, that women should leave the workforce and stay home, partly as a backlash against earlier Communist idealizations of women as workers and partly in response to a rising rate of real unemployment (Pukhova 1988).

In Uzbekistan, women's expectations of the state are also shaped by their role in the family, a role that is informed by Islamic culture.[16] Throughout Islamic societies, including those in Central Asia, there are common ideas about family relationships and gender roles: men are women's guardians, providers, and protectors; women's primary role is motherhood; and male honor depends on controlling women's sexuality.[17] With the revival of religious expression in the late 1980s in Uzbekistan, widespread citation of hadith, or teachings attributed to the prophet

16. Many Islamic countries articulate ideologies that state that women are equal to men but declare that a woman's primary role is that of mother and wife. Both law and social welfare regulations often restrict a woman's mobility and make her dependent on men. Examples can be found in Haddad and Esposito (1999) and Joseph (2000). When, in 1997, Uzbekistan instituted a law placing restrictions on women and girls in travel abroad, they echoed the restrictions that other Islamic states place on women, though those restrictions are far more severe in many Middle Eastern countries than would be conceivable in Uzbekistan.

17. The Qur'an, 4:34, says, "Men are the protectors and maintainers of women" (Yusuf Ali translation). Although a normative source does not dictate lived realities, scriptural and other religious sources have long informed ideas about family life among Muslims (Fernea and Bezirgan 1977, xix).

Muhammad, regarding motherhood seemed to reinforce Soviet gender ideology.

In the late-Soviet period, Uzbekistan's women's councils were not ad-hoc, spontaneous organizations; rather, they were headed by women of some stature in the local party or soviet or trade unions. Women's committees could advocate for the collective interests of groups of women by calling for better working conditions, but their seemingly most significant role was to give assistance to individuals, especially single mothers (Abdurazakova 1986, 188–89).

In the late 1980s, when glasnost made it permissible not only to say that the "woman question" had not been resolved in the Soviet Union but to openly discuss discrimination against women and the sources of ongoing inequality, the women's councils became a more active force. In Uzbekistan, the wave of women's suicide by self-immolation pushed the women's councils to collect information, investigate cases, and discuss openly the reasons for this suicide wave.[18] The Women's Committee of Uzbekistan had a thorough top-to-bottom network made up of the local women's councils; their role, though limited, was well known to many women.

When Uzbekistan became independent and began to change its structure, the Women's Committee remained (and now its divisions are usually referred to as committees, not councils) and was given a substantially higher profile when its leader was named to a new position, deputy prime minister and chairwoman of the Committee on Women's Affairs.[19] (It should be noted that, except for the head of Human Rights, this set-aside position is the only cabinet post in the Uzbek government held by a woman.) At the *viloyat* (province), region, and local level, the Women's Committee has offices and appointed, paid staff members. Turkish researchers Ayse Saktanber and Asli Özataş-Baykal write, "According to a decree of President Karimov on 2 March 1995, a female vice-chair is compulsory for each administrative unit (mahalla, rayon, province), thus providing women with much more authority." The women's committee in the mahalla is made up of volunteers, who are "elected according to the advice of mahalla inhabitants" (Saktanber and Özataş-Baykal 2000, 234). In prac-

18. In June 1991, I attended a meeting of members of the Tashkent Women's Council at which this topic was discussed; the chair praised Karimov's decision to suppress press coverage of self-immolation, noting that in the previous quarter the number of such incidents in Tashkent had dropped to one. Suicide remains a problem, but self-immolation is less widespread than it was in the 1980s.

19. As of 2001, this post is filled by Dilbar G'ulomova. Http://www.uzland.uz/gov_staf.htm, accessed 3 June 2001.

tice, this seems to mean that they may be approved by public opinion but, like the mahalla committee members, they are not chosen through competitive elections. Rather, they are volunteers who come from respected families and possess social capital and who may advise and influence the mahalla committee. The women's committee remains separate from the mahalla committee; it has a separate budget and is not part of the local administration. At higher levels, paid women's committee members are appointed and come from a variety of employment backgrounds; the government seeks their advice.

The women's committee occasionally can provide women with emergency aid, but it does not share any of the mahalla committee's authority over social welfare payments. However, women turn to both the women's committees and the mahalla committees in search of aid, as is evident from focus group data.

Women's Expectations in the 1990s

In 1996, with a grant from the Ford Foundation, focus group research was undertaken in various regions of Uzbekistan to assess social identity in the transition. Focus group participants in Tashkent, rural Fergana, Bukhara city, and rural Bukhara described the difficulties and problems that arose during the transition, and in discussing them, mentioned many of their own strategies for coping with economic and social problems. Moderators asked the groups which individuals or organizations they saw as responsible for problems and which they saw as helpful in ameliorating the social cost of the transition. In their responses are widely repeated statements that reveal some of their expectations concerning the state's role in welfare.[20] Not surprisingly, because they are the recipients of far more direct government aid then men, women in the focus groups commented far more than men about child subsidies and expectations of aid from various social welfare organizations.

Although the extension of child subsidies to almost all children and the laws extending maternity leave are fairly recent, women in the 1996 focus groups regarded both subsidies and extended maternity leave as entitlements. Sociologist Deniz Kandiyoti points out that in household surveys

20. "Social Problems and Identity Formation in the Transition: Estonia, Ukraine, Uzbekistan." A study carried out by the Center for Russian and East European Studies at the University of Michigan as part of the International Institute's grant from the Ford Foundation for "Crossing Borders." This research was supported by the Ford Foundation (grant no. 950–1163) and the National Council of Soviet and Eastern European Research (NCSEER) (contract 812–11).

respondents did not necessarily mention their income from pensions and subsidies: "It became apparent that benefits were not perceived as income since this was something they were entitled to" (Kandiyoti 1999, 517).

From the focus groups, it was also clear that women throughout Uzbekistan counted on receiving child subsidies to provide cash for goods that they could not produce themselves. Urban women complained the amounts were so small as to be meaningless, but rural women, whose salaries often went unpaid seemed to regard the child subsidies as a somewhat reliable source of cash, along with retirement pensions. However, child subsidies are not always paid in cash. Shoira, a woman from a village near Bukhara, said:

> There are monthly allowances for children, but they aren't paid on time, only once in ten months. And they pay them with a check that is taken only at the store in the village. The store does not give food. They have some crummy china dishes and they say, "Here, take some of these!" If they would give out food instead of checks, that would be all right.

Women from rural communities near the city of Fergana also commented that children's subsidies were not paid on time. Although government policy was to pay pensions and child subsidies before salaries, some of those payments were not being made.

In 1996, responsibility for welfare had recently been transferred to the mahalla committees. When asked whether she would turn to her local mahalla committee for help, Zebo, from the Bukhara Tajik women's focus group, said, "If you want to talk about the mahalla board, is the chairman a leader? He never issues a single piece of paper without money; he will ask money for it. Instead of helping you, he is looking for a bribe." Aziza concurred, "Yes, it is really true." And Leila added, "And even then you have to beg and humiliate yourself."

When the moderator of the Fergana rural women's focus group asked whether there were leaders in their mahalla committees who spoke out on their behalf, she was greeted with a chorus of responses: "No, there are no such people in mahalla committees. The mahalla committees only distribute flour!"

Some of the participants' expectations of the mahalla committees were based on what had been those committees' primary role, providing services to the community for life-cycle events. In urban neighborhoods and villages, weddings and circumcisions are often large, open events; each family considers it an obligation to send at least one representative to any major event in the neighborhood, and the host family is obligated to provide hospitality to all. At the time of independence, the mahalla committees' main service was to provide tables and benches, dishes, and some labor for these events.

One rural Fergana woman, Laylo, thought the mahalla committee ought to help out more by providing monetary support for these events. She complained:

> What are the mahalla what's-it-called doing? I do not work anywhere; my husband is the only one who works. I have a child, and this son is growing up. We need to have a *toi* [a circumcision celebration]. People from the mahalla said that if you go to the mahalla committee and apply, they will allot monetary aid to you, since you are not working and not getting a children's allowance. So I went. They sent three commissions to our house, they came and inspected, and said, "You have a gold ring; sell it and use the money for food. When you have used that up, then we will give you material aid." I sold my wedding ring and we lived on this money for a month and a half. . . . We are still in this situation.

Laylo's comments suggest that some people may not know exactly what the mahalla committee is supposed to do; she apparently went to them looking for some extra funds for her son's circumcision. To her surprise, she had to go through a needs assessment and was not judged needy enough for aid as long as she held one valuable gold asset.[21]

In the Fergana group, Shahlo said, "Help is given, but if people like me come to the *hokims* [regional governors], they do not treat us well and do not give aid." Shahlo was a single mother, and she alluded to that status as "people like me." Malika commented that even though they were aware of President Karimov's directives, local leaders would not fulfill those directives to help single mothers: "If someone like Shahlo-opa comes and asks, they will send her away and say, 'Come tomorrow or the next day,' isn't it so? They *have* to give aid to single-parent families!" In Bukhara, Aziza said, "We mothers who bring up our children alone used to be given one-room apartments for free, at the expense of the budget, and the women's council used to help us with an allowance. At present we also receive an allowance, 600 *som*. What can that buy?" (The monthly minimum wage was about 1,500 som at the time of this focus group.) She

21. In anecdotal evidence from June 2001, some mahalla committees assess need according to income while others include assets. In one case, a family that owned an old car that had not run for years was told they could not qualify for aid until they sold the car — but they could not sell the car without repairing it, and they had no money to do so.

added later, "A single mother will never get anything from the government!"

Divorcees face severe social disapproval in Uzbekistan. The mahalla committees that are now responsible for giving allowances to single mothers such as Shahlo and Aziza may not be giving them equal treatment with other needy families. A 1999 survey of mahalla residents' perspectives on the mahalla confirms this thesis. Surveys asked two thousand residents about their level of reliance on the mahalla in their daily lives. Although reliance varied with region and nationality, the most significant difference among residents was that divorcees relied on the mahalla far less than other residents (Sievers 2002, 124).

Expectations that the women's councils would help ordinary women meet practical needs formed in the 1960s, when the councils began directing small amounts of aid to women in need. In the Bukhara Tajik women's focus group in 1996, one participant, Aziza, remembered that the women's council had provided a subsidy to her single mother when she was raising children; the council also helped her mother get a plot of land.

Other participants expected the women's committees to continue this role: Leila and Mavluda both reported going to the women's committee for aid and being disappointed that the committee could not provide any. The women's committee could do no more than help Leila place her child in a day-care facility that she could not afford.

In the rural Fergana group, Laylo thought that the women's committees might be able to help with rural women's unemployment: "In these mahallas there used to be these women's [committees], specially appointed, working there. For example, they compile lists, going from door to door. If small businesses were organized for unemployed women, they would study their conditions, and if family conditions were not alleviated, they would bring work to the women's homes."[22]

The evidence from focus groups conducted in 1996 strongly suggests that women recipients of aid were not convinced that the newly implemented welfare policy would meet their needs. Yet, five years have passed since then. To assess the welfare system's present effectiveness and fairness, and thus whether women's attitudes have changed, follow-up research needs to be conducted.[23] The 1999 mahalla surveys, discussed

22. It should be noted that the Women's Committee is the umbrella organization to which the Business Women's Association of Uzbekistan belongs. The BWA has established micro-loan programs for women in a few areas.

23. The Mahalla Initiative Program run by Counterpart Consortium, an NGO working in Central Asia, proposes to do local assessments that may elucidate this question. http://www.cango.net/news/archive/october–26-00/a0002.asp, accessed 6 January 2002.

above, strongly suggest that while married women with children appreciate mahalla support, divorcees have been alienated and do not believe the mahalla will help them (Sievers 2002).

The government's policy of guaranteeing a basic standard of living for all by giving priority to paying pensions and child subsidies has been successful insofar as the indicators for living standards have fallen slowly during the decade of independence, rather than precipitously, as they have in neighboring states that adopted more radical economic reforms (Falkingham et al. 1997). Direct government aid has benefited women and children and has brought cash into needy homes. To the extent that promised payments are met, the government is fulfilling the expectations of several large constituencies, mothers of young children and pensioners. The continuation and, indeed, expansion of the Soviet pronatalist and antipoverty policy, giving significant allowances to mothers on the birth of a child and for two years thereafter, makes the government of Uzbekistan a direct patron to the majority of Uzbek women. Most of this patronage is funneled through, or obstructed by, the local mahalla committees.[24] Although the central government remains the source of welfare transfers, its devolution of decision-making authority to the mahalla committees means that it cannot guarantee the delivery of welfare to all those who are entitled; as Kelly McMann proposes, the "paradoxical strong-weak state" controls resources but lacks capacity to achieve its goals.

Ideology and Policy

In return for its patronage, the government of Uzbekistan wants women to raise children who will be loyal citizens of the state.[25] The relationship between the citizen and the state in Uzbekistan is formed by the state's response to a perception of the citizen's need, but it is also constitutive, as the state relates to women primarily as mothers and helps to create women who will also think of themselves primarily as mothers.

24. Incidents of mahalla committees threatening to withhold subsidies in order to pressure women to stay in unwanted marriages are found in the Human Rights Watch report, *Sacrificing Women to Save the Family?*, in the section titled "Mahalla and Other Community Government Bodies."

25. This idea is articulated across the Uzbek press, but a particular example is M. Kuronov, "O'zbek oilasining milliy tarbiaviy xususiatlari" in *O'zbekistonda Oila, Davlat va Jamiiat Qurilishida Ayollarining Roli va Gender Muammolari*, a collection of papers from a conference of the same name held 17 June 1999 and sponsored by the Uzbekistan Academy of Sciences and the Uzbekistan Republic Women's Committee (Tashkent: Fan, 1999).

In independent Uzbekistan, the state ideology regarding women draws on the Soviet legacy, makes explicit reference to Islamic discourses on motherhood, and is creating a newly emergent but rather ordinary nationalist linkage of women and the nation. In independent Uzbekistan in the early 1990s, Islamic teachings on women and family promoted women's primary role as mother and advocated that women stay at home. Such writings emphasized women's character, instructing women to be kind, righteous, good teachers to their own children, and compliant so as to create good relations with their husbands.[26] Since the early 1990s, secularized versions of these Islamic messages have also emerged from Uzbekistan's intelligentsia: in the context of nationalist teachings, they stress to girls that their role is to become wives and mothers, that they must be kind and obedient and get along.[27] The government of Uzbekistan has seen a need to include in its educational programs attention to "preparing girls for family life" (Xolmatova 1999). *Soadat*, the Uzbek women's journal, which traditionally has had close ties with the Women's Committee, has led the way in publishing the new ideology, offering little to the woman who wants change and much to reinforce tradition.[28]

26. Example: Fotimaxon Sulaymon qizi (Mudaris, or woman religious teacher at the Fotima-tuz-Zahro Madrasa, or Islamic school for girls), "Ilm" in *Saodat* 3–4 (1992): 26–27. Saktanber and Özataş-Baykal (2001, 242–47) also note these qualities in the types of booklets popular among women in two traditional Tashkent mahallas in the early 1990s.

27. Marfua Tokhtakhodjaeva, "Traditional Stereotypes and Women's Problems over the Period of Transition," http://www,undp.uz/GID/eng/UZBEKISTAN/NGO/uzneg_res.html accessed 3 May 2001. There are many examples of this genre. Some examples include Rahima Shomonsurova's *Er Eplamoq oson, lekin . . .* (Tashkent: O'zbekiston millii entsiklopediiasi 1998), in which a wise and loving mother-in-law has an entire book to tell her daughter-in-law how to get along as a good Uzbek wife; Dilbar G'ulomova (the minister of women's affairs) wrote *Xotin-Qizlar Entsiklopediiasi* (same publisher, 1999), a comprehensive volume of instructions for women on being a wife and mother, and not a word on how to combine career and family.

28. My favorite example: Tursunoy Sodiqova, "Yigitlarg'a Maktub," *Saodat* 4–5 (1993): pp. 8–9, a letter to her son before his wedding. She gives him advice such as: "Tell your wife, 'Never say anything bad about my parents or relatives, and don't do things that make me look bad.' Be proud; women don't love a man who doesn't know how to get upset or has no sense of honor. Don't agree to everything your wife wants; let her wait to find out whether you agree. If you agree too quickly, you'll lose your authority. Don't forget occasions that are important to her: bring her flowers and gifts. Have two faces: one that you show your wife, and one that you show to others. Don't let your wife get into fights with you over housekeeping. Try to help with housework. Don't ever open your heart completely to your wife. Let her always worry about whether or not she pleases you. Then she will always try to please you."

Emphasizing women's roles as wives and mothers bears some similarity to the discourse of the "reform of women" in the early twentieth century. In neglecting attention to women's roles as workers, though, the discourse is unrealistic, and more disciplinary than emancipatory (Najmabadi 1998).

This emphasis on women as wives and mothers complements government policies that have reduced support for working mothers. Although the government of Uzbekistan has generally paid child subsidies, other kinds of services have been cut. The provision of day care and kindergarten has decreased; the rate of enrollment in these preschool programs in Uzbekistan fell 32 percent between 1991 and 1996 (Falkingham 1999, 30). Between the late 1980s and 1997, the percentage of able-bodied women in Uzbekistan who were employed fell from a high of 48 percent to 35 percent, and that figure includes women listed as holding positions who have taken three-year maternity leaves. The figure leaves out the many women who work as day laborers and private vendors. The 1999 *Report on the Status of Women in Uzbekistan* observed that "women were forced to abandon jobs in industry or agriculture not only because of redundancies, but also because of diminished numbers of preschool institutions. The budgetary allocations for maintenance of kindergartens and creches [was] reduced greatly." Preschools either charge parents for their services or close (*Zhenzhshiny v. SSSR* 1989; *Report on the Status*, chap. 2, p. 5).[29]

In Uzbekistan, women's participation in the labor force is low compared with other former Soviet states and high compared with less developed countries, but it is declining. This decline is the result, in part, of economic factors. When unemployment is high (officially it is low, but government statistics do not take into account fictive employment, underemployment, and those who have given up looking for work), employers show a preference for male employees. By law, employment discrimination is illegal, but many employers are not eager to hire women to whom they may have to pay maternity benefits for several years. In addition, government protections of women mean they cannot take certain jobs, and employers face restrictions on the kinds of labor they can require of women (*Report on the Status*, chap. 5). Although a few women have found new and better-paid employment with foreign employers in Uzbekistan, many, who have fallen out of the official work force, earn a living as private entrepreneurs, producing or selling goods, or work as day laborers. This sort of work

29. The decrease in day-care facilities has been seen across all former Soviet states, and in some it has been more drastic than in Uzbekistan.

often pays better than official employment, but it provides no social welfare benefits.

Women's NGOs and Possibilities for Change

Recently, scholars have examined women and the state in Uzbekistan in comparison with other post-Communist and post-Soviet states, in works such as *Post-Soviet Women: from the Baltic to Central Asia* (Buckley, 1997) and *Making the Transition Work for Women in Europe and Central Asia* (Lazreg 2000). Although the political systems of most East Central European and Soviet successor states have moved toward greater openness and more dramatic economic change, Uzbekistan, like many states in the Middle East, has moved toward an authoritarian system. Scholars who write about women and the state in the Middle East have analyzed their situation in ways that seem applicable to Uzbekistan as well, not because of a commonality of Islamic culture but because of the commonalities of authoritarian systems. For example, Deniz Kandiyoti remarks on the contradictions that emerge for women's status and their ability to organize under authoritarian regimes in the Middle East: "Measures for the emancipation of women did not as a rule coincide with a drive for democratisation and the creation of a civil society where women's gender interests could be autonomously represented" (Kandiyoti 1991, 12–13). Opportunities for such autonomous representation are similarly limited in Uzbekistan.

Is it possible for women to pressure the government to change policies? Women's own activism in independent Uzbekistan takes place either in organizations that are government directed, such as the women's committees which are direct successors from a long Soviet past, or in nongovernmental organizations, many of which have connections to international development agencies. The NGOs are not controlled by the government, but they have to meet certain conditions to be officially registered, may receive government funds, and participate in government planning forums; and some appear willing to toe the line when the government wants their support for its ideological initiatives.[30] Although there are outspoken representatives in many NGOs, whether women will organize autonomously and be able to exert pressure on the government to

30. See, for example: "National Plan of Action for the Improvement of the Status of Women," http://www.undp.uz/GID/eng/UZBEKISTAN/GENERAL/GGA/act_plan.html, accessed 23 February 2001.

defend their rights and interests is questionable, because the current regime is authoritarian and because there is a general sense among women that fighting for one's rights is objectionable.[31]

In Uzbekistan, women's NGOs appear to be growing in a number of ways that represent a substantial departure from the past: they have international links; they draw on international gender critiques; and they are developing programs that are distinctly more feminist than those of the Soviet period, such as teaching women about sexuality and birth control and combating domestic violence. Can their activism make a dent in the *mentalité* of a society with decidedly patriarchal norms? Reports from NGOs are mixed.[32] Although women's NGOs have been given some government encouragement in Uzbekistan, the growth of NGOs is not taking place within a context of widespread democratization, and popular participation in NGOs is very low. One wonders whether women will be able to represent their interests autonomously in the future, or whether their activism will continue to be overseen, and to some extent controlled, by the state.

As activist and NGO leader Marfua Tokhtakhodjaeva makes clear, the voices in the media promoting a conservative role for women are strong, and many of them come from organs that are associated with the government, especially the Women's Committee, although it includes the defense of women's employment in its official priorities. The only substantial counterpoint — arguing strongly for women's full freedom of choice about work, motherhood, marriage, childbearing, and so on — comes from women's NGOs. The government of Uzbekistan apparently is willing to allow NGOs to use foreign aid for education about birth control and to establish crisis centers for victims of domestic abuse. Women's NGOs are able to advocate on women's behalf in these limited spheres (*Report on the Status*, chap. 2). However, the government of Uzbekistan faces the same issues that Middle Eastern countries faced in their 1980s "transitions": a serious economic downturn, a lack of democratic channels, Islamist opposition, and widening social stratification:

31. Typical of this phenomenon, in an interview with an Uzbek scholar Uzbek singer Dilarom Omonullaeva said, "By my nature I am not a fighter, so I too would not associate myself with feminism." "Prizvanie — eto dar, dannyi Allakhom," in *Zhenshchiny Tsentral'noi Azii, Sbornik Statei* 8 (Tashkent: Tashkentskii Zhenskii Resursnyi Tsentr, 2001), 97–98.

32. Central Asian Non-Governmental Organization Net posts reports from women's NGOs in Uzbekistan, as well as others, at http://www.cango.net.kg.

> The ways in which women are represented in political discourse, the degree of formal emancipation they are able to achieve, the modalities of their participation in economic life and the nature of the social movements through which they are able to articulate their gender interests are intimately linked to state-building processes and are responsive to their transformations. (Kandiyoti 1991, 2–3)

The government of Uzbekistan has not permitted the free emergence of a civil society and limits the roles that NGOs can play. Women's NGOs have not challenged the revisions of the state welfare system and have not yet established a discourse that would encourage women to organize for their own interests.

Conclusion and Recommendation

The structures of and approaches to social welfare in independent Uzbekistan are modifications of those inherited from the Soviet period, although now the mahalla committees perform functions that were transferred from the social welfare committees. The emphasis on a woman's role as nurturer likewise is inherited from the Soviet period, though now it is bolstered with Islamic sayings. The concept of separate women's organizations is inherited from Soviet practice, as well as from the gender-segregated forms of sociability in Central Asia that preceded and persisted throughout the Soviet period. So what has changed? Women's own activism, and its increasingly feminist themes, on one hand; on the other hand, the channels of patronage.

The transition from Soviet republic to independent state in Uzbekistan has been an unpredictable one for women. Aspects of the Soviet programs for women have remained, but the independent state has expanded emphasis on payments for and protection of motherhood, while decreasing support for women's work outside the home. Not only in the state's programs but also in its discourse, women in Uzbekistan are now, more than ever, told that their role is in the home, as wives and mothers. In this situation, women become more dependent on the state's subsidies for children, and it seems essential to ensure that these are, at least, paid out in a nondiscriminatory fashion so that divorced mothers will be given aid along with those from more socially approved categories.

Rather than adopting the model used by much of the developed world for the implementation of welfare through professional social workers, Uzbekistan has chosen a community-based system that depends on the character, knowledge, and inherent fairness of elders in the community.

The Uzbek state, like the Soviet state before it, retains a redistributive ideal difficult to uphold in a time of economic hardship. Its local sites of policy implementation, however, present a unique experiment: poor citizens are to turn to an unelected committee of their neighbors, generally elder men with substantial social and cultural capital, to ask for the aid to which they are entitled by law. Although it is nice to believe in the good will of community elders, a system based on the use of social work professionals who know the law and are accountable to it might provide the poor with a better guarantee of fairness, and it would prevent arbitrary power over the lives of community members from being concentrated in the hands of community elders.

The government's policy of entrusting more and more authority to the mahalla committees can be regarded as a form of decentralization and a means of creating more efficient and responsive government. However, citizens of very few countries would be happy with a decentralization in which police authority and authority for the division of spoils, from welfare to land to business credit, are placed in the hands of an unelected body whose elected head holds office only with the approval of the central government. Lawyer and sociologist Eric Sievers (2002) argues that rather than creating a base for democratization, "Uzbekistan is pioneering grassroots absolutism" (152). Democratization of the mahalla committees, with election of the candidates of local choice using the secret ballot, might make the committees more responsive to local majorities and reduce their manipulation by central authorities. But at the same time, it would be wise to place some of the functions of the mahalla committee in professional rather than elective or volunteer hands. Welfare may be a clear example, depending on the government's goals. If the goal of welfare is provision of aid modified by local prejudice — provision of aid in a discriminatory fashion with leverage for social control — then the current system should be maintained. Only the marginalized and the unpopular, those without effective access to social capital, will object, and the government may not see them as an important constituency. However, if the government is committed to its constitutional guarantees, and sees fairness as being as important as efficiency, then professionalizing social work would be a better policy. The mahalla committee would allocate welfare more fairly if work were shared with a professional, paid welfare worker, whose responsibility was to know the law and the government's policies and to implement those in an accountable way and to make allocation determinations. Welfare workers should have no connection to the mahalla committees' other functions, such as policing or allotting property. The most effective system, though not necessarily the cheapest, would be one more like the Japanese system, in which mahalla committee members and women's committee members would help identify families in need and provide an interface with the welfare system but not act as welfare workers, assessing need and making allocations.

2. Women, Marriage, and the Nation-State

THE RISE OF NONCONSENSUAL BRIDE KIDNAPPING IN POST-SOVIET KAZAKHSTAN

CYNTHIA WERNER

One night during the spring of 1994 while I was living with a rural Kazakh family, a loud knocking at the door woke me from a deep sleep. Everybody in the house got up to greet our close neighbors, Gulnara and Zharkyn, and we all drank tea as they recounted their disturbing news.[1] Their eighteen-year-old daughter Aiman was missing and they suspected that she had been kidnapped by an admiring suitor! Her parents didn't know what to do, but they wanted to ask us if we knew anything about her whereabouts, and they mentioned that they might need to borrow the family car. A few hours later, the kidnapping was confirmed when members of the groom's family arrived to apologize for the kidnapping. Aiman's parents arranged for several relatives, including another daughter, to return with the groom's relatives in order to check on Aiman's condition.

The next day, upon their return, they described Aiman's version of the events. On the evening of the kidnapping, she was home with her younger siblings doing household chores, while her parents were attending a

This chapter is based on fieldwork conducted in Kazakhstan between 1992 and 2001. The author thanks the following organizations for funding various stages of research that contribute directly to this paper: the Social Science Research Council (SSRC), the International Research and Exchanges Board (IREX), the Wenner-Gren Foundation for Anthropological Research, the National Council for East Eurasian and European Research (NCEEER), and the Lowry Mays College of Business and the Women's Studies Program at Texas A&M University. Some of the funds from the SSRC, IREX, and NCEEER grants were provided by the U.S. Department of State (Title VIII). Aigul Baituova, Tarbiye Orazbekova, Zhanna Torebaeva, Kamshat Torebaeva, Maria Parks, and Andy Scherer all provided research assistance. None of these organizations or individuals is responsible for the views expressed here.

1. Pseudonyms are used throughout this paper to protect the identity of those who participated in this study.

dinner party. While she was outside washing clothes, four young men entered her family's fenced compound. They grabbed her, forcibly placed her inside a waiting car, and drove a few kilometers to a nearby village. Once she was in the car, she recognized one of the men from school. Having realized that she was being kidnapped, Aiman assumed that this was the man who wanted to marry her. Only when the car arrived at its final destination did she find out that instead she had been kidnapped by a virtual stranger! Apparently, her new husband Serzhan had fallen in love with her at first sight after seeing her at the local bazaar. They had never so much as exchanged a few words. Through friends, he learned enough about her to know that he wanted to marry her. He also found out where she lived. Not knowing the young man, she was not excited about the prospect of being married to him. She was also disappointed to find out that he was almost ten years older than she was and his family was not very prosperous. Nevertheless, she did not want to deal with the shame of being a "girl who returned home" so she reluctantly decided to accept her fate.[2] Although they were extremely upset, her parents agreed that this was the right decision.

In the months and years that followed, I heard many more accounts of bride kidnapping. And, in the fall of 2000, I conducted extensive interviews on this topic. I found that Aiman's kidnapping is an extreme but not an isolated case. Although most brides are kidnapped by men they know and many are kidnapped with their full consent, there are other women such as Aiman who are kidnapped by strangers without their consent. Cases like these appear to be increasing, first in the late Soviet period and now in the post-Soviet period. Despite the illegal nature of these kidnappings, few women return home and even fewer take the case to court.

After seventy years of Soviet rule, the practice of bride kidnapping, let alone the existence of nonconsensual bride kidnapping, provides a fascinating case study for examining state-society relations in Soviet and post-Soviet Kazakhstan. From its inception, the Soviet state tried to transform the patriarchal nature of Central Asian society. In addition to providing women with new opportunities for education and employment, the state attempted to reduce gender inequality by banning a number of marriage

2. I use the term "girl" to refer to an unmarried woman. This is consistent with Kazakh language usage, which distinguishes "girls" (*qyz*) from "women" (*aiyel*) through the act of marriage and consequently sex. The term "girl" is synonymous with "virgin," and the term "woman" is synonymous with "wife." Contemporary American English, in contrast, distinguishes "girls" from "women" based on their age, though the distinction is often ambiguous. When it comes to men, the term "young man" is less problematic as a translation for the Kazakh term *zhigit,* and thus it is used consistently in this paper.

practices that limited a woman's freedom of choice, including child betrothals, arranged marriages, and kidnap marriages. Despite these policies, bride kidnapping did not disappear. In the Soviet context, especially in the southern regions of Kazakhstan, the practice of bride kidnapping was transformed in a way that reflected women's new position in society. By the 1970s, the practice of bride kidnapping had clearly been transformed into a practice of consensual elopement, disguised as abduction. In the post-Soviet context, the practice of bride kidnapping is being transformed yet again in a way that reflects the withdrawal of the state from gender-sensitive social issues.

Women, Marriage, and the State in Central Asia

Historical and Ethnographic Accounts of Marriage in Pre-Soviet Central Asia

Although the historical and ethnographic record is incomplete and biased by ethnocentric source material and Soviet interpretations, these accounts of pre-Soviet Central Asian society offer a glimpse into pre-Soviet social life. According to all available sources (Akiner 1997; Argynbaev 1978, 1996; Bacon 1966; Massell 1974; Michaels 1998; Taizhanov 1996), unmarried Central Asian girls did not have much say about their life or their marriage. The Kazakh proverb, "A girl's path is narrow," aptly expresses the social constraints on a Kazakh girl's life. Most girls' marriages were arranged by parents and relatives, especially the father, when the girl was still very young. The girl did not have any choice in the matter, and she rarely saw the groom before her wedding night. Once married, the girl left her natal family to live with the groom's family. Arranged marriages always involved transfers of bridewealth (*qalyn-mal*) and dowry (though Soviet sources placed more emphasis on bridewealth as an indication that women were viewed as commodities). Because of the difficulty of acquiring bridewealth and the practice of polygyny, the groom was often older than the bride.

Although the practice of bride kidnapping has received much less attention in the literature, there is sufficient evidence that bride kidnapping did exist in the pre-Soviet period.[3] Levshin (1832, 337), a Russian ethnogra-

3. Anthropologists also provide evidence that the practice of bride kidnapping has been found in other societies. In the nineteenth century, the evolutionary anthropologist John McLennan's (1865) treatise on the origins of marriage included a detailed survey of bride kidnapping. After McLennan, Firth (1936) and Levi-Strauss (1949) made cursory reference to bride kidnapping in their respective studies of Tikopia and comparative kinship. Then, the topic largely disappeared from the anthropological record until 1974, when a special

pher, describes the ritual enactment of bride abduction among some Kazakh clans in the eighteenth century. American historian Virginia Martin (2001) refers to a court case in the 1870s in which a father was seeking restitution from a man who abducted his daughter after he refused to allow them to marry.[4] Taizhanov (1995), a Kazakh ethnographer, mentions that bride kidnapping would occur when the girl's father requested a higher bridewealth (*qalyn-mal*) than the groom could afford or the bride's father violated the original conditions of matchmaking. In a more serious offense, the girl might be betrothed to one young man yet be stolen by another young man who was in love with her. This second type of case could lead to a battle between tribes or negotiation in the court of traditional judges (*bilar*). Karmysheva (1967), a Soviet Kazakh ethnographer, argues that the practice allowed pre-Soviet tribes to show their power vis-à-vis other tribes and allowed young men to display their boldness. She also refers to a case in which a young girl was kidnapped by a man after the death of her older sister, his betrothed bride. Argynbaev (1996), another Soviet Kazakh ethnographer, mentions that bride kidnapping also occurred in cases where the bride's father did not like either the groom or his family.[5] Elizabeth Bacon (1966, 40), an American ethnographer, mentions that Kazakh men preferred young brides in part because it "precluded the possibility of her elopement with a man of her own choice." Finally, Gregory Massell (1974, 114), referring to the works of early Soviet ethnographers Nukhrat and Brullova-Shashkol'skaia, indicates that genuine bride theft, as well as symbolic bride theft, also existed among

---

volume of *Anthropological Quarterly* was devoted to bride kidnapping with case studies from Turkey (Bates 1974; Kudat 1974), India (Brukman 1974), Bosnia (Lockwood 1974), Mexico (Stross 1974), and East Africa (Conant 1974). In an introductory piece that examines bride kidnapping across cultures, Barbara Ayres (1974) distinguishes a number of different marriage practices: "genuine bride theft" (which does not involve knowledge or consent of bride); "mock bride theft" (which allows the girl to defy her parents' wishes while giving the appearance of obedience); "ceremonial capture" (which involves a pretended struggle between members of both families); "elopement" (which involves neither genuine nor pretended use of force or resistance); and "raiding" (which involves the abduction of an unknown and unspecified woman). Often, more than one of these practices can be found in a society at any given time.

4. I would like to thank Virginia Martin for pointing out this reference to me. In a personal communication, she also noted the importance of not generalizing marriage practices across all three hordes of Kazakhs.

5. It is interesting to note that Argynbaev does not describe bride kidnapping in a Soviet-era article (1978) on pre-Soviet marriage rites, yet does mention it in a post-Soviet book (1996, 137–38).

the Turkmen in pre-Soviet periods. Their accounts of this practice emphasize the use of force and rape. Taken together, these sources suggest that bride kidnapping in the pre-Soviet period was just as complex, varied, and misunderstood as bride kidnapping in the present.

Women, Marriage, and the Soviet State

Women's lives and marriage practices changed during Soviet rule. All modern states set controls on marriage by establishing minimum ages for marriage, banning certain forms of marriage, and establishing official procedures for marriage and divorce. In democratic states, regulations on marriage might be contentious but they tend to reflect the consensus of the voting populace. In contrast, in Central Asia, the early Soviet state introduced radical social policies based on Marxist ideology. Regarding women as the "surrogate proletariat" in need of emancipation, the Bolshevik leaders tried to widen the path of Kazakh girls by passing laws that outlawed patriarchal marriage practices (Massell 1974). In the early 1920s, the state passed laws that banned various "crimes of custom," including the payment of bridewealth, polygamy, child betrothals, forced marriage, and levirate. The state also established sixteen as the minimum age of marriage; the minimum age was later increased to eighteen. The Soviet state also pushed for gender equality in other spheres, including education and employment.

There is no consensus among scholars regarding the extent to which Soviet policies improved the lives of Central Asian women. On the one hand, Soviet scholars have pointed to the many achievements of Soviet rule in health care, education, and employment opportunities. Such studies also point out how Soviet policies have changed family relations and marriage practices in ways that benefited women. For example, the Kazakh ethnographer Karmysheva (1967) presents a rosy picture of family relations and marriage practices in a Kazakh village in Taldyqurgan Oblast. According to her account, the village women are free to marry men whom they choose, and their families no longer receive bridewealth from the groom's family. Moreover, women are treated fairly by their husbands and mothers-in-law. In reference to bride kidnapping, Karmysheva explains that the former practice of bride kidnapping is only imitated in the ethnographic present (the 1960s). Girls are only abducted with their full consent. According to Karmysheva, the "initiative and invention of youth" serves to simplify the complex and burdensome wedding customs, without detracting from the significance of the celebration.

Western sources tend to be more critical of the Soviet success story. In contrast to some Soviet scholars who portray radical change, some scholars argue that Soviet policies did very little to change the status or lives of Central Asian women. Martha Olcott (1991) and Sergei Poliakov (1992), for example, paint a grim picture of women's lives in Soviet Central Asia. According to Olcott (1991, 235), "A woman's place is generally still predetermined at birth." Both Olcott (1991) and Poliakov (1992), one of Olcott's primary sources, go on to explain the life cycle of Central Asian women. Before marriage, young girls are expected to help with household chores as their families want to get some benefit from them before they leave home. Central Asian women, especially in rural regions, are usually married by the age of sixteen. Most marriages are arranged by parents, and the payment of bridewealth is still observed. Once married, women are emotionally and sometimes physically abused by their husbands and mothers-in-law. In addition, they are expected to have large numbers of children. Women who can't bear children may be beaten, divorced, or subjected to a polygynous marriage. Because of poor hospital conditions, rates for infant mortality and maternal deaths are relatively high. Women may work, but women from traditional families are restricted from taking certain jobs, and most women do not control their earnings. Women who are unhappy with their situation often commit suicide, sometimes through a dramatic self-immolation. This depiction of women's misery might apply to women in some parts of Central Asia, but it does not provide a balanced assessment for understanding the lives of the women I encountered in southern Kazakhstan, a region known for being more traditional. A more balanced assessment would consider the love and nurturance provided by natal families, the extent to which women do control their earnings, the fact that many husbands and mothers-in-law treat their wives and daughters-in-law with respect, and the fact that children (including girls) are not viewed as a burden.

Other scholars acknowledge the ambitious nature of Soviet objectives yet point to the numerous discrepancies between Soviet policy and actual practice. Bacon (1966, 139–40), for example, points out several instances where the local population understood yet chose to circumvent Soviet laws that challenged customary marriage practices. For example, men continued to marry multiple women, but they only registered one as their official wife. Families managed to avoid the law requiring a minimum age for marriage by registering a marriage at a later date. And bridewealth payments were made in cash more often than in livestock in order to conceal the transfer. Massell (1974, 338) similarly describes how the ban on bride kidnapping was ignored in the early Soviet period under the following circumstances: "(a) if the abductor proved his honorable intentions by actually marrying the girl; (b) if the abducted and violated girl refused, out of shame or lack of viable marital alternatives, to lodge a complaint in court; and (c) if the girl forced into marriage by her parents and kinsmen refused, out of loyalty to kinfolk and custom, to testify against them."

Finally, some scholars are critical of the Soviet state's ability to solve women's problems. In studies of Soviet women, Buckley (1989) and Lapidus (1978) argue that the state successfully increased women's participation in the workforce but did little to change gender relations at home. Thus, they argue that Soviet women were stuck with the "double burden" of doing all the housework and working long hours outside of the home. Similarly, Michaels (1998) points out that Kazakh women who "freed" themselves from unhappy marriages faced new economic burdens and unequal wage structures. Despite these critiques, most scholars do acknowledge that the Soviet state was responsible for making significant changes in women's lives. And, as Elizabeth Constantine (2001) and Marianne Kamp (chap. 1) point out, Soviet policies were quite effective in changing women's expectations of the state and expectations for a certain quality of life.

Women, Marriage, and the Post-Soviet State

Although the Soviet state was unable to eliminate gender inequality, Soviet women experienced a state that provided a number of economic and social benefits for women: free education, guaranteed employment, a generous maternity leave, free day care, and monthly supplements for women with children. In the post-Soviet period, women in the former Soviet Union and Eastern Europe are coping with the realities of a post-socialist economy in which the state has terminated its social contract with women and transferred many of the costs of social reproduction to the household level (Zhurzhenko 2001). Many Central Asian families cannot afford the new costs of higher education, and some cannot even afford the costs of clothing and school supplies (Bauer, Green, and Kuehnast 1997). Employment is no longer guaranteed by the state, and many girls and women have turned to small-scale trade to ensure household income (Bauer, Green, and Kuehnast 1997, 67–69; Bauer, Boschmann, and Green 1997, 35–41; Werner 2001). In addition to putting economic strains on households, unemployment has brought a sense of helplessness to Central Asian women and men who were raised with Soviet attitudes toward work (Bauer, Green, and Kuehnast 1997, 25–27, 55). Cutbacks in the socialist system of subsidized day care have made it more difficult for women to gain employment outside the home in either the formal or informal economy (Klugman, Marnie, Micklewright, and O'Keefe 1997). Finally, the value of monthly supplements for children has decreased because of inflation, and extended maternity leave is sometimes forced upon women by employers with limited budgets (Bauer, Boschmann, and Green 1997, 28). As Kamp points out (chap. 1), post-Soviet Uzbekistan has maintained and expanded welfare programs (such as supplements) that protect motherhood per se while cutting back on subsidies (such as day care) that support working women. Taken together, the postsocialist transition has brought new hardships to many Central Asian women. However, some enterprising women, especially younger women with foreign language skills, have managed to benefit from the transition to capitalism by working for foreign companies and international NGOs (Berg 2001; Ishkanian 2001; Michaels 1998).

The impact of the post-Soviet transition on women goes beyond these new economic hardships and opportunities. A number of studies indicate that postsocialist states in Eastern Europe and the former Soviet Union are promoting nationalist agendas that involve the "re-traditionalization" of society (Gal and Kligman 2000; Graney 2001; Marsh 1998; Tohidi 1998; Verdery 1996). Among other things, this process is characterized by antiabortion policies (in Eastern Europe) and pronatalism, the decline of women's political power, and political discourse stressing the need to return to "traditional" gender roles. In post-Soviet Azerbaijan, for example, two contrasting images of women can be found — one emphasizing "physical beauty, Western fashion, consumerism, and Turkish identity" and one displaying "modesty, morality, Islamic values and Muslim identity" (Tohidi 1998, 137). According to Tohidi, Azeri women are increasingly opting for the second image, as their morality has become a sign that they are loyal to their ethnicity. In particular, "authentic" Azeri women do not appear in public without a male or an elder female chaperone, do not wear pants, do not drive cars, and do not smoke or drink in public (Tohidi 1998, 152).

Although the Central Asian states remain secular and wary of Islamic fundamentalism, there has been more acceptance of Islam and Islam's place in national identity formation (Abramson 2001; Michaels 1998). Throughout Central Asia, gender relations are being redefined as Islamic values are reinstated as the "guiding ethic for society," national histories and national traditions are rewritten and revived, and patriarchal authority (symbolized by the male head of state) is reasserted (Akiner 1997, 284). In particular, Akiner points to the growing number of mosques and madrasas in Central Asia and the greater acceptance of polygamy and bridewealth in public discourse. Marianne Kamp (chap. 1) explains that the shift from Soviet to Islamic ideology toward women started as early as the 1980s in Uzbekistan and continued in the 1990s. Discussions of these issues in popular magazines and newspapers encourage women to leave the workplace and resume their proper role as mother and wife. On a related point, Roy (2000, 183) mentions how Islam Karimov, the president of Uzbekistan, has "established a presidential contest for the best daughter-in-law, whose most valued quality is of course to obey her mother-in-law." And, in her study of Uzbek dancers, Doi (2001) notes that Uzbek women in post-Soviet Uzbekistan are increasingly turning to the traditional role of getting married and having children.

Gender identities in post-Soviet Central Asia, however, are shaped by the introduction of Western fashions and lifestyles as well as by the revival of traditional culture and Islam (Akiner 1997; Kuehnast 1998; Michaels 1998; Tadjbaksh 1998). Tadjbaksh (1998) similarly argues that many post-Soviet Tajik women have welcomed the return of traditional culture, including the expectation that women will stay home with the children and the possibility of legalized polygyny, and view the acceptance of Western values as a rejection of their national culture. Different attitudes toward Western culture can be found in Kazakhstan and Kyrgyzstan, where the titular groups are known for being less influenced by Islam and more influenced by Russian colonial rule. Kuehnast (1998) and Michaels (1998) both suggest that young women in Bishkek and Almaty, respectively, are more influenced by Western capitalism and consumerism than by the revival of Islamic ideals of modesty.

Though there is a similar pull toward the West in Southern-Kazakhstan Oblast, this chapter on bride kidnapping indicates that the revival of traditional culture is playing a fairly strong role in shaping post-Soviet gender identities in that region of Kazakhstan. Although there have been many studies of gender identity and women's poverty, little attention has been devoted to the study of marriage practices in the post-Soviet context. A few studies have made cursory reference to bride kidnapping in Kazakhstan, Kyrgyzstan, and Azerbaijan (Bauer, Green and Kuehnast 1997, 24; Tohidi 2001; Weatherford 2000, 268; Werner 1997, 6–7). In a previous publication (Werner 1997), I indicated that some brides conspire in their own kidnapping while others are kidnapped without their consent. And, similar to Kyrgyzstan (Bauer, Green, and Kuehnast 1997), I mentioned that bride kidnapping provides a less expensive option because a lower bridewealth is expected. Amsler and Kleinbach (1999) provide the only detailed study of bride kidnapping in the post-Soviet context. Their study of Kyrgyzstan focuses on the issue of consent. They conclude that approximately one-fourth of the women consent to the kidnappings while three-fourths are taken by deception or force, and they argue that nonconsensual kidnappings represent a violation of basic human rights. Here, I build on their research by providing data on the frequency of bride kidnapping in general and nonconsensual bride kidnapping in particular in Kazakhstan and by placing the practice of kidnapping within a historical and political context. I have found that there has been a rise in nonconsensual bride kidnappings in the 1980s and 1990s, and this rise can be linked to economic and political change in Kazakhstan.

Research Methods

This chapter is based on ethnographic fieldwork in the Southern-Kazakhstan Oblast of Kazakhstan (in 1994, 1995, 1998, and 2000). During the fall of 2000, I collected data on bride kidnapping through the use of structured surveys and informal interviews. Because of the lack of previous research on this subject, I chose to collect both qualitative and quantitative data. While the qualitative data is critical for exploring local understandings of this practice, the quantitative data is useful for determining the prevalence of bride kidnapping, in general, and the prevalence of nonconsensual bride kidnapping, in particular, over time.

During the course of my research, I collected interview and/or survey data from 187 informants. I used a nested sample. From the total sample of 187 informants, 177 answered survey questions about how they met and married their spouse.[6] Fifty-four of the survey respondents were selected for additional open-ended interview questions about the practice of bride kidnapping. These qualitative interview questions were continuously updated in the field as I became more familiar with the kidnapping practices. Ten additional informants, mostly unmarried individuals, answered interview questions only.

All of the interviews and surveys were conducted in Southern-Kazakhstan Oblast, a region known for being more patriarchal and traditional than the rest of Kazakhstan. Although bride kidnapping occurs in other regions, it is considered to be more widespread in the southern oblasts of Kazakhstan. The survey sample was not specifically stratified along socioeconomic lines because this is difficult to measure. However, I attempted to get a broad spectrum of society by interviewing in both urban and rural areas. I collected data from one small city (Turkestan, with approximately one hundred thousand residents), one large village

6. Before starting the research for this project, I contacted Russell Kleinbach, who had previously conducted research on bride kidnapping in Kyrgyzstan with Sarah Amsler. Kleinbach generously provided me with a copy of his survey questions. Although I modified some questions and added others, and I used a different interview format, their survey was very helpful for my project.

TABLE 2.1. *Survey Sample by Location and Sex*

Location	Female	Male
Turkestan city	36	19
Shauildir village	39	37
Talapty village	23	17
Otyrar village	5	1
Total (177)	103	74

TABLE 2.2. *Survey Sample by Age and Sex*

Age	Female	Male
18–27	31	28
28–37	20	17
38–47	26	21
48–57	12	5
58–67	12	1
67 and older	2	2
Total (177)	103	74

(Shauildir, with approximately eight thousand residents), and two smaller villages (Talapty and Otyrar, with approximately fifteen hundred residents each) (see table 2.1).[7] Of the 177 survey respondents, 103 were women and 74 were men. The sample was also stratified by age (see table 2.2). Younger generations were intentionally oversampled because I was primarily interested in more recent trends. All of the survey informants had been married, but several were either divorced or widowed at the time of the interview.

Methodological issues arise in any ethnographic study. For example, informants may not be able to remember certain events in detail. Or, they may have some conscious reason to present a story from a certain angle. Both of these issues are relevant to this study of bride kidnapping. When it comes to the issue of memory, there is no guarantee that the men and women who were married twenty or thirty years ago remember the details

7. The population of Shauildir is about 96 percent Kazakh; the populations of Otyrar and Talapty are 100 percent Kazakh. In contrast, the population of Turkestan is ethnically diverse with a large Uzbek population. Bride kidnapping is limited to the Kazakh population in Turkestan. Though it is not unheard of for a Kazakh young man to kidnap an Uzbek girl, it is very rare for an Uzbek man to kidnap a bride. One informant mentioned an unusual case where an Uzbek young man had recently kidnapped an Uzbek girl.

as well as the men and women who were married more recently. And, when it comes to bias, there may be a number of reasons why people choose to exaggerate certain elements of a story or exclude other elements. In other words, my informants might have had certain agendas as they explained their version of how they got married and how they view nonconsensual bride kidnappings. In some interviews, several informants seemed eager to entertain me as they shared stories of nonconsensual kidnapping cases that they knew about. Other informants seemed just as determined to conceal the existence of nonconsensual kidnappings, possibly out of a concern that this would embarrass their nation. There might also be significant gender biases in the interpretation of a kidnapping case, as indicated by Amsler and Kleinbach's study (1999) of bride kidnapping in Kyrgyzstan. Although these methodological issues could be viewed as a weakness, they were often used as a vehicle for gathering more information. In other words, the particular difficulties that arose in the course of the survey revealed a number of interesting things about how people categorize the different paths to marriage and why it is not so easy to define "consent." Acknowledging the inherent biases in ethnographic and survey research, I do not set out to tell the "truth" per se. Rather, I set out to explore how different people describe their own experiences with bride kidnapping and other forms of marriage.

The Practice of Bride Kidnapping in Southern Kazakhstan

A General Overview of Bride Kidnapping

Bride kidnapping in its various forms is just one of several paths to marriage in southern Kazakhstan. The Kazakh word for bride kidnapping, *alyp qashu* (literally "to take and run"), is a general term used to refer to both consensual and nonconsensual bride kidnappings. Depending on the linguistic context, Kazakhs may choose to distinguish further the form of kidnap marriage: (1) *kelisimsiz alyp qashu* ("to take and run without agreement"), and (2) *kelisimmen alyp qashu* ("to take and run with agreement"). To emphasize the girl's consent, they might even state that the "girl ran away" (*qyz qashyp ketti*). Other paths to marriage include a modern variation of the arranged marriage and a marriage based on mutual consent and a civil ceremony. The modern variation of the arranged marriage (*quda tusu*) hardly resembles arranged marriages of the past. Young couples describe arranged marriages in which they have as much, or more, input in the marriage decision as their parents, who are mostly expected to deal with the formalities of "arranging" the marriage, which involves a series of exchanges between the new in-laws. In contrast, elderly women describe arranged marriages in which they had little if no input in a marriage to a complete stranger. Besides arranged marriages, another alternative is for a couple to get married in a more simple fashion with an official yet simple ceremony at the civil registry (*ZAGS*) and perhaps a small celebration at home. This type of marriage is sometimes referred to as a Komsomol marriage.

Bride kidnapping varies from case to case in terms of the level of consent and the primary motive for kidnapping, yet there is a normative pattern of events at a general level. Each event represents a further step toward the completion of the marriage. Once all the events have taken place, the marriage is considered to be finalized.

The first event is the abduction. Traditionally, this was done on horseback. The potential suitor would sneak into the girl's encampment (*aul*), grab the girl and put her on a horse, and then ride off to his home. In contemporary times, it is more common for the abduction to be carried out with a car, and the groom is usually accompanied by a few male friends or relatives. In a few cases, the bride was kidnapped by tractor or train. The girl may be abducted from home or she may be kidnapped from another location, such as a workplace, a café, or a party.

Young men cite different and multiple reasons for kidnapping their wives. When asked to describe the possible origins of bride kidnapping, many Kazakhs suggested that the practice developed as an option for a besotted young man when the parents of a desired girl objected to a marriage. This motive is depicted by the Kazakh proverb: "If they give, take from the hand; if they don't give, take from the road" (*Berse qolynan, bermese zholynan*). Surprisingly, very few informants claim that this motive was relevant in their own kidnapping. Instead, one of the most commonly cited explanations is that the costs of an arranged marriage are much higher than the cost of a kidnap marriage. In particular, the bridewealth and dowry are expected to be more expensive and more elaborate in an arranged marriage, and there is the additional expense of a "girl leaving home" feast (*qyz uzatu toi*).[8] In addition to saving money,

8. The young men are not necessarily "marrying up," as they might have done in the past; rather, they are simply avoiding these extra expenses. In the 1990s, it is true that arranged marriages are more expensive than kidnap marriages, as the revival of the arranged marriage is clearly limited to those who can afford it. But, it is difficult to say whether this explanation can be projected back in time, when the expectations for feasts may have been different. Previous research on feasting (Werner 2000a) indicates that the costs associated with feasting increased in the 1970s when wedding feasts were transformed from intimate family affairs inside the home to large parties in a family courtyard. Perhaps it is not a coincidence that this is the time when kidnap marriages started to become even more popular.

many men cite the need to save time. With an arranged marriage, not only do the in-laws have to meet and agree to the marriage but both sides are also required to host an in-law feast (*qudalyq*) before the large wedding feast (*uilenu toi*). Because of these costs, the wedding (and thus consummation of the marriage) may be delayed for a long time. There are a number of reasons that the groom or his family does not want to wait a long time to complete a marriage. One reason is that another young man may kidnap the girl, especially if she is attractive and desirable. In other situations, the young man's parents might need a daughter-in-law to help with housework. It is also likely that some of the young men kidnap a girl simply because they don't want to wait several months to have sex with her. On a related point, there are cases in which the boy kidnaps a girl because he has already had sex with the girl and she is now pregnant. Virginity is expected before marriage, but unwed pregnancies are not considered to be too scandalous as long as the girl is quickly married to the father of the child.

When it comes to kidnap marriages that involve minimal or implicit consent, the motive for kidnapping is often based on a belief that the girl might otherwise refuse a marriage. When this is the primary motive, the young man is taking advantage of the fact that a girl, once kidnapped, will probably stay. In some cases, the boy is simply afraid to ask the girl if she is interested or he perceives that the girl is not interested in him. In other cases, the subject has come up and the girl has specifically told the boy that she does not want to marry him. Although this motive most often applies to nonconsensual kidnappings, it can also apply to situations in which the girl has told the boy that she is "not ready" to marry him.

Although some girls know the full plan ahead of time, deception is a recurring theme. Even in cases in which the girl is kidnapped with her consent, it is not uncommon for the young man to deceive her into being kidnapped. Forty-one of the 106 abduction stories I collected involved some form of deception. Typically, an acquaintance or boyfriend offers the girl a ride home (possibly from work or from a feast) and then proceeds to drive her to his own house. The young men I interviewed explained that it is more fun this way. One informant added, "If asked, the girls will always say 'I'm not ready yet,' so it's just better this way." Though Kazakh girls generally look forward to getting married, young girls are also apprehensive about the idea of leaving their familiar home and adapting to a new person and his family. Moreover, one of the conflicting messages they hear while growing up is that leaving their home to become a bride is a traumatic event. They are expected to be reluctant beforehand, and they are expected to cry during their departure. So, even girls who are eager to marry a certain boy may hesitate to marry him immediately. I interviewed several girls who said that they were eager to marry their husband after they finished the university, but their husband was unwilling to wait and thus kidnapped her with the use of deception before she completed her studies. In cases like this, it is important to distinguish deceit from consent. From a Kazakh perspective, a kidnapping may involve deceit yet still be viewed as consensual. The young man, for example, may receive the girl's explicit consent by asking her if she is interested in marrying him or receive her implicit consent by noting her interest in him. Despite this consent, the kidnapping itself is a surprise because the girl does not know ahead of time when and how she is going to be kidnapped.

Only 9 percent of the kidnapping stories in my survey involved the use of physical force.[9] For example, I heard stories where the young men would physically grab the girl, force her into the car, and then restrain her while driving to his house. In one case, the young men put a sack over the girl's head before putting her into the car. When the girl is a willing participant, such physical force is obviously not necessary. When the girl is deceived into being kidnapped, physical force is less likely to occur, at least until the moment she discovers that she has been deceived.[10]

After the abduction, the boy takes the girl to his home. The boy's parents are almost always informed ahead of time, and thus they know to expect the girl. The second element of a kidnapping occurs when a female member of the groom's household presents the girl with a kerchief (*oramal*). This is the first opportunity for the girl to acknowledge publicly her willingness to marry the groom. The kerchief, which covers the hair

9. Although I did ask about the "use of physical force," I chose not to include a survey question about rape during kidnappings. I knew that understandings of what constitutes rape vary cross-culturally. I also knew that it would be even more difficult to get an honest answer to this question, and I did not want to offend or embarrass my informants. During the interviews, however, the issue of rape did come up a few times. Those who discussed rape indicated that it occurs very rarely with the kidnappings, despite the fact that the purity and virginity of a "girl who returns home" is put into question. I was told of two different cases of girls who were threatened with rape on the way to the groom's house as a way to force them to calm down and consent to the marriage. I also interviewed some impudent young men who boasted about how they would probably rape a girl they had kidnapped if she were to testify in court that the kidnapping was nonconsensual.

10. When it comes to questions like this, it is important to emphasize that the percentage refers to the reported number of instances, not the actual number. The "use of physical force" involves some ambiguity and it is likely that some of the survey informants did not answer this question honestly. Not surprisingly, women were more likely than men to report the use of physical force when asked to describe how they entered marriage.

but not the face, is a symbol of a married woman.[11] Even if the girl wants to marry the boy, she is expected to feign some reluctance and resistance to the marriage, and thus most girls do not want to appear too eager to put on the marriage scarf. Though there are no serious repercussions, older women do gossip about young brides who are "laughing and smiling" on the day they are kidnapped. To express her genuine or feigned resistance, the girl may refuse to take the kerchief or may simply refuse to wear it. Meanwhile, the groom's female relatives keep insisting over and over again that she put it on. If the girl is truly resisting the marriage, she might not put the scarf on for hours or even days. But, if the girl is excited about the marriage, she will probably put the scarf on within the first hour or two.

In the third element of a kidnapping, the girl is asked to write a letter to her family stating that she came of her own free will. By this time, she is sitting in a back room behind the white curtain that is used to decorate a new couple's bedroom. The letter is taken to her parents as evidence that the girl has not been harmed and that she has already agreed to stay. Although nobody could remember exactly when this tradition started, it certainly developed after literacy was achieved in the Soviet period as a way to avoid arrest for the crime of nonconsensual kidnapping. Similar to the kerchief, the writing of the letter theoretically provides the girl with another opportunity to decline the marriage. However, the girl's freedom to choose her own future at this point should not be emphasized. There is extreme social pressure "to stay" and most girls make this "choice" even if it goes against their true wishes. The groom's relatives often try to reassure forlorn brides that he loves her and that she will be able to adapt to this new life and new family. The girl also realizes that she and her family will be the subject of malicious gossip if she returns home. It is almost impossible to keep a kidnapping a secret and a "girl who returns" is labeled as such and thus becomes a less desirable marriage partner. Finally, in some kidnapping situations, the girl's family has some kind of tie to the groom's family that makes it difficult for her to renounce and disgrace his family.

11. In more traditional households, the daughter-in-law (*kelin*) is expected to wear the kerchief in front of her husband's parents and other older relatives. Actual practice and preference varies from one family to the next. In some families, not wearing the kerchief is considered to be a grave sign of disrespect. Some young women are uncomfortable wearing the kerchief, and others resent it as a symbol of their subservient status in the household. Acknowledging these issues, I met several families where the groom's parents have granted permission to their young daughter-in-law to make her own decision about when and where to wear the kerchief.

The amount of time that transpires before the girl writes the letter, rather than the fact that she does write the letter, indicates the extent to which she consents to the marriage. I listened to several stories of girls who were completely distraught for hours, screaming at anybody who approached them, throwing things around the room, and even breaking windows. One young woman described how she repeatedly wrote: "I don't want to stay here! I did not agree to this!" The groom's relatives kept telling her that they could not take this note to her parents. They kept bringing her a fresh piece of paper and dictated the words that they wanted her to write. Eventually, like the others, her will was broken and she wrote the letter.

The letter is usually a crucial precursor for the next event, when the groom's relatives send an official apology (*keshirim*) to the bride's house. By the time the apology arrives, the bride's parents may have already heard what happened to their daughter or they may at least have their suspicions. However, it is not until the informal apology delegation arrives that they know for sure. This event is usually postponed until the girl has prepared the letter. The delegation usually consists of two or three respected males from the groom's side. If the kidnapping is nonconsensual and the girl is stalling, her family has to wait longer before they find out what has happened to her. If the groom's family is concerned that the bride's family might contest the marriage, they will be very determined to send persuasive and powerful relatives (or close family friends).

The purpose of the apology visit is to explain what happened to the girl and to present an amount of money in lieu of the bridewealth. (When talking about this money, informants use the terms *keshirim* and *qalyn-mal* interchangeably.)[12] Families who kidnap a bride are not exempt from paying money to the bride's family. However, the standard amount for a kidnapped bride is less than the standard amount for an arranged marriage bride. The exact amounts vary according to the family's wealth, but in the late 1990s, less than the equivalent of two hundred dollars is generally considered to be low for a kidnap marriage, and less than five hundred dollars is considered to be low for an arranged marriage. The difference in part reflects the fact that arranged marriages are more common among the elite, who have more money to give in the first place. In addition to presenting the apology fee, the apology delegation tries to console the parents who might be upset that their daughter has been kidnapped.

12. Aware of Soviet bias against bridewealth, many Kazakh informants argue that the Kazakhs do not "sell" their daughters. They insist that this money is used to purchase dowry items, the total cost of which almost always exceeds the amount given for the bridewealth.

Some informants noted that it is not uncommon for the apology delegation to be met with angry words and physical violence.

The apology delegation is followed by another small delegation, called "the pursuers" (*qughynshy*), who are sent from the bride's house to the groom's house. The girl's parents do not go to the groom's house unless they intend to take their daughter back home. If the girl's parents believe that the girl wants to stay or they think that she should stay, they will organize a delegation of two to five relatives. They often send relatives who fit into the following categories: the bride's aunts, her uncles, her siblings, and her sisters-in-law. During this visit, the *qughynshy* delegation is able to check on the bride's condition. The delegation stays the entire night as honored guests, celebrating the union of the bride and groom. As they leave, they are presented with the first installment of in-law gifts (*kiit*).

On the following day, after the bride's relatives have departed, the groom's family arranges for the "face-opening" or *betashar* ceremony. The face-opening ceremony also takes place in the case of an arranged marriage, soon after the bride starts to live at the groom's house. The ceremony formally introduces the bride to the groom's family, relatives, and close friends. After the guests have gathered, the veiled bride is led in front of the guests where she stands next to two sisters-in-law. They assist her as she gives "one hello" (*bir salem*) after another to her husband's relatives, as an invited *dombyra* (a guitar-like instrument) player sings out their names. Each "hello" consists of a brief bow to the audience, as the named relatives place a small amount of money in a collection jar. When all of the names have been called, the bride is formally "unveiled." Until this time, the bride has been treated as a special guest in her new home. After this event, she starts to take on some of the duties of a new daughter-in-law. For example, she might help her mother-in-law prepare dinner and wash the dishes.

Variations in Bride Kidnapping Experiences

Despite the general sequence of events, kidnap marriages vary remarkably from case to case when it comes to the issue of consent and the motive behind each kidnapping. Sometimes the kidnappings are consensual, and sometimes they are not. Sometimes, they are something in between. To explore this issue, I am going to describe three different kidnapping cases, each representing a different level of consent. Each of these cases took place in the 1990s.

The first case (a consensual kidnapping) describes the marriage of Kairat and Zhamila in 1994. I was living with Zhamila's family in a Kazakh village while doing research for my dissertation on post-Soviet economic and social change. Kairat and Zhamila were from the same village and they were both attending a university in the small city of Turkestan. They were dating regularly, and they often got together with friends in the dorm or they met at an outdoor café. They were clearly in love with each other and they hoped to get married. His family approved of the marriage, but Zhamila knew that her parents did not approve. They found out that she had been dating him, and they angrily warned her to stop seeing him. Her parents did not know Kairat's family very well, but they had heard some bad rumors about his family, including that his father was often drunk. More importantly, they had already discussed the idea of marrying her to the son of her father's college friend. That young man lived in another town, and she barely knew him. Against her parent's wishes, Zhamila continued to date Kairat in secret. One day, shortly after she heard her parents discussing the other boy, she and Kairat talked about the possibility of elopement. She agreed that kidnapping was their best option. They did not discuss the details. The kidnapping occurred about a month later while she was doing a summer internship in a nearby city. She was temporarily living at her uncle's house, and she simply didn't return from work one day. Kairat surprised her by arriving at lunchtime. They went out to lunch, they went for a walk in the park, and then without asking, he drove her to his family's home in the village two hours away. Though she didn't know ahead of time, she happily accompanied him. Kairat's parents and relatives were waiting for them. Kairat's mother offered a kerchief, the symbol of a married woman, and Zhamila accepted it. Meanwhile, Zhamila's aunt and uncle were concerned about her whereabouts, and eventually they alerted her parents in the village. Although they had not yet received the "apology," they were able to guess where Zhamila was. Still unwilling to accept this match, they quickly drove to Kairat's house and asked to speak to Zhamila. She came out of the house wearing the kerchief, and where before she was afraid of disrespecting her parents by speaking back to them, she was now willing to plead her case. She reminded her mother that she herself had been able to marry the man she loved, and she asked her why she wouldn't let her daughter do the same thing. Realizing that there really wasn't much they could do at this point, her parents reluctantly returned home without their daughter.

When I returned to the village several years later to conduct research on bride kidnapping, it was perhaps with a little irony that Zhamila recounted the details of a popular Kazakh film that seems to glorify the merits of a love-based "kidnap" marriage. The film, *Shangyraq*, was produced and set in the 1970s. It tells the story of a young man named Aman who lives alone with his poor, widowed mother. He is in love with Maira, a girl who comes from a wealthy and powerful family. Maira is also in love with Aman, but the young couple faced opposition from her maternal uncle. To prevent the union, the uncle insists on an exorbitantly high bridewealth. Unable to pay this amount, Aman discusses the possibility of a kidnap marriage with Maira. Once she agrees, he informs her when and where to wait. On the appointed day, she happily accompanies him to his house, and his relatives warmly welcome her into their family. This, however, was not the happy ending of the film. When her uncle hears the news, he drives to the house with the police. They immediately arrest Aman and his "accomplices." The uncle then forces his niece Maira to sign a legal affidavit claiming that she was kidnapped against her will. When the case comes to trial, the judge asks her directly whether she had been kidnapped against her will. She sobs violently and does not answer for a long time. Aman pleads with her to tell the truth. Eventually, out of fear and respect for her uncle, she lies and tells the court that Aman had kidnapped her *against* her will. Aman is then sentenced to prison in Siberia for several years. While in jail, Aman befriends a Russian orphan girl who works at the prison. When he is released early for good behavior, he proposes marriage to her. While she considers the offer, he returns to his native town in Kazakhstan. Meanwhile, Maira has been unhappily married to a man she does not love. When she hears that Aman has returned, she goes to see him and begs him to forgive her and to run away with her. He does not say a word and refuses to make eye contact with her. In the end, the Russian girl arrives in the village and accepts his marriage proposal. And Maira throws herself over a cliff after witnessing their happiness.

Consistent with Soviet ideology, stories recounting the tragedy of arranged marriages were commonly portrayed in Soviet literary works (Allworth 1989). The film draws a definite contrast between the love-based kidnap marriage (where Maira was temporarily happy) and the nonconsensual arranged marriage (where she was so unhappy that she chose to commit suicide). In so doing, the film defends the practice of bride kidnapping in situations in which the young people themselves are making the decision. At the same time, the film delivers a powerful message that runs counter to "traditional" Kazakh values: devastating results occur when relatives interfere in the matchmaking process!

Many of the kidnap marriages in Kazakhstan today occur in ways that resemble Zhamila and Kairat's marriage, and Aman's first marriage to

Maira. My survey data suggests that consensual kidnappings were a popular form of marriage by the 1960s and 1970s. It can be argued that kidnap marriages provided a solution to an intrinsic conflict between Kazakh and Soviet values. On the one hand, traditional Kazakh cultural values stress that girls should not appear overly eager to get married (and consequently to start having sex). Girls were expected to listen to their parents and their elders when it came to their marriage choices. Several elderly informants told me how it used to be really shameful if a girl "ran away" to marry a man for love, but now girls do it all the time without any social sanctions. On the other hand, Soviet values stressed that girls should play an active role in choosing their marriage partners. Young men who kidnapped girls with their consent did not violate any Soviet laws, while girls who were "kidnapped" did not appear to be "running away" and thus did not violate Kazakh customs. Further, because it is also shameful for the girl "to return home" after being kidnapped, this makes it difficult for the girl's parents to do anything after the fact.

In the second case (a semiconsensual kidnapping), Erlan was a young man from a prosperous family in Turkestan, and Raikhan was a girl from a modest family in Otyrar village. Erlan's mother had studied in the same village class as Raikhan's parents. She visited Otyrar regularly to keep up with her relatives and friends. On one visit, she ran into Raikhan's mother and asked about her family. During this conversation, she learned that Raikhan, the eldest child in a family of six, was studying to be a teacher at the university in Shymkent. Kazakhs have a proverb, "See the mother, take the daughter" (*Sheshesin korip, qyzyn al*), and this is exactly what Erlan's mother did. Knowing that Raikhan's mother was an honorable woman and a good housewife, she started to think that Raikhan might be a good match for Erlan. She even went to Raikhan's house to see for herself whether or not the girl's character resembled her mother's. When she returned home, she told her son that there was a girl that she wanted him to meet. Erlan trusted his mother and wanted to marry somebody that his parents approved of. About a month later, Erlan and his mother returned to Otyrar village where he first met Raikhan. Although she was shy about meeting him at first, they had a mutual attraction. Later, he visited Shymkent twice to take her out on "dates" with a small group of friends.

Erlan and his parents agreed that a kidnap marriage would be more appropriate because her family would have a hard time paying for an arranged marriage. At this point, he heard a rumor that another boy was planning to kidnap her. He didn't want to lose her, so on the third "date," he decided to kidnap her. He never asked her whether she wanted to marry him, but he felt he had received implicit consent from both Raikhan and her parents. He didn't think it was necessary to ask directly because she would just be afraid and say that she wasn't ready yet. His older sister added that it is better this way, because if a girl knows that she is going to be kidnapped on a certain day from a certain place, she will get "all weirded out."

So, he used deception to get her to his house. First, he invited Raikhan and her two girlfriends to Turkestan for a city tour, and then, after they had dinner at a café, he promised to take them to a discotheque. Instead of going to the disco, he drove them to his house where his relatives were waiting. His grandmother offered her the marriage kerchief, and she accepted it almost immediately. The apology delegation was sent to Raikhan's house a few hours later to deliver the good news that the young couple had been married.

While the first two stories involve kidnappings with happy endings, the next case reveals the other side of bride kidnapping. In this case (a non-consensual kidnapping), Marat and Aizhan were two youths from Shauildir who were both studying law at Turkestan University. Marat lived with his widowed mother and his divorced older sister. Aizhan, the daughter of the village police chief, was an attractive, intelligent, and well-disciplined girl. The story of this kidnapping was told by a young woman who had heard two different versions of the story: one version from Aizhan, who was her good friend, and one version from her husband, who was one of Marat's accomplices. As she explained it, Marat's mother and sisters decided that it would be useful if Marat married into a family with good connections. They decided that Aizhan was an ideal choice, as she would make a good daughter-in-law and her father had the appropriate connections. From their perspective, it was irrelevant that Marat was not terribly excited about the marriage and that Aizhan had her own boyfriend.

Marat's mother convinced her son that this was the right choice. So, one day, as Aizhan was returning from Shauildir to Turkestan on the train, Marat and three of his friends stalked her. They secretly watched her and an aunt get on the train in the village, and then they raced in their car to meet the train in Turkestan. At the train station, they politely offered the two women a ride. Aizhan and her aunt accepted the offer, and her fate was sealed. Cleverly, the young men dropped off the aunt first, and then, instead of driving Aizhan to her dormitory, they started to drive in the direction of Shauildir. Once Aizhan understood what was happening, she became very distressed and angry. She knew that she had to act fast. If only she could avoid going to his house, then maybe she could get out of this situation and still manage to marry her boyfriend. At this point, the boys were holding down her arms so she couldn't get out of the car. Her feet were still free so she tried to get the boys to stop the car by kicking at the dashboard and damaging the stereo. Eventually, they stopped the car to get a drink. Although she was in an area with no houses for miles, she made a run for it. She took off her high-heeled shoes and ran off into the steppe. Maybe she would run into a shepherd tending his sheep? Unfortunately, in her bare feet, she was not able to outrun the four boys who came at her from two different directions. They grabbed her and forced her back into the car.

When the entourage arrived at Marat's house, the despondent bride was greeted by his extended family. They offered her the kerchief, which she refused, and then took her to a back room and asked her to write the letter, which she also refused. After a few hours, in an unusual move, his family decided to send the "apology" delegation to her house without the letter. About the same time that the apology delegation left for her house, Aizhan's parents received disturbing news from their friends who happened to live next door to Marat. The friends told them that Aizhan had been kidnapped, and that they suspected that she was kidnapped against her will because she was screaming and crying. When the apology delegation arrived without the letter, her parents knew that their fears had been confirmed. They angrily refused to accept the apology fee. Concerned for their daughter's happiness, they decided they would retrieve their daughter and deal with the possible shame. As chief of police, the father must have been surprised that anybody would dare to kidnap his daughter against her will. After all, there are severe penalties for committing this crime. So, they headed to Marat's house, hopeful that the situation could be resolved. When they arrived, they immediately understood why Marat's family had acted so brashly. Marat's paternal uncle, the very man who had mentored and assisted Aizhan's father during his studies, was now sitting on the front porch. Unaware of the circumstances, he had been invited from Almaty to celebrate his nephew's marriage. When Aizhan's father approached him, the uncle said that he thought Aizhan would make a fine daughter-in-law. Out of respect for this man, Aizhan's father decided that he could no longer rescue his daughter from this undesirable fate. Instead of taking her home, he asked to speak to her. As she begged him to take her home, he explained the circumstances and told her that it would be too shameful for her to return home. He later accepted the second apology fee, and the marriage was complete. Although Aizhan ended up staying, the couple was not happy. They stayed together for seven years and had two sons, before they ended up getting a divorce.[13]

Kidnapping Trends over Time

These three case studies reveal the amount of variation in kidnapping practices. Using survey data, I tried to come up with a rough estimate of the prevalence of bride kidnapping in general and the prevalence of nonconsensual bride kidnapping in particular. As these stories demonstrate, a number of ambiguities make it difficult to determine whether or not a kidnapping case is "consensual" or "nonconsensual." There is no single question that gets at this issue. For example, a question about whether or not a girl expressed resistance during the kidnapping could be misunderstood, as girls are expected to act a little upset. Similarly, the issue of implicit consent does not arise in questions about whether or not the girl knew the kidnapping plan ahead of time. Because of these issues, I decided to create an index of consensus, by compiling the answers to seven different survey questions.[14] And, because of cases like Erlan's, I decided that it would be more useful to think in terms of high consent, medium consent, and low consent.

The survey results represent 177 different marriages formed between 1946 (the year of the earliest marriage in the survey) and 2000. Based on the survey, 60 percent of the marriages were kidnap marriages, 14 percent were arranged marriages, and 26 percent were nontraditional marriages. Figure 2.1 illustrates how these trends have changed over time. During this period, arranged marriages experienced a sharp decline from the 1940s to the 1970s, and continued to decline slightly in the 1980s and 1990s. I believe the decline of arranged marriages reflects the efficacy of Soviet laws against

13. Though most brides stay when they are first kidnapped, it is not uncommon for divorce to occur after several years. Sometimes, the man initiates the divorce. But, I heard of several instances in which the woman initiated the divorce because her husband physically abused her or was an alcoholic. In these cases, her parents, who initially encouraged her to stay in the marriage, tend to favor her decision to leave the marriage and provide a place for her and her children to stay.

14. These are the questions that were used for the index: (1) Were the bride and groom acquainted before the marriage? If so, how well? (0–2 points); (2) Before he kidnapped her, did she know that he was going to kidnap her? (0–1 point); (3) Did he ask her if she wanted to marry him? If yes, did she agree? Did he tell her when and how he planned to kidnap her? (0–2 points); (4) Did he use deception to kidnap her? (0–1 point); (5) Did he use physical force to kidnap her? (0–1 point); (6) Was she upset when she was kidnapped? Did she resist the kidnapping? (0–1 point); (7) How long did she wait before she consented to the marriage? (0–2 points). Higher points were scored for items if the answer revealed greater consent.

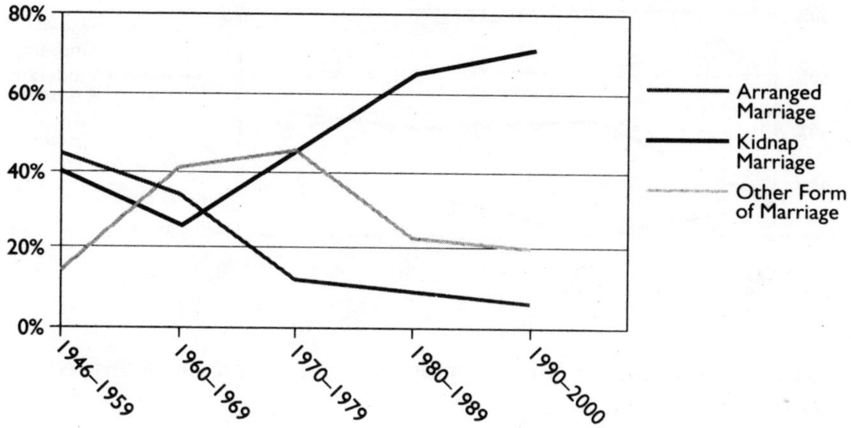

FIGURE 2.1. *Frequency of Marriage by Type in Ten-Year Intervals, 1946–2000*

traditional marriage practices. Interestingly enough, the practice of bride kidnapping did not experience a similar decline in the Soviet period. Although bride kidnapping did decline between the 1940s and the 1960s, the percent of kidnap marriages has been on a constant rise since the 1960s. The percentage of kidnap marriages was 25 percent in 1960s, 44 percent in the 1970s, 65 percent in the 1980s, and 71 percent in the 1990s. I believe that the resurgence of bride kidnapping in the 1970s reflects the state's acceptance of consensual kidnap marriages as a form of elopement that involves the girl's consent. At the same time, I argue that the subsequent rise of nonconsensual bride kidnapping in the 1980s and the 1990s can be traced to political and economic change. Finally, it is important to note the appearance of nontraditional forms of marriage, such as the Komsomol marriages. As traditional forms of marriage declined in the 1950s and 1960s, nontraditional forms of marriage appeared to increase. By the 1970s, nontraditional marriages represented 44 percent of all new marriages. Then, in the 1980s and 1990s, as the percentage of kidnap marriages increased, the percentage of nontraditional marriages declined to a low of 26 percent and then to 21 percent of all new marriages.

Figure 2.2 illustrates how the level of consent in kidnap marriages has changed over time. From 1946 to 2000, the percentage of kidnap marriages with strong consent declined from 75 percent (1946–1970) to 35 percent. The percentage of kidnap marriages with moderate and minimal consent have correspondingly increased, especially in the 1980s and 1990s. In the 1990s, 35 percent of the kidnap marriages involved strong consent,

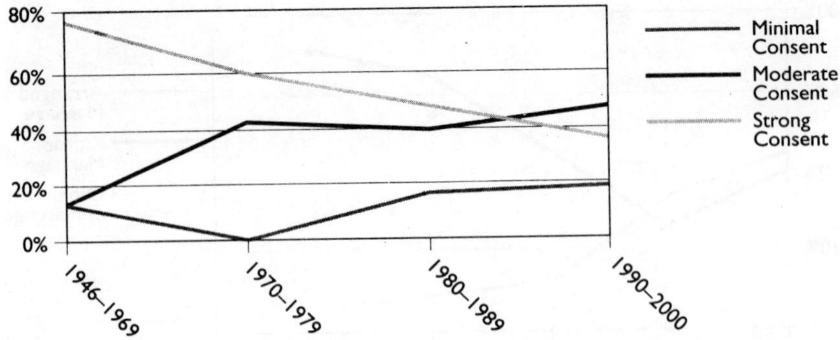

FIGURE 2.2. *Frequency of Kidnappings by Level of Consent in Ten-Year Intervals, 1946–2000*

47 percent moderate consent, and 18 percent minimal consent. These findings correspond to a popular perception that the percentage of nonconsensual kidnappings is on the rise. Informants who were married in the 1960s and 1970s point out nostalgically that the kidnappings in the past were almost always with the girl's consent, and she was typically informed where and when the kidnapping would take place. Today, consensual kidnappings still occur regularly, but people say that it is increasingly common for the young man to use deception to kidnap a girl who has only implicitly given her consent. In addition, an increasing number of cases involve girls who are kidnapped completely against their will.

The Post-Soviet State and the Rise of Nonconsensual Bride Kidnapping

The rise of nonconsensual bride kidnapping provides an interesting lens for examining state-society relations in post-Soviet Kazakhstan. Nonconsensual kidnappings are not new. They existed in the pre-Soviet period and they did occur during the Soviet period. However, there seems to be a definite contrast between the 1970s, when the majority of kidnappings were completely consensual, and the 1980s and 1990s, when an increasing percentage of kidnap cases were nonconsensual and semiconsensual. The rise of nonconsensual kidnapping can be explained by looking at the transition from a socialist state, which sought to protect women's rights and to provide economic security for its citizens, to a postsocialist state, which has substantially reduced its provisions and promoted a nationalist agenda that is less concerned with women's rights. The changing nature of the state's social contract with its citizens has changed the social environment in which marriages take place. This transition started in the 1980s with glasnost and perestroika, and accelerated in the 1990s after Kazakhstan achieved independence. Here I will point to three ways in which the post-Soviet state has helped foster new conditions that have contributed to the rise of nonconsensual bride kidnapping.

First, the introduction of state discourse that glorifies Kazakh traditional culture helps to explain the rise of nonconsensual bride kidnapping. As discussed above, postsocialist states throughout Eastern Europe and the former Soviet Union are redefining national identities in the post-Soviet period (Gal and Kligman 2000; Graney 2001; Marsh 1998; Tohidi 1998; Verdery 1996). This process started in the late Soviet period, when glasnost policies allowed nationalists to criticize Soviet versions of history and traditional culture. No longer constrained by Soviet ideology, state discourse in post-Soviet Kazakhstan has introduced new attitudes toward traditional gender roles. In the post-Soviet context, there has been a plethora of newspaper articles and books describing Kazakh traditional culture, including marriage practices. These marriage practices were generally disadvantageous to Kazakh women, but, not surprisingly, these descriptions of Kazakh traditional culture do no contain harsh Soviet-style critiques of practices that are "feudal" and "patriarchal." Rather, these publications seem to suggest a need to return to some of these traditions in order to recapture the glory of the pre-Soviet past. The retraditionalization of Kazakh society goes beyond these publications. The issue of polygyny, for example, has been discussed in parliament in a new, positive light. Further, arranged marriages, once banned by the Soviet state, were given renewed status when the president of Kazakhstan and the president of the Kyrgyz Republic publicly arranged a marriage of their children to each other. In this light, the post-Soviet state is seen to be withdrawing from gender-sensitive social issues.

Though bride kidnapping is not explicitly condoned by the state, this public discourse has influenced local attitudes toward nonconsensual bride kidnapping because there is no ideological pressure to defend women's rights. When it comes to nonconsensual bride kidnapping cases, there is a paradoxical situation that mirrors the conflict between Soviet values and the nationalist return to "traditional" values.[15] Most Kazakhs believe that nonconsensual bride kidnapping is morally wrong, yet many also believe that a girl who is kidnapped against her will is obligated to stay. Inspired by the national return to "traditional" values, Kazakh grooms and their relatives actively manipulate the Kazakh belief that it is shameful for a kidnapped bride to return home. A few girls do return home, but

15. Bride kidnapping is viewed as a Kazakh tradition, not an Islamic practice.

most agree to stay. Girls who are kidnapped against their will often insist on returning home, and they refuse to write the letter expressing consent. But they are pressured by the groom's elders who remind her of the shameful consequences of returning home. Eventually, many girls succumb to this pressure. The girls know that it is almost impossible to keep a kidnapping a secret, and a "girl who returns" is labeled as such and thus becomes a less desirable marriage partner. In addition, in some cases, the girl's family has some kind of tie to the groom's family that makes it difficult for her to renounce and disgrace his family. The few girls who do return home experience psychological and social difficulties. And, unfortunately, there are no state organizations or NGOs that provide services to help these women cope with their decision.

Second, the rise of nonconsensual bride kidnapping is influenced by a growing perception that the legal system is corrupt and does not protect the interests of women. Many of the people I interviewed believe that lawlessness and corruption has increased in the late Soviet and post-Soviet period and that these processes contribute to the rise of nonconsensual bride kidnapping. Women in particular feel that the Soviet state did more to enforce laws that promoted gender equality. When it comes to bride kidnapping, they believe that the state does not regard this as an important issue. Young men are aware of these issues, and those who choose to kidnap girls know that the odds are good that there will be no legal repercussions from kidnapping a bride.

Although many of the men I spoke to are strongly opposed to nonconsensual kidnapping, I also encountered a few that did not think that there was anything wrong with this. I interviewed a small group of men with these attitudes in a dingy café within the Turkestan bazaar. They admitted that they had all acted as accomplices on a number of kidnappings, including some cases with minimal consent. When asked whether they ever thought of the girl's happiness, they laughed, and one said, "Oh, we don't worry about that, she'll be happy after one week." The others chimed in, "Yeah, let her be happy!" — a common refrain used in wedding toasts. They could probably tell that I was uncomfortable with their brazen manner, but this only seemed to encourage them to tell even more stories and perhaps to embellish some of the details. One of the things that came up in these conversations was the fact that they were not at all worried that they might be prosecuted and tried for kidnapping. In their estimates, only about 5 percent of girls would return home if kidnapped against their will, and fewer would take the case to court. One of the boys claimed that they were able to "talk to a girl and determine whether she was likely to return home." Then, they added that if a girl's family does take the matter to court, the boy's family has the option of paying off the court or paying off the girl's family.

The final factor that helps explain the rise of nonconsensual bride kidnapping is the changing economic environment. Following the lead set by the Soviet state in the late 1980s, the post-Soviet state has introduced structural reforms that have substantially changed the economic security of Kazakhstan's citizens. Inspired by capitalist notions of economic management, the state has curbed its expenses by reducing the number of state employees and the magnitude of state subsidies. Employment is no longer guaranteed by the state. A substantial number of citizens, including state farm workers, have lost their state salaries and future pensions. Some have secured employment within newly established private enterprises while others have found employment in the informal economy, most notably the local bazaars. However, because of low wages, many of those who are employed in one way or another do not receive enough income to offset the effect of reduced subsidies for food, transportation, education, and consumer goods. Further, they cannot afford the cost of expensive imported goods that have flooded local markets and increased consumer desires. The problem of poverty is even worse for households without any employed adults (Bauer, Boschmann, and Green 1997; Bauer, Green and Kuehnast 1997).

Although the Soviet state certainly had its shortcomings, the state did provide Central Asian households with basic economic security after the 1950s. For this reason, families that are now experiencing poverty tend to remember the Soviet past with some nostalgia. In addition to guaranteeing basic survival needs, the Soviet state created a sense of expectation for a certain quality of life. Although the post-Soviet state is no longer honoring the economic promises made by the Soviet state, expectations of economic security persists in the popular conscience. These expectations affect marriage because marriage choices always involve economic considerations. Unmarried Kazakh girls and their parents want marriages with good families that can provide for the girl's economic well-being. When asked to describe the ideal marriage candidate, girls and their parents consistently hope for young men who have a secure form of employment. They don't want wealth so much as a sense of security. In the post-Soviet context, many young men and their families simply cannot offer girls the kind of economic security that they have learned to expect from their Soviet upbringing. Fear of rejection is one of the common motives for kidnapping a bride. Men who cannot offer as much economic security have more reasons to fear rejection. In addition to providing a less expensive alternative to an arranged marriage, kidnapping reduces the chance that the young man will be rejected by the bride or her family. As discussed above, there is a heavy stigma attached to "girls who return home," so even reluctant brides usually agree to stay. This does not mean that men use kidnapping to marry girls from relatively wealthy families. In fact, most choose to marry girls from similar economic backgrounds. One of the advantages of kidnapping, however, is that a young man does not have to worry about the embarrassment of being rejected by a girl and her family because of his economic situation. All of these three factors contribute to the rise of nonconsensual bride kidnapping in Kazakhstan.

In this chapter I have used ethnographic research to explain the practice of bride kidnapping in Kazakhstan. Bride kidnapping is a complex phenomenon that can be traced to the pre-Soviet period. In Soviet and post-Soviet Kazakhstan, this practice was and is more widespread in the southern regions where this research took place. The motives for kidnapping and the level of consent from the bride vary greatly from instance to instance. In addition, the practice of bride kidnapping has adapted and been transformed over time. In contrast to arranged marriages, which experienced a large decline in the Soviet period, kidnap marriages persisted and increased. By the 1970s, most kidnap marriages could be described as elopements that were staged as kidnappings. This practice corresponded to Soviet laws that banned forced marriages and Kazakh values that discourage girls from initiating their own marriages. In the 1980s and 1990s, the percentage of consensual bride kidnapping cases decreased as the practice of bride kidnapping was transformed yet again. By the 1990s, 35 percent of the kidnap cases involved strong consent, 47 percent moderate consent, and 18 percent minimal consent. The rise of nonconsensual bride kidnapping is attributed to the transition from a socialist state where women's rights were protected and economic security was provided to a postsocialist state where nationalist ideologies are more important than gender equality, perceptions of legal corruption are high, and economic security is uncertain.

This empirical study of bride kidnapping in Kazakhstan has several implications for understanding state-society relations in Central Asia. As Jones Luong (introduction) points out, previous studies of Central Asia offered two conflicting interpretations: while some scholars suggested that the Soviet state had succeeded in changing Central Asian society, in particular by creating strong national identities (Carrerre d'Encausse 1981; Rakowska-Harmstone 1970; Rywkin 1963), other scholars argued that the state was unable to change indigenous traditions and Islamic practices (Allworth 1989; Akiner 1995b; Fierman 1991). The second category of studies typically assumed that traditional beliefs and practices persisted throughout the Soviet period and thus would play an important role in the post-Soviet period. Particular emphasis was placed on the revival of Islamic practices (Bennigsen and Broxup 1983; Bennigsen and Wimbush 1985; Rywkin 1982), as Islamic practices are often conflated with traditional practices (Saroyan 1997).

This study suggests that neither interpretation is valid for understanding bride kidnapping. The Soviet state did succeed in changing this practice, but not in the way intended. Rather than eliminating the practice altogether, the practice was transformed in a way that reflected Soviet ideology. Further, though the practice of bride kidnapping today bears some resemblance to that of the past, this practice should not be regarded as the revival of a practice that persisted throughout the Soviet period. The practice changed in the Soviet period, and in the post-Soviet period the practice is being transformed yet again in a way that reflects the state's withdrawal from gender-sensitive issues. The increase of nonconsensual bride kidnapping reflects the retraditionalization of society, a process that is influenced by new social attitudes toward Kazakh national tradition and by state policies that encourage traditional gender roles. These processes, however, have little to do with Islam. Bride kidnapping is considered to be a Kazakh practice, shared by other groups (such as the Kyrgyz), but not an Islamic practice. The post-Soviet state appears to have some interest in reviving Kazakh national traditions, but it has much less interest in reviving Islamic faith.

Other authors in this book suggest that state-society relations are increasingly characterized by regionalism and influenced by international organizations. On the one hand, my work suggests that the practice of bride kidnapping, which is more commonly found in the southern regions of Kazakhstan, illustrates the growing relevance of regional policies. Anecdotal evidence suggests that residents of southern Kazakhstan, including state actors, are more willing to accept the practice of bride kidnapping. Future research could assess whether the state's reluctance to crack down on instances of nonconsensual kidnapping is confined to the southern oblasts of Kazakhstan, thus demonstrating the increasing authority of regional leaders (chap. 6). On the other hand, the evidence here is that certain aspects of state-society relations have not been affected by international organizations. Although international NGOs are interested in women's issues (McMann, chap. 7) among other things, the existing NGOs have not paid much attention to the problem of nonconsensual bride kidnapping in Kazakhstan. It is likely, however, that this issue will receive more attention in the future, as knowledge of this practice becomes more widespread.

2

LINKING STATE AND SOCIETY

Culture and Language

3. Cultural Elites in Uzbekistan

IDEOLOGICAL PRODUCTION AND THE STATE

LAURA ADAMS

In the realm of totalitarian kitsch, all answers are given in advance and preclude any questions. It follows, then, that the true opponent of totalitarian kitsch is the person who asks questions. A question is like a knife that slices through the stage backdrop and gives us a look at what lies hidden behind it.
—Milan Kundera

Any observer of public culture in Uzbekistan will tell you that kitsch is winning the battle against its question-asking opponents. In any country, major social and political events are staged to some degree to carefully craft a particular message, be it nationalist or consumerist. However, in Uzbekistan, more than in most countries, politics is conducted on a symbolic level, promoting the state's domination over the shared meaning of concepts such as heritage and progress. Nearly all public events are gaudily dressed up in a costume of Uzbek national culture and pop-culture kitsch in order to promote a particular vision of Uzbek national identity. For this, the government requires the cooperation of culture producers who share the government's goal of promoting social solidarity and state legitimacy through the renewal and propagation of Uzbek culture. However, while this experience of participation in nation-building and meaning creation has a powerful impact on the experience and identities of the political and cultural elites, it is not clear that the elites are enhancing a system of shared meaning in the broader society. It does not necessarily follow that a strong concept of national culture will ensure the loyalty of the people to the regime. Unlike the situation in Kazakstan and Kyrgyzstan (chap. 4), the

Research for this chapter was supported by the International Research & Exchanges Board (IREX) with funds from the National Endowment for the Humanities, the U.S. Department of State (Title VIII), and the U.S. Information Agency, and by the Berkeley Program for Soviet and Post-Soviet Studies. For their enormous assistance in helping me refine the ideas presented here, I want to thank my fellow participants in the Olin Seminar, especially Pauline Jones Luong and Kelly McMann, as well as David Abramson, Gulnora Aminova, Farhad Atai, Douglas Blum, Todd Horowitz, Adeeb Khalid, and Niaman Rzaeva.

state is strong in Uzbekistan's cultural realm, but perhaps strength in culture is a minor triumph when the state is weak in other ways.

Political communication in Uzbekistan consists mainly of the one-way transmission of ideology from state to citizen. Cultural elites[1] are, along with the state-controlled media, the main agents of these transmissions. The people are invited to receive these messages, but they are not normally invited to respond or to initiate communication themselves, resulting in a deceptively unified public discourse about culture and national identity. The intermediaries in this relationship between state and citizen, such as cultural elites, have some opportunities to initiate communication with the bureaucrats above them and to affect the government's nation-building program, but for the most part, the flow of political communication moves in one direction.[2] However, we cannot assume that the system works like a radio broadcast, with cultural elites simply transmitting the words they are given by the "announcers." Cultural elites have interests of their own, shaped by their institutional location within the state, that can put them in conflict with other state actors and shape the production and transmission of ideology, albeit within the parameters acceptable to the regime of President Islam Karimov.

Here, I will explore the experience of Uzbekistan's cultural elites in the 1990s by way of data gathered during my fieldwork in Tashkent between 1995 and 1998.[3] Changes in the Soviet-style command system of culture

1. I use the term "cultural elites" to refer to the general category of people I was studying who (1) received higher education in the arts (either in performance, administration, or criticism) or in cultural studies (such as folklore); and (2) who are now or were during the Soviet period employed professionally in the arts or culture. I avoid the term "*the* cultural elite" because I do not want to imply that this group of people who share similar educational and working environments constitute a cohesive social, economic, or political category. I do believe, however, that the similar experiences of these individuals have led them to think in similar ways about culture. Because I ended up studying this particular group, I also want to stress that cultural elites are but one segment of the intelligentsia as a whole, and my observations of these cultural elites cannot necessarily be generalized to all academics or the technical intelligentsia.

2. Some cultural elites have key roles in ideology production at the top levels, especially historians whose expertise centers on key time periods, such as the Timurid era. Others have more peripheral roles, such as some of my interviewees who were called to consult with the President's Council on issues directly related to their work. One choreographer, for example, was called to the council on two occasions, once to consult about how to best present the extravaganza for the Amir Timur 660 celebration in 1996, and on another occasion to give his advice about the future of dance education in Uzbekistan, including how to best preserve the distinct regional styles of dance while at the same time "developing" them.

3. Between 1995 and 1998 I conducted twelve months of fieldwork in Uzbekistan, based in Tashkent, interviewing cultural elites and observing cultural events ranging from folk

were slow in coming during this period, and the content of culture continued to be restricted by the dictates of state ideology. Although I am often critical of the actions and policies of the government of Uzbekistan during this period, I recognize, as anthropologist Valery Tishkov put it, "that when a society is accustomed to a one-dimensional symbolic system, it cannot become a multidimensional space over night" (1997, xiii). New ideas were introduced and new opportunities arose for culture workers during the 1990s; thus, my analysis must be seen in the context of a culture production system in transition and at a particular moment in time.

However, there is a real danger for the future of pluralism in Uzbekistan if the society's elites simply accept the trade-in of a monolithic discourse of communism for a monolithic discourse of nationalism. As Mansoor Moaddel (2001) argues, each ideology in a pluralistic system is enriched and diversified through its competition with other ideologies, whereas alternative ideologies developed in response to a monolithic ideological system tend to be unitary, formulaic, and conservative: "In attacking a monolithic target, ideological producers often tend to reproduce in a different form an idea system similar to what they are criticizing" (675). Not only are cultural elites reticent to draw on internationally available alternatives to a Soviet-style nationalist discourse but they keep at arm's length from the indigenous sources of alternative discourses that allowed "autonomous culture" to develop and take on totalitarianism in East Europe (Goldfarb 1991). Cultural elites in Uzbekistan might play a more organic role in responding to discourses emerging from the societal sphere, but, like other state actors, they are insulated from public sentiment by the absence of feedback mechanisms such as customer flight, audience research, or an independent press.

I argue that cultural elites play a somewhat contradictory role in mediating state-society relations in Uzbekistan. On the one hand, they support the state's goals by accepting and working within the parameters of official ideology and they use their institutional locations within the state as the resource base for their own goals, thus unintentionally legitimating and reproducing these state institutions. On the other hand, each of these activities has unforeseen consequences that sabotage the nation-building

---

games to Uzbek language theater. The focus of my research in 1996 was on the production of the mass theatrical extravaganzas that take place on major national holidays, though I also attended other cultural events such as neighborhood celebrations, theatrical performances, and folklore contests. I also conducted archival research on cultural institutions in Uzbekistan during the late Soviet period.

project of the state. By accepting the parameters of official ideology, cultural elites fail to provide any real aid to people searching for meaningful belief systems. By working within the institutional limits of the old Soviet system, the democratic inclusion of the people, of "society," in the culture-production process is severely limited. Interestingly, in my interviews, many culture producers went out of their way to point out that they knew what the people wanted and were doing what was best for the people and the nation. Thus, cultural elites in Uzbekistan engage in a pleasurable self-deception by believing the idea that they are serving the nation, while in reality they are serving short-term interests of their own and of the state that claims to be the legitimate representative of the nation. There is nothing inherently wrong with this; most people's actions are directed by self-interest. The people I interviewed and observed are no more and no less noble than their co-nationals or their peers in other countries. However, Uzbekistan's cultural elites are different in that the creativity and aesthetic demands that are at the heart of cultural work are limited by their participation in the existing system. Thus, we must try to understand how it is they continue to work within that system.

Understanding the experience of cultural elites helps us understand the state as something other than a monolithic and omnipotent force in Uzbek society, and, as I discuss below, it also helps us see the process of ideology creation and transmission in this type of state as a contingent and sometimes haphazard process. This understanding requires a thoughtful exploration of the structural and discursive possibilities available to cultural elites as a group and an understanding of the play of power within the state. In this I follow Michel Foucault's lead in seeing power as actions at work on a field of possibilities, enabling or hindering certain actions. Cultural elites in Uzbekistan face a particular field of possibilities that is constituted largely by Soviet legacies and contemporary state priorities. Their apparent lack of resistance to state power must be seen in terms of the actions they take within this field of possibilities and their institutional location as state actors themselves. First, I will give a broad overview of the working conditions of culture producers in Uzbekistan, and then I will explore the way that the resistance of cultural elites to the state reproduces the state both ideologically and institutionally. In my conclusion, I will speculate about the future of culture and ideology in Uzbekistan.

Culture and Ideological Production in Uzbekistan

In many ways, the Soviet Union was organized as much around principles of nationality as around principles of communism. Nationality featured prominently in many Soviet institutions, and nationality was defined by common language, history, and traditions (Brubaker 1994; Slezkine 1994; Suny 1993). This meant that Soviet cultural elites (especially writers, historians, and ethnographers) were placed in positions of unusual influence and danger compared to cultural elites in other societies. The prestige of being a member of the intelligentsia was higher in the Soviet Union than in other countries, but of course the restrictions were also much greater. National cultural elites in the Soviet Union had the resources of the state at their disposal so long as they propagated a version of national culture that fit with the current trends in Soviet socialist ideology. With the collapse of the Soviet Union, the support for and prestige of cultural elites also rapidly declined in most of the post-Soviet republics.

Although other Central Asian states have moved away from Soviet–style centrally funded and directed culture production, leading to greater freedom as well as greater economic hardship for culture producers (Eurasianet 2001; Megoran 2000; Odgaard and Simonsen 1999), in Uzbekistan the state maintains a close relationship with cultural elites. This has ideological as well as institutional repercussions. In Uzbekistan, most cultural production, whether academic or aesthetic, must relate on some level to one of the key symbols of independent Uzbekistan such as President Karimov, Amir Timur (the new national hero), the Great Silk Road, or, at the very least, Uzbek folk motifs, all of which have a standard interpretation that is repeated formulaically, ad nauseum.[4] This prevalence of state ideology is made possible by the government's control over most cultural production, through its various professional arts organizations and by the vast reach of the Ministry of Culture.

The government of Uzbekistan, with occasional support from international cultural organizations such as UNESCO,[5] finances nearly all cultural activities, ranging from the restoration of architectural monuments to the

4. President Islam Karimov has been in power since before independence and has created a cult of personality by proxy using the fourteenth-century ruler, Amir Timur (known in the West as Tamerlane the Great). While Turkmenistan's president has created a true cult of personality, President Karimov has elevated Amir Timur and cleverly restricted himself mainly to making analogies between his reign and Timur's, stressing the progressive, humanistic side of Timur's government and downplaying its brutal conquests. The Great Silk Road, a trade route of the first millennium that passed through the territory of today's Uzbekistan, is a metaphor for the economic integration with the world community to which the government currently aspires.

5. UNESCO is the United Nations Educational, Scientific and Cultural Organization, whose main objective is "to contribute to peace and security in the world by promoting collaboration among nations through education, science, culture and communication in order to further universal respect for justice, for the rule of law and for the human rights and

organization of film festivals to the physical maintenance of concert halls. The government is still the main source of material support for all cultural institutions including theaters, libraries, museums, concert halls, and educational institutions. During my visit in 1996 it looked like the Ministry of Culture was giving greater autonomy to cultural organizations than they had during the Soviet period, but in 1998 the ministry seemed to have not only reversed directions but gone beyond the centralization of the Soviet era. Administrative bodies that operated as independent professional organizations, the equivalent of trade unions for dancers, composers, and theater artists, lost a great deal of independence between 1995 and 1998 (see Adams 2000). Four of the main professional national dance ensembles, Lazgi (specializing in Khorazmi dance), Zarafshan (Bukhoran dance), and Bahor and Tanovar (pan-Uzbek and syncretic dance), lost their former sovereignty when they were all incorporated under the directorship of the new organization Ozraqs, which is directly responsible to the ministry (Gray 1998).

Most culture producers in Uzbekistan today receive a government salary, which, although meager, is not out of proportion with the prevailing wage scale. Additionally, culture producers supplement their income with government bonuses for special projects such as working on national holiday celebrations and profit from side ventures such as renting a spare flat or performing at a private function. There is an important realm of culture in the private sphere, such as weddings, where musicians are and always have been free to play to the taste of the public rather than to that of the state (Levin 1996). But virtually all the art, music and dance one sees in public is funded by the state, and virtually all culture producers continue to be dependent on the state for their livelihood.[6]

Given this picture, it might seem that cultural elites resign themselves to working on the state's nation-building projects because they have no

---

fundamental freedoms which are affirmed for the peoples of the world, without distinction of race, sex, language or religion, by the Charter of the United Nations." UNESCO provides research, information exchange, and recommendations to further member nations' advancement of knowledge (http://www.unesco.org/general/eng/about/what.html).

6. In the last few years, popular music appears to be breaking away from the state-sponsored model. Although pop stars are still enlisted in various nation-building efforts such as holiday concerts and patriotic song contests, the daily work of many popular musicians appears to be more and more independent of the state. Foreign, especially Turkish, business interests and the increasing availability of cheap recording technology and digital music files make the realm of popular music a very exciting one for anyone interested in autonomous culture production in Uzbekistan. For more on Uzbek pop culture, see the Uzland website: http://www.uzland.uz.

other choice. However, most culture producers do what they do for the state because their work is inherently pleasurable. Many of the cultural elites who haven't left their profession (for economic freedom) or left the country (for cultural and economic freedom) are deeply invested in their identities as artists or scholars. The state allows them to preserve those identities. It would be a mistake to think of cultural elites as being co-opted or coerced away from their proper place in "society" by "the state," as if they weren't themselves part of both the state and society. The elites seduce themselves (in the Foucaultian sense) into the state's project, but, in doing so they become part of the complex dynamic of resistance to the state that comes from within the state itself. As Ilkhamov (chap. 5) and Jones Luong (chap. 6) also show, resistance to the state can often come from within the state structure itself because of the way different institutional locations shape actors' interests. Cultural elites have their own interests, both as professionals who enjoy and are committed to their work and as members of a society that is facing numerous economic and social problems. Even though many members of the cultural elite in Uzbekistan view their work as an uphill battle for excellence and authenticity in the face of mundane bureaucrats and simpleminded ideologues, few of them publicly question the role that they play in supporting the regime.

This assessment may seem discordant with the assumptions we make about the moral obligations of cultural elites, especially given the role of intellectuals in resisting and bringing down Communist regimes in the late 1980s. In all the countries of Eastern Europe there was some form of political opposition, and intellectuals played a leading role in the transformation of the state and society. In Central Asia, however, cultural elites were ineffective or uninterested in opposing or transforming the authoritarian state during this period, and protest was focused more on cultural goals than on political change. Why was this so? Is it not the duty of the intellectual class in any society to stand up and speak truth to power?

For various reasons, in part because of the political insecurity caused by Moscow's crackdown on corruption in the government of the Uzbek SSR in the mid-1980s, sovereignty movements emerged relatively late in Uzbekistan and advocated mainly cultural goals such as legislation guaranteeing the status of the Uzbek language. These cultural issues were quickly co-opted by the Karimov regime, and the collapse of the Soviet Union made moot other issues of national sovereignty. In 1991–92, some cultural elites in Uzbekistan — for example, the writers who supported independent political movements such as Birlik and Erk — attempted to bring about a more democratic society, only to be violently repressed (Fierman 1997; Polat 1998). Most of Uzbekistan's cultural elites don't lead such perilous lives, however, and have continued to play the key role that intellectuals played in all Soviet-type societies: that of the producers and propagandizers of official ideology.

In the face of state repression, did intellectuals lack the resources to mobilize resistance to the Karimov regime, or were they cowardly and lazy? Some scholars argue that the resources to mount an opposition in Uzbekistan were available around the time of the collapse of the Soviet Union but that cultural elites failed in their central role of providing intellectual leadership "not just because of institutional legacies and old habits of scholarship, but because they were weak and hesitant, thus allowing state bureaucrats to usurp their intellectual prerogatives in defining discourses about culture and spirituality" (Smith et al. 1998, 84–85). This perspective puts the blame for the current cultural (and spiritual) domination of the state over society squarely on the shoulders of a group that failed to take up the mantle of their societal responsibility.

This view is shared by some among the cultural elites in Uzbekistan, such as Hamid aka,[7] a young postsecondary teacher at a Tashkent institution of arts education. One day when it was just the two of us at lunch, Hamid aka startled me with his surprisingly open contempt for his colleagues who were complicit with the Karimov regime's ideology. He bemoaned the ridiculous contortions of academic discourse in the post-Soviet period, giving me examples of how scholars found absurd ways to relate their work to the heritage of Amir Timur. "Someone is even writing a dissertation on the choreography of Timur." Seeing my incredulous expression, he asked in mock surprise, "What? You didn't know Timur was a ballet master?" Because most people I interacted with were concerned that I have a positive impression of cultural change since independence, I rarely glimpsed this kind of sarcasm. He continued, "Uzbekistan is like a dog that has lived all its life kept inside the courtyard, and suddenly the door to the street is opened, but it refuses to go out." I suggested that it was a problem of leadership: if even the elites were afraid to "leave the courtyard," how could anyone else? He agreed: "The elite, they're just puppets. Puppets and parrots!"

The cultural elite failed to articulate a coherent and viable alternative to the ideology of the Karimov regime. But why should intellectuals, more than trade unionists or entrepreneurs, be the vanguard of democratic reform? Underlying most arguments about why intellectuals failed to

7. Rather than using titles such as Ms. and Mr. when respectfully addressing someone, Uzbeks use first names with the honorific *aka* (for men older than oneself) or *opa* (for women older than oneself). The names I use in this paper have been changed and identifying information has been modified to protect my informants from exposure.

reform Uzbek society is the assumption that the role of the intellectual is inherently a subversive one. In his sociological analysis of the relationship between intellectuals and politics Jerome Karabel calls this the "moralist tradition . . . [which] treats intellectuals not as they actually are, but as they should be" (Karabel 1996, 205). Karabel proposes an alternative "realist" analysis that identifies "the conditions and processes that shape the actual political consciousness and actions of different groups of intellectuals" (Karabel 1996, 206). Following Pierre Bourdieu's characterization of intellectuals as occupying a position tied more closely to the dominant groups in a society than to the masses, Karabel argues that intellectuals generally have an interest in the status quo. Intellectuals have a relatively privileged position in the social order, but they are dependent for resources on their links to political and economic elites. This relationship is often a complex and ambivalent one, but Karabel points out that "what needs to be explained is less why intellectuals reach accommodations with the status quo than what it is that causes some of them, at certain historical moments, to rebel" (Karabel 1996, 209). Karabel outlines a theory of the conditions under which cultural elites compete with, rather than cooperate with, political and economic elites (Karabel 1996, 211–14).

When we see Uzbekistan through this theoretical framework, several aspects of the "field of possibilities" upon which Uzbekistan's cultural elite act are clarified. The lack of organizational and social diversity which serve as bases for developing oppositional ideas, the high level of professional integration of intellectuals with the state fostered by the Soviet system, and the consistent repressive nature of the Karimov regime all structure the support of cultural elites for the status quo. Additionally, the past models of state-society relationships in Uzbekistan all point to the role of intellectuals as one of resistance or reform from within the system, rather than one advocating revolutionary change.

As Karabel argues, one set of factors that makes it more likely, though by no means inevitable, that cultural elites will oppose the existing social order is the presence of well-organized and politically radical subordinate social groups, such as trade unions, that generate "organic intellectuals" and a high ratio of "relatively unattached" intellectuals to those employed by large-scale organizations. Given the unitary nature of the Soviet state and its successor in Uzbekistan, it has been nearly impossible for any group to organize independently of the government. This does not mean that the government is not internally differentiated, but the possibility of radicalization is very limited under such conditions. The fact that in post-Soviet Uzbekistan the former Communist Party and the state have been organizationally merged means that even fewer institutional bases for alternative thought exist than before. What's more, occupations in the Soviet Union were highly professionalized, one of the factors that makes it *less* likely that intellectuals will become radicalized, because the rigorous certification process and network ties associated with professionalization bind individuals more tightly to the system. However, if a society is "overproducing" intellectuals, the underemployed intellectuals are far more likely to be radicalized than if they are absorbed by institutions integrated in the social order. During the Soviet period, overproduction of intellectuals wasn't a problem, but today it is, and while some of Uzbekistan's unemployed intellectuals have found employment in other sectors, others are committed to what Karabel calls the accumulation of "moral capital — a resource that permits one to speak forcefully and convincingly to a wider public on fundamental issues of morality and truth" (Karabel 1996, 223). Although the state continues to monopolize economic and political resources, normative resources may be accruing to members of social movements, such as Hizb-ut-Tahrir, that are providing new discursive frameworks for interpreting the policies and actions of the government of Uzbekistan.[8]

Another factor that increases the likelihood of intellectuals turning against the state is the presence of a moderately repressive regime that lacks the means or the will to stamp out dissent. Studies of social protest mobilization show that the relationship between state repression and social protest looks like an inverted "U" curve, with the highest levels of social protest occurring at moderate levels of state repression. Although the Soviet regime relaxed its attitude toward dissent during the glasnost period, producing the predicted increase in protest activity, the Karimov regime acted swiftly and violently against most forms of social protest during the 1990s, successfully raising the cost of dissent. There is no indication that the repressive apparatus in Uzbekistan is faltering or wavering in its support for the president, so the most likely choices for dissidents are silence or exile. Intellectuals would be more likely to challenge the current order if the regime showed weakness, either in divisions within the government that are apparent to cultural elites or in succumbing to external threats such as incursions by militants or by returning to the Russian sphere of influence (both of which look increasingly unlikely since September 11, 2001 given the effects of U.S. military presence in the region).

8. Hizb-ut-Tahrir is an international Islamic political party that aims to restore the caliphate throughout the Muslim world (see http://www.hizb-ut-tahrir.org). Although (or perhaps because) Hizb-ut-Tahrir is one of the main targets of the Uzbek government's repression, the party seems to be gaining in popularity.

One other factor that Karabel mentions is the existence of historically grounded cultural repertoires of resistance to authority (see also Tilly 1993) shaping the way that actors see the field of possible actions. Some types of activity have precedents that lend legitimacy to those that choose them, while other activities may be seen as alien or inappropriate. Indigenous repertoires of resistance in Uzbekistan could potentially be based on early twentieth-century Jadid activities, such as publishing manifestos and oppositional newspapers, forming independent political organizations, engaging in peaceful public demonstrations in support of state policies they favor, and creating cultural works such as theater and literature that critique contemporary social and political conditions. These forms of protest and critique almost always took place within the rubric of reform rather than revolution, however (Allworth 1990, chap. 10; Khalid 1998, chap. 4). Some groups and individuals use pamphleteering and peaceful demonstrations to spread their views, but Soviet repertoires of resistance dominate the public sphere. These tactics included using official newspapers catering to the cultural elite, such as *Adabiyot va Sa"nat*, to express points of view that diverge from official policy as well as continuing the tradition of subtle critique through literature and the arts.

Veiled critique through the arts is still a mode of expression for Uzbekistan's cultural elites. The most dramatic example of this that I witnessed was the Hamza Theatre's 1998 production of *Cholpan*, a play about the persecution of a famous Uzbek writer who supported the Bolshevik Revolution but later fell victim to an early Stalinist purge. The production was pretty standard except that it used a film projection screen as part of its staging. In the first part of the play, this screen was used as part of an Uzbek Communist Party cell meeting to show an early Soviet documentary about the glories of progress that the Revolution had brought to Uzbekistan: chugging tractors tilling cotton fields, happy workers in newly built factories, and farmers celebrating Soviet socialist holidays. Throughout the rest of the play, the attendees of the meeting turn against each other as the fear and paranoia about "nationalist deviations" builds, eventually resulting in the arrest of the idealistic Cholpan. At the end of the play, just before the police arrive, Cholpan's student begs him not to burn his papers, to save them for a better day in the future. As the stage lights dim, the projection screen is used again to show propaganda footage, this time the standard fare of contemporary UzTV: babbling brooks, scenic mountain flowers, tractors tilling cotton fields, and President Karimov holding a smiling child on Independence Day. Is this the better day Cholpan's student was hoping for? Given the overall tone of the play, that seemed to be the intended meaning. However, another meaning was equally clear given the parallel uses of the projection screen: the propaganda about the glories of the revolution has simply been traded for propaganda about the glories of independence. Afterward, I asked the director what the ending meant, but his only response was an enigmatic smile.

Critique through the arts and newspapers and direct protest through peaceful demonstrations were relatively common throughout the early 1990s and are the types of actions we can expect to find when looking for resistance in the future. With the spread of mass media technology, the repertoires of protest of other cultures are increasingly available to Uzbekistan's cultural elites, should they wish to adapt them to their own society's situation. However, the lack of existing repertoires for directly confronting the state makes it more likely that reform-minded cultural elites will opt to work within existing channels. The irony of resistance from within, however, is the almost inevitable reproduction of the system itself.

When Resistance Is Reproduction

Cultural elites in any society play a key role in the transmission of ideology, whether the ideology is capitalist, communist, or nationalist. But what does this transmission process consist of? There are three elements of a generic view of ideology transmission that I would like to explore and complicate with empirical examples. The first element is the assumption, especially prevalent in simplistic descriptions of state ideologies, that a group of "puppet masters" formulates a coherent set of ideas that justify their power. The second element is the assumption that cultural elites play their role by grudgingly taking orders from these puppet masters and dutifully expressing these ideas in aesthetic or scholarly form. In contrast to this stereotypical notion of ideology transmission, I will show how ideology transmission in Uzbekistan is sometimes more of a pastiche than a coherent plan, and that elites make use of ideological formulas in ways that allow for improvisation, playfulness, and the advancement of their own interests. Again, I want to stress the institutional location of cultural elites in relation to other state actors, and the way their interests and priorities differ from both political elites and ordinary people.

In February 1996, I was invited by my advisor at the Tashkent State Institute of Culture to accompany him and a number of artists on a trip to Samarkand. This trip was billed as the "Amir Timur Scientific Expedition." I assumed that this meant it was going to be some sort of pilgrimage to historic sites associated with Timur. The poets, writers, and entertainers on the expedition had made the same assumption, because we were all rather disgruntled to find, at the end of the trip, that we had only spent about four hours out of three days learning about Timur. The rest of the trip was devoted to an interesting form of spectacular propaganda, engineered by state-employed ideologues and by the needs of the television crew accompanying us.

The trip was sponsored by the Youth Union (formerly Komsomol, now called Kamolot) and by the director of Uzbekelectroapparat, one of the largest complexes of electronics factories in the Soviet Union. His sponsorship surprised me, but this man was known for being a leading citizen and patron of the arts through his sponsorship of a factory drama club and four previous expeditions, among other civic-minded projects. We met with the director and a hundred or so employees at the factory where he gave us a send-off breakfast and speech. Delivering his message in Russian so that all of his employees would understand, he said: We don't know our own culture or language and therefore we don't know ourselves. This Timur expedition is very important for us to reclaim our heritage, which has been destroyed. Thanks to independence and our great president, we can all become richer spiritually and go and do great things for our country. Moments such as these show the complexities of nationalist discourses in Uzbekistan, which sometimes include non-Uzbeks in the "we" (as in "our heritage") and at other times ignore or downplay the role of non-Uzbeks in the nation-building process.

We then boarded a bus and headed for Samarkand. No sooner did we catch sight of Timur's tomb than we were heading out of town. After another hour, we came to a building, the Nurpay House of Culture, in the middle of the semiarid farmland and set up what turned out to be our song-and-speech routine for the next three days. First, the local dignitaries, the writers, and the academics (myself included) were seated at a table on the stage. In the first half of the program, the poets read their poetry, the academics gave little lectures, the officials made really long speeches, and I was asked to get up and say a few words in Uzbek.[9] I was usually introduced with the words "this person has come from America to learn about our traditions and customs and to honor our respected grandfather, Timur." The second half of the program was emceed by a well-known comedian. The musical groups played, a famous singer performed, and people got up to dance in front of the stage. We performed this same routine at the "planting of the first cotton seed" festival at a local kolkhoz, at Samarkand State University, and at the Samarkand Medical Institute.

9. For an analysis of the methodological implications of this type of fieldwork situation, see Adams 1999b.

I dubbed this expedition "the traveling ideology show" because I could see quite clearly how it was a transmission belt of ideology from the center to the periphery. Again, this is not to say that ideology transmission is a simple process of someone in the center deciding what ideas are official, telling intermediaries what to do, and the people passively receiving the information. There are several ways the activities of this "expedition" help us gain insight into the role of cultural elites in transmitting ideology in Uzbekistan. First, I will talk about the reproduction of ideology both in this particular example and in other cases from my fieldwork. Then I will continue the analysis of this anecdote in light of the institutional reproduction of state power.

Ideological Reproduction

Against a background of deteriorating economic conditions, little tolerance for diversity of political expression or dissident activity, and the increasingly apparent rapaciousness of the few families at the top of the political elite, how has the Karimov regime ensured its support? Through repression of dissent, apparently, but also through the time-honored formula of "bread and circuses." The Karimov regime has pursued a three-part strategy to ensure its success: stability, oligarchy, and national identity. The first component of the regime's legitimacy involves a continual emphasis on peace and stability, implicitly and explicitly contrasted with the civil war and social disruptions in Tajikistan and the fear of Taliban-style fundamentalism. For this part of the strategy, the regime relies heavily on the security forces as the guarantor of both domestic and trans-border stability. The second component involves neutralizing potential challenges to the regime from other factions with substantial political capital. As Ilkhamov notes in chapter 5, this requires balancing the interests of various segments of the economic and political elites through doling out control over various ministries and valuable resources, effectively creating an oligarchy within which internal conflicts are settled through bargaining among factions, away from the public eye.

The third component of legitimacy involves the creation and propagation of a national identity and ideology that supports particular expressions of both "national" and "universal" values. The "traditional" Uzbek culture (expressed in the material culture of *piyola* teacups and *atlas* silk as well as the emblematic Uzbek values of hospitality and the extended family) that is glorified in the nation-building program is largely an extension of the national culture institutionalized during the Soviet period, while the "universal" aspects of the Uzbek nation (Uzbekistan's constitution, its role in international organizations, and its support for "peace" and other values that are seen as being shared by all humanity) are an expression of post-Soviet equivalence with others in the world community of nation-states (Adams 1999a). The message is that citizens of Uzbekistan are part of a rich cultural heritage encompassing the Great Silk Road and the empire of Amir Timur, that they should be proud to be part of a multiethnic nation that celebrates friendship between all peoples, and that they have a bright future as a "normal" nation-state in the world from which they were isolated during the Soviet period. Although a great deal of time and money are spent producing products that express this "new" national identity, the message is often delivered in ways that trivialize the ideals or bore the viewers[10] because of the rigid bureaucracy of culture production and the strict limits set by the state on historical and cultural exploration.

The purpose of these cultural products is more than entertainment. Culture producers hope to create (1) social solidarity on a horizontal dimension (binding members of society together) and (2) on a vertical dimension, an identification of the individual citizen with the president. This nation-building project in Uzbekistan is messy and problematic, relying as much on Soviet ideas about Uzbek culture as on any novel construction of identity (Adams 1999a), as much on vacant slogans as on solidarity-building programs.

The "traveling ideology show" illustrated the formulaic consistency and internal inconsistency of this nation-building ideology in action. Not only was there no omnipotent state telling these people what to say, most of the speechmakers didn't know that they were even going to be called on to make a speech. They thought they were on an expedition to learn, not to teach. But they rose to the occasion by repeating familiar catchphrases and illustrating them with rather idiosyncratic examples culled from their own area of specialization. I didn't understand Uzbek well enough at the time to give an exact account of what was actually said, so I am merely conveying my impressions. The speech would begin with an orienting phrase that was familiar to everyone, something that would resonate because it is part of the official ideology and properly signals an official, authoritative, and "correct" statement, such as the obligatory quoting of Lenin (and now Karimov) in academic texts. Then, framed by phrases such

10. Although I didn't do any research on culture reception, casual conversations led me to believe that a lot of television audience members aren't all that interested in the formulaic cultural programs seen on national holidays and the repetitive national culture programs featuring twirling dancers in atlas silk dresses, the "national costume." Even some of the cultural elites expressed their fatigue with the repetitiveness of the standard national dance theme.

as "a thousand thanks to our president" and "our grandfather, Timur," the speaker would extemporize on an unrelated topic, such as the history of the "planting of the first cotton seed ritual." Thus, the strict official ideology is a framing device for the more subtle content of national culture and heritage. This framing and improvising is only prevalent in spontaneous situations that aren't prescripted, however. The very unexpectedness of the performances on the expedition allowed a wider range of playfulness with the ideology, but all within the prescribed ideological forms.

The form of ideology comes automatically, picked up from cues everyone receives from the media. The speeches by the officials were the same tired rhetoric found everywhere in Uzbekistan's public sphere, but the speeches by the academics, which could have given depth to this rhetoric, were thematically incoherent. The speeches by the local government officials at each of the events echoed the refrain "our grandfather, Timur" along with the usual repertoire of slogans about the gifts independence has brought, the wisdom of Karimov, and the importance of peace. This information was nothing new to anyone there and I would guess that most people didn't even pay attention. It was a one-way, closed-ended transmission that was mainly about the engagement of the elite in the nation-building project.

Though some members of the cultural elite have little interest in the nation-building project, others see the opportunity to define Uzbek national culture as one they have been waiting for their whole careers. Not all of these people work closely with the state, as my Tashkent interviewees did, and they are freer to experiment with reviving traditional culture in ways the Tashkent elites might find radical or even distasteful (see Levin 1996, 137–46). Though the state provides fewer rewards to those who work with it than it did during the Soviet period, the ideological project of the state in independent Uzbekistan is one that many members of the cultural elite take pride in. Many were quite happy under the Soviet system, and now they are all the more so because the state is working with their desires, instead of channeling them away from patriotism and national pride. Today, these artists look back with disdain on the politicization of culture during the Soviet period and profess no affinity with the ideology of communism that they played a part in disseminating. However, they see the political elements of culture today as a natural extension of the will of the Uzbek people to manifest their identity fully and freely, with the help of the state. Within the parameters set by the state, such as the exploration of the Timurid heritage, artists and scholars are relatively free to engage in the creativity and discovery that is at the heart of their identities.

One of Foucault's insights into relations of power is that power is not solely a negative, constraining, and external force; it is not always, or even often, the exercise of one's will in spite of opposition:

> What makes power hold good, what makes it accepted, is simply the fact that it doesn't only weigh on us as a force that says no; it also traverses and produces things, it induces pleasure, forms knowledge, produces discourse. It needs to be considered as a productive network that runs through the whole social body, much more than as a negative instance whose function is repression. (Foucault 2000, 120)

This insight is very important for understanding the relationship of cultural elites to the state in Uzbekistan. If knowledge and power are mutually constituting, then we must understand what sort of knowledge the state is producing. At the same time, we also must understand that the state, as embodied in particular bureaucrats and government officials, does not coerce artists into producing particular products all or even most of the time. The state is coercive in its relationships with cultural elites in that it sets the parameters of acceptable discourse, exercises censorship, and punishes open dissent. The state doesn't simply threaten, though it does do that when self-discipline fails, and it doesn't just offer rewards (which can be seen as coercive in the current economic situation). State power is exercised in the desires of the cultural elites to please their leaders and, even more, to please themselves.

Returning to the example of the "traveling ideology show," we need to understand the pleasures that this expedition provided to the people involved to understand the role of the cultural elite in the transmission of ideology. During the Soviet period, the pleasures of travel with the purpose of combining work and play was provided for elites on a grander scale, internationally. The opportunity to tour on a more modest budget has its appeal still, and many of the people on the expedition looked forward to the excuse to stop and get some special honey on the road from Tashkent to Samarkand, to buy Samarkandi *patir* bread in the bazaar, and to see the sights. Because cultural elites have a job in which they take pleasure, they enjoyed the opportunities this trip provided to do their work, to connect with audiences, to play with ideas about Uzbek traditions and Timur, to show off their authority or virtuosity while enriching the cultural milieu of the audience (especially in the rural areas), and to receive praise from officials. They also enjoyed the opportunities to socialize with one another, to shop, to sightsee, and to eat and drink in restaurants on someone else's tab.

I saw many other instances where cultural elites genuinely wanted to create works on nationalistic themes or to write articles demonstrating the parallels between Timur and Karimov. This desire stems in part from knowing where their next meal is coming from, but it is also a part of their nationalist sentiments and the pleasure they get from playing with ideology. It isn't so hard to imagine that it could be a pleasurable challenge to write that piece on Timurid choreography that Hamid aka derided. The game becomes seeing how you can play with the material inside the boundaries that clearly delineate the forbidden from the possible. But how do these parameters become known and how are they tested and resisted?

Knowing the parameters is a problem in some areas but not in others. When it comes to official policies or historiography, the parameters are clear and the content is formulaic. Through picking up cues from the media and from official statements passed down from the President's Council and other elite ideology-producing bodies, cultural elites working on historical themes are well aware that if they want their work to be free of unnecessary frustration, they should explore topics from the Timurid era, not the Shaibanid era.[11] When it comes to folklore and elements of national tradition, the parameters are less clear and there is more room for specialized knowledge. Culture producers working with folk themes have greater room for individual interpretation but also face a greater risk that their work will be censored. This happened after the dress rehearsal for the 1996 Navroz extravaganza,[12] when the representatives from the Cabinet of Ministers put the kibosh on a dance representing fire, one of the key symbols of Navroz. The official parameters of Uzbek national identity were much more friendly to Islamic practices than Zoroastrian prac-

11. There are many possible reasons why the Timurids (fourteenth-fifteenth century, C.E.) have been favored over the Shaibanids (sixteenth century, C.E.), even though the latter are ethnic Uzbeks. The Timurids' lasting monuments and international reputation are greater, and the Timurids are thought of as "sedentary" people whereas the Shaibanids are thought of as "nomadic," and therefore more primitive in the historical-materialist perspective that dominated Soviet scholarship. Additionally, the stature of the figure of Timur allows for President Karimov to develop a cult of personality by proxy, by creating analogies between his rule and Timur's. The decision to favor the Timurids and discourage research on the Shaibanids was probably made at the level of the Presidential Council, in consultation with academic experts, in the early 1990s.

12. Navroz is the Zoroastrian New Year, celebrated on the spring equinox in many parts of Central Asia. The holiday is one of Uzbekistan's most important national holidays and is celebrated on March 21 with a spectacular show that is broadcast on television.

tices,[13] and in their minds, the dance looked too much like fire worship. This was frustrating to the dance's creators who saw an opportunity to engage their creative vision in a genuine exploration of their people's heritage:

> In my opinion, you can't erase history, good, bad or average, it's all ours. At one time, in the ancient past, there weren't Uzbeks or Turks, there were some kinds of tribes here and they were fire worshippers. But in general, Navroz is considered a Muslim holiday even though that's all relative, since it wasn't originally Muslim but was adopted by the Muslims. But our [pauses] boys in politics decided that wasn't allowed. . . . They explained that "this isn't ours."

This incident was also frustrating for them because it demonstrated the power of bureaucrats over the creative vision of the artists. The response of cultural elites in Uzbekistan to this friction between political and creative interests is usually resignation and rationalization rather than rebellion. As another member of the team working on the holiday explained:

> I don't think that anything terrible would have happened if it [the fire dance] had been left in, but it's not like it was a great loss, either. As a director, as an artist, it simply would have been interesting: how to communicate the idea, the theme, of fire worship . . . through the arts, you know? It was interesting in and of itself. But, since different viewers would see it, since it would be transmitted by television and tapes would go to different countries, it was an issue of Uzbekistan being a Muslim country, a Muslim state, and then "there's something about a fire . . . what are they up to there anyway?" You get it? There are these political nuances . . . it's obvious that there are politics that we can't fully comprehend.

In testing the parameters, cultural elites often attempt to add new dimensions to the state's ideological program, pursuing their creative impulses in directions that will be more pleasurable intellectually and aesthetically. Unfortunately, the state, again in the person of bureaucrats employed by the Ministry of Culture and other government bodies, is rigid in its enforcement of a very narrow and one-dimensional interpretation of its main ideological tropes, such as that of Amir Timur. I spoke to two theater directors who had attempted to put on plays that diversified the portrayal

13. Thanks to Marianne Kamp for anecdotal evidence that since Uzbekistan's crackdown against Muslims in the late 1990s, the official ideology appears to be stressing the Zoroastrian roots of various "folk" practices much more often, sometimes to the point of confabulation.

of Timur; one wanted to show him as a dramatic, sad figure, looking back on his life with regrets in spite of his accomplishments, and the other wanted to show him as a devout Muslim, humble before Allah. Both were told by representatives of the Ministry of Culture and of the executive branch of government to stick to the ubiquitous heroic interpretation of Timur as a great leader and patron of the arts and sciences. This rigidity not only alienates and frustrates the cultural elites, it creates cultural products that have much less chance of engaging their audiences and creating the basis for any sort of depth of connection to the nation-building project. The monolithic interpretation of heritage produces few opportunities for people to engage in debates about national identity with any depth or pluralistic breadth.

Institutional Reproduction

To understand the role of cultural elites in mediating the state-society relationship, we need to understand the variety of interests and agents of the state. Going back to the example of the "traveling ideology show," we can't even separate the cultural elites on this expedition from the state, because they all earned their primary income from government salaries. However, it would be a mistake to assume unitary interests on the part of all these social actors simply because the government pays their salaries. We need to understand the institutional bases for conflict among state actors in Uzbekistan and other centralized authoritarian states, rather than positing the state as a single agent apart from society. The state as a monolithic, centralized source of coercion and support has never existed in Uzbekistan. Individuals are responsible to and rewarded by their peers and superiors within their own institutional context.

The cultural elites on this expedition had very similar institutional bases: performing arts organizations, the writers' union, and academic institutions. Their goals for this trip were similar: to engage in the pleasures of work, learning, and play. There were other people on this trip with very different institutional bases, with very different interests, not all of which were clear to me. I am most clear on the goals of the representative from Kamolot, because I interviewed him afterward. He was the most stereotypical "state" actor, genuinely passionate about educating the masses about the greatness of Timur. He was also concerned, and rightly so, about the future of his organization, which, later that year, would see its funding and personnel drastically cut. His goal on that trip was to perform as many shows as possible, thus reaching as many people as possible both for its intrinsic ideological value as well as to show the worth of his organization in general and himself in particular. He was in charge of organizing and coordinating the "work" part of the expedition that interfered with the cultural elites' goals of "learning" and "play." However, because the representative from Kamolot was officially in control of the agenda, the cultural elites weren't able to control how their time was spent. They complained, but in the end they complied.

The television crew played a similar role. Their goal seemed to be to capture as much entertaining and educational footage as possible, so they collaborated with the Kamolot representative in scheduling extra performances. They also attempted to enhance the spectacular aspects of the trip, capturing the "planting of the first cotton seed" ritual on tape and interviewing the exotic American about a particularly interesting dream she had had. They interfered with the desires of the cultural luminaries to play tourist and shop at the bazaar when they dictated only a half-hour stop so that they could get footage of an archaeological site that the rest of us weren't allowed to see. This especially irked the academics, who would have found a trip to this site an especially interesting learning experience. They had assumed this trip would be full of such learning experiences, and instead found themselves put on a strict schedule dictated by a twenty-five-year-old ideologue and, of all things, a television crew. As a gesture of resistance, they dawdled at the bazaar for well over an hour.

When the state penetrates all realms of life, as it does in totalitarian states and, to a lesser degree, in authoritarian regimes such as Uzbekistan, it becomes difficult to judge where the state ends and society begins. But even in authoritarian regimes, state institutions mediate between the agents representing governing bodies and those that are more involved in reproducing society. As Goldfarb (1980) demonstrated, totalitarian states unintentionally provide space within state organizations for mediation and dialogue between state and society. The state in any society is built on multiple institutional locations and furnishes its agents with differing and sometimes conflicting goals. Thus we must disaggregate the state into multiple institutional bases and look beyond the "commanding heights" to the other levels at which the state connects with society (Migdal 1994, 16). Resistance, complicity, and negotiation may be hidden within the processes of carrying out the daily work of the state, behind the closed doors of rehearsal halls or inside "houses of culture."

Resistance to the state is often seen as being a clear indication of societal interests in conflict with state interests, but resistance to the state takes place within state institutions as well as in other societal institutions and is carried out by individuals who, in other roles, are likely to be the target of resistance to the state. The very same culture producers at one moment might be resisting "the state" and in the next be the representative of "the state" that is meeting resistance from another state or social actor. "Just as we must abandon the image of the state as a free-standing agent issuing orders, we need to question the traditional figure of resistance as a subject who stands *outside* the state and refuses its demands. Political subjects and their modes of resistance are formed as much *within* the organizational terrain we call the state, rather than in some wholly exterior social space" (Mitchell 1991, 93).

Conflict between different state actors was evident every day in the staff meetings for the 1996 Independence Day holiday extravaganza.[14] Each of the members of the creative staff was cognizant that they were acting on behalf of the state, often represented discursively in the phrase "the president wants . . ." as a claim to the legitimacy and authority of their actions. However, the meetings were rife with conflict between various state actors with different institutional locations and different interests. For example, the deputy mayor of Tashkent yelled into a phone every morning to someone at the Ministry of Culture that they had not yet sent anyone over to assume their share of the holiday production burden: "Do I have to tell Jurabekov [the Prime Minister] about this? This isn't personal business, it's a republican matter! Why can't we draw up papers?" As far as I could tell, the ministry's resistance was due in part to the desire of its officials to concentrate their efforts on projects they were directly responsible for and would get credit for (credit for the holiday went mainly to officials from the Tashkent city government), and in part it may have actually been personal business: a deliberate attempt to thwart or embarrass the director of the extravaganza, against whom some in the ministry apparently carried a grudge that stemmed from ideological and artistic conflicts going back to the mid-1980s.

Another way that authoritarian systems can create a space for resistance is by fostering situations in which culture producers see their relationship to government and party bureaucrats as an "us versus them" relationship. Once this dynamic is put in place, usually by the arbitrary and aesthetically offensive directives of bureaucrats, artists find opportunities to resist and sabotage the party ideology whenever possible. In cases where the party dictatorship is seen as imposed by an alien power, such resistance is even considered a patriotic duty. (See Goldfarb 1991 for an analysis of these dynamics in the Polish case.) However, when Uzbekistan

14. Uzbekistan celebrates its independence from the Soviet Union on September 1. Every year the government produces a spectacular concert on the eve of the holiday.

became independent, it became harder for cultural elites to sustain this antagonistic relationship, and for a while many of them held off on sabotaging or even criticizing political elites because they were "our own." Resistance is now potentially unpatriotic and must be framed carefully when state actors come into conflict with one another.

Acting on behalf of the state, indicated by invoking the phrase "I am fulfilling the decree of the president," legitimates claims on resources within the frame of patriotic duty. One morning the director of a stadium showed up at the holiday production staff headquarters and confronted the lead directors about using his stadium for rehearsals of the "children's block" of dances in the Independence Day extravaganza. "You'll have three hundred little feet tearing up the grass in there! The president of the soccer team won't stand for it!" he exclaimed. One of the lead directors of the holiday told him to quit arguing because it was going to happen anyway, and the holiday directors proceeded to talk among themselves about what time rehearsals would begin. The stadium director got exasperated at being ignored and said hotly, "I cannot compromise on this matter. I am fulfilling our president's decree" (presumably a decree on sports). The lead director, who was in the process of storming out of the room, said, "Let's not have this conversation. We're fulfilling the president's decree, too." The deputy mayor nodded as if it were settled and said, "Okay, so we'll be rehearsing in the stadium from 7 to 11:30." A few days later, another employee of the stadium showed up demanding 150,000 som (about $4,000) for the use of the stadium, but only got grief for his trouble. "What's this about? We never had to pay before!" one of the directors yelled and dismissed him. In this case, despite the appeal to the authority of the "president's decree," the stadium administrators lacked sufficient institutional resources to protect their soccer field from damage. They would either have to pay for repairs themselves, or, if they had sufficient political capital, they could appeal to the Ministry of Finance, the body responsible for making sure the balance sheets of ministries, city agencies, and private vendors came out even after the holiday.

Thus, conflicts between state actors in Uzbekistan are not likely to be framed in ideological terms but rather as struggles over the allocation of resources and the apportioning of credit and blame. To see resistance to the state only in terms of democratic opposition or liberalism versus authoritarianism is to overlook the mundane modes of resistance *within* states such as Uzbekistan's, which take the form of assertions of personal or organizational autonomy. In situations where the state demands resources but fails to provide adequate incentives, such as the conflict over the Independence Day participation of the Ministry of Culture, resistance can be quite strong, but in the end, it changes virtually nothing. In essence, by invoking state power to resist state power, the relations of power are simply reproduced.

Cultural elites in Uzbekistan are not free thinkers who have simply been browbeaten into working for the state. They are state actors who pursue their own interests, some of which come into conflict with the interests of other state actors. Both the institutional and the ideological analyses presented here show how even the "resistance" of cultural elites contributes to the reproduction of a closed ideological system that supports state power in Uzbekistan. The nation-building project may have its greatest effects on the culture producers themselves, who want to believe that what they are doing is for the greater good of the nation. But they may be seduced by the spectacular nature of the work they create.

Uzbekistan's government has a penchant for spectacle because spectacle has properties that enable elites to close opportunities for input from below without making the masses feel left out (Baudrillard 1983, 207–17; Debord 1995 [1967]; Ritzer 1999, 105–7). Spectacle enchants and persuades, its audience feels included without feeling responsible for the action. Ideology, when cloaked in spectacle, takes on a vibrant quality of democratic participation, even though there is nothing democratic or participatory about it. Spectacle produces a hum of excitement and physiological arousal that, as Emile Durkheim noted, binds us more closely to the group sharing the experience and fixes in our minds the ideas and symbols portrayed therein (Durkheim 1915, 236–45). Of everyone involved, this excitement and intensity is most keenly felt by the spectacle producers themselves. Thus is their solidarity with the nation-state cemented, regardless of the lasting effects of the spectacle on the masses. The elite is seduced by the nation-building project and the rest of the population is left to find some meaning in the shows put on by the elite for one another.

The Next Generation of Cultural Elites

Examining the role of cultural elites in Uzbekistan helps us see the state as a multifaceted entity and helps us understand the foibles of ideology transmission. Culture producers are neither enslaved by the state nor are they merely automatons fulfilling decrees from above. Cultural elites play along with the nation-building project because they enjoy their work, even when it happens to serve the purely ideological goals of the state. Whether the cultural branch of this project will be successful will likely depend on the ability of Uzbekistan's cultural elites to introduce gradual innovations that gratify the desires of the public and keep the official version of culture tied in meaningful ways to the vernacular culture.

By way of conclusion, I would like to explore two issues that have implications for the future role of cultural elites in Uzbekistan. The first issue is that of the next generation of culture producers in Uzbekistan. The majority of people in positions of creative control in Tashkent in the 1990s were from a cohort that completed higher education in the 1970s. This cohort was trained at the height of the Brezhnev era and came to the apex of their career in the eras of perestroika and independence. Under the Soviets, cultural elites were well rewarded and occupied a position of high social status. Promising young artists and academics received free, high-quality education, after which they went on to a guaranteed job that offered a decent salary and opportunities for international travel. They had additional opportunities to earn money through participation in special projects and, if they were quite good, from the stipend of "People's Artist" awards. Artists' unions provided housing in convenient locations and provided various social services to artists and their families. Culture was highly valued by the Soviets, and artists enjoyed the respect and admiration of both the political elite and the masses.

Clearly, things have changed. These middle-aged men and women of the contemporary cohort are in a bad spot: fully invested in the old way of doing things yet at an economically vulnerable stage of life, facing the challenges of financing their children's weddings and educations in a system that requires annual bribes in the thousands of dollars. The generation nearing retirement has no incentive to abandon their powerful positions in the cultural sphere, but the middle-aged generation is faced with unpleasant and frustrating choices. Odgaard and Simonsen observe that what matters for this mature generation in Kazakhstan is "to be able to define and formulate projects where they, as scholars, can contribute to the development of the country" (1999, 38), thus retaining their identity and avoiding what they see as a distasteful descent into the market economy (Adams 2000, 36–39). This generation has already been depleted, however, by emigration of many of its brightest talents, and by defection to more lucrative careers. Those remaining are capable of innovation, but are hemmed in by their conservative elders and by the constraints of working on the state budget.

Many observers of Uzbekistan pin their hopes for positive social change on the coming generation, which will allegedly be free of Soviet bad habits and will have been exposed to a broader range of thought than their predecessors. In the realm of culture, the outlook is even less rosy than in the economic and political realms because of the bleak prospects for earning a living as an artist in Uzbekistan. Enrollments in the programs that train culture producers have dropped, and the slow development of a market-based cultural economy has provided little incentive for the next generation to choose a career in the arts. A further disincentive might be the lack of opportunities to pursue their interests in modern and international culture within the current administrative and ideological constraints.

A survey of young artists indicated that they are not as excited about the renewal of traditional Central Asian art as their predecessors were. The next generation sees independence as an opportunity not to explore their repressed cultural traditions but to become acquainted in a less politicized way with the art of Western Europe and to develop an indigenous avant-garde movement (Chukhovich 1998). Whether the state will accommodate these interests remains to be seen. As Jones Luong and Weinthal also show (chaps. 6 and 8), foreign resources are very important in the formation of social spheres not dominated by the state. With the help of new types of financing for the arts (such as ECOLOT, a joint-venture lottery whose proceeds go to a variety of causes, and OSI, the Soros Foundation–sponsored Open Society Institute), a segment of the younger generation will have opportunities to innovate, take risks, and work outside the confines of state ideology. Another segment will continue to work within the state-funded system inherited from the Soviet era and provide a stable flow of cultural products that meet the ideological demands of the political elite.

The second issue is whether the current method of nation-building through culture can sustain the existing oligarchy. The Karimov regime has pursued a three-part strategy to ensure its success: stability, oligarchy, and national identity. This strategy is probably not viable in the long term and it attempts to address only short-term issues of security and solidarity. Longer-term solutions must also address economic development and political reform, and successfully building national solidarity through shared identity will rely on the development of feedback mechanisms that will put the elite in closer touch with the symbols and practices that are actually meaningful to the people. The state's domination of communication is not only antidemocratic, it is dangerous for the elite because it only gives the illusion of control over society. When the state insulates itself from societal input, it looses touch with social reality and makes decisions based on biased or absent data. Werner (chap. 2) also argued that the state in Kazakhstan doesn't have a meaningful influence on society, but in the case of Uzbekistan, as Ilkhamov also argues (chap. 5), the lack of influence occurs despite a strong centralized state. In the first case, perhaps it is society that has isolated itself from the state, but in the second it may be the state isolating itself from society. Cultural products designed to build a sense of national identity and solidarity end up being by and for the elite, rather than an opportunity for society to reflect on itself or for the state to reflect on society. Instead, society is invited to reflect on the state, in silence.

4. A Shrinking Reach of the State?

LANGUAGE POLICY AND IMPLEMENTATION IN KAZAKHSTAN AND KYRGYZSTAN

BHAVNA DAVE

Why would a state or, to be precise, its ruling elites enshrine a particular language as the state language, when that language does not possess a standard vocabulary for day-to-day administration, education, and other modern tasks and is widely seen as "backward" or "less developed"? This seems particularly baffling when the ruling elites themselves are more at ease using a more established language and lack a popular base or the credibility to pose as ethnic or cultural leaders. Assuming that the two aforementioned concerns were either manageable or irrelevant, switching official documentation into a less developed language and attempting to alter the sociolinguistic repertoire of the population would still require enormous state capacity, investment of resources, meticulous planning, and widespread societal support. Even the congruence of these factors does not ensure the success of language policy, as the latter is determined by a fortuitous coincidence of favorable demography, political framework, and global context, so why would a state undertake this change?

It becomes clear when we consider this question in comparative perspective. For example: Why has reviving Hebrew and implementing it as the state language succeeded in Israel whereas efforts to revive Celtic Irish in Ireland have had only a limited success, though both endeavors were supported by huge state investment and legislation? A preliminary hypothesis would be the difference in timing and context: most Irish had adopted English as their first language, leaving a very small percentage of people monolingual in Irish. In contrast, the advantage of Hebrew was precisely in its literary and liturgical status. Having adopted the language of their geographical homes, Jews had no common language that they could claim to have "lost." The newly founded Jewish state needed a lingua franca for establishing effective administration and a common code of communication among its linguistically diverse citizenry, whereas English had already filled that role for the Irish. Both states invested vast resources in promoting the respective languages with varied outcomes. The gains made by Irish were of profound symbolic salience — it did not become the de facto state language but made enormous symbolic gains in terms of enhancing its prestige and the number of English-Irish bilinguals.

The linguistic choices and constraints facing Central Asian states have more parallels with the Irish revival than with the promotion of Hebrew as a lingua franca. This is because Russian, now regarded as the "colonial" or metropolitan language, remains the primary language of the elite, of the urban and the educated strata, in all five former Soviet Central Asian republics, where the language of the eponymous or titular nationality was relegated to a secondary status. However, this was done with a backdrop of enormous language planning undertaken by the Soviet rulers in the 1920s and 1930s to develop the national languages through standardization, changes in orthography, and institution of primary education.[1] Kazakhstan and Kyrgyzstan were the two most Russified republics because of their large percentages of Slavic inhabitants and because of significant Russification of the titular urban elites. According to the last Soviet-era census (1989), proficiency in the "second language" (i.e., Russian) was 64.6 percent among Kazakhs, 35 percent among Kyrgyz, and significantly low at 22.3 percent among Uzbeks. Kazakhstan was the only republic in which the titular nationality did not have a majority. Kazakhs formed 39.7 percent of the population, slightly more than Russians, who made up 37.7 percent, though the Slavs and Germans together constituted almost half the population. Kyrgyzstan was "ahead" of Kazakhstan in establishing the numerical ascendancy of the titular nationality in the republic. Kyrgyz constituted a clear majority at 52.4 percent in 1989; Slavs and Germans together constituted 26.4 percent, while the Uzbeks formed 12.9 percent. It seemed plausible, then, to consider whether Kazakhstan, and perhaps Kyrgyzstan too, could be an exception to the overall trend of defining the titular language as the state language.

The above statistical indicators also suggest that the battle against Russian would be far more difficult to wage in Kazakhstan than in Kyrgyzstan, where presumably a critical mass of Kyrgyz speakers already existed to facilitate the promotion of Kyrgyz as the state language. Kazakhstan's vast territorial expanse, dispersed ethnic settlements, large pockets of Russian-speaking population in the northern and eastern

1. For the elaborate language planning efforts undertaken by the Soviet state in its formative years, see T. Martin 2001 and Slezkine 1994. For detailed accounts focusing on Central Asia, see Fierman 1985 and Kreindler 1991.

regions and the former capital Almaty (Alma-Ata) implied that devising, let alone implementing, a unified language policy could be a task fraught with divisive consequences. Yet, over the past decade, Kazakhstan has managed to manufacture a working consensus on the language question and has considerably depoliticized both language and ethnic issues. The 1999 census statistics showed that 99.4 percent of Kazakhs were proficient in the state language, and, more astonishingly, 15 percent of Russians were proficient in it as well. Even more astonishing were the figures of 27 percent of Russians who were "learning" the state language. At the time of the 1989 census data, fewer than one in a hundred Russians had any proficiency in Kazakh.

Kyrgyzstan, in contrast, has continued to muddle through the issue and has been unable to take a decisive stand. It underwent heated debates over the past decade on whether to hold a nationwide referendum on the status of Russian and whether to grant "official" or "state" language status to Russian, including debate on the difference between the definition of "state" and "official" languages. The law granting "official" status for Russian, which was passed finally by the Kyrgyz Parliament in October 2000, had been stymied for almost five years. Neither the parliament that adopted the constitution nor the subsequent one elected in February 1995 (with Kyrgyz obtaining 82 percent of seats) was able to agree on the status of Russian (Kosmarskaia 2000, 68). Having tentatively resolved the issue of Russian, Kyrgyzstan has yet to address the question of status for Uzbek. According to the 1999 census, Uzbeks, who now form 14 percent of the population, have surpassed Russians, who now form 13 percent and are the largest minority. Because of their ongoing emigration, especially of the youth, and zero birthrates, the Russian share of the population is steadily declining.

Kazakhstan's apparently successful language legislation and acclaimed success in implementation of the language law stands in contrast to the prolonged contestation on language law in Kyrgyzstan and its ineffective implementation. A host of factors — such as the vast gap in the size and resource base of the two countries as well as the size and relative share of the two ethnic groups, differential demographic trends, and the extent of literary development of the two languages in the pre-Soviet period — sheds light on the differences in the process of formulating and implementing language policy between the two states. However, these cannot be viewed as independent variables that determine language policies. What is more salient is how state leaders respond to these structural constraints and accordingly deploy cultural or identity symbols for acquiring the support and compliance of key segments of the society. Therefore, I focus here on the differences in state capacity, particularly the extent to which the titular elite is able to pose as a relatively unified entity and is able to capture the state apparatus and define some coherent course of nation building by using language as a salient identity symbol, as well as a political instrument.

Language Policy and the Trajectories of Nation and State Building

Language is a particularly contentious issue in multiethnic or ethnically divided societies, as the symbolic cultural issues are inextricably tied with economic and political opportunities available to members of a group (Horowitz 1985). Cultural or linguistic homogenization, prevalent in several western European states, is not simply a product of the functional requirements of industrialization and bureaucratization, as Ernest Gellner (1983) argues, but is also a result of active pursuit of modernity and cultural standardization by the state (E. Weber 1976). From this standpoint, "nation building" refers to measures taken by the state to unify and homogenize its diverse population under a commonly shared civic identity that prevails over ethnic, linguistic, religious, or regional markers (Geertz 1963). The homogenizing thrust of nation building makes it an inclusive or assimilationist process, in which membership in the state is not based on ascriptive ethnic criteria but defined by territorial or civic markers. The high culture represented by a language is also mass culture, and a culturally homogeneous society is also the most egalitarian one (Gellner 1983). Gellner sees a common state language as a crucial factor in forging a cohesive sense of nationalism and closer correspondence between the cultural and ethnic boundaries of the state. Milton Esman (1992) has argued that integration of a country's diverse social domain is often a prime rationale for the adoption of a language as the "state language." David Laitin (1992), however, has shown that a recognition of multilingualism has been pivotal in state consolidation in several African states, contrary to the Gellnerian "one culture, one nation" paradigm.

The states of Central Asia (and several other post-Soviet states) face a scenario that is fundamentally different from that faced by postcolonial states in Africa. Russian is already established as the lingua franca of the various Central Asian peoples as well as the language of convenience for day-to-day administration. Seventy years of Soviet rule has significantly standardized and streamlined the cultural and linguistic landscape. The concern of post-Soviet Central Asian states has not been that of standardization and identification of a lingua franca but of asserting (and in turn, inventing) their cultural and linguistic heritage and defining their statehood by evoking ethnocultural symbols. In this regard, statehood is potentially an exclusive concept rather than a necessarily inclusive one. Similarly, the issue of state language in the post-Soviet sphere has focused on entitlements for the titular nationality and the exclusion of minorities.

Despite the tide of nationalism and the urgency of forging a shared national imagination in the newly decolonized entities, postcolonial elites in several countries of Asia and Africa were cautious about the choice of a national or state language. The choice of the language of the majority or of the "indigenous" group as the state language was perceived as consolidation of the domination of the majority. This is illustrated by the case of Sri Lanka where the choice of Sinhala (the majority language) as the sole state language in 1956 negated Tamil claims of cultural and territorial autonomy that gradually led the country into a brutal civil war. Scholars of the linguistic scene in India have paradoxically attributed the commonly shared national Indian identity, despite a profoundly diverse ethnic and linguistic structure, to the absence of a national language: "India is a nation that has no national language, perhaps *that is why* it is a nation" (Trivedi 2002). The niche for a lingua franca there has been filled by English, showing how a former colonial language can transform itself into a crucial axis of cultural unity among the educated strata of the most disparate linguistic communities. Contrasting India's experience with that of the Soviet Union, Paul Brass (1991, 112) astutely noted that "the major contrast here between India and the Soviet Union — and one which perhaps holds lessons for the Soviet future — is that the Indian solution to the official language question in practice has been both multilingual and permissive at the *center* itself."

In contrast, the Central Asian states have sought to realize the Soviet-era unfulfilled promise of recognizing the language of the titular nationality as the state language together with the pursuit of what they see as the universal model of the nation-state based on the centrality of one language.[2] Uzbekistan has solved the language issue by imposing a

2. In my various conversations, academics and activists engaged in cultural-linguistic issues, as well as lay people, endorse views such as "if English is the language spoken in Britain or America, German in Germany, French in France, Russian in Russia and so on, then why not Kazakh in Kazakhstan." What is curious is that none of the contrary examples (India, most African states, or even Belgium or Canada) are ever mentioned. Indeed, the prevalent ideological framework here determines the lack of awareness of the complexity of bilingual or multilingual situations.

rigid monolingualism that does not grant any special status to Russian or to Tajik. Tajik is spoken by an estimated 5 to 15 percent of its population. Both Kazakhstan and Kyrgyzstan have opted for a ranked bilingualism at the center. Kazakhstan has permitted Russian to function as an official language, while fortifying Kazakh with higher status as the state language. Bilingualism is required only in Russian-speaking areas and not in Kazakh-dominated oblasts such as Kzyl Orda and Southern Kazakhstan. Kyrgyzstan has tentatively endorsed bilingualism at the center, though parliamentary debates on the status of Russian have not ceased. The question of the status of the Uzbek language, the language of the largest minority (14 percent), has not yet been addressed. Finally, both states have formally endorsed the Soviet view that each nationality should be encouraged to preserve its national language, while qualifying that the financial responsibility for this lies with the kin state as well.[3]

Soviet nationalities theory has conferred a fixed salience on nationality (or national identity) by forging a natural or primordial connection with language and designated territory. The Soviet institutional legacy has produced an enduring conception of the new states as repositories of the titular nation, closely entwined with its cultural symbols, myths, and language. Nation building is also construed as "remedial" in nature (Brubaker 1995) in that the goals of regeneration of the titular nation, development of its culture, language, revival of history, genealogy, and symbols, including demographic growth are seen as most pressing concerns. These remedial or corrective aspects have taken precedence over inclusive or civic attributes as the titular nationality is seen as entitled to special status and protection. Indigenization or "nativization" of the polity (understood in ethnic terms) is a defining attribute of the state. While it places an ideological emphasis on accommodation or representation of nontitular groups in the state, such a representation is based on a ranked or hierarchical positioning of ethnic groups in the state structure.

The Soviet state did not just shape the cultural salience of nationality but also turned it into a central criterion for distribution of socioeconomic benefits. Deeply embedded in one's attachment to nationality are perceptions of power and entitlements, the latter shaping access to housing, jobs, and education, as well as career mobility and security of tenure. Language

3. Indeed the state-recognized national-cultural centers that represent various nationalities, whose leaders are made members of the "assembly of nations" in both states, are encouraged to seek support of their kin state to promote the cause of their "national" language.

laws in all the former Soviet republics have been enacted primarily to enhance the autonomy and power base of the titular elites as a way to counteract the actual or perceived hold of Russians on the institutions of power. There is nothing natural or inevitable about the proclamation of the titular language as the sole state language.

The immediate and short-term goal of the legislation favoring the national language was to establish the autonomy of elites as distinct from the former imperial or colonial rulers and assert the primacy of the titular nationality over Slavs in the state administration, economy, and education. Both states may have achieved this objective. However, favorable legislation is only a first step in establishing titular control. A state's efficacy in enacting and implementing its language policies is influenced by the extent to which it is able to exert control over the contending factions within the government and outside it.

Common Soviet Legacy

There are some fundamental similarities between the development of the titular language and their political fate (or as sociolinguists point out, between "language corpus" and "language status") in Kazakhstan and Kyrgyzstan during the Soviet period. First, both languages were transformed into standardized literary and modern languages along the modular path laid down by Soviet language planners. The Bolsheviks standardized these languages by first discarding the Arabic script and writing them in the Latin alphabet in the early 1920s and subsequently changing the Latinized alphabets into Cyrillic in the late 1930s. Kazakh and Kyrgyz were languages with a rich oral tradition that had not been codified in writing. The bulk of printed material is in Cyrillic, as these two languages — along with all other Turkic languages and Tajik — have been written in Cyrillic from the late 1930s onward.[4]

The Soviet *korenizatsiia* (nativization) policies of the 1920s and early 1930s placed great emphasis on nativizing the Communist Party by hiring national cadres and promoting the national languages of the republics. Slavs were not only formally required to learn the national languages of the republics they inhabited, they were expected to do so, which caused considerable resentment and ethnic strife (Payne 2001). With the formal end to korenizatsiia in the early 1930s, the de jure bilingualism endorsed by the party increasingly turned into asymmetrical bilingualism, as the key emphasis no longer was on the development of national languages but on

4. Uzbeks have begun a switch to the Roman alphabet, to be completed by 2005.

enhancing proficiency in Russian. As educated strata among the titular groups became proficient in Russian, the latter became the language of intraethnic communication for the titular group in urban areas and other Russian-dominated regions in Kazakhstan and Kyrgyzstan. By the 1950s Russian had become the dominant language all over the Soviet Union and was officially referred to as the "language of interethnic communication," though it had no juridical status (Kreindler 1991). The most telling indicator of the low prestige of the national languages in Central Asia was the near total lack of proficiency in these languages among Slavs or European settlers in the region. Only 1 percent of Russians (or even fewer) in Kazakhstan and Kyrgyzstan were proficient in the titular language — the lowest level in all the republics. Russians in Uzbekistan tended to be more proficient and more inclined to say greetings and be able to count in Uzbek.

The 1989 Soviet census data showed that about 97 percent of the titular Kazakhs and Kyrgyz claimed proficiency in the language of their own nationality. However, it should be noted that the questions about "nationality" and "mother tongue" (*rodnoi iazyk*) in the Soviet censuses were first and foremost questions of primordial or ascriptive ethnic self-identification and not a measure of cultural attachment or actual proficiency in the language (Silver 1976). The statistics on mother tongue compiled by Soviet census takers reflected, at best, the symbolic identity choices of the respondents, rather than their actual language repertoire or proficiency in the native language. Figures showing the extent to which members of a certain nationality claimed proficiency in Russian as a second language were more reliable indicators of the extent to which the mother tongue had been pushed out. The 1989 statistics showed that 64 percent of Kazakhs claimed fluency in Russian as their second language. Among the Muslim groups, only Bashkirs (83.4) and Tatars (82.2 percent) were ahead of the Kazakhs in proficiency in Russian as their second language (Kaiser 1994, 290–91, 276–77).

The ability of Central Asians to proficiently use their native language was much lower than what the census data indicated. Sociological surveys and articles in the late 1980s and early 1990s referred to the pervasive Russification of urban Kazakhs, particularly those under forty. My own ethnographic observations during the period 1992–95 suggest that two-thirds to three-fourths of Kazakhs living in urban settings spoke Russian almost exclusively, though many of them claimed to understand Kazakh and speak it if necessary. Kazakh scholars also corroborate these findings, though there is disagreement as to how proficiency in the native language is to be measured and on the precise numbers of those lacking proficiency in their native language.[5] Research by Eugene Huskey (1995) confirms similar trends in Kyrgyzstan.

It was hardly surprising that in the post-1991 scenario, Russians and other Russian-speaking nontitular groups would press for official bilingualism or for having two state languages. However, few Kazakhs or Kyrgyz have openly demanded two state languages, though many have privately expressed the need for official bilingualism (Dave 1996b, Laitin 1998). As a result of the underlying assumption by titular language activists that the Russified co-ethnics could eventually be reclaimed, these language activists exclusively attributed demands for official bilingualism (two state languages) to Russians and other nontitular Russian-speaking groups.

Kazakhstan: Language Legislation and the End of Language Debate

In its initial stages of sovereignty, Kazakhstan witnessed an assertive language revival campaign. The intensity of the language debate was closely connected with the desire to establish numerical and political control in that Kazakhs did not then constitute a majority in their "own" sovereign state. Here we will look at how Kazakhstan has used language as an instrument for promoting indigenization and ensuring a balance between regional and sectarian claims. The cultural and linguistic barrier between Russified and rural Kazakhs has not acquired a political dimension.

Among the most vocal opponents of proposals for having two state languages in the early 1990s were the literary intelligentsia and academics, many of whom were members of Qazaq tili — the organization championing the cause of Kazakh language (Dave 1996b). Their initial pronouncements unequivocally labeled Russian as the "colonial" language, responsible for pushing out Kazakh from its legitimate domain. Consistent with the nationalists' perception of Kazakhstan as a Kazakh state, they demanded that Kazakh alone should serve as the state language. The arguments favoring Kazakh can be summarized in the following: "A nation can

5. Abduali Qaidarov (*Kazakhstanskaia Pravda*, 20 August 1992), the head of the language revival society *Qazaq tili*, estimated that some 40 percent of Kazakhs were not able to speak the language. Demographer Makash Tatimov (1993) claims that the native language proficiency of Kazakhs should be determined not by the extent of public usage (in multiethnic settings) but by the extent to which the language is spoken in the family (i.e., the intraethnic setting). Following this criterion, the number of Kazakhs who do not know their own language is only 28 percent.

have only one mother tongue" (a retort by Rakhmankul Berdibaev, a Kazakh folklorist, to Khrushchev's reference to Russian as the "second mother tongue"). "There can be no nation without its language" (A common refrain among Kazakh language activists). "Russian is the language of Russians and the Russian state, therefore it cannot become that of Kazakhstan" (from a Kazakh writer). "Where else will Kazakh be spoken if not on its own ancestral Kazakh lands?" (from the rector of a university in Almaty). In the nationalist imagination, the Soviet-defined territorial framework inherited by Kazakhstan was coextensive with their ancestral homeland. Although the regime of President Nursultan Nazarbaev did not endorse the intense tenor of the demands of language activists, it nonetheless rewarded them by recruiting them as policy advisors and appointing them to the various committees and organizations involved in promoting the language issue.

The nationalist euphoria and narratives of discrimination and cultural and linguistic "genocide" abated after Kazakhstan adopted its first constitution in 1993, which defined Kazakh as the state language and Russian as the "language of interethnic communication." This formulation pleased neither the proponents of Russian, who wanted nothing short of a state language status for Russian, nor the nationalists, who were perturbed by the continuation of the Soviet-era accent on Russian as the language of interethnic communication. The 1993 constitution also made conflicting claims to both ethnic and civic conceptions of statehood. It opened with a civic emphasis by referring to "the people (*narod*) of Kazakhstan" as the architects of the constitution. However, the very first article declared that the state of Kazakhstan is based on "the Kazakh people's statehood," thus endorsing an ethnically based concept of the nation. Russian activists questioned the juxtapositioning of the notions "the people (*narod*) of Kazakhstan" and "Kazakh people," which implied that they were synonymous. In 1992 President Nazarbaev had, indeed, linked the notion of sovereignty with the principle of "national self-determination" of the titular nation, describing the country as the historical land of the Kazakhs.

This clause was retained in the draft version of the subsequent constitution, but it was eliminated from the final version adopted in September 1995. Instead, the civic categories "Kazakhstani" and "Kazakhstani patriotism" were enshrined in the new constitution. However, it added a new formulation referring to Kazakhs as the "primordial" owners of their land. The preamble of the constitution stated: "We, the people of Kazakhstan, united by a common historical fate, have created a state on the ancient land (*iskonnaia zemlia*) of the ethnic Kazakhs" (Kolstø 1999, 618). This clumsy phrasing nonetheless served to underscore the ethnic definition of statehood. In conclusion, one can say that the 1995 constitution and the legal framework have judiciously sought to combine ethnic and civic conceptions of statehood while promoting a de facto policy of Kazakhization.

As Russian speakers in Kazakhstan continued to demand recognition for Russian as a second state language, proponents of Kazakh justified the need to retain Kazakh as the sole state language more forcefully in terms of equity and affirmative action. This can be summarized in views such as: "Where else can Kazakh be spoken, if not in its own homeland?" and "Kazakh needs protection as the state language precisely because it is a weak language, unable to withstand a natural competition with Russian." The overall agreement was that Kazakh could not survive if bilingualism, that is, the existing status quo, were to prevail and that it needed extensive state support in order to revive and flourish in its homeland. These arguments endorsed a primordialist view of nationality — *nyet iazyka, nyet natsii* ("there is no nation without a language") — while calling for affirmative action to fortify Kazakh's status as the sole state language.

Advocates of "Kazakh only" argued that even if Russian were to be accorded the status of second state language, a person seeking a position in state administration and in service spheres would still be required to be bilingual (Aldamzharov 1995, 3). Furthermore, as a Kazakh nationalist went on to ask: "And who are the bilinguals in the country? At the moment, it is the Kazakhs . . . and they will, of course, have greater opportunities to occupy key posts." Thus bilingualism was understood as competence in both languages and not in only one of the two proposed state languages. This implies that even if the status of Russian were restored, the ensuing nationality-based corrective measures, accompanied by the upgrading of Kazakh, would still favor the titular group. Ultimately, it is nationality and not the (spoken) language that is taken as the defining marker of identity.

Since independence, which has led to the emergence of a "nationalizing state" (Brubaker 1995), the share of Russians and nontitular groups in governmental offices has steadily decreased. Their share in legislative and executive branches at oblast level in 1989 was 50 percent, in 1992 it had dropped to 38 percent, and in 1994 it was reduced further to 25 percent.[6] In 1994, when Kazakhs formed 45 percent of the population, they occupied 60 percent of the seats in the Kazakh Supreme Soviet. The parliament had only 28 percent Russian members, though they formed 35

6. Data from parliamentary proceedings on Russian-Kazakh relations, 18 April 1995, by the State Duma Committee on Ties with CIS and Compatriots Abroad.

percent of the population and were a much higher percentage of those over twenty-five. Nazarbaev's staff in spring 1994 had 74 percent Kazakhs, 23 percent Slavs, and 3 percent non-Slavs (Galiev et al. 1996). A radical change of personnel was reported in the top positions within the oblast *akimat* (the office of the *akim*) between 1992 and 1995 (*Kazakhstanskaia Pravda*, 28 June 1996), though several akims of non-Kazakh nationality were appointed.

The ongoing emigration of the Slavic and German population and an influx of Kazakh diaspora from Mongolia, Turkey, and other neighboring countries has accelerated the process of nationalization. Kazakh officials have reasoned that a favorable demographic balance (i.e., becoming a majority) will eventually restore the status of the Kazakh language. However, the state has utilized demography as a political instrument for consolidating the status of Kazakh while projecting it as a natural process that reflects linguistic and political change (Dave 2002). Kolstø (1998) commented on the intense pace of kazakhization in the government and administration, stating that the dynamics of ethnic representation *anticipate*, and thus jump ahead of, rather than result from changes in the ethnodemographic structure.

The 1993 language law, growing kazakhization, and anxiety over a deterioration of their status are among the key factors that have triggered an exodus of the Russian-speaking population from Kazakhstan since 1991, even from Russian-dominated regions in the northeast. The crucial tipping point for nontitular emigration was reached between 1994 and 1996 when almost 1.2 million (481,000 in 1994, 309,600 in 1995, and 229,400 in 1996) left Kazakhstan (*Statisticheskii Biulletin* 1997, 12–15). Altogether, about two million Russian speakers (including 750,000 ethnic Germans, out of about a million ethnic Germans living in Kazakhstan) left Kazakhstan between 1989 and 1999, with the combined European share of the population dropping to less than 40 percent compared with 50 percent in 1989. Since then emigration has become the norm, no longer needing a trigger. Exit has been the dominant response by culturally and politically disgruntled Russians, who perceive the nationalizing course as irreversible and see little future for their children in the ethnically reconfigured landscapes of the Caucasus and Central Asia. Demographic changes in Kazakhstan between 1994 and 1997 (peak of emigration 1994–95) provide the context for a more "liberal" language policy, which followed two years later. Russian emigration was in response to anticipated discrimination.

In July 1997 when the new Kazakh language law was passed, the demographic situation had become more favorable to the titular nationality as a result of the critical mass of Slavs who had emigrated between 1991 and

1996. The law recognized Russian as an official language on a par with Kazakh, dropping the additional proposed clause "only when absolutely necessary (*pri neobkhodimosti*)," insisted upon by nationalists in the previous versions. Two other controversial proposed clauses, one requiring Kazakhs to master their language by the year 2003 and all others to gain a proficiency in it by 2006; and the other creating a list of positions in the government where Kazakh would be mandatory, were scrapped. No formal means for testing proficiency in the state language exists, nor is any documentation attesting to the proficiency required. Such tests could disqualify many natives.

The belated concession to Russian may not have convinced the nontitular Russophone population to see Kazakhstan as their long-term home, but it certainly lifted the pressure off Russian-speaking Kazakhs, particularly those in the various governmental and administration offices. Most Kazakh officials at the top levels of administration and government have better facility in Russian than in Kazakh, which has contributed to the ineffective implementation of the language program. The law also deems that learning Kazakh is "the duty of each Kazakhstani," but there is no clear statement of what resources the state will invest in order to facilitate the learning of Kazakh.

A ten-year state program on language policy was approved in 1999. It defined strategic priorities and objectives and how they should be implemented. The law requires official bodies to complete the majority of their documentation in Kazakh and stipulates that at least 50 percent of all TV and radio broadcasting should be in Kazakh (*RFE/RL Newsline* 9 February 1999; also 20 January 1999).

Assessing the Implementation of the Language Law

Since the adoption of the language law, Kazakhstan has streamlined its implementation, ironically without causing a drastic shift in the established language repertoire. A presidential decree, "The Conception of the Language Policy of the Republic of Kazakhstan," issued in November 1996 (*Kazakhstanskaia Pravda* 6 November 1996), called for a well-coordinated language policy to ensure effective results. Two years later, the minister of Information and Public Concord, Altynbek Sarsenbaev, declared that the implementation of the language law was in "full force" and that "at long last we have moved away from fruitless discussions on the fate of the Kazakh language, which only made the situation worse" (*Karavan*, 9 October 1998, 6).

Indeed, there seemed to be a high number of competing individuals and agencies involved in devising and implementing appropriate language policy during the period 1992–96.[7] Personal and ideological differences between the heads of the various committees and departments appeared to have generated much internal dissent over the language policy, particularly in regard to setting the timetable for the various regions to begin conducting official business only in Kazakh. In 1994, the director of the Department for Coordination of Language Politics under the Ministry of Education and Culture, Sultan Orazalinov, expressed his displeasure with the pace of progress on implementing Kazakh as the state language, blaming both the government for dragging its feet on the issue and the Qazaq tili activists for "all talk and little action" (author's interview, August 1994). Bakhytzhan Khasanov, head of the Center for Language Development Strategy of the Ministry of Science and the Academy of Sciences, clarified that the language law was about devising a strategy for promoting "bilingualism" (though he failed to provide a definition) and complained that "too many agencies and amateurs" were involved who spent their energy on discussing "irrelevant language issues" (author's interview, March 1993).

The Nazarbaev leadership has since then appointed more moderates to leadership positions, while allowing nationalists and linguists to maintain a certain social status (i.e., through granting dachas and housing) but keeping them out of politics. In other words, nationalists are able to operate as watchdogs and have freedom to agitate on language issues but to not wield political influence.

Erbol Shaimerdenov, the head of the Committee on Implementation of the State Language, told me the increasing official documentation in the state language was a measure of the "success" of the language policy (author's interview, 9 September 1999). He assured me that a comprehensive law and a detailed language plan had already been worked out and that the task of his agency was to facilitate its implementation and not to carry out "inspections." He claimed that a major task of his committee was to "increase" the demand for the use of the state language and that the committee had already achieved the targets. He repeatedly emphasized the success in "meeting targets" and put forward the central aim of "increasing the need for Kazakh" rather than a qualitative improvement and widening of the linguistic domain.

7. The three most prominent of these were the organization Qazaq tili headed by Abduali Qaidarov, which wielded influence and enjoyed visibility but had no juridical status; the Center for Language Development Strategy at the Ministry of Sciences; and the Department for Coordination of Language Politics under the Ministry of Education and Culture.

Although in 1993 Nazarbaev challenged questions from Russian journalists about the plight of the "Russian-speaking population" of Kazakhstan by asserting that "all Kazakhstanis are Russian speakers" and, therefore, no separate problem of "Russian speakers" exists, seven years later he described Kazakhstan as a Turkophone state (*Kazakhstanskaia pravda*, 15 December 2000). In the same speech, Nazarbaev also proclaimed that the language issue had been "solved."

Although this claim is very much mired in the Soviet Marxist canon that key material and cultural issues can be "solved" with a degree of finality, here it also suggests that language is no longer a thorny issue at the state or policy-making level. In other words, the issue has been pushed down to the bureaucratic level; the responsibility of promoting and expanding the use of Kazakh now rests with the various agencies entrusted with implementing (or "fulfilling") the state directives. This suggests that the legality of the language legislation has already been established, and the task of various agencies is to implement the law and ensure the provision of "bilingualism" by producing (mainly translating) the relevant literature into Kazakh. In 1995, Nazarbaev had chastised the parliament (which he dismissed earlier that year) for failure to pass an adequate number of laws because it was more involved in debates than in getting the work done (Dave 1996a). From this standpoint, the parliament's "success" is to be assessed on the basis of how many laws it manages to pass in a relatively short period, rather than spending time on prolonged debates.

The 1999 census has contributed to the institution of Kazakh as the "state language" by revealing enhanced levels of state language proficiency, both among Kazakhs and the nontitular population. Unlike previous Soviet-era censuses, the 1999 census did not require citizens to indicate what their "mother tongue" was. Instead, it inquired about "proficiency" in the state language. It revealed that 99.4 percent of Kazakhs say they know the state language; over 70 percents of speakers of other Turkic languages — Karakalpak, Kyrgyz, and Uzbek — claim knowledge of Kazakh. This was up from 97 percent of Kazakhs who claimed proficiency in the their native language in 1989. However, the use of the category "state language" rather than "mother tongue" is a clever political spin in that it transfers the data on native language proficiency to the state language, representing all Kazakhs as proficient in the state language. It also demonstrates that the state leaders care more about the symbolic significance of the language than its actual use or survival. The census data reveal that only 15 percent of the ethnic Russians claim to know the state language, illustrating their remoteness from a major state symbol. Nonetheless, this is a remarkable improvement from 1989 when less than 1 percent claimed proficiency in Kazakh.

The 1999 census did not ask any detailed questions about proficiency in state language, nor did it inquire into proficiency in various domains, such as speaking, reading, writing, or as to degree of competence. (The available categories in the census were: "know," "know weakly," "learning," and "do not know.") Moreover, the instructions state that "knowledge" of the state language refers to those who "use the state language without difficulties as a mode of communication in various social spheres and understand it well, *irrespective of whether they can read or write in it*" (*Instruktsiia* 1998, 17, emphasis added). Thus the question on "state language" is about a basic familiarity and not proficiency or command. The determination of proficiency is left strictly to the self-evaluation of the respondents. Since a near universal knowledge of the state language is attributed to Kazakhs, it is obvious that the response reveals a "primordial" link with the native language and not actual proficiency or use of the language. Quite consistent with the Soviet-era practices, the 1999 census results indicate that citizens' responses tend to endorse the official line and confirm, rather than challenge, the identity categories employed by the state. The conformity required in this case has very little cost in that no strenuous demands to alter language repertoire are made.

It was presumably on the basis of this statistical endorsement of state language proficiency that in celebration of Kazakhstan's anniversary of independence, President Nazarbaev said, "As the leader of the state, I have already solved this [language] problem from the political point of view. Kazakh language is codified as the state language in the constitution. We have successfully adopted the law on state language" (*Kazakhstanskaia pravda*, 15 December 2000). From Nazarbaev's standpoint, the absence of a public debate on the issue or of overt resistance to the language policy indicates that the issue is "solved." In fact, the state has had a very limited impact in inducing a major language shift. Emerging market forces, globalization, and the spread of English have mediated the space between state and citizens to allow the latter greater options to shape their own language repertoire while formally complying with the state objectives. Though Kazakh has established itself as the uncontested symbol of the state and has gained in prestige, it is too early to say whether its new status has brought fundamental changes in people's language repertoire and instituted an effective system of school education in the state language.

Kyrgyzstan: Discontent and Contestation over Language Status

Although in 1989 the extent of bilingualism (proficiency in Russian as second language) was more limited among Kyrgyz than among Kazakhs (35 percent of Kyrgyz claimed proficiency in Russian in contrast to 64.6 percent of Kazakhs), the Kyrgyz language was seen as even less advantaged than Kazakh. According to Huskey (1995, 549), "Kyrgyz was one of the least robust Union-republic languages in the USSR." The capital Bishkek (Frunze) and the northern areas contained several Russophone clusters; 84 percent of Kyrgyz living in Bishkek claimed to speak Russian fluently in 1989, a situation comparable to that in Almaty.

Kyrgyzstan conferred the status of "official" language on Russian only in 2000, despite numerous pronouncements by President Askar Akaev since 1995 to institute bilingualism by making Russian an official language. The prolonged language debate in the parliament and persistent amendments to the language law are the result of the weakened capacity of the state, which has found itself increasingly dependent on powerful regional and clan interests, particularly from the more densely populated southern regions that dominate the current parliament. The regime is also faced with the potential for ethnic secessionism or irredentism on the part of the Uzbek minority, which constitutes almost a fourth of the population of Osh Oblast and two-fifths of Jalalabad Oblast. Here we will look at how intraelite struggle, which coincides with existing regional and clan divisions, has made the language issue more contested in Kyrgyzstan than Kazakhstan.

In addition to regionalism, the exacerbation of the divide between urban or Russified Kyrgyz and rural and recent urban migrants has contributed to the sustained politicization of the language issue and the weakness of the state in formulating an effective policy or aiding its implementation.

The 1993 constitution (Article 5) elevated the status of Kyrgyz to sole state language, while guaranteeing equal rights for Russian and all other languages prevalent in the republic (Smith et al. 1998, 151). This was a victory for the nationalists in that it codified the law passed by the Kyrgyz parliament in 1989 to make Kyrgyz the sole state language. A presidential decree issued in 1994 made Russian an official language in predominantly Russian-speaking areas as well as in "vital areas of the national economy," which emphasized its role as the language of interethnic communication (Smith et al. 1998, 201). In 1995, President Akaev requested from parliament a positive assessment of Russian's role and initiated measures to institute bilingualism, which were persistently stymied by the parliament.

Constitutional changes in the structure of the parliament since 1994 have reduced the power of the parliament, though they have made it a more rancorous institution. In 1994, a referendum ordered by Akaev transformed the unicameral parliament into a bicameral body consisting of a forty-five seat legislative assembly and a sixty seat assembly of people's representatives. The new bicameral structure provided for regional executive officials to join one of its chambers. Of the 105 members of the parliament elected in 1995, eighty-five were Kyrgyz, eight Uzbek, six Slav, and the remaining six belonged to other nationalities. As a result, the nontitular groups were underrepresented; although they formed 41 percent of the population, they won only 19 percent of the seats.

Many liberal and democratically oriented parliamentarians lost their seats to powerful representatives of the regional elites or to wealthy leaders of local clans. Even more salient than the ethnic composition is the representation of individual regional leaders, or strongmen — such as those Pauline Jones Luong describes in chapter 6, who were elected as "independent" candidates — and the decline in political party representation. Seventy-three of the 105 parliamentary deputies elected in 2000 were "independent" candidates, not affiliated to any political parties, and only thirty-two belonged to the various political parties, with the majority of these being propresidential parties. The downsizing of the parliament has particularly hurt small, independent political parties and benefited powerful regional bosses and other entrenched interests in the state bureaucracy. This also makes achieving a consensus on policies very difficult.

The divide between the urban and rural population, coinciding with linguistic repertoire (urban Kyrgyz are more Russified, whereas rural Kyrgyz are more proficient in the native language), is much sharper in Kyrgyzstan, which has significantly lower levels of urbanization, than in Kazakhstan. The rural population, 62 percent in 1989, had increased to 65 percent by 1999. The demographic share of Russians is smaller and concentrated in urban areas. Quite predictably, support for Russian or bilingualism has come mainly from the northern regions, mainly Talas, Chu, and Issyk-Kul, which have a high number of Russians as well as Russian-speaking Kyrgyz. Russians constituted majorities in several areas of Chu and Talas Oblasts. Russification of the northern provinces not only affected the language and culture of the local Kyrgyz but also shaped their political orientation (Huskey 1995, 244). The southern region, mainly the Fergana Valley (Osh and Jalalabad Oblasts) and Naryn Oblast in the east are more rural with a very small number of Russians or Slavs.

As noted above, Kyrgyz nationalists exerted a strong influence over the drafting of the 1993 constitution, which initially failed to make a clear reference to the existing status of Russian as the language of interethnic communication (Huskey 1995, 564). The arguments for defining Kyrgyz as the sole state language were very similar in tone and content to those for Kazakh. The proponents of "Kyrgyz only" were united in the belief that granting official status to Russian would be suicidal for Kyrgyz and that Kyrgyz could not survive without extensive state support. Article 43 of the 1993 constitution declared that knowledge of the state language was mandatory for the presidency of the country. In a state where about one in a hundred Slavs has any proficiency in Kyrgyz, the law effectively bars any Slav from becoming president.

According to Huskey (1995, 564) Kyrgyzstan's cultural and language policies have divided the elites into three competing groups — "internationalists," "indigenizers," and "moderates," with the Akaev leadership representing the "moderate" group as of 1995. The "internationalists" consist of leaders of the European communities and Russified Kyrgyz and are keen to slow down the pace of language indigenization, wishing to dilute or block the language law and elevate Russian to a state language. The "indigenizers" include leaders of various nationalist parties and movements such as Asaba, some Kyrgyz intellectuals and *aksakals* ("white beards" or respected elders in the community), and, most importantly, numerous local officials from predominantly Kyrgyz areas, especially the south.[8] This group is least inclined to make concessions to non-Kyrgyz speakers and instead urges greater protection for Kyrgyz ethnic interests vis-à-vis "stronger" groups such as Slavs or Uzbeks. Finally, the "moderates" are caught between the two poles, "granting concessions to both sides in order to avoid deepening existing social or economic crises" (Huskey 1995, 564–65).

Since 1994, the Akaev leadership has made repeated attempts to push through a constitutional amendment that would elevate Russian to the status of "official language." A bill proposing to amend the constitution by conferring "official language" status on Russian was introduced in the legislative assembly in 1996. The bill was passed by the lower house but held back in the upper house (assembly of people's representatives) because several deputies contended that the phrasing of the bill was ambiguous. Article 2 of the proposed legislation stated that "Russian language may be used in official capacity" but did not state in clear terms that it was to have the status of an "official language" (*Slovo Kyrgyzstana*,

8. Huskey's article, written in 1995, focuses on representatives of various political parties but not on regional elites, who have come to the fore since the new parliamentary structure of 1995.

19–20 July 1996, 6). Others objected to Article 4 of the proposed law, which stated, "There will be no violation of rights and freedom of citizens on grounds of nonproficiency and lack of knowledge of the state and official languages." They argued that the proposed law sought to put Kyrgyz and Russian on a par, which invalidates the status of Kyrgyz as the sole state language enshrined by Article 5 of the constitution. Other deputies said that the difference between "official" and "state" language was not clear.

The bill was referred to the Constitutional Court to determine the legality of the proposed constitutional amendment. After the Constitutional Court ruled that the proposed amendment was legal, the bill was presented again to the parliament. The bill was still not passed because of numerous alleged voting irregularities in the upper house (Smith et al. 1998, 266).

Interestingly, in 1997, while the parliament was dragging its feet over the language legislation, both Akaev and Almambet Matubraimov, the former Speaker of the lower house, were making repeated references to Russian as an official language. In 1998, Akaev made concessions to nationalist pressures by issuing a special decree "On the Further Development of the State Language of the Kyrgyz Republic," which placed a more unequivocal emphasis on the state language. The decree provided for the creation of a special twenty-one-member national commission on state language in the president's office and entrusted it with coordinating the activities of all governmental organs and public institutions toward the development and implementation of the state language. Its decisions were described as binding on all governmental organizations (Landau 2001, 76). The state secretary, Ishenbai Abdurazakov, was appointed chairman of the commission. Jolbors Jorobekov, a member of parliament, was appointed head of the group working on language legislation. Kazat Akmatov, a writer and former member of parliament, was appointed a head of the National Fund of State Language. Nonetheless, the commission lacks a constitutional status, and, because its members are appointed by the president, it is also deprived of autonomy. Both Abdurazakov and Akmatov were fired by Akaev a year later for criticizing the implementation of the state language at a meeting devoted to the tenth anniversary of the Law on State Language passed in 1989. The 1998 presidential decree also provided for the creation of a special National Fund of State Language under the commission for devising measures on development of the state language and a special program for 1998–2007. In the mean time, Kambaraly Bobulov, president of Kyrgyz Til, argued that the Kyrgyz language was too weak to survive on its own (*Kyrgyz News*, 23 September

1998). He cautioned against proclaiming Russian as a second state language until adequate measures were taken to strengthen Kyrgyz. A group of Kyrgyz scholars consisting of Bubuina Oruzbaeva, Toktosun Akmatov, and Kachynbay Artykbaev argued that until the law on the state language was fully implemented — according to the 1993 law all official documents were to be written in Kyrgyz by the year 2000 — granting official language status to Russian would further undermine the work done to promote Kyrgyz.

Although regional elites in the south have taken a hard line in support of Kyrgyz, the Communist Party, which has a sizeable base in the southern region, has continued to champion an "internationalist" agenda. In May 2000, Turdakun Usubaliev, the former first secretary of the Kirghiz Communist Party (1961–86) proposed that the parliament open up a debate on giving Russian the status of an official state language. Although Usubaliev himself comes from the Kyrgyz-dominated oblast of Naryn, he represents the "internationalist" group of Russian-speaking Kyrgyz. As the first secretary of the Communist Party of Kyrgyzstan, he had authored a detailed work on the Kyrgyz language question, embellished with characteristic references to the greatness and glory of the Russian language (Huskey 1995, 567). Even though forty-seven of the sixty deputies of the upper chamber supported that proposal, the debate was postponed because of protests by a small but vocal group of deputies. Deputy Adaham Madumarov, for example, lashed out at the proposal by saying that it was intended as "a gift" from unnamed "pro-Russian forces" to President Vladimir Putin for his inauguration (*RFE/RL* Kyrgyz Report, 3 May 2000).

The proposed amendment conferring the status of "official language" on Russian was eventually passed in May 2000 when the lower house voted 43–2 in favor (Landau 2001, 120). The amended Article 5 of the constitution stated that Kyrgyz is the state language and guaranteed an "equal and free development and functioning of the Russian language and all the other languages used by the population of the Republic." It is important to note that Uzbek, the language of the largest minority, is not specifically mentioned. Article 1 of the law qualified that the new legislation does not affect the status and use of the Kyrgyz language as the state language, including its special status in the constitution and in the law on state language (*Khabar News Agency*, 29 May 2000).

In August 2001, just when proponents of Russian, both "moderates" and "internationalists," appeared to have gained significant ground, a draft law, "On the State Language," was proposed in the lower house by some deputies demanding priority status for Kyrgyz in official contexts (*AKI Press*, 28 August 2001). The draft bill was rejected by Prime Minister

Kurmanbek Bakiev, who argued that the proposal was unconstitutional, adding that it was also too expensive to implement (*Central Asia Report*, 6 September 2001). There is little evidence that the Communists have relaxed their stance on fortifying the status of Russian. Proposals were debated to make Russian the second state language. The Kyrgyz parliament debated a bill on introducing a Kyrgyz language proficiency test, but eventually withdrew it in April 2001 (*RFE/RL Newsline*, 27 April 2001), justifying the withdrawal as a desire to stem the emigration of Russian speakers. Such a measure could open up a Pandora's box of acrimony between Russified and nationalist Kyrgyz.

Language Implementation and Nationalist Discontent

Faced with an increasing resurgence of rural, regional, and clan-based demands, along with political opposition, social unrest,[9] and international pressure for reform and liberalization, Kyrgyzstan has been unable to pursue indigenization in as resolute a manner as Kazakhstan. It has also oscillated between supporting ethnic entitlements and embracing civic norms, as the section below illustrates. Paradoxically, as a result, the outcome in Kyrgyzstan is a more liberal (that is, contested) language policy.

Kyrgyzstan's constitution displays an ambiguous position between ethnic and civic conceptions of nation by juxtaposing the term "people" or narod of Kyrgyzstan and the Kyrgyz "nation" (*natsiia*). The preamble states: "We, the people of Kyrgyzstan, strive to secure the national renaissance of the Kyrgyz and to defend and develop the interests of the representatives of the other nationalities, who together with the Kyrgyz make up the Republic of Kyrgyzstan." Akaev (1995, 104) himself noted that Kyrgyzstan has elements of an "ethnocratic" statehood, though it is also a political association of diverse people sharing the common homeland.

Kyrgyzstan was the only Central Asian state to propose deletion of the mandatory nationality entry from its new passports, which were to be issued from late 1996 onward (*RFE/RL Newsline* 15 March 1996). The proposal was motivated by the desire to obtain international approval and particularly to convey to the Organization for Security and Cooperation in Europe (OSCE) High Commission on National Minorities Kyrgyzstan's commitment to embracing civic statehood. The Akaev leadership encountered restiveness from ethnic minorities as well as ethnic Kyrgyz on its decision to replace the category "nationality" with "citizenship" on its new passports. The nationality stamp on passports is not merely an ethnic

9. For details, see International Crisis Group, August 2002.

marker but also a crucial criterion in determining the distribution of privileges and positions among the titular and nontitular nationalities. Uzbeks, who make up over a third of the population of the Osh Oblast, have resisted the deeply entrenched practice of preferential treatment for the titular nationality and have lobbied for increased representation in the government after the bloody interethnic riots of 1990 (Tishkov 1997).

The nationalists or "indigenizers" who had a major say in the making of the 1993 constitution have been the most zealous proponents of an ethnic vision of the state. Political movements such as Asaba have been at the forefront of mobilizing demands of ethnic Kyrgyz, particularly the new rural migrants to Bishkek.[10] Asaba champions the goal of realizing "one state, one nation, and one language" (Landau 2001, 98) and endorses certain pan-Turkic symbols, especially shifting the alphabet to Latin. It was presumably in anticipation of a mounting discontent with the proposed removal of nationality among ethnic minorities, particularly Uzbeks and Uighurs, as well as from the active proponents of Kyrgyz ethnic interests that the government soon retreated from its earlier position and "nationality" was reinserted in the new passports. A special governmental decree on ethnic minorities in 1998 further institutionalized the salience of nationality by granting permission to change the "nationality" listed on a person's passport to reflect the individual's "true" nationality (*RFE/RL Newsline*, 24 March 1998). Though the decree formally allowed anyone to change the "nationality" entered in his or her passport, the decree was geared toward small minorities who in the past had felt compelled to adopt "larger" or more "visible" ethnic identities. During the Soviet period many Uighurs had been registered as Uzbeks, Turks and Kurds as Azerbaijanis, and Meskhetian Turks as Georgians.

Although the nontitular share has shrunk at the upper echelons of power, the top elite is still predominantly Russian speaking with some ability to speak Kyrgyz. The status of Kyrgyz as the state language has done little to introduce any fundamental shift from the diglossic nature of bilingualism prevalent during the Soviet era.[11] The impact of nationalization and the induction of Kyrgyz as the state language are more visible at the lower and middle levels of administration. Kyrgyz speakers, overwhelmingly of rural origins and less proficient in Russian, tend to be

10. Asaba was founded in 1990 as an ultranationalist political grouping of opposition forces.

11. Diglossia refers to an asymmetric bilingual condition where matters of importance are the reserve of a "high language" while matters of affection or private affairs are discussed in a "low language" (Laitin 1992, 16).

among the more depressed strata of the society (Korth 2001). However, Kyrgyz has an economic salience for people at the lower rungs of power, predominantly in rural areas in the south. In the last ten years, the rural population has grown by 18.3 percent and now stands at 3.13 million, whereas the urban population has been in a state of decline.[12] Out of a total population of 4.8 million (an increase of 13 percent over the 1989 figures), 34.9 percent are urban dwellers and 65.1 percent are rural residents.

The state has issued numerous decrees and directives emphasizing the expansion and use of Kyrgyz in various fields. However, most of these make no reference to resources to be allocated or how these are to be made binding. These directives are more of a wish list than policy statements (*Erkin Too*, 11 March 1998). They contain "a list of priorities, carefully thought out, for the promotion of Kyrgyz — without however attempting a ranking by importance and urgency" (Landau 2001, 77).

In the absence of a clear policy, commitment, and financial support from the state, Kyrgyz has made very little progress in attaining some form of market value. As noted above, criteria for assessing proficiency in Kyrgyz remain subjective and fairly relaxed. Korth (2001, 19) observes that "very often the naming of a fixed set of objects, the counting up to one hundred and the use of some greeting phrases are certified as 'knowledge of Kyrgyz' although the learner has not learnt to speak, let alone communicate, in Kyrgyz." As with Kazakh in Kazakhstan, proficiency in Kyrgyz is of value only when accompanied by fluency in Russian. Nor is it profitable to publish in the titular language alone. Apart from some literary works and works concerning aspects of history and culture of the titular nationality, almost all publications in the titular languages are translations from Russian or other languages. Paradoxically, the rapid opening up of the Kyrgyz economy to global market forces and to international actors has provided it with some material base and contributed to enhancing the role of Kyrgyz. Korth (2001, 21) notes that some foreign companies and international organizations have contributed remarkably to the publishing of scientific literature in Kyrgyz at a time when the Kyrgyz government has fallen short in making economic investment to promote the state language. Kyrgyz proficiency, when combined with knowledge of Russian and English (or other European languages), can be a prized asset for those seeking employment with foreign companies and international organizations. However, such positions are very limited, and estimates suggest that

12. The urban population increased by 54,000, whereas the rural population grew by 511,000.

no more than about 1 percent of the population — overwhelmingly youth — has such multilingual facility.

Some 70 percent of the population claimed fluency in the state language in the 1999 census, up from 54 percent in 1989. Of these 54 percent, at least 50 percent presumably were Kyrgyz (the Kyrgyz share of the population was 52.4 percent, and almost 98 percent claimed proficiency in Kyrgyz), and the remaining belonged most likely to Uzbek and other Turkic nationalities. The 70 percent who claimed fluency in the state language in 1999 include nearly all Kyrgyz (64.9 percent) and some Uzbeks and Kazakhs and other Turkic groups. These figures, however, do not give an accurate account of how many Kyrgyz actually are proficient in their native language.

The language issue has acquired a triangular dimension in Kyrgyzstan because the Uzbeks, mainly concentrated in the Osh Oblast in the south, now constitute the largest minority in Kyrgyzstan. Unlike Russians, who are a continually shrinking population, the Uzbeks, along with rural Kyrgyz, have registered higher birthrates than urban Kyrgyz.[13] As the Uzbek share of the population is likely to increase further, demands for granting an official status for the Uzbek language in the region are likely to escalate. As Brass (1991, 100) reminds us, struggles between state authorities and nondominant groups tend to focus on issues of local control in general, especially in relation to the peripheral regions of a country.

Fearful of Uzbeks, who are seen as a stronger nationality with a more advanced language, the Kyrgyz authorities have so far resisted granting any local concessions to Uzbek. It is feared that an official recognition of bilingualism would open up avenues for demands for recognizing the special status of Uzbek in the southern regions, whereas the emphasis on a single state language makes it more difficult to fortify Uzbek with a legal status. Demands for granting an official status to Uzbek in the southern regions is rejected on the grounds that the Kazakh and Uzbek languages spoken in the region are mutually comprehensible, therefore no valid grounds exist for granting a separate status to Uzbek.[14]

Kyrgyz nationalists tend to see ethnic Uzbeks, particularly those in the Osh Oblast, either as posing a separatist threat or as wresting control of the local economy. The prevalent ethnic stereotypes portray Uzbeks as entrepreneurial, shrewd, and calculating, whereas the native Kyrgyz see

13. Osh and Jalalabad Oblasts have the highest birthrates in the country, 35.9 and 35.2 per 1,000 respectively. Cited in Buckley (1998). The average birthrate in Kyrgyzstan in 1990 was 29.1 per 1,000.

14. I thank Arslan Koichiev for clarifying this point.

themselves as naïve, trusting, and hospitable to a fault. While Uzbeks are seen as benefiting from the transition to market conditions, Kyrgyz see themselves as victims of the market economy and generally as unable to compete (*nekonkurentsposobnyie*) in market conditions. These perceptions of the self and of rival groups reflect the subjective typology of "advanced" and "backward" groups portrayed by Horowitz (1985) and have become further entrenched since the 1990 riots in Osh in which 120 Uzbeks, 50 Kyrgyz, and one Russian were killed (Tishkov 1995, 135). Uzbek alienation from the higher echelons of power and their underrepresentation in the regional apparatus was recognized as an important factor in the riots. By the mid-1990s Uzbeks held only 4.7 percent of key posts in the Osh regional administration, only two positions in the Jalalabad town government, and had only six deputies in the country's parliament (Anderson 1999, 43). There are no Uzbeks in the regional judiciary or law-enforcement bodies (*Eurasianet Report*, 26 March 2001). The general economic depression of the region has exacerbated interethnic tension and created a fertile climate for blaming the "other" group for limiting economic opportunities. At the same time, Uzbeks in Kyrgyzstan remain resistant to any purported measure of introducing a civic identity that is nonetheless seen as closely connected with the titular nationality. As elsewhere in the former Soviet Union, and particularly in the Russian Federation, ethnic minorities have strongly resisted proposals for obliterating the "nationality" entry from passports and other identity documents. Indeed, it is the stamping of "nationality" on identity documents that has been the most effective instrument for sustaining a primordialization of ethnic identities and providing a platform for making claims for cultural and linguistic rights and political autonomy.

It should be noted, however, that the southern Uzbeks supported Akaev in the 1995 elections, whereas the majority of Kyrgyz in the south voted for the Communist contender Absamat Masaliev, the former first secretary of the republic (Melvin 2001, 181). The Uzbek support was presumably an act of faith in the civic nationalism espoused by the Akaev regime in its initial years.

As a representative of the more Russified northern regions, Akaev rallied for the support of non-Kyrgyz groups and made numerous concessions to various regional elites, enabling them to enhance their political positions at local and national levels (Melvin 2001, 180). The center's handling of the Uzbek issue is closely related to its dealings with the various regional leaders.

Tensions surfaced between the northern and southern leaders in the aftermath of the Osh riots in 1990, which contributed to the termination of Masaliev's (a southerner) tenure as head of the republican Communist party, and the election of Akaev as his successor. The erosion of southern dominance over key posts, traditionally within their purview, led the southern elites to propose some federal features, which were incorporated in the new bicameral legislature introduced in 1995 (Melvin 2001). As Akaev has sought to garner the support of incumbent regional elites, local Uzbeks as well as the Communists have become increasingly restive. The Communists continue to advocate an official status for Russian, whereas the incumbent regional leaders have been pushing to expand the role of Kyrgyz. Melvin (2001, 181) argues that "the rise of ethno-politics in the south during the late 1980s had produced an uncoupling of the Uzbeks from the leading regional political networks." As a result, the Uzbek minority, which had been important in the early part of the decade as an ally of the president, was increasingly politically isolated. The former Communist elite and the Uzbeks are the two key politically marginalized strata. However, the deeply entrenched status of ethnicity prevents formation of cross-ethnic alliances based on the common experience of political exclusion.

While Uzbeks in Osh remain excluded from politics at the center, there is little indication that Uzbekistan is seeking to mobilize their support and loyalty. Uzbekistan appears to be more anxious to hold at bay suspected "Islamists" among their ranks than to garner kin support. According to Morgan Liu (2000, 4), "Osh Uzbeks are tantalized by the seductive rhetoric of 'Uzbek nation' on one hand, but shut out by the logic of the Uzbekistani state on the other."

The language issue in Kyrgyzstan is an arena of contestation that engulfs numerous aspects of national identity, state capacity, economic opportunities, and conflicts over resources. Nationalist elements, on the one hand, are combating what they see as the continuing structure of domination and mobility associated with the Russian language. On the other hand, they are equally threatened by the demands of the self-confident and aggressively nationalistic Uzbeks, who are associated with the Uzbek State, which is numerically and politically more powerful than the Kyrgyz (Uzbekistan's population is around 27 million), and endowed with a stronger and more developed language and culture. They do not see Uzbeks of Kyrgyzstan as detached from the Uzbek state and its ostensible hegemonic aspirations. More recently, nationalist opinion, combined with discontent with the ailing economy, has focused on anxiety over China's growing encroachments on Kyrgyzstan's fragile sovereignty. Kyrgyz nationalist groups are caught between their opposition to Russian, the language of their former "colonial" rulers, resentment toward Uzbeks who are seen as the regional "big brother," and alarm over China's rapidly growing influence over the country.

In July 2002, Azimbek Beknazarov, a member of parliament and head of the Parliamentary Committee for Law and Legal Reforms, led a widespread protest against the Kyrgyz government's decision to transfer 125,000 hectares of Kyrgyz land to China in the border demarcation treaty and called for Akaev's resignation. His arrest on "criminal charges" and the ensuing hunger strike in protest led to mobilization of widespread public demonstrations that ended in shootings by police, which let to six deaths. Beknazarov was eventually released, but a movement demanding Akaev's resignation and the return of lands ceded to China has gained increasing support. Since these events, a powerful grassroots movement against Akaev's policies and bowing to China, led by various Kyrgyz nationalists and supported by depressed strata of Kyrgyz society, has gained momentum.

The state in Kyrgyzstan does not have the coercive strength and ideological control that neighboring Uzbekistan is able to wield, nor does it have the economic resources of Kazakhstan to boost its cultural identity. As a result, the symbol of language, including the self-perception of the Kyrgyz as a small nation sandwiched in between several powerful states and larger ethnic entities, has continued to be a focal point of debate about statehood and sovereignty.

Varying Salience of Language as an Instrument and Identity Symbol

The constitutions of both Kazakhstan and Kyrgyzstan mandate that candidates for presidential election be fluent in the state language. Article 43 of the Kyrgyz constitution states that the president must have lived at least fifteen years in the republic and be fluent in the state language, but it does not say the language proficiency is to be tested. As a large number of contenders for the presidential post began to prepare their candidacy for the 2000 election the Kyrgyz Central Election Commission demanded that they submit certificates of state language proficiency, available upon passing a language test administered by the National Linguistic Commission.

Two prominent presidential candidates, Anarbek Usupbaev and Iskhak Masaliev (son of Absamat Masaliev), both nominated by the Communist Party, failed the Kyrgyz language examination administered by the National Linguistic Commission. The candidates claimed good knowledge of Kyrgyz, complaining that very special linguistic questions were posed at the exam. Five of the twelve presidential candidates failed the language examination. Nine of the candidates, including some of those who passed the test, appealed to the Constitutional Court to rule on the legality of the mandatory tests. Feliks Kulov, seen as the most powerful contender, who heads the opposition Ar-Namys (Dignity) Party, refused to take the language examination, arguing that the language proficiency test was imposed for political reasons by the current regime and is not required either by the constitution or the election code of the country (*RFE/RL Newsline*, 12 September 2000). Kyrgyz officials claimed that Kulov's refusal to take the language examination showed his contempt of the Kyrgyz language, which he had "failed to learn" (quote from a Kyrgyz official). Kulov's retort was rooted in a "primordial" understanding of nationality and language. In a statement issued on 18 September 2000, he said: "I am Kyrgyz by my nationality and took it in with my mother's milk. One can deprive a person of life, health, liberty and even Motherland, but no one will be able to deprive me of belonging to a people, to the native language, which belongs to me upon my birth." The Kyrgyz Constitutional Court upheld the mandatory language examination as legal and other candidates were disqualified from contesting the elections (*RFE/RL Newsline*, 12 September 2000).

As the case of Kulov and other candidates show, there is no impartial and independent body that can administer language tests and set objective criteria for determining language proficiency. Such laws are invoked for political expediency, and the decision is made on the basis of subjective assessment by officials.

Though the presidential candidates in Kazakhstan are also required to pass a state language proficiency test, the language test issue was a neutral factor in the elections of 1999. Contrary to initial fears that he might fail the language exams on political grounds, Akezhan Kazhegeldin, the ex-premier of Kazakhstan and an opposition leader living in the West, did pass the Kazakh language proficiency test in October 1998. However, his "failure" on nonlinguistic grounds appeared to have been preordained, as his candidacy for the 1999 presidential elections was invalidated on the spurious grounds of court conviction. (Kazhegeldin was fined in 1998 for not appearing before an Almaty court to answer charges of corruption.) Kazhegeldin nearly failed the test when he was asked to explain why he had a Russian wife (author's interview, November 2001). What this shows is that the "identity" or "language" issue is not politically salient enough in Kazakhstan to bar an opponent from contesting elections as it was in Kyrgyzstan.

Language proficiency is tested only for the highest office in the country. Although demands to introduce language tests for civil and administrative positions are frequently made, none of these have become law. In April 2001 the Kyrgyz government withdrew the controversial state language bill, which would have required officials to be tested for proficiency in Kyrgyz (*RFE/RL Newsline*, 27 April 2001).

The different political fates of the Kazakh poet Olzhas Suleimenov and the Kyrgyz writer Chingiz Aitmatov — the two most famous Central Asian writers of the late Soviet period and who wrote exclusively in Russian — reveal an interesting contrast.[15] Both men were mentioned as possible candidates for president in their respective countries in the mid-1990s. After initial interest, Aitmatov decided not to run and threw his support to Akaev in 1995. As Suleimenov's candidacy remained a distinct possibility (his National Congress Party had declared itself as an "opposition" in 1995), Nazarbaev hastened to announce a referendum on the extension of the presidential term by five years in April 1995 and adopted a new constitution later in September. In the meantime, Suleimenov was already being sidelined as attacks on his "patriotism" toward Kazakhstan and lack of facility in Kazakh collided with numerous charges of corruption and financial mismanagement as the head of the anti-nuclear Nevada-Semipalatinsk movement, ending with his being bought off through diplomatic exile as ambassador to Italy (in mid-2002 he was appointed ambassador to UNESCO). This case shows how the Kazakhstani regime disempowered one of the most influential challengers of its cultural and linguistic policies. Although Aitmatov also served as a diplomat during the initial years of Kyrgyz independence, he has retained much of his Soviet-era reputation and prestige. The Kyrgyz leadership maintained a moderate stance, which was coupled with Aitmatov's own unwillingness to politicize the language issue and risk inviting censure because of his own tentative command of the native language.

Language Policy as an Indicator of Changing State-Society Relations

The insecure sense of statehood, the limited repertoire of cultural symbols available to the ruling elites, and the lack of their own cultural "authenticity" raise the question: How does a state go about implementing its language policies when it lacks legitimacy as well as resources? Clearly, nationalization or indigenization — through a preferential treatment of the titular group in state employment, education, and social services — has served as an instrument of implementing language policies. As Horowitz (1985) has argued, affirmative action or preferential policies, at

15. Aitmatov's early works were in Kyrgyz.

least in the short run, are perhaps the cheapest and most effective means of appeasing an economically disadvantaged or "backward group" and easing ethnic tensions.

The degree of success these states have had in implementing their respective language laws in the first decade of independence is an outcome of the elites' capacity to wield control over the institutions of power and to deploy ethnic symbols as state symbols. The more divided the elites are on core issues of national interest and identity, the greater is the ambiguity in the law and in the proliferation of contending claims.

This is the case in Kyrgyzstan where historical, geographical, and cultural divisions between the north and south have coincided with differences in economic power and political status, exacerbating perceptions of a politically salient regional divide within the country. As a small state it has been called on to negotiate the cultural hegemony of the Russian language, Chinese economic power and perceived imperial interests, and the big brotherly roles of Kazakhs and Uzbeks.

The Russification of the northern regions is an outcome of its longer association with Russian colonial rule and subsequent incorporation into the Soviet state. The southern regions, especially the Fergana Valley, were part of the Kokand khanate and have been more influenced by Islam as practiced by sedentary groups such as the Uzbeks. These regions were incorporated into the new Soviet entity of Kyrgyz ASSR only in 1924–25. Since becoming president, Askar Akaev, a northerner who lacked a *nomenklatura* background and a clientele of supporters and allies when he came to power in 1991, has increasingly turned to clan leaders, regional strongmen, and former party notables in the north for support. The personal "friendship" and political bond between Akaev and Dastan Sarygulov, an important member of the Talas regional elite and the head of the state gold company, blocked efforts to investigate the alleged financial misdeeds of the Sarygulov family.[16] In his initial years as president, Akaev also formed a tactical alliance with the former party boss Turdakun Usubaliev from the predominantly Kyrgyz oblast of Naryn (J. Anderson 1999, 40). Notwithstanding his "internationalism" and eulogy for the progressive role of Russian, Usubaliev was able to mobilize support for Akaev in his home oblast of Naryn during the 1995 presidential elections. In the process of building his clientele, Akaev has faced growing challenges from various

16. Sarygulov accused the two editors of *Res publica*, Zamira Sydykova and Aleksandr Alianchikov — who detailed the wealth acquired by Sarygulov by using his official position — of libel for which they were sentenced to eighteen months in prison, though the sentence was subsequently reduced. See Sydykova (1997).

political elites from the south. Despite the alleged manipulation of votes in favor of Akaev, the opposition candidate Absamat Masaliev (another ex-Party boss) polled 50 percent votes in the southern Osh region in the presidential elections of 2000.

Regionalism remains deeply embedded in Kazakhstan (Jones Luong 2002), and clan or *zhuz*-based identities have increasingly come to the fore as a corollary to nation building (Schatz 2000). However, these differences are not acutely reflected in parliament as far as issues of language and cultural identity are concerned. The political elites in Kazakhstan present a unified image in which their unity or solidarity is orchestrated through the use of presidential patronage, co-optation, and prospects of mobility within the governmental structure (Khliupin 1998). The move of the capital to Astana, at least in the short term, has eased the tensions and competition between the three zhuz or hordes. Kazakhs affiliated to the elder zhuz, encompassing the southern territories, had benefited the most from ethnic preferences and enjoyed a rapid mobility in the then capital Almaty. The political loyalty of the Kazakhs belonging to the middle zhuz, which historically has had the closest ties with Russia, was particularly looked upon with suspicion. The transfer of the capital to Astana has created a new framework for integration of Kazakhs in the more remote and Russified northeastern regions, as well in as the restive western oblasts.

Kyrgyzstan seems to have emulated Kazakhstan's example in dealing with regional challenges by designating the city of Osh as the southern capital and launching a ten-year program of social and economic development for Osh in 2001 (*RFE Central Asia and Caucasus Report*, July 2001). One significant motivation for President Nazarbaev's transfer of the Kazakh capital to the economically depressed northern steppe bordering Russia was to neutralize potential separatist tendencies on the part of the ethnic Slavs who heavily populate that area. Establishing the new capital in the Slavic heartland not only re-anchored those regions to Kazakhstan but also stimulated economic development, which could ease the intensity of ethnicity-based discontent and grievances. A major objective of launching a socioeconomic development program for Osh is to reduce the appeal of militant Islamic groups who are able to exploit the discontent arising from economic deprivation.

Central Asian states differ from postcolonial African and Asian states in that they have inherited a strong institutional infrastructure and an extensive surveillance apparatus over the society. These have endowed them with a greater capacity to render their societies "legible" (Scott 1998) and thus able to undertake large-scale social engineering, even though the capacity to use coercion or invest resources has been severely curtailed since the collapse of the Soviet state. As Beissinger (2002) has demonstrated, the erosion of the state's capacity to use coercion in light of the growing waves and cycles of nationalist mobilization eventually triggered the collapse of the Soviet state.

Uzbekistan and Turkmenistan are somewhat of an exception in that the emergence of strong patriarchal regimes promoting a personality cult has strengthened the coercive apparatus of the state. As Adams (chap. 3) has shown, Uzbekistan in particular has succeeded in invigorating the Soviet-era repertoire of ideology and engineered periodic mobilizations in the form of grand spectacles that show societal conformity to the state's goals.

In Kyrgyzstan, the state has shown itself to be quite weak in the domestic and regional context in its inability to effectively intervene in social or cultural matters. Its ability to employ coercion has been challenged by contending groups. The weakness of the state and the growing authoritarian turn taken by the Akaev regime has sparked protests and group actions. Language activists have blamed the president and the government for failure to develop the Kyrgyz language, confirming the overall desire to seek governmental assistance, as argued by McMann (in chap. 7).

Although it has not been averse to using coercion, the Nazarbaev regime has for the most part relied on patronage and co-optation to gain allies and buy off its political opponents. It has also wielded firm control over language or cultural activists, including nationalist Kazakhs. Some of the visible parties or groups that champion ethnic Kazakh interests, such as the Renaissance Party, Azat, and Alash, are supported by the ministry of Interior Affairs and are authorized to champion the notion of special rights for the indigenous Kazakhs against the "settlers" and foreigners, including opposition parties and activists.

Having established a legal basis for implementing their language policy, the state has progressively withdrawn from intervention in the cultural-linguistic arena in Kazakhstan. As Werner demonstrates in chapter 2, the post-Soviet Kazakhstani state has showed only a limited and very instrumental interest in reviving Kazakh national traditions. Lacking (or unwilling to invest in) adequate financial resources and trained personnel, and unwilling to use muscle or vigilance, perhaps because of its own deficient "cultural" credentials, the state has refrained from imposing formal requirements or rigorous means of testing proficiency in the state language.

Indeed, the erosion in the state's capacity to implement policies and to wield coercion has in turn reduced its expectations as to what constitutes "success" and "compliance" in language matters. The policy of implementing the state language has fundamentally been reduced to counting and monitoring the conversion of all official business in the akimats to the state language and translating all existing documentation into the state language.

When Nazarbaev claimed that the language issue has been "solved" in Kazakhstan, he also noted: "The development of the language is not just the task of the state, or of the president, but also of the intelligentsia of the country. People should be concerned about developing the language. Let's talk with children and grandchildren in the native language."[17] In the same speech he added: "Intelligentsia must not always ask others for help. I would like to ask them: What have you done since [to ensure that] the problems have been solved? Why are you waiting for the president to again offer some idea?" This indicates that Nazarbaev has shifted the responsibility to the intelligentsia and the people for advancing the cause of the language. His statements also show a clear separation between the state, symbolized by the president, and the society and intelligentsia. Nazarbaev is also prevailing upon society not to lag behind and to carry out its obligation to speak the national language.

The language arena reflects radically different patterns of state-society relations emerging in the two states. Ordinary citizens in Kyrgyzstan, particularly the titular Kyrgyz, as well as political parties and public organizations, have increasingly tended to make claims on the central authorities to enact favorable legislation on a range of issues pertaining to language and nationality. On the other hand Kazakhs — whether as individuals or social groups — have tended to shun the state apparatus and carried on with day-to-day business through overt compliance as far as "identity" issues are concerned.

An implicit social contract of noninterference between the state and society in cultural and national identity matters appears to have emerged in Kazakhstan, which has helped to depoliticize the language issue.[18] In contrast, in Kyrgyzstan a close, though contested, interaction between the state and social forces has precluded the two sides from negotiating a social contract or making a pact. On one level, various Kyrgyz nationalist groups are urging greater action on the part of state to strengthen its

17. Also available on http://eurasia.org.ru/2000/ka_press/12_15_ka_nan.html

18. Jowitt (1992) refers to the social contract that emerged during the Soviet rule in which society offered the state political quiescence in exchange for cradle-to-grave waelfare.

fragile statehood and social base. At the opposite end, the Uzbek minority is growing more restive; unlike Russians who have voted with their feet, the local Uzbeks are more likely to mobilize to realize their cultural claims. These factors portend a further politicization of cultural and identity claims.

As these countries continue through cataclysmic changes and a tortured and uncertain path of transition, one can only make tentative conclusions about the success or failure of language policies. At least in the short term, the rapid pace of indigenization, the steady "exit" of the Russian-speaking population, an absence of overt social conflicts, and the statistical increase in the number of people claiming proficiency in the state language in Kazakhstan tentatively indicate "success" in that these have enabled the titular elite to firmly establish itself in control.

Unlike neighboring Uzbekistan, which has developed — perhaps fabricated — the most cohesive and well-articulated conception of a national idea and orientation, the ruling elites in Kazakhstan and Kyrgyzstan have failed to work out a viable and overarching national ideology or "state idea."

Kazakhstan has managed to maintain a formal or de jure basis that provides for integration and civic statehood while developing a de facto ethnocratic structure. On the surface, Kazakhstan has devised a clear, comprehensive, and apparently balanced language policy, which has paved the way for a rather uncontested and smooth implementation. The language question has been bounced back at the society, especially at intelligentsia, language activists and watchdogs, school and university officials, and, ultimately, the large pool of young pupils. The clear message is this: The state has done its duty by enacting clear and comprehensive legislation; it is now the task of various social actors to carry through with the job. And ultimately, it is the duty of every Kazakhstani to facilitate the cause of the state language. Indeed, the pervasive terminology "state language," rather than "Kazakh language," has taken the edge off the issue and served to neutralize it. The census data is a convincing illustration. The ruling elite is torn and ambivalent on the issue and lacks the cultural authenticity (legitimacy) to undertake a gigantic identity transformation (restructuring of the language repertoire) of the population; it is also limited in its ability to invest in and lead a fundamental restructuring of the linguistic domain. In addition, it is eager to define the state as "Turkophone," "Russian speaking," "multinational," and "Eurasian" (read, "closer to Europe").

Kyrgyzstan has been muddling through at the level of legislation, unable to develop a clear legal base. It has vacillated between ethnic and civic notions of statehood and is likely to encounter more active resistance from the Uzbek minority as well as a resurgence of Kyrgyz nationalist sentiments particularly in densely populated rural areas and in Bishkek. The language question still remains high on the central as well as regional agendas.

3

THE STATE AGAINST ITSELF

Central-Regional Relations

5. The Limits of Centralization

REGIONAL CHALLENGES IN UZBEKISTAN

ALISHER ILKHAMOV

Sociological analysis has often focused on relations between the center and the periphery, both at the level of the international system (or interstate) and the domestic level (or intrastate). Although this analysis usually concerns relations between advanced capitalist countries that constitute a metropolitan "center" and developing countries in the "periphery," it can also be applied to center-peripheral relations within a particular country (Marshall 1998, 63). The very factors that distinguish developed and underdeveloped countries and frame their relative position in the "modern world-system" (Wallerstein 1974) — such as rates of economic development, access to strategic resources, and geographical location — can also define the struggles between central and subnational governments. Both relationships undoubtedly affect the trajectories of developing countries, yet only the latter is intimately tied to the state-building process. As the literature on state-societal relations has shown, these struggles can also have a direct effect on the ability of developing countries to build sufficient state capacity to achieve their policy goals, and perhaps even to maintain their territorial integrity (see, e.g., Migdal 1988). Understanding the nature of center-periphery struggles in new states, then, is crucial to understanding the state-building process itself.

The integral role that center-peripheral relations play in the state-building process is also clear in the emerging literature on the Soviet successor states. In the Russian Federation alone, for example, the relationship between central and subnational governments has been linked to state survival (Gorenburg 1999; Solnick 2001; Treisman 1997), prospects for economic growth (Treisman, 1999; Stoner-Weiss, 2001), efficient public service provision (Zhuravskaya 2000), tax collection (Treisman 1999), corruption (Treisman 2000), and monetary consolidation (Woodruff 1999).

The author kindly acknowledges the other authors of this book for their critical comments, and especially Pauline Jones Luong for her judicious editing of multiple drafts. She not only improved the English version of the chapter but significantly enriched its content by sharing her data, sources, and arguments.

Across the former Soviet republics, however, tensions between central and regional authorities have presented perhaps the greatest challenge to both the capacity and territorial integrity of the state.

In some cases, this challenge has taken the form of an ongoing struggle among national and subnational leaders for spheres of influence, which has constrained the central government's ability to achieve its policy goals. During Boris Yeltsin's decade-long presidency, for example, regional governors in Russia often ignored federal laws and refused to consistently adhere to revenue-sharing arrangements with the federal government (see, e.g., Stoner-Weiss, 1997, 2001). Not surprisingly, therefore, the hallmark of the presidency of Vladimir Putin (Yeltsin's successor) has been a concerted effort to restrict regional sovereignty and reassert federal control over policy-making and revenue collection. Similarly, central and regional authorities have been engaged in an intense battle over policy jurisdictions and, in particular, the right to control budgetary revenues in Kazakhstan and Ukraine, both of which are unitary states (Jones Luong, chap. 6; Way, 2000).

In many other cases, this challenge has taken the form of organized separatist movements and civil war. To prevent several regions from seceding from the Russian Federation, for example, Yeltsin was forced to negotiate, and ultimately sign bilateral treaties, with several regional leaders (e.g., Tatarstan, Chuvashia) and to fight a protracted civil war with Chechnya, which the Putin administration has continued and intensified (see, e.g., Kovalov 2000). Several other former Soviet republics — Georgia, Azerbaijan, and Moldova — have experienced the realignment of the state's 1990 borders along regional lines as a result of violent conflict. Similarly, one of the primary causes of the civil war in Tajikistan was the united democratic opposition's attempt to challenge the long-standing political and economic dominance of one region (Leninabad) over several others, whose elites were excluded from power during the Soviet period (Rubin 1993; Schoeberlein 1994).[1]

The purpose of this chapter is to examine the link between center-peripheral relations and the state-building process in post-Soviet Uzbekistan. I begin with the premise that this vantage point provides greater insight into several aspects of the country's political and economic development, including why the post of vice president was introduced and then shortly afterward abolished, why the new political party Fidokorlar was established, which group interests it was intended to serve, the meaning of the results of Uzbekistan's December 1999 parliamentary

1. Others have (erroneously) attributed this civil war to interclan and regional animosities. For examples, see the introduction to this book.

elections (as well as the 2002 parliamentary reforms), and the motivation for President Islam Karimov's periodic purges of regional cadre. Yet, with few exceptions (see, e.g., Jones Luong 2002), scholars have paid insufficient attention to the nature of central-peripheral relations in Uzbekistan since independence, in large part because scholars and policy makers alike have portrayed Uzbekistan as a consolidated nation with a strong central government (see, e.g., Akbarzadeh 1996; Kubicek 1998). Instead, more attention has been paid to the central government's brutal crackdown on the country's nascent political opposition (see, e.g., Anonymous 1993; Kangas 1994; Fierman 1997), Islam and the rise of Islamic radicalism (see, e.g., Haghayegdi 1994; Olcott 1994), and the activities of nongovernmental organizations (NGOs) and the development of civil society (see, e.g., Abramson 1999) — that is, to actors and processes that have been more visible because of the closed nature of the Uzbek state and society — and much less to the tensions between central and regional authorities.

My central claim is that center-peripheral relations in Uzbekistan since independence present a paradox. Although it is a highly centralized regime, it nonetheless faces serious challenges from regional elites, particularly those dissatisfied with post-Soviet shifts in the distribution of national economic resources. Politically, this discontent manifested itself in the results of the 1999 parliamentary elections, in which President Karimov failed to promote members of the political party he had created (Fidokorlar) to key positions in the national parliament.[2] Economically, it is demonstrated by the common practice of diverting state-ordered cotton to the black market. From this point of view, the political regime in Uzbekistan is actually less stable than it might appear to an outside observer. The loyalty of regional forces, and therefore stability in general, must be achieved much as it was during the Soviet period — that is, by maintaining a fine balance between concessions and reprisals rather than through mass participation in a democratic electoral process.

To explain this paradox, I rely on a combination of sociohistorical and contemporary evidence that points to the development of center-peripheral relations in Uzbekistan over time and the strength of regional actors vis-à-vis other possible sources of political opposition in the country. In short, the historical tendencies toward regionalism have been inadvertently strengthened in the contemporary period by the policies of the Karimov regime. The repressive political and economic conditions have

2. The Fidokorlar (Self-sacrificers) National Democratic Party was established in January 1999 and joined forces with an existing party, Vatan Taraqqiyoti (Progress of the Homeland), in April 2000 primarily for this purpose.

not only provoked tensions with regional elites, encouraging them to defy central authority, but also left these elites as the primary source of political opposition in the country — with the sole exception of Islam. Although the central state is not as weak in Uzbekistan vis-à-vis the periphery as Jones Luong (chap. 6) describes in Kazakhstan, stability remains based on continuous negotiations between layers of the state that largely leaves out society.

The Paradox of Center-Periphery Relations in Uzbekistan

The first decade of center-periphery relations in post-Soviet Uzbekistan has consisted of two seemingly contradictory trends. On the one hand, we have witnessed the extreme concentration of power in the hands of the central government, particularly Islam Karimov's presidential apparat. On the other hand, recent years have demonstrated growing forms of resistance by the country's regional elites. The latter are experiencing pressures from three forces: (1) from above, as agents of the central government in the regions, (2) from the ground, where the living standard of the population, especially in the provinces, has been significantly declining in recent years, and (3) from their own group interests, which have suffered because of the shift in control over the key natural resources in the country. This section provides some empirical evidence for these trends.

Concentration and Centralization of Power

At the end of the first decade of post-Soviet rule in Uzbekistan, by most accounts, Islam Karimov's regime had consolidated its power and created a strong central state. Yet, this consolidation and centralization was by no means a preordained outcome. In the late 1980s and early 1990s, Uzbekistan's government was widely perceived as one of the weakest in the Soviet Union. Part of the reason for this is that the Soviet government in Moscow initiated a sweeping purge of Uzbekistan's top republican leadership in 1986, accusing them of embezzling funds and taking bribes in connection with the "cotton scandal" following Sharaf Rashidov's twenty-four-year reign (1959–1983) as first secretary of the Uzbek SSR (see, e.g., Critchlow 1991 for details). This resulted in a leadership more pliant to Moscow's demands that suffered from an inferiority complex vis-à-vis other Soviet republics. It appeared that Uzbekistani society had also lost some degree of faith in its government. The sense of the government's relative incapacity was confirmed in 1991 when the government failed to prevent the outbreak of violent conflict among various ethnic groups over scarce resources in the Fergana Valley, which led to the destruction of property, mass disorder, and hundreds of deaths.

In sum, Karimov's regime achieved such consolidation and centralization of power through a series of administrative and legal measures, the systematic replacement of regional (*obkom*) first party secretaries with those considered to be more loyal to the president, and the elimination of any independently organized political opposition (Jones Luong, 2002, chap. 4).

Administrative and legal reforms after independence consisted primarily of establishing strong presidential rule, reinvigorating a centrally created and managed party system to replace the Soviet-inspired Communist Party of Uzbekistan (KPUz), and strengthening direct links between the central and local levels of government so as to usurp and contain regional leaders' authority (see Jones Luong 2002, chap. 4, for details). After his election to the presidency in December 1991, Işlam Karimov immediately began to concentrate political authority effectively within this newly created office. The adoption of a new constitution in December 1992, which gave the president several exclusive powers, was the first major step toward institutionalizing these changes.[3] Anointing a worthy successor to the KPUz was the next step. In contrast to his counterparts in Kyrgyzstan and Kazakhstan, almost immediately after independence, Karimov and his supporters created a government party — the People's Democratic Party of Uzbekistan (PDPU) — to replace the KPUz in form and function.[4] The PDPU was a change in name only, because the leadership, core membership, and function of the party remained the same (Akbarzadeh 1996, 26; *Srednaia Aziia i Kazakhstan* 1992, 70). Regional and local leaders were compelled to become members of the PDPU, just as their predecessors' had been required to have Communist Party membership (Jones Luong 2002, chap. 4).

At the same time, Karimov deliberately built direct links with local leaders to establish closer central supervision over local affairs, and, hence, diminish the influence of regional leaders vis-à-vis the central government. Toward this aim, in January 1992 he created a new state agency — the State Control Committee under the president of the Republic of Uzbekistan — to place direct supervision over the implementation of laws and decrees issued by the central government under central rather than regional control (*Pravda Vostoka*, 15 January 1992, 1). Satellite offices of this committee were then established in each oblast, Karakalpakstan, and

3. For details, see the Konstitutsiia Respubliki Uzbekistan (1992) and Saidov (1993).

4. The PDPU held its founding congress on November 1, 1991.

the capital city of Tashkent and charged with monitoring the activities and evaluating the performance of regional administrations. Karimov also supported legislation and structural changes that usurped some of the regional leaders' "traditional" spheres of influence — such as appointing regional legal bodies and administrative heads at the rayon, city, and village levels — and accorded the sole authority "to punish or pardon heads of administration [at all levels] to the president" (*Pravda Vostoka*, 14 May 1992, 2). He took measures to assert his exclusive authority in selecting and dismissing both regional- and local-level officials. By mid-1993, in all thirteen oblasts he had appointed new regional hokims whom he considered loyal (or "less of a political threat to the center") and replaced several leaders at the rayon- and city-level whom he accused of being disloyal (Jones Luong 2002, chap. 4).[5] Furthermore, he implemented sweeping reforms in order to streamline power into the local administrative organs (*hokimiats*) and place their activities and relations with the regional hokimiat under tighter central supervision.[6] By 1993, for example, it became the responsibility of rayon-level and other local leaders to establish a system of *mahalla* (or neighborhood) committees to deal with local problems and report these directly to central authorities rather than to regional hokims (Jones Luong, 2002, chap. 4).

In addition to these administrative and legal changes, beginning in 1992 President Karimov actively suppressed or expelled from the country any real and potential political rivals, including such prominent opposition leaders as Mukhammad Solih (Erk political party), Abdurahim Pulat (Birlik political movement), and Tohirj Yuldashev (Adolat political movement in Namangan) and such well-known religious figures as Mufti Mukhammad Sodyq (former head of the Spiritual Department of the Muslims of Central Asia and Kazakhstan) and Abduvali Qori Mirzoev (imam in Andijon).[7] The first step was to make it more difficult for new

5. Although the appointment of regional hokims has to be approved by local councils of representatives, this is essentially a cosmetic procedure.

6. This included the Law on Local Government of the Republic of Uzbekistan, issued on September 2, 1993. For a discussion of this law, see "Beseda po Kruglom Stolom" (1993). It also consisted of revitalizing and co-opting the local mahallas (or neighborhoods — see Kamp, chap. 1), beginning in 1992. This is documented in Jalilov (1994).

7. For an overview of the regime's tactics during this period, see "Karimov's Way" (1994). Since August 1999, Tohirj Yuldashev, also known as Tahir Yuldash, has been one of the leading figures in the Islamic Movement of Uzbekistan (IMU), an organization that advocates the establishment of an Islamic state in Uzbekistan through violent means and can be linked directly to international terrorist networks. Mukhammad Sodyq fell out of favor with the Karimov regime when he was put forth as a presidential candidate (to challenge Karimov) in 1991.

parties and movements to register by amending the 1991 Law on Public Organizations in the Republic of Uzbekistan to require all public organizations to register with the government after holding an organizational conference of ten or more people to adopt a charter and elect officers.[8] These requirements made it virtually impossible for independent political organizations to operate legally in the republic because they were either denied permission to hold a conference or were refused registration by the Ministry of Justice. Compounding these difficulties, in March 1993 Karimov declared that all registered political parties must reregister by October 1993. The second step was to severely restrict the activities of independent groups, for example, by instituting a national ban on public demonstrations. Karimov's campaign to establish direct links between the central government and mahallas was also a way to circumvent the local popularity of independent movements and organizations that utilized the mahallas as both an organizational and popular support base.[9] Thus, by the end of 1992 independent parties and movements faced insurmountable obstacles to either reaching initial stages of organization or maintaining and expanding their existing popular support base (Jones Luong 2002, chap. 4).

At the same time, by virtue of its independence alone, the Uzbekistani state inherited direct control over the country's economic resources, which were not insubstantial. In the mid-1980s, Uzbekistan's cotton sector produced more than 65 percent of its gross output, consumed 60 percent of all production inputs, and employed approximately 40 percent of the labor force. It also accounted for about two-thirds of all cotton produced in the Soviet Union (Rumer 1989, 62). Thus, at independence, Uzbekistan became the world's fourth-largest producer of cotton (World Bank 1993b, xi). This provided the new government with a viable export, and hence a direct source of revenue after the breakup of the Soviet Union (Jones Luong and Weinthal 2001). During the Soviet period, cotton production in Uzbekistan was an important source of hard currency for Moscow, which paid well below market value for Central Asian cotton and then resold it abroad at market prices. Following the Soviet Union's collapse, Uzbekistan was able to substitute foreign buyers for its reliance on Moscow as the "middleman," because those who had traditionally bought Soviet cotton from Moscow instead began to conduct business with

8. Refer to articles 8 and 11 of *Zakon ob Obshestvennikh Obyedinenniiakh v Respublike Uzbekistan*, adopted on 15 February 1991 and amended in July 1992.

9. Adolat (Justice) in Namangan, for example, was the first independent organization to invoke the mahalla and did so quite successfully. For details, see Jones Luong 2002, chap. 4.

Uzbekistan and Turkmenistan directly. Thus, in 1991 cotton already comprised approximately 84 percent of Uzbekistan's foreign exports, and by 1992 it provided over three-quarters of Uzbekistan's total export revenue (International Monetary Fund 1992, 2; World Bank 1993b, 24).

In addition, Uzbekistan's new government acquired the ownership of substantial natural resources, including precious and nonferrous metals as well as oil and gas reserves. As of July 2001, Uzbekistan was the third-largest natural gas producer in the Commonwealth of Independent States (CIS) and one of the top ten gas-producing countries in the world (USEIA July 2001). Moreover, both its gas and oil production have increased dramatically since independence, which has enabled the country to attain complete energy self-sufficiency (USEIA March 2001).[10] This, in turn, allowed the country to achieve another of its primary goals — economic and political independence from Russia, which its leaders perceive to be its greatest competitor for influence in the region. The threat of dependence on Russia is real, because prior to 1992 oil was one of Uzbekistan's major imports from the other Soviet republics, primarily Russia, for which it was compelled to use its modest hard currency income (World Bank 1993, 7).

Karimov's ability to establish Uzbekistan's right of ownership and control over what are widely considered to be the country's strategic resources gave him two advantages with respect to the centralization and concentration of power. First, he gained the respect and loyalty of the republican *nomenklatura*, who credited him with standing up to Moscow. With less reliance on Russia, Karimov's government was able to negotiate the withdrawal of Russian troops from Central Asia and to rehabilitate those who had been implicated in the aforementioned "cotton scandal," including Rashidov. Second, he used this opportunity to redefine the relationship between the republican (now central/national) and regional governments. When he became first secretary of the KPUz in the late 1980s, just as the Soviet Union was undergoing sweeping reforms under Mikhail Gorbachev, Karimov feared that Moscow and regional elites would make a deal to evade the republican center's authority; thus, in the first few years of independence he flirted with regional leaders by continuing to recognize their jurisdiction over the production and sale of cotton and even allowing them to obtain limited authority over cotton exports. As soon as the proverbial umbilical cord connecting the republic with Moscow was severed in 1991, however, Karimov believed he had greater latitude

10. Uzbekistan achieved independence in gas production in 1985. It achieved oil self-sufficiency in 1996. For details, see Jones Luong and Weinthal 1998, 5–6.

over the regional elites. Soon thereafter, the central government established state commodity (or marketing) boards for buying and selling cotton that continue to set artificially low prices at which the government purchases cotton and then resells it for world-market prices to foreign countries (World Bank 1993, 121) (Ilkhamov, 1998).

Increasing Regional Autonomy

Given this degree of centralization and concentration of power, it seems unlikely that Karimov's regime would be challenged from below: those leaders of the political opposition who remain alive and in the country are under close scrutiny by the internal security apparatus, and the regional hokims are appointed by the president himself, allegedly based on their personal loyalty. Yet, in addition to attacks by Islamic extremists, the central government faces growing resistance from among regional elites.

Most recently, this resistance has manifested itself primarily in two forms: the battle for jurisdiction over cotton production and export and the struggle for control over Uzbekistan's national parliament (Olii Majlis). This resistance continues, moreover, despite the central government's ability to use tactics developed under Soviet rule — that is, periodically reshuffling regional hokims and purging regional hokimiats.

The Battle for Cotton

The Karimov regime's efforts to centralize control over land distribution and the proceeds from cotton and other agricultural products has deprived regional and local hokims, as well as chairmen of collective farm, of their share of revenue extracted from the agricultural sector, while leaving them responsible for fulfilling production targets set by the central government.[11] This situation has not only created resentment and hardship it has forced these regional elites to find an alternative source of revenue. They began to support themselves by exploiting their freedom to cultivate the one-third portion of irrigated land that was not engaged in export crop production. Officially, these lands were intended primarily for households, so that they could support themselves at subsistence levels in light of the shrinking subsidies from the center, including job cutbacks, devaluated

11. According to a recent government resolution, for example, two-thirds of irrigated land is to be used to grow cotton and wheat. See "On the sowing area of cotton, cereals, rice and potato for 1998–2000," decree of the Cabinet of Ministers, Republic of Uzbekistan, June 24, 1997, no. 317. Source: Database "Pravo," Tashkent, 1997.

salaries, and long wage arrears. Under these circumstances, however, regional elites were compelled to raise their personal income by exploiting the sector of household economy. They have achieved this through imposing various levies in the form of unpaid wages, fines for traffic violations, marketplace duties, and illegally appropriating and privatizing the assets and lands of collective farms (*kolkhozes*) while protecting their own private businesses from such exploitation. At the same time, regional elites discovered that they have a stake in developing the household economy and began leasing land to households on commercial terms, including some of the land that the central government has reserved for cotton and wheat. Their abuse of land distribution quotas, however, has resulted in *shirkats* (cooperative farms) being frequently visited by representatives from the prosecutor's office and the state militia who have been charged with enforcing cotton and wheat land quotas and preventing farmers from growing crops that are more lucrative — for them as well as for regional elites. (Ilkhamov, 1998, 2000a)

The center's encroachment on the regional elites' traditional sources of revenue has also led to an increase in social tensions within the regions. Farm workers are suffering from a double burden imposed on them by the central government and their local bosses. The appropriation of crops, wage arrears, and misuse of land resources have led to a contraction in the local population's economic base and, hence, its growing impoverishment. Their responses have taken two forms — either to openly protest against the center's appropriation policy or to "adapt" to it. Public protests over crop seizures are less common, but appeared to be on the rise in 2001 (see, e.g., ICG August 2001). Adaptation, which is more common, very often constitutes using public resources to grow private crops and diverting state-ordered cotton and wheat to the black market. In this, moreover, the regional and local elites are often complicit. For example, to keep workers from leaving the kolkhoz — where salaries are often not paid for months and even years — kolkhoz chairmen ignore the use of kolkhoz farmlands for grazing privately owned cattle.

The failure of several regions to fulfill cotton production quotas has prompted the central government to widen its use of law enforcement agencies, such as the militia, police, and prosecutor offices, and enlist them in the "battle for cotton." For example, four times since 1994 Karimov has enacted measures to prevent crop damage caused by grazing cattle on kolkhoz farmlands. The first such decree made provisions for "preventive measures and . . . tough prosecution for the offenders," and courts were instructed to "promptly address and investigate cases of crop damage . . . and apply drastic measures to those found guilty, up to imprisonment."[12] Another decree, adopted two years later, however, admitted that in spite of the actions taken "crop damage by cattle had not decreased," and thus, additional measures were needed.[13]

The use of law enforcement agencies to combat these offenses has become necessary in large part because of the divided farm economy in Uzbekistan, in which one subsector is oriented toward cotton export and highly centralized and the other subsector is based on livestock and fruit and vegetable production, oriented toward domestic markets, and more decentralized (Ilkhamov 1998, 2000a). Because local elites have significant control over the second subsector, they have a vested interest in its expansion, at the expense of land allocated for cotton production. In response, the central government has attempted to induce compliance through administrative and punitive levers directed at the local and regional hokims — including conducting periodic cadre purges and reshuffling the top ranks of regional bureaucrats and managerial elites — without any positive incentives except perhaps the prospect of career advancement (or at least preservation).

As table 5.1 demonstrates, since 1993 the average term for regional hokims is only three years. Only the hokim of Andijan Oblast, Kayum K. Khalmirzaev, has enjoyed being indispensable, while the hokims of Kashkadarya, Samarkand, Surkhandarya, and Tashkent city have been replaced every two years on average. This unstable cadre policy is very characteristic of Uzbek's authoritarian regime. It demonstrates both the hokims' lack of genuine loyalty to the president and the latter's fear of rebellions in the provinces. In fact, rebellion takes place in the form of underreporting of resource use (such as land) and hiding a share of locally acquired wealth from the center's strict fiscal accounting. The frequent hokim turnover isn't necessarily determined only by the fight over cotton revenue, but it is notable that the untouched Andijan hokim persistently demonstrates ardor exactly on this point: the oblast for the last several years is the first to report meeting targets for the cotton harvest. The fiscal approach of the center, in the spirit of mercantilism, has turned the management in the cotton sector into the cat-and-mouse game played by the center and hokims. Under conditions in which the center prefers simply to pump resources from the provinces it remains reluctant to implement any major reforms in the agricultural sector.

12. "On strengthening measures preventing crop damage," decree of the president of the Republic of Uzbekistan, November 21, 1994, No. UP-1005. Database "Pravo," Tashkent, 1994.

13. "On Additional Measures to Prevent Agricultural Crops Damage by Cattle," decree of the Cabinet of Ministers of the Republic of Uzbekistan, November 25, 1996, No.416. Database "Pravo," Tashkent, 1996.

TABLE 5.1. *Regional Hokim Turnover in Uzbekistan, 1993–2002*

Region	Number of replacements	Average number of years served by each hokim
Andijan Oblast	1	8.0
Bukhara Oblast	3	2.7
Ferghana Oblast	3	2.7
Jizzak Oblast	3	2.7
Karakalpakstan Oblast	3	2.7
Kashkadarya Oblast	4	2.0
Khorezm Oblast	3	2.7
Namangan Oblast	2	4.0
Navoi Oblast	3	2.7
Samarkand Oblast	4	2.0
Surhandarya Oblast	4	2.0
Syrdarya Oblast	3	2.7
Tashkent Oblast	3	2.7
Tashkent (city)	4	2.0
Average	3	3.0

Source: Data complied by Alisher Ilkhamov and Pauline Jones Luong, based on appendix 2 in Jones Luong, 2002, and the *Pravo* database.

The Struggle for Parliament

The December 1999 parliamentary elections provide another indicator of the growing tensions between central and regional elites, as the latter seek to display their discontent with increasing centralization and to reassert their authority. Uzbekistan's national parliament, the Olii Majlis, was established in 1993 along with a new electoral law based on a series of negotiated compromises between central and regional leaders (see Jones Luong 2002, chap. 5, for details). Although the structure ultimately adopted largely favored the center's preferences, the regional leaders were granted some important concessions, including the right of local legislatures to nominate candidates to the 250-seat, one-chamber parliament, which in most cases meant the hokims themselves. In addition, in contrast to other officials, hokims did not have to resign from their existing positions once elected to the national parliament.[14] These concessions

14. This, of course, continued the practice of oblast party secretaries occupying the majority of seats in the republican-level soviet. For details, see Jones Luong 2002, chap. 3.

became all the more meaningful when the hokims won a majority of the seats — 167, or 67 percent — in the first parliamentary elections, in December 1994. Together with representatives of the PDPU, which from its inception was directly tied to regional hokims, they constituted 94 percent of seats, an overwhelming majority.

Since 1995, Karimov has encouraged the creation of several progovernment parties, both to provide a check on the PDPU's power and to give the appearance of a multiparty system to the international community, while at the same time increasing his own control over the national parliament. These include the Social-Democratic Party Adolat (Justice), which purposefully adopted the name of an Islamic movement in Namangan that was banned in 1992; the Democratic Party Milliy Tiklanish (National Rebirth); and the aforementioned National Democratic Party Fidokorlar. Only the latter, however, has rivaled the PDPU's closeness to President Karimov, who many believed called for the creation of this new party to provide a counterweight to growing opposition among regional elites.[15] Whereas previously Karimov could depend on regional and local hokims to support most of his policies and to bring out the vote during elections, this was becoming less and less certain as he continued to pursue policies that effectively reduced their share in the proceeds from cotton production. He intended to secure his dominance over the parliament, then, by creating a new presidential party that would demand the loyalty of hokims, who are appointed by the president. Yet, this plan appears to have backfired. Despite its strong presidential endorsement in the December 1999 parliamentary election, Fidokorlar only won 34 seats or 16 percent of the nominated candidates. In contrast, the hokims' parliamentary bloc was only slightly reduced, from 167 to 110, and remained a majority in the parliament. Thus, it is by far the most numerous parliamentary faction, holding 44 percent of all seats, and together with the PDPU constitutes 63 percent of all seats. Even after Fidokorlar was ostensibly strengthened by a merger with another propresidential party, Vatan Tarakkiyoti (Progress of the Homeland), it only occupied 22 percent of all seats.

The Historical Roots of Uzbekistan's Paradoxical Center-Periphery Relations

Central-peripheral relations in Uzbekistan are best understood in a historical perspective. The balance of power between central authority and regional elites has been shaped most directly by Soviet policies and institutions, which fostered a system of power sharing both between the repub-

15. Karimov remained the head of the PDPU until he resigned in 1996.

lican and regional (oblast) administrations and among the regions. This sheds light not only on Karimov's ascendancy to the top leadership position in Uzbekistan at the end of the 1980s and early 1990s but also on his ability to consolidate this power over time.[16] When viewed in this context, it also becomes clear that the growing tensions between central and regional elites in recent years are a direct consequence of Karimov's attempts to transform the system in which the power of the republican elite was restricted by the authority of both Moscow and the oblast elites into a new one where authority is supposed to be concentrated within the presidential apparat. This seizure of power by the republican elite, personified in the change from a weak Rafik Nishanov and Inamjon Usmankhodjayev to a strong, Tamerlane-style leader, Karimov, was undertaken at the expense of a diminished role for Moscow and oblast elites. It could not help but provoke resistance from the latter and therefore a new impulse toward increased regionalism.

Yet, regionalism's role as one of the two primary sources of opposition to the current regime must also be understood in the context of escalating political repression under Karimov. The elimination of independent political parties and movements and the persecution of religious leaders and practicing Muslims throughout the country has created a vacuum of viable opposition that regional elites as well as religious leaders have attempted to fill, radicalized the Islamic opposition, and galvanized support behind militant Islamic organizations (see Jones Luong and Weinthal 2002).

Sources of Authority over the Periphery

Perhaps the most important consequence of Soviet rule in Central Asia in general and Uzbekistan in particular was that it imposed two new centers of power on the periphery — one in Moscow and the other within the Soviet Socialist Republics themselves. In some respects, this system mirrored the administrative system established after the Russian conquest in the mid-nineteenth century, which divided the region into three governorate-generals (*guberniya*) — the Steppe, Turkestan, and Transcaspia — for the sake of administrative efficiency, yet left intact two states they had encountered — Bukhara and Khiva — which had become Russian protectorates.[17] The designated local authorities over these new administrative

16. Karimov become first secretary of the KPUz in 1989 and Uzbekistan's first elected president in December 1991.

17. The Steppe included north-central parts of present-day Kazakhstan; Turkestan included southern Kazakhstan, Kyrgyzstan, and the eastern part of Bukhara; Transcaspia consisted of today's central and western Turkmenistan; and most of the Bukharan and Khivan Khanates eventually became part of Uzbekistan (Jones Luong 2002, 60).

divisions were subordinate to the region's appointed governor-general, who in turn was subordinate to the tsarist government in Saint Petersburg. The governor-general, himself appointed by the War Office, was charged with appointing officials to serve in the administrations at the oblast and *uezd* levels, while the lower levels of administration (*volost*, town, and village) were formed mostly with elected representatives of the local population (Tolstov et al. 1962, 180). Similar to the Bolsheviks' experience in the 1920s, the local response to the imposition of external rule was a mixture of resistance and acceptance, and local elites who pursued the latter strategy were given a greater role in local governance with all its rewards. Even those local elites who initially resisted external rule and refused to participate in the new local government administration — including the tribal aristocracy, wealthy *ishans*, landowners, and a new urban bourgeoisie — eventually realized the financial benefits of holding such positions within the new government (see, e.g., Tursunov 1962; Pale 1910, 101). Yet, because some of these local elites, particularly the bourgeoisie, appeared to abandon traditional norms and ethics, they could not depend on the loyalty of the local population.

Yet, there were also several key features of Soviet rule that departed significantly from Russian colonial policy in Central Asia. First and foremost, Soviet rule was more direct and aimed at transformation rather than merely domination. In contrast to the tsarist government, for example, the Soviets engaged in nation building and the cultivation of indigenous cadre to exercise local rule in accordance with their policy of self-determination (Hirsch 2000; Martin 2001). Thus, from the beginning, there was a much greater role for local elites who accepted Soviet power. In particular, they influenced the boundaries that were drawn to delimit Central Asia into five national republics by manipulating the Bolsheviks' desire to create nations based on common language and territory as well as appearing to quickly assimilate these newly ascribed categories (Hirsch 2000; Edgar 1997). The Bolsheviks then assigned leading positions in the local administration to their supporters among the indigenous population, many of whom were viewed as local nationalists for their participation in the delimitation, which fundamentally restructured the relationship between the new center and the preexisting social and political organization in the periphery. In this respect, Soviet rule succeeded in achieving what tsarist rule could not: it was able to create a new system of local administration that was not wholly rooted in tradition and yet could win the loyalty of the local population.

Yet, while some elites participated directly in establishing Soviet rule, others led the resistance against it known as the Bosmachi movement.

This movement represented the revolt of the "old" (or preexisting) center and periphery against the "new" (or Soviet) center and periphery and regional leaders' rejection of a central authority that ignored their traditional rights and privileges. It incorporated a variety of different actors and interests: some remained loyal to the Emir of Bukhara, who was allowed to maintain his throne under the tsarist government but was forcibly deposed by Bolsheviks; some followed the call of Muslim clergy for jihad against the infidels; while others fought for tribal independence of their tribes from any central authority. Although the Bosmachi ultimately failed to rid themselves or Central Asia of Soviet rule, it took more than ten years for the Bolsheviks to completely suppress this armed resistance movement and thus to demonstrate, above all, the superiority of a strong central power over the anarchy of regional and communal high-handedness.

Finally, the triangular hierarchy between the central and peripheral governments (where the second to Moscow was the union republican center, and the third was the local (oblast) authority) created under Soviet rule was much more closely linked to the distribution of scarce political and economic resources than to access to military power. As mentioned previously, under both Russian colonial and Soviet rule there were effectively two centers and two peripheries because the middle level (that is, the gubernaia and the republics, respectively) was both subordinate to Moscow and presided over the local-level governments. Whereas in the tsarist empire supreme power in the region rested in the hands of military officers, under the Soviets this power was concentrated in the party structure — specifically, the CPSU Central Committee — and disseminated through the lower ranks (from republic to region to local levels) in a hierarchical fashion.

Despite declarations of the right to self-determination for all nations, the Soviet regime initially retained full control over the governments in the newly created Central Asian republics. Before establishing the Union of Soviet Socialist Republics (USSR) in 1924, the Bolsheviks governed the region from Moscow by maintaining close scrutiny over the Communist Party's personnel and functions. The first secretaries of the republican Communist Parties, for example, were to be recruited from representatives of the indigenous population, and yet second secretaries chosen from among loyal Russian Communists were entrusted with supervising ideological requirements, cadre policy, and the work of law enforcement.

This situation, however, changed dramatically over time as regional elites gained increasing control over scarce political and economic resources. The importance of second secretaries vis-à-vis first secretaries,

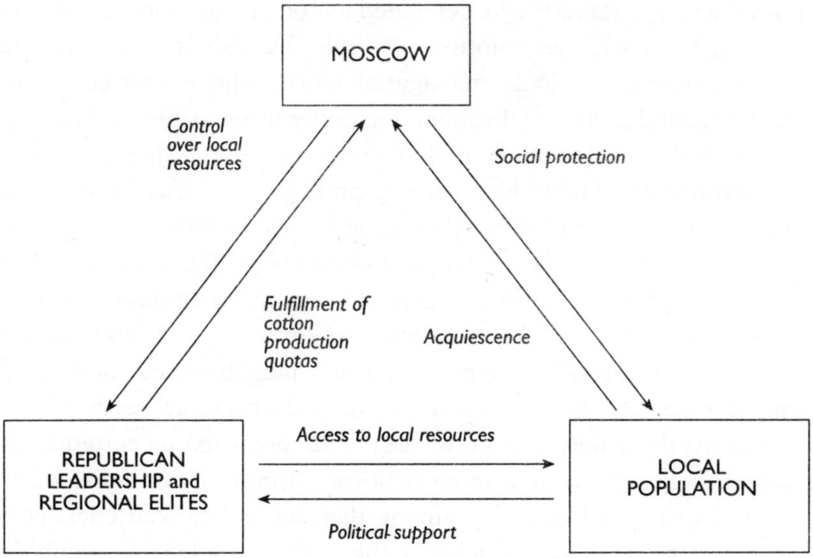

Source: Adapted by Pauline Jones Luong from Weinthal, 2002, 98.

FIGURE 5.1. *The Role of Cotton in Forging Reciprocal Relations*

for example, gradually declined as regional and local cadre recruitment fell under the purview of republican and regional Communist Party elites, respectively. At the same time, regional leaders gained significant influence in their respective republics, stemming both from their contribution to the republic's economy, which the Bolsheviks used as a basis for recruiting and promoting cadres, and their crucial role in managing distribution networks (Jones Luong 2002, chap. 3). In Uzbekistan, this pertained to cotton-producing regions, whose leaders were automatically elevated to a higher political and economic status in the republic (Lipovsky 1995, 534).[18] As depicted in figure 5.1, cotton production and distribution both forged a reciprocal relationship between Moscow, the republican leadership, and the regional elites and served as the primary basis for creating and sustaining patronage networks within the regions, which, in turn, sustained Soviet power. Thus, it served to both balance power between the different levels of governance and exert control over the population (Weinthal 2002, 97).

Throughout the republic, moreover, regional elites competed for direct control over a substantial share of those resources connected to the local economy, such as trade, services, housing construction, and communal

18. The republican-level leadership, for example, continuously rotated between Tashkent and Fergana, and later Samarkand. See Jones Luong 2002, chap. 3, and app. 2 for details.

utilities. Victory in this struggle depended not on military force or alliances between tribes, as it had before Soviet rule, but rather on competition between groupings of local managerial elites, who employed various tactics to expand their social capital, including using bribes and intrigue, searching for powerful allies, and obtaining compromising data about their adversaries. These local-elite groupings are often erroneously referred to as *clans*, or an ethnically homogeneous sociopolitical unit based on common descent (see, for example, Collins 2003). Yet, it would be more appropriate to term them *quasi clans* (or regional patronage networks) because they were not based exclusively on kinship but on informal partnerships and reciprocal exchanges between neighbors, coworkers, and classmates that served the various social and economic needs of their members. As these networks grew, they were mobilized by entrepreneurial regional elites to serve a more political purpose. Having divided the resources of the local economy among themselves, regional elites could claim the right to hold positions in the higher echelons of republican power and to gain control over additional resources — both formally and informally. Moreover, because Central Asian elites rarely served outside of their republics and regions of origin they had more opportunity to build and sustain extensive patronage networks (see, e.g., Burg 1986; Rakowska-Harmstone 1994, 32).

This expanded social, economic, and political role for regional elites was institutionalized under Sharaf Rashidov, who served as first secretary of the KPUz from 1959 until his death in 1983. Rashidov's long tenure was part of a general trend in the Soviet Union Leonid Brezhnev's reign as general secretary of the KPSS in the 1970s. Hoping to rebuild trust between the center and the union republics, Brezhnev allowed long tenures for republican first secretaries with little interference in the internal selection of personnel (see, e.g., Rigby 1978). Yet, it was also a testament to Rashidov's somewhat unusual ability to achieve an enduring consensus between Moscow, the republican leadership, and regional elites. Moscow considered him a loyal Communist and an exemplary leader, and he gained the support of the republican leadership and regional elites by giving them carte blanche to manage a large portion of the economic and political resources within their jurisdiction. Thus, while Brezhnev's "stability of cadres" policy affected all of the union republics, in Central Asia it secured a preexisting system. Republican and regional leaders alike could now openly access the political and economic power bases they had consolidated.

It is not surprising, then, that the shadow (or informal) economy in Uzbekistan also became a vibrant political and economic force under

Rashidov. To profit from their official control over local resources, regional elites also had to gain exclusive access to and control of unofficial and illegal distribution channels, which they established in such sectors as trade, communal and other services, and housing construction. These distribution channels were based on a division of labor between elites with official positions in the party structure and elites with unofficial positions in shadow structures; the former secured political and legal protection while the latter converted public economic resources into private ones.[19] Thus, they facilitated the expansion of the shadow economy from serving as a means of personal enrichment for quasi-clan members to a method of accumulating capital for exploring and investing in new areas of political and economic influence.

Gradually, the reciprocal relationship between official and unofficial distribution channels encompassed those sectors of the economy that had been directly controlled by the republican leadership — namely, the cotton and water management/irrigation sectors. Because these were the most important sectors in Uzbekistan's contribution to the Soviet Union's economy, they were significantly better financed than other economic sectors. These sectors also benefited from the Soviet system's emphasis on cost-based management, which meant that an economic entity was considered more successful the more capital investment it utilized — that is, the more resources it expended. Irrigation, in particular, required huge capital investment because Uzbekistan was mostly desert, and these costs increased over time as a result of poor water management and the erosion of topsoil. Moreover, the cost-management system generated perverse incentives such that economic entities were interested in increasing their costs rather than in efficient resource management. Excess capital and material resources could then be easily skimmed off the top without notice. In irrigation and water management, this was relatively simple to do because the recipient of inputs was the agricultural production unit, which was not an end user. Thus, an unofficial alliance formed in which the cotton sector was assigned the function of fulfilling production quotas and the irrigation sector was responsible for resource "consumption." Regional elites in Samarkand, Bukhara, and Jizzak, for example, rose to prominence and increased their presence in the republican leadership precisely through this unofficial alliance between the cotton and irrigation

19. One of this system's most notable figures in late 1970s and beginning of the 1980s was Akhmadjon Adylov, a legendary boss of the Pap RAPO, a district branch of an agromanufacture corporation in Namangan. Enjoying protection from Rashidov and managing a criminal network, he could afford to appropriate material resources allocated to Namangan Oblast for his private use.

sectors.[20] It is for this very reason that they were also the primary targets of Moscow's aforementioned anticorruption campaign in Uzbekistan launched shortly after Rashidov's death in 1983 (see, e.g., Carlisle 1991, 114–16, for details).

Karimov's Rise to Power

The historical development of center-periphery relations in Uzbekistan provides the backdrop for Islam Karimov's own rise to power. From Moscow's perspective, he was an appropriate choice to succeed Rashidov's successors, Inamjon Usmankhodjaev (1983–88) and Rafik Nishanov (1988–89), because he was neither directly implicated in the infamous "cotton scandal" behind the anticorruption campaign nor considered to have a strong connection to any of the most powerful regional groupings.[21] Yet, more importantly, Karimov had the support of the leaders of these groupings — most notably, Ismail Djurabekov, the minister for Water Management and a fellow native of Samarkand Oblast, and Shukrullo Mirsaidov, the mayor of Tashkent city and a colleague with whom Karimov had developed a close friendship during their years working together in the government bureaucracy. Mirsaidov represented the Tashkent city–based elites and could provide the support of mid-level technocrats responsible for managing the central government bureaucracy. Djurabekov represented the elite groupings that controlled the cotton and irrigation/water management of the economy as well as regional elites, because the regional economy was based primarily in these economic sectors. In return, Mirsaidov and Djurabekov became the most powerful figures, de facto and de jure, in the Uzbek leadership after independence as prime minister and deputy prime minister, respectively, with the latter controlling the agricultural and water-management sectors. Regional elites generally lent their support to Karimov because they expected him to fully restore their rights to directly control and benefit from the cotton and water management/irrigation sectors, which Moscow's anticorruption campaign had begun to reverse.

Karimov cleverly took advantage of his broad support in negotiating with Moscow over the right to manage local resources. In the first few years he was in office as first secretary, and then as president, he seemed

20. Jizzak Oblast, located in the Mirzachul Steppe, was founded in 1973. It was one of the virgin land areas and began receiving enormous investments in its irrigation system beginning in the 1950s. It is noteworthy that Rashidov, as well as Prime Minister Normuhammad Khudaiberdiyev, originated from Jizzak. Ismail Jurabekov, the minister of Water Resources under Rashidov, was from Samarkand.

21. At the time of his appointment, Islam Karimov was the first secretary of the Kashkadarya Oblast party committee.

to concentrate on fulfilling the republican and regional elites' expectations. The republic's (and then independent state's) leadership gained control over the most important economic resources, including cotton and precious and nonferrous metals and other minerals, while regional elites regained to some degree their control over cotton production and distribution alongside expanded but still limited authority over cotton exports. After independence, Karimov also presided over the rehabilitation of Rashidov and the amnesty of dozens of other government officials and regional elites who were arrested and jailed in connection with Moscow's anticorruption drive in the late 1980s (see, e.g., Carlisle 1995).

Once Karimov had firmly established Uzbekistan's political independence from Moscow, however, his attention turned to the consolidation of his own power. The first sign of resistance came from Mirsaidov. Just before Karimov's well-orchestrated presidential election in December 1991, the parliamentary deputies loyal to Mirsaidov unexpectedly attacked Karimov by sharply criticizing him at the December session. Karimov reacted by simultaneously strengthening his ties with the other regional leaders in the parliament and driving the rebellious prime minister from the government.[22] He even went so far as to abolish the post of vice-president, which was widely deemed a concession to the powerful Tashkent elite for their support. But as soon as Mirsaidov was forced from the political arena, it was time to make amends with the remaining Tashkent elite. This was not a difficult task, because both sides were keen to make peace: Karimov did not want to have a latent opposition deeply rooted among the capital-city officials right in his midst, and the Tashkent quasi clan was also ready to demonstrate its loyalty in exchange for continued access to political power. The Tashkent elite was thus put in charge of the Ministry of Foreign Economic Relations (MVES), which was granted extensive rights for issuing export and import licenses, as well as over the National Bank for Foreign Economic Relations (NBU), which was to manage the distribution of international loans. Ironically, these administrative levers eventually enabled the Tashkent elite to gain control over the revenues from cotton as well as fuel exports.

Regional Backlash

Not all regional leaders, however, fared as well as the Tashkent elite. Having reached a rapprochement with the Tashkent quasi clan, Karimov

22. Mirsaidov remained under house arrest for several years afterward. All his attempts to reenter politics, including his leadership in the Democratic Opposition Coordination Council, failed, and he finally withdrew completely from politics in 1998 (ICG 2001, 10).

began to distance himself from the provincial leaders, even from the Samarkand elite to which, until that moment, he was believed to firmly belong. As previously mentioned, beginning in 1992 Karimov instituted several measures to diminish the influence of regional leaders in both the political and economic spheres. Most importantly, he centralized cotton production, distribution, and exports and requisitioned all rights to participate in sharing cotton revenues that had been previously granted to regional elites. Although regional leaders viewed this as a direct violation of his verbal contract with them in 1991, they also felt powerless to reverse this trend for several years because of their perceived weakened status vis-à-vis the center (see Jones Luong 2002, chap. 4, for details). Instead, they opted to demonstrate their loyalty to the president by, for example, joining the PDPU and endorsing his call for early parliamentary elections (Jones Luong 2002, chap. 4). As their formal sources of power continued to erode, however, they responded by bolstering the informal power they possessed through their control of patronage networks. Whereas under Rashidov they had sought to make their de facto control over material resources become de jure control, under Karimov they sought to seize de facto control over what de jure was no longer theirs.

Implications for the Uzbekistani State

Regional recalcitrance not only threatens the stability of the Uzbekistani state but also undermines its ability to govern effectively. Under the cover of formal loyalty, the proliferation of hidden disobedience to the center by regional elites has created a dangerous situation in which the state itself is on shaky grounds. Its territorial integrity may be compromised if regionalism grows unchecked, and especially if regional elites ally with militant Islamic groups or if Islamic opposition begins to supercede regional opposition. Yet, in the short run, the most serious implication for state-building under Karimov's regime is that some of its core polices are not being implemented and its primary source of revenue is being compromised.

This realization has forced central authorities to once again, in the very Soviet style of center-periphery bargaining behind closed doors, try to find a compromise with regional elites. Indeed, this is precisely what is behind several recent (albeit minor) reform efforts in the cotton sector and concerning the national parliament. Regional resistance in the form of the diversion of state-ordered cotton to the black market has prompted the central government to alter the mode of distributing cotton output. A new decree issued in September 2001, for example, retains the highly centralized system of management in the cotton production sector yet envisages concessions to regional elites in the cotton sector by codifying their share of revenue from the cotton gins that was already de facto under their control.[23]

Likewise, the failure of Fidokorlar to win a majority of seats in the December 1999 elections instigated the president's decision to embark on parliamentary reform. At the May 25, 2000 session of the Olii Majlis, President Karimov unexpectedly proposed transforming the current parliamentary structure from a unicameral into a bicameral body in which the lower chamber (Olii Majlis, or Supreme Assembly) would be made up of representatives of political parties and independent deputies working year-round, and the upper chamber (Olii Kengash, or Supreme Council) would be elected from among deputies of regional, district, and city-level councils and convene only three or four times a year, as is the practice of the current unicameral parliament (*Milly Tiklanish* 13 June 2000).[24] This proposed reform, which was adopted in January 2001, introduces a legally palatable way for Karimov to pacify regional parliamentary elites and consolidate his power. While it makes concessions to regional elites by guaranteeing them continued representation in the national parliament, at the same time it reduces the risk that Karimov will be impeached. Under the new system, the parliament must embark on a lengthy and complex procedure to initiate impeachment, which allows the president time to undertake sufficient countermeasures to remain in power (Ilkhamov 2000b).

Thus, the loyalty of regional forces, and stability in general, is achieved much as it was during the Soviet period — that is, by maintaining a fine balance between concessions and reprisals — rather than through mass participation in a democratic electoral process. The result is a central state vis-à-vis the periphery based on a precarious (that is, continuously renegotiated) "stability" between layers of the state that largely leaves out society. In other words, stability is very much predicated on the continuing ability of central and regional leaders to reach mutually satisfactory agreements based on their perceptions of shifts in their relative power.

23. Decree of the Cabinet of Ministers, Republic of Uzbekistan, September 18, 2001, no. 377: "On the approval of the rules for the cotton fiber centralized export organization order."

24. For details about the structure and composition of the previous parliament, see Jones Luong 2002, chap. 6.

6. Economic "Decentralization" in Kazakhstan

CAUSES AND CONSEQUENCES

PAULINE JONES LUONG

Since the breakup of the Soviet Union in 1991, we have witnessed a pattern of increasing subnational autonomy over economic policy making and implementation in Kazakhstan and several other Soviet successor states — particularly Russia and Ukraine — that both contradicts existing models and understandings of why, when, and how economic decentralization occurs and highlights some of the particular challenges of state formation in the postcommunist world.

Decentralization departs from conventional expectations in two important ways. First, the impetus for decentralization in these states has come more often from below (the regional-level government) rather than from above (the central government). This explicitly places the central government in the role of responding or reacting to regional leaders' independent actions, and in some cases outright demands for more autonomy, rather than in the position of initiating decentralization. Second, as a result, initially decentralization has taken on a much more de facto (unofficial or "in practice") than de jure (official or "on paper") form. In many cases, this has spurred the central leadership to issue decrees or authorize legislation in order to recognize officially what is already occurring unofficially; in others, the central government has chosen to feign ignorance in an attempt to maintain regional leaders' support and avoid the appearance of "weakness." President Boris Yeltsin of the Russian Federation, for example, signed a series of bilateral agreements with regional governments in the early to mid-1990s that legally granted them additional

The author is grateful to Laura Adams, Sally Cummings, Keith Darden, Anna Grzymala-Busse, Marianne Kamp, Lawrence King, Kelly McMann, M. Victoria Murillo, Valerie Sperling, James Vreeland, Lucan Way, Erika Weinthal, Cynthia Werner, and the Post-Communist Workshop at Yale University for comments on earlier versions of this chapter. Funding for fieldwork and data collection was provided by the Yale Center for International and Area Studies and the William Davidson Institute, University of Michigan.

spheres of autonomy and institutionalized a system of asymmetrical federalism (see, e.g., Slider 1997; Stoner-Weiss 1999). Similarly, as I demonstrate in this chapter, central authorities in Kazakhstan have moved to codify regional governments' de facto control over certain spheres, particularly fiscal and budgetary matters. These two characteristics of decentralization in the former Soviet Union (FSU) amount to the informal usurpation of power from below that is often, though not always, followed by the formal recognition of this newfound authority from above.[1] Yet, the existing literature seems willing to define away this possibility by equating "decentralization" with the "formal transfer of power from above to below" (see, e.g., Agrawal and Ribot 2000, 4).

These differences also reveal some distinguishing features of the state-building process in the former Soviet Union, particularly Central Asia. The fact that decentralization has both occurred from below and been largely de facto demonstrates that the central state apparatus is not as "strong" as it is often portrayed — whether measured in terms of its coercive or infrastructural capacity to achieve its policy goals — or at least that it is "weak" in comparison to the corresponding regional governments.[2] Kazakhstan in particular gained an international reputation during the second half of its first decade of independence as a highly centralized state governed exclusively by its authoritarian ruler President Nursultan Nazarbaev — an image that remains largely undisputed by scholars and policy makers alike (see, e.g., Cummings 2000; George 2001; Hyman 1997; Kubicek 1997; Moser 2002). This image, however, presents a view from above that relies on formal state institutions and overlooks the informal bargaining and tacit agreements that take place between central and regional leaders. Moreover, because central-peripheral relations are such a key component of the state's structure and functions, the fact that the center has responded to de facto decentralization by officially recognizing it suggests that the state-building process in Kazakhstan is being driven as much from below as it is from above.

This chapter illuminates both the causes of economic decentralization and its implications for state-building in Kazakhstan. Although Kazakhstan is formally defined as a unitary state and its central leadership is often

1. In contrast to Russia and Kazakhstan, for example, there has been little willingness in Ukraine to officially recognize the de facto dual subordination of the tax administration, commercial banks, and the treasury department to regional administrations (Way 2001).

2. State "strength" is usually meant to denote its ability to achieve its policy goals. According to Mann (1993), states can employ a combination of coercive and infrastructural means to achieve their ends. Some also consider legitimacy to be a crucial component of state effectiveness (see, e.g., Jackman 1993; M. Weber 1953).

assumed to exert authoritarian control throughout the country, I argue that de facto decentralization has been occurring in Kazakhstan since independence. In other words, subnational leaders have exercised much greater influence over the economy in practice than they are granted on paper. The de jure decentralization that has been enacted since 1999, moreover, is in fact an official recognition of what had already been occurring in practice. The impetus for decentralization in Kazakhstan, then, has come largely from regional (or subnational) governments rather than from the central government, as is commonly argued (and often assumed) in the theoretical literature.[3]

Thus, the mode of decentralization in Kazakhstan indicates that the central state must engage in ongoing negotiations with regional authorities in order to both make and implement economic policy. This finding is significant not only because it suggests that the mode of center-periphery bargaining developed under Soviet rule has persisted into the post-Soviet period but also because it reflects the nature of the state-building process that is occurring in Kazakhstan. Although the practice of informal bargaining between central and regional elites over economic matters is certainly not a wholly new phenomenon, particularly with regard to budgetary policy (see, e.g., Bahry 1987), it has accelerated and expanded following the collapse of the Soviet Union and in the context of a shrinking central state since independence.

These findings have several key theoretical implications for the study of the state. First, they contribute additional evidence to the growing contention, particularly among those who study the developing world, that the state cannot be treated as either a unitary, coherent actor or an integral whole, but instead should be viewed as a set of competing actors and institutions (see, e.g., L. Anderson 1986; Migdal 1988; Migdal, Kohli, and Shue 1994; and Waldner 1999).[4] Second, this competition can occur between governing elites within the state apparatus itself. The greatest obstacle to building effective states in Kazakhstan as well as Uzbekistan (see Ilkhamov, chap. 5) is not the struggle for domination between those actors that make up the state and those that constitute social forces, as is commonly depicted in the literature on state-building in the developing world (see, e.g., Migdal 1988; Migdal, Shue and Kohli 1994). Rather, it is a geographically based struggle between state elites for control over access to both public and private resources that is likely to intensify when

3. For an excellent overview of the literature on decentralization, see Agrawal 1999, esp. chaps. 2–3.

4. For an elaboration of this argument and its application to the postcommunist world, see Grzymala-Busse and Jones Luong (2002).

existing resources become scarce or new resources are generated. Third, owing to the lasting imprint of Soviet rule on central-peripheral relations in Kazakhstan (and Central Asia in general), "winning" this struggle depends much more on the art of negotiation and compromise than it does on the nature of the political regime and its ability to employ coercion. Alisher Ilkhamov's (chap. 5) findings suggest that this is also the case in Uzbekistan, which has an arguably much more repressive and authoritarian regime that is prepared to use force to impose its political will. At the same time, as the chapters by both Ilkhamov and Erika Weinthal (chap. 8) demonstrate, although nonstate actors who constitute society have the most to lose (or gain) from the elite bargaining that determines the allocation of resources, they are essentially excluded from this process. Finally, in the context of a weak central state, further decentralization only serves to exacerbate the struggle among governing elites for control over spheres of influence — particularly where the actors engaged in this struggle view it as zero sum — and thus to undermine the potentially positive economic effects of greater subnational autonomy. Policy makers, therefore, have good reason to pause before endorsing such an outcome, at least in the short term.

The first section of this chapter provides a brief overview of the impetus behind growing international support for decentralization throughout the developing world. I then present compelling empirical evidence that economic decentralization has been occurring de facto in Kazakhstan since independence, and that the recent move toward de jure decentralization occurred in direct response to this. Finally, after considering several alternative explanations for decentralization in Kazakhstan, I elaborate the empirical and theoretical implications for state-building in Kazakhstan, the former Soviet Union, and beyond.

International Support for Decentralization

In recent years, economic decentralization has become an increasingly popular policy recommendation among international development organizations and lending agencies around the world.[5] Its strongest advocates often point to the "successes" of several developing countries, such as China and India, which have experienced significant market reform and

5. This includes the United States Agency for International Development (USAID), United Nations Development Program (UNDP), International Monetary Fund (IMF), and World Bank. One indication of the growing support for decentralization is the amount of seminars and working papers that have recently been devoted to decentralization. See, for example, http://www.imf.org/external/pubs/ft/seminar/2000/fiscal/index.htm.

economic growth in the aftermath of devolving economic decision-making authority to local governments (see, e.g., Montinola, Qian, and Weingast 1996; Echeverri-Gent 2000).[6]

The main rationale behind the growing international impulse to promote decentralization in the developing world is that it will provide the necessary structural incentives to foster market-promoting behavior at the local level, and hence, stimulate economic growth. These incentives can be crudely summarized as predictability, efficiency, and accountability.[7] Proponents of fiscal decentralization, for example, argue that devolving control over the generation, collection, and distribution (or expenditure) of tax revenue will provide local leaders with a stable revenue base. They will then use this to provide public goods such as social services more efficiently both to satisfy the demands of their constituents and to create surplus revenue that can be reinvested in the local economy (e.g., to build infrastructure) to attract more investment. Most accounts endorsing decentralization also stress the role that interregional competition over mobile sources of revenue (e.g., capital and labor) plays in reinforcing these incentives by motivating local governments to guarantee property rights, implement rational fiscal and regulatory regimes, and provide public goods (see, e.g., Weingast 1995, 5).

Advocates of decentralization have gained ground most recently in several postcommunist states, including the Czech Republic, Poland, Hungary, Russia, Ukraine, and Kazakhstan.[8] Yet, these states do not appear to possess the fundamental structural conditions that either necessitate decentralization or guarantee its effectiveness. Decentralization requires, first and foremost, a strong central state. Indeed, the driving force behind efforts to devolve political and economic authority to the local level is the assumption that the main obstacle to establishing or maintaining efficient markets, and hence to promoting economic growth, is the predatory central government. Returning for a moment to the example of fiscal federalism, this is often illustrated by central governments setting a revenue collection target for local governments and then "punishing" them for generating any amount above this target by repeatedly confiscating or "clawing back" the excess revenue. Local governments, therefore, have a

6. In actuality, the desirability and effectiveness of decentralization in these countries have received mixed reviews. See, for example, Rodden and Rose-Ackerman 1997.

7. For a comprehensive overview, see Tanzi 1995. On fiscal federalism in particular, see Oates 1972.

8. Author's personal communication with Gulnara Kurbanova, UNDP project manager for decentralization in Kazakhstan, Almaty, November 1999. See also, e.g., Bryson and Cornia 2000; Treisman 1999; Way 2000; Zhuravskaya 2000.

compelling disincentive to either increase tax collection or expand their revenue base. The value of decentralization, then, it that it "ties the hands" of the central government so that it can "credibly commit" *not* to confiscate revenue (see, e.g., Weingast 1993). At the same time, however, a strong central government is crucial to the success of decentralization because it must have the administrative and legal capacity to assure economic actors that it can enforce contracts and property rights as well as to regulate interregional economic activity (see, e.g., Montinola, Qian, and Weingast 1996).

The assumption of a strong central state is a particularly powerful one in the postcommunist setting because most attribute the failures of communism to an overgrown and intrusive socialist state. This is often accompanied by an underemphasis on the state's crucial role in enforcing contracts and regulating economic activity. Yet, in reality, central governments throughout Eastern Europe and particularly the former Soviet Union have exhibited signs of administrative weakness and severely limited fiscal capacity (see, e.g., Cirtautas 1995; Jones Luong 1999; Stoner-Weiss 1999; Way 2000). In both Russia and Ukraine, for example, there is substantial evidence that central authorities have failed to enforce revenue-sharing arrangements with subnational governments that they themselves designed precisely because regional governments exert a great deal of informal control over this formally centralized process (see, e.g., OECD Economic Surveys 1997, 2000b; Stoner-Weiss 2001; Way 2000). Throughout the former Soviet Union, moreover, central governments frequently fail to honor formal commitments, including subsidies to subnational governments, because they have suffered from severe fiscal crises and sharp declines in growth since independence (see, e.g., Jones Luong and Way 2001).[9] What, then, is the effect of increased local autonomy in the context of a weak central state? The case of Kazakhstan provides some insight into this question.

De facto Economic Decentralization in Kazakhstan

There are three basic types of economic decentralization: (1) fiscal (e.g., revenue collection, generation, and distribution), (2) administrative (e.g., providing social services), and (3) regulatory (e.g., issuing licenses and permits, monitoring safety and environmental compliance). All three have been a feature of Kazakhstan's political landscape since shortly after

9. From 1992 and 1998, GDP fell by over 40 percent in Russia and Ukraine and by over 20 percent in Kazakhstan (see *Transition Report* 1999, and Way 2001).

independence, and began accelerating in 1995. Yet, they have emerged and persisted unofficially, or de facto, rather than officially, or de jure, until 1999. According to both its 1993 and 1995 constitutions, Kazakhstan is a unitary state with a highly centralized budgetary system that operates in much the same manner as the Soviet one. The key difference between de facto and de jure decentralization is that in the latter subnational control is legally codified while in the former subnational control is illegal but nonetheless exists in practice. We must thus find ways to separate the official delimitation of authority for economic policy making from the actual degree of autonomy that subnational leaders are exercising unofficially. This is no easy task. In this section, I attempt to demonstrate that de facto economic decentralization has indeed occurred in Kazakhstan and is widespread, based on a variety of indicators and using a combination of qualitative and quantitative data.

At the most general level, de facto decentralization can be said to exist where the central government's economic directives diverge from local practices and outcomes. We need to ascertain, therefore, the degree to which agencies located at the subnational level actually respect and implement central policy, particularly when it contradicts regional or local policy preferences, or to what degree local agencies are "captured" by regional or local interests. More specifically, for each type of decentralization mentioned above there are several possible indicators of de facto subnational autonomy. I explore each of these in turn below.

Fiscal Decentralization

A key indicator of de facto fiscal decentralization is the degree of subnational discretion over revenue generation and collection. Several questions serve to ascertain this: (1) Are tax administrators dually subordinated to central and subnational authorities? (2) Do subnational governments issue tax exemptions at their discretion? (3) Do they have access to extrabudgetary funds? (4) Do tax collection efforts vary? On paper, the central government in Kazakhstan has the sole authority to collect taxes at all levels of government and set tax rates for the country (with the exception of a few local taxes). Yet, there is sufficient evidence based on these indicators to suggest that this is not the case in practice. The central tax agencies operating at the subnational levels are not under the exclusive control of the central government and tax rates are not uniform; rather, they are subject to the needs and interests of subnational government officials.

Concerning the dual subordination of tax administrators, interviews that I conducted with members of the regional administrators and representatives of the central tax agencies in several regions (Almaty, Atyrau,

Kyzl-Orda, Mangistau, Pavlodar) in the fall of 1999 and summer of 2000 confirm that tax administrators receive directives from both the central and regional levels of government. When the two conflict, moreover, they are also more likely to fulfill those of the regional governments. Thus, for example, they frequently "avoid putting pressure on state enterprises that cannot afford to pay [their] taxes" and willingly accept noncash payments.[10] Regional leaders explained the common practice of issuing directives to these agencies, despite their official subordination to the central government, as a matter of both "convenience" and entitlement. They explained that the tax agency representatives are actually local employees because they receive similar privileges, such as housing subsidies, and that "they should [therefore] . . . be given local instructions . . . be managed by local authorities."[11] When asked to reflect on their own tendency to follow regional officials' directives, some tax agency representatives explained that the regional leaders were often better equipped to "understand the needs of the local population" than central authorities.[12] Several others also alluded to the fact that they had close personal relations with the regional administration or had once served in the regional administration and planned to return at some point.[13] An additional reason for the de facto dual subordination of tax agency representatives is that regional and local administrations control their access to key resources such as office space, telephones, and might even finance their activities.[14] Thus, similar to the situation for local NGOs that Kelly McMann (chap. 7) describes in Kyrgyzstan, they must rely on local governments in order to carry out their basic functions.

Recent surveys of foreign investors operating in the aforementioned regions as well as several others (including Aktyubinsk, Karaganda, and Semipalatinsk) that I conducted with Erika Weinthal between 1997 and 2000 provide additional evidence that regional leaders consistently prioritize regional tax policy over national tax laws and regulations. In fact, this occurs to such an extent that foreign investors often described

10. Author's personal communication with tax administration representative in Almaty, name withheld, November 1999.

11. Author's personal communication with regional administration in Pavlodar, name withheld, June 2000.

12. Author's personal communication with tax administration representative in Almaty, name withheld, November 1999.

13. It is worth noting here that, as in several other Soviet successor states, when these agencies were created they recruited staff from the regional and local administrations (see, e.g., Norris, Jorge Martinez-Vasquez, and Norregaard 2000).

14. Author's personal communication with Gulnara Kurbanova, op. cit.

the entire process as "extremely arbitrary." They complain, for example, that it is not sufficient to keep up with the central tax codes in order to avoid fines because they are "subject to the whim of the local tax authorities, who are often unfamiliar with the tax code."[15]

These interviews and surveys also confirmed that subnational tax authorities routinely offer tax exemptions in exchange for "donations" to the regional administration's discretionary funds and prefer to concentrate more on fining for noncompliance with tax laws (usually caused by minor accounting or procedural errors) than on collecting taxes owed. Both of these activities contribute directly to the creation of a source of extrabudgetary income for regional leaders. The latter in particular converts the regions' power to tax into the power to fine, such that, ironically, tax administrators are often encouraged to vigorously enforce central tax codes in order to extract larger fines. Because of the complex bureaucratic process, which requires that taxes be calculated and accounting records be reviewed on a transaction by transaction basis, that an excessive amount of paperwork be filed for each transaction, and that specific rules be followed for bookkeeping, the relevant regional authorities can and do employ frequent tax audits to penalize the (mostly foreign) companies under their jurisdiction. As one financial officer of a major oil company commented,

> the line-by-line accounting method and excess bureaucracy actually increases the amount of money owed because there is so much room for error. Every single individual transaction is subject to regulation. Every single regulation is treated as an opportunity for the company to be fined.[16]

Whether or not there is variation in tax collection efforts is more difficult to determine. One way to do this without relying on more anecdotal evidence is to think of the amount of revenue collected as simply a function of the tax base, tax rate, and collection effort: $R = F\ (TB, TR, CE)$. Because the central government officially sets tax rates, which are uniform across regions, it is reasonable to expect, *ceteris paribus*, higher tax collection in regions with a larger tax base or in wealthier regions. As table 6.1 clearly illustrates, however, tax revenue — whether broken down into personal income tax (PIT), property tax, or measured in aggregate — is only very weakly correlated with either the level of industrial production

15. Author's personal communication with representative of foreign oil company, Almaty, Kazakhstan, November 1999. See Weinthal and Jones Luong (2000) for more detail on the evolution of Kazakhstan's tax code.

16. Author's personal communication, name withheld, November 1999, Almaty, Kazakhstan.

TABLE 6.1. *Variation in Tax Collection Effort*

	PIT	Property Tax	Total Tax Revenue
Industrial Production			
Pearson Correlation	.254	.478	.407
Sig. (2-tailed)	.342	.61	.117
N	16	16	16
GDP			
Pearson Correlation	.727[a]	.444	.286
Sig. (2-tailed)	.001	.085	.283
N	16	16	16

Source: Calculations based on data from the Ministry of Finance, Republic of Kazakhstan.

[a]Significant at the 0.01 level.

in a given region or its GDP. The only exception is GDP and PIT, which has a correlation of .73 (significant at the 0.01 level), yet here we might expect an even stronger correlation if wealth alone is driving tax collection receipts. Thus, we can conclude (albeit rather tenuously) that tax collection efforts vary across the regions.

Some additional evidence that tax collection efforts vary across regions, or at least that they are not as high as the central government demands, comes from examining the differential between the targeted rates of tax collection and the actual rates. Although I was able to obtain this data only for 1998 — a year in which Kazakhstan suffered a sharp decline in both GDP and revenue[17] — it nonetheless suggests that not all regions are as vigorous as others when it comes to fulfilling revenue targets. (See table 6.2.) The "ability" to fulfill revenue collection targets, moreover, is clearly not a function of a region's wealth. The five wealthiest (or "donor") regions in table 6.2 — Almaty city, Atyrau, Mangistau, Karaganda, and Pavlodar — were among that year's biggest slackers.[18]

There is also some evidence to suggest that collection effort varies by the type of tax — that is, whether it provides revenue exclusively to the

17. Kazakhstan's GDP fell by 2 percent in 1998 in conjunction with the drop in world oil prices and the August financial crisis in Russia.

18. This is particularly the case in Mangistau and Pavlodar (see table 6.2). One could argue that these regions failed to meet revenue targets because the bulk of their revenue depends on oil. Yet, this is also true for Kyzl-Orda, which is the only region that exceeded its revenue target. Astana (formerly Akmola), the country's capital as of December 1997, also exceeded its revenue targets.

TABLE 6.2. *Actual Revenue and Expenditures Compared to Planned (1998)*

	Difference between Actual and Planned Revenue (%)	Difference between Actual and Planned Expenditures (%)
Akmolinsk	−24.7	−20.5
Aktyubinsk Oblast	−30.8	−23.5
Almatinsk Oblast	−9.4	−11.9
Almaty City	−8.1	−9.3
Astana City	2.6	−1.9
Atyrau Oblast	−11.1	−13.3
East Kazakhstan Oblast	−19.7	−19.5
Karaganda Oblast	−23.4	−22.4
Kostenai Oblast	−29.6	−13.9
Kzyl-Orda Oblast	0.0	−0.2
Mangistau Oblast	−29.5	−30.7
North Kazakhstan Oblast	−19.8	−20.9
Pavlodar Oblast	−38.2	−24.6
South Kazakhstan Oblast	−1.4	−6.0
West Kazakhstan Oblast	−32.9	−28.3
Zhambul Oblast	−12.8	−13.5
Totals	−16.9	−15.3

Source: Calculations based on data from the Ministry of Finance, Republic of Kazakhstan.

region or is shared with the central government. Although tax revenue has increased across the regions over the past few years, revenue from the land tax, property tax, and vehicle tax, all of which remain at the local level, has increased at a higher rate. Property tax, for example, doubled as a percentage of GDP from 0.4 percent in 1996 to 0.8 percent in 1997 (Republic of Kazakhstan 1999, 42). Moreover, because of the de facto dual subordination of tax agencies illustrated above, representatives of tax agencies often comply with instructions to focus on the collection of these local taxes over central ones. Although the Almaty city and Atyrau Oblast budgets for 1999, for example, exceeded collection targets for all taxes the greatest "excesses" were in local taxes.[19]

19. Author's personal communication with Marcia Occomy, resident advisor, USAID Fiscal Reform Project, August 2000.

Another key, and commonly utilized, indicator of fiscal decentralization is the degree and mode of revenue sharing. Here, again, several questions are relevant: (1) What is the share of subnational budgets in consolidated revenue and expenditures? (2) To what degree do subnational budgets consist of revenue raised on their territories as opposed to transfers? (3) Is revenue-sharing based on negotiations between regional and central governments or does it follow a predetermined target set by central authorities?

Answering the first two questions enables us to compare the level of decentralization in Kazakhstan, which is a unitary state, to several other postcommunist states and developing countries, many of which are federal systems. Subnational budgets in Kazakhstan contributed approximately 18 percent to consolidated revenue in 1999 (Ministry of Finance, Republic of Kazakhstan). If we compare this to Russia, where this figure was over 40 percent in 2000, it appears that Kazakhstan is not very decentralized (*OECD Economic Surveys* 2000b). Yet, in comparison to other federal states, such as Mexico, where this figure was approximately 22 percent in 2000, Kazakhstan appears to be more decentralized than one would expect for a unitary state (*OECD Economic Surveys* 2000a). Concerning the degree to which subnational budgets rely on revenue generated within their territories versus transfers, the situation in Kazakhstan is much closer to Russia's. For Russia, transfers made up approximately 15 percent of regional budgets in 1999 while in Kazakhstan they accounted for 23 percent of regional budgets in 1995 and then dropped to approximately 17 percent in 1999 (*OECD Economic Surveys*, 2000b; Ministry of Finance, Republic of Kazakhstan). Both of these figures are much lower than federal states at similar levels of economic development, such as Mexico and India, as well as unitary states with a high degree of decentralization, such as China (*OECD Economic Surveys* 2000a; Arora and Norregaard 1997).

I combine qualitative and quantitative data to ascertain the extent to which revenue sharing is based on negotiations or a "tug-of-war" between the regional and central leaders. This is an especially important indicator of de facto versus de jure decentralization because it demonstrates the extent to which regional governments can unofficially "renegotiate" what has already been officially determined.

The aforementioned interviews with regional leaders in Almaty, Atyrau, Kyzl-Orda, Mangistau, and Pavlodar provided compelling evidence that they not only negotiate with central leaders over annual revenue-sharing rates but that it is their expectation that this should be the case. The akims (regional administrative heads) clearly consider officially determined rates as the beginning, not the end, of a long bargaining process. As one

TABLE 6.3. *VAT Collection and Contribution to Central Budget*

	1996	1997	1998
Pearson Correlation	.26	.158	.222
Sig. (2-tailed)	.925	.559	.409
N	16	16	16

Source: Calculations based on data from the Ministry of Finance, Republic of Kazakhstan.

akim boldly proclaimed, "if it were up to me, of course, I would keep all the revenue here. . . . But we are forced to share [it]. So, I say, let Astana [referring to those in the capital] come and get it."[20] The expectation that informal negotiation and agreements would trump official sharing rates is also evident in the rationale for exceeding revenue targets. When asked why their region or city regularly exceeded revenue targets, for example, akims uniformly responded that this increased their ability to "convince" the center to let them keep more of the excess revenue. In other words, the more revenue they collected the stronger their bargaining position vis-à-vis the central government.

Questions remain, however, as to whether this practice extends beyond these five regions and, if so, how widespread it is. Two types of quantitative measures help me address these questions. First, if the rate of revenue sharing is officially determined then we should expect to find that wealthier regions contribute more to the national budget. As table 6.3 illustrates, however, there is only a weak correlation between a region's overall level of wealth (measured in terms of VAT) and its contribution. Second, we can calculate the effective rate of revenue sharing between the central and regional government in Kazakhstan and compare it to the official rates. (See table 6.4.) These figures clearly show that the effective rate of revenue sharing fluctuated considerably between 1997 and 1999 and, moreover, that it differed considerably from official rates, particularly for the corporate income tax (CIT), personal income tax (PIT), and social tax.

Administrative Decentralization

A state is administratively decentralized when either the main locus of state expenditures is at the subnational rather than the national level or

20. Author's personal communication with oblast akim, name withheld, October 1999. Note that the reference to "Astana" to denote the central authorities is similar to the reference to "Moscow" under Soviet rule.

TABLE 6.4. *Effective versus Official Rates of Revenue Sharing*

	Official Share	Effective Rates[a] 1997	1998	1999
Tax Revenue, of which		33.1	34.8	48.9
CIT	0.0	52.3	54.2	50.0
PIT	0.0	81.9	84.1	97.5
Social tax	0.0	0.0	0.0	97.8
Property tax	100.0	100.0	100.0	98.2
Land tax	100.0	100.0	100.0	97.2
Vehicle tax	100.0	100.0	100.0	100.0
VAT	0.0	15.6	14.3	0.0

Source: Republic of Kazakhstan 1994, 44.

[a]Based on the percentage that is officially assigned to the regional government versus what is actually receives.

TABLE 6.5. *Distribution of Expenditures between Levels of Government*

	As a Percent of Total Revenue			As a Percent of GDP		
	1995	1997	1998	1995	1997	1998
Kazakhstan						
Central government	48.6	55.1	55.4	9.2	10.5	11.1
Regional governments (consolidated)	51.4	44.9	44.6	9.7	8.6	8.9
Total	100	100	100	18.9	19.1	20.0
Russia						
Central government	54.9	53.0	58.8	18.6	19.0	16.6
Regional governments (consolidated)	45.1	47.1	47.2	15.3	16.8	14.8
Total	100	100.1	96	33.9	35.8	31.4

Source: Based on Norris, Martinez-Vasquez, and Norregaard 2002, 25–26.

when the national and subnational governments have comparable levels of expenditure. Table 6.5 demonstrates not only that this is indeed the case in Kazakhstan but that the distribution of expenditures between levels of government in Kazakhstan is very similar to that of Russia. The simi-

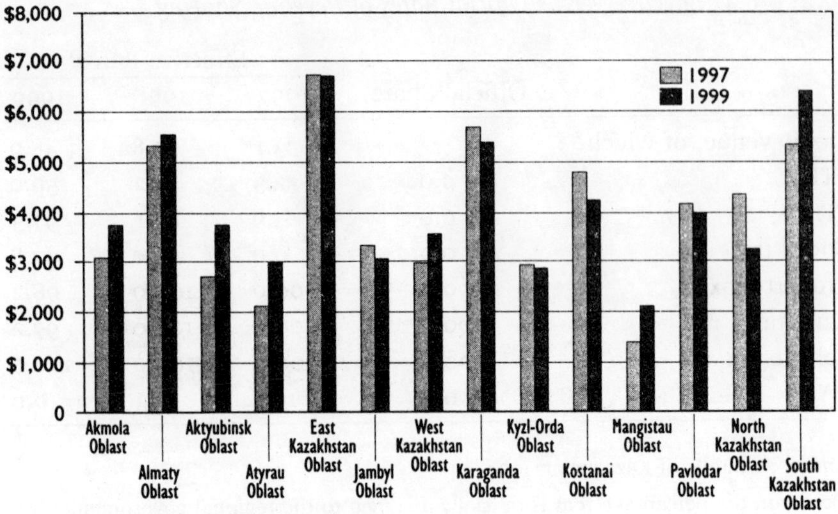

Source: Ministry of France, Republic of Kazakhstan

FIGURE 6.1. *Expenditures on Education per Capita*

larity is striking because Russia is a federation and thus should automatically have a much higher portion of expenditures at the subnational level.

At the same time, Kazakhstan differs dramatically from Russia because the central government has no formal expenditure responsibilities. For each budgetary year, it can decide which responsibilities it will assume and dump the remainder onto subnational budgets. The central government has done this to a greater degree since independence, without transferring the necessary funds to regional budgets.[21] Thus, regional governments in Kazakhstan have assumed increasing responsibility over providing social services without the financial resources to provide these services.[22] They must make difficult choices about whether and how to allocate scarce resources, and they often fail to meet national expenditure targets (see table 6.2).

Yet, the lack of formal requirements also provides regional leaders with a great deal of discretion over social spending. Thus, as table 6.2 illustrates, they fail to meet their expenditure targets to varying degrees. Their ability to fulfill these targets, moreover, is once again not determined by wealth. The discretion of regional leaders over expenditures is also apparent in the wide variation across regions in per capita expenditures on specific areas. Figure 6.1 and figure 6.2 demonstrate that the level of spending

21. In some cases, this is deliberate while in others it is circumstantial — for example, the collapse of state enterprises that previously provided social services.

22. Author's personal communication with Kurbanova, op. cit.

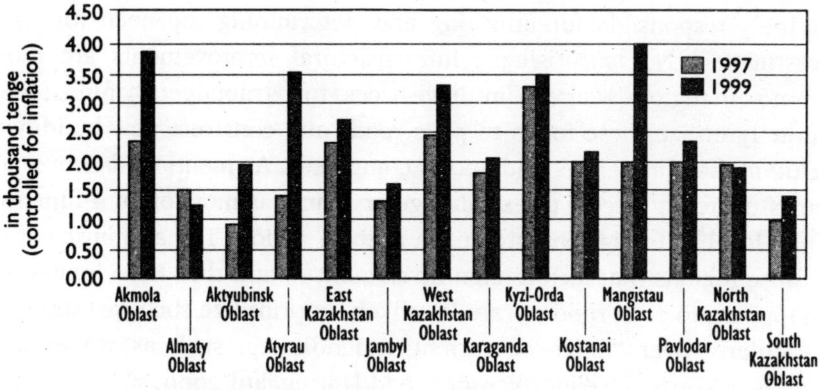

Source: Ministry of France, Republic of Kazakhstan

FIGURE 6.2. *Public Health Expenditures per Capita*

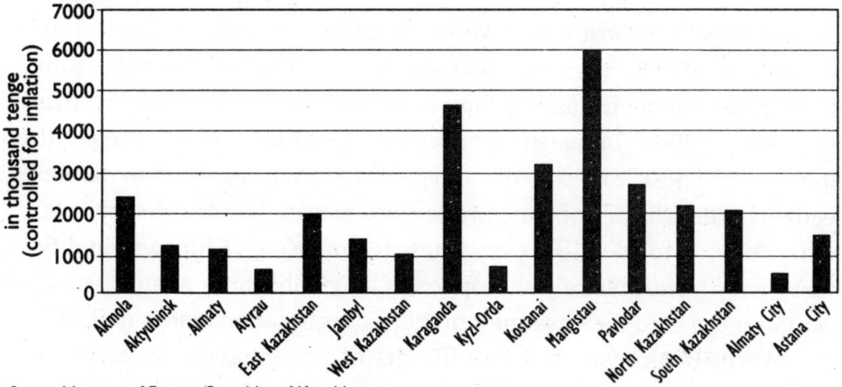

Source: Ministry of France, Republic of Kazakhstan

FIGURE 6.3. *Variation in Wage Arrears by Region, 1998*

on education and public health varies not only across regions but also from year to year within the same region. Such discrepancies become more visible when they are directly compared to the targets set by the central government. In 1997 and 1999, for example, Atyrau Oblast failed to meet its expenditure targets for public order and security and environmental protection, but exceeded these targets in education and health care (Department of Finance, Atyrau Oblast). As figure 6.3 illustrates, regional governments also meet their salary obligations to state employees to varying degrees, though none do so completely.

Another area with significant variation in regional expenditure is investment in local infrastructure. Although this obligation is formally assigned to the central government, regional governments complain that they are routinely responsible for financing and determining the need for such investment.[23] Not surprisingly, infrastructural improvements are most common in regions where akims have access to extrabudgetary funds; they routinely utilize these funds to pave roads and construct new buildings, including bowling alleys and sports complexes. As mentioned above, an akim's degree of access to extrabudgetary funds is most often a function of the level of foreign investment in a given region. The administrations in those regions that lack foreign investment — and thus have limited (if any) access to such funds — are less likely to prioritize such investments, particularly over "items of current expenditures, such as wages and salaries" (Norris, Martinez-Vasquez, and Norregaard 2000, 7).

Regional leaders' record on implementing economic policies formulated at the central level provides another key indicator of the degree to which regional leaders are exercising greater control over the local economy in practice than they are granted on paper. Since independence, Kazakhstan has launched the most extensive privatization program in Central Asia.[24] Its "success" in the regions, however, has been mixed from the start. In many cases, regional leaders simply refused to implement privatization programs, created bureaucratic obstacles to hinder private-sector development, or chose to "look the other way" when local akims refused to recognize the transfer of state property to private hands (see Jones Luong 2002, chap. 4, for details). Only a few regions (e.g., Chimkent and South Kazakhstan) did precisely the opposite by establishing a single-step procedure in order to increase the number of registrations more quickly (see, e.g., World Bank 1993, 70). The results of privatization, therefore, have also been mixed. Figures 6.4 and 6.5 provide some indication that the regions vary considerably according to the degree of private economic activity and the amount of budgetary receipts from privatization.

Regulatory Decentralization

De facto regulatory decentralization overlaps somewhat with fiscal and administrative decentralization because it describes a situation in which subnational officials exercise greater authority over setting and enforcing regulations in practice than they are empowered to do on paper. Three main questions help us to determine the degree of regulatory decentralization: (1) Are national regulations and standards inconsistently enforced

23. Author's personal communication with regional administrations in Atyrau and Mangistau, October 1999; Almaty city, November 1999; and Pavlodar, June 2000.

24. See, for example, the *Law on Destatization and Privatization of the Republic of Kazakhstan*, June 1991.

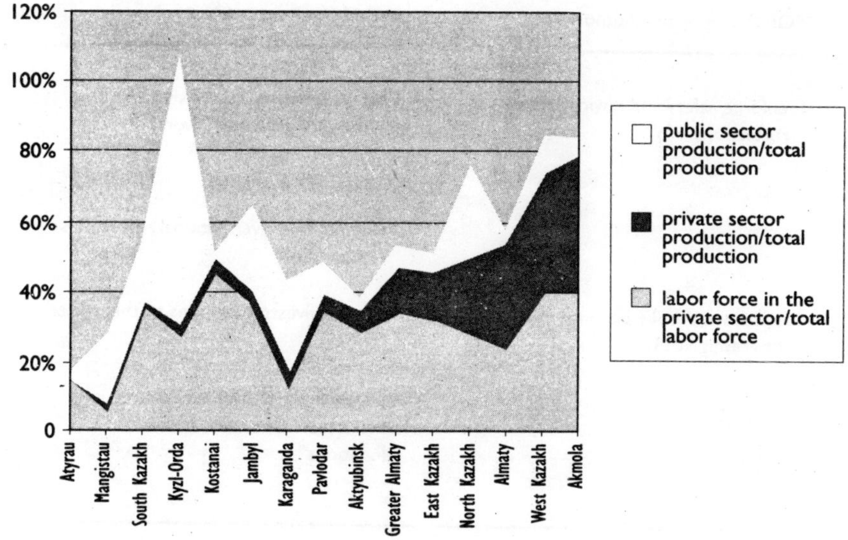

Source: Ministry of France, Republic of Kazakhstan

FIGURE 6.4. *Size of the Private versus Public Sector, 1996*

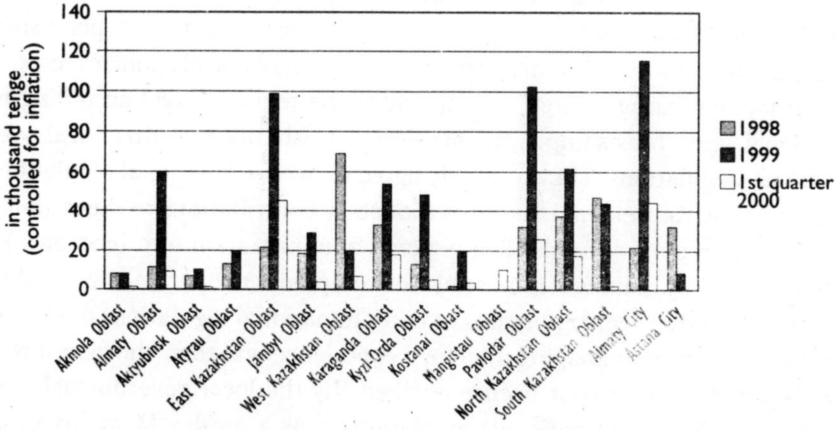

Source: Ministry of France, Republic of Kazakhstan

FIGURE 6.5. *Revenue from Privatization, 1998–2000*

at the subnational level? (2) Are licenses and permits to contractors (foreign and domestic) issued arbitrarily — that is, at the subnational leadership's discretion? (3) Are regulatory authorities dually subordinated to central and subnational authorities?

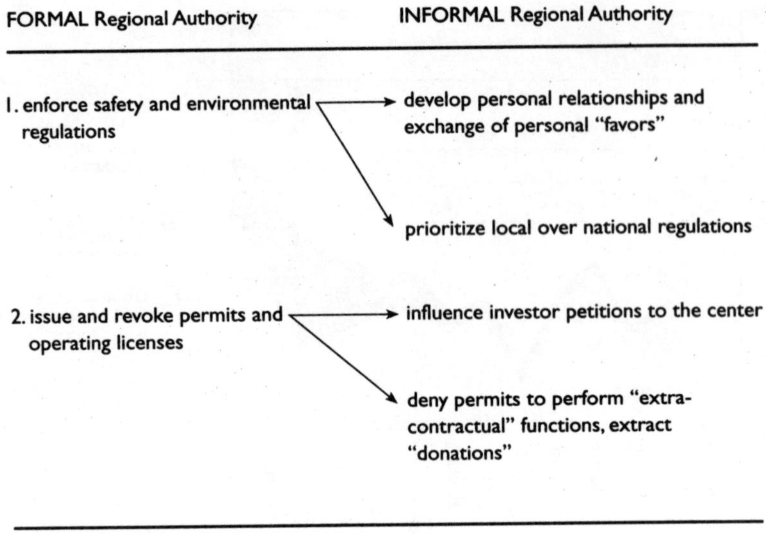

Source: Jones Luong-Weinthal Survey of Foreign Investors Operating in Kazakhstan, 1997–2000

FIGURE 6.6. *Regulation and Monitoring of Foreign Investors*

According to surveys conducted with foreign investors throughout Kazakhstan from 1997 to 2000, all three of these features are pervasive. (Their experiences are summarized in figure 6.6.) Central agencies responsible for regulating foreign investment at the regional level according to national laws, for example, nonetheless consistently prioritize local over national regulations. They routinely agree to overlook national regulations in exchange for personal favors or monetary contributions to the regional akim's discretionary funds. The regional administration also promotes its own agenda by making it impossible for companies to operate if they either refuse to follow local regulations or defer to national regulations over local ones. One former managing director's experience was that "the fastest way to be fined or have your license revoked [by the local government] is to ignore the local [not national] regulations.[25] As a result, "Many investors have found that it is worthwhile to resolve oblast concerns first before approaching the republican authorities for contracts," and in some cases to "always give the oblast level the first opportunity to comment before sending applications to the central government" (Biddison 1999, 6).[26]

25. Author's personal communication, name withheld, October 1999, Atyrau, Kazakhstan.

26. Author's personal communication with former managing director, name withheld, op. cit.

Investors nearly uniform experiences provide a clear indication that regional authorities have a much more direct influence on regulatory policy than the central government originally intended.

The testimony of regional officials I interviewed corroborates that of foreign investors, and sheds some additional light on the dual pressures that regulatory authorities face at the subnational level. Where national and regional regulations conflict, they are legally obliged to enforce the former over the latter. Yet, similar to tax administrators, they are considered local employees and often receive subsidized housing as well as their salary and bonuses from the regional government. They are thus more likely to enforce regional over national regulations. Regional akims also use their de facto authority over local regulatory agencies to extract additional funds from foreign investors by putting pressure on the employees of these agencies to revoke a company's operating license, deny them a permit, or cause an "endless delay" in these procedures.[27]

De Jure Economic Decentralization in Kazakhstan

Measuring de jure decentralization is much more straightforward. In this case, the key is to ascertain whether the official locus of authority over the economy, as codified in a country's laws and institutions, is at the national or subnational level. Some relevant indicators for fiscal decentralization in particular include first, whether shared revenue sources between different levels of government are clearly delineated and consistent, and second, whether subnational governments have the legal authority to generate their own revenue and to independently determine budgetary expenditures.

According to these indicators, since 1999 the central leadership in Kazakhstan has enacted several measures that would officially devolve greater fiscal and administrative authority to regional governments. The most recent budgetary law, approved in April 1999 and amended in February and then August 2000, establishes a revenue-sharing system between the central and regional governments in which several taxes are reserved for either the central or regional budget exclusively, and several others are shared equally. (See table 6.6 for details.) A few of these taxes, such as the land tax and environmental protection tax, are local taxes for which regional governments also have the power to determine rates.[28]

27. Author's personal communication with members of the regional administration in Atyrau, names withheld, October 1999.

28. For an overview of Kazakhstan's tax regime, see Weinthal and Jones Luong 2000.

TABLE 6.6. *Revenue Sharing According to Kazakhstan's 1999 Budgetary Law*

Central	Regional	Shared (50/50)
1. VAT (as of 1997)	1. PIT	1. CIT
2. Excess profit tax	2. Social tax	2. Excise tax on alcoholic beverages
3. Excise taxes (except alcoholic beverages)	3. Property tax	
4. Customs duties	4. Land tax	
5. Royalties and bonuses	5. Vehicle tax	
6. Administrative fees		

This same law also includes an explicit assignment of central and subnational expenditure responsibilities and grants regional governments the right to generate their own revenue through borrowing directly from foreign sources, albeit on a limited basis.[29] It was amended again in 2000 to give regional governments even greater budgetary authority by assigning "regional representative bodies as opposed to centrally appointed executives . . . [the] sole authority to approve tax sharing rates and transfers to local governments" (Norris, Martinez-Vasquez, and Norregaard 2000, 18). Finally, the 1999 draft law "On Subventions and Withdrawals," which has not yet been adopted, would make the revenue-sharing system more reliable, at least on paper, by fixing the rate of subventions to and withdrawals from the regions.

This limited form of de jure decentralization is nonetheless significant in that it legitimizes what was already occurring de facto in fiscal and budgetary matters. The new official revenue-sharing rates, for example, codify the effective rates of revenue sharing that resulted from annual negotiations between central and regional leaders before 1999. For example, the CIT, the revenue from which previously went exclusively to the central government on paper but was shared almost evenly with regional government in practice, was changed to a shared (50/50) tax. Similarly, the PIT, the revenues from which previously went exclusively to the central government on paper but in practice went almost exclusively to the regional government, was changed from a central tax to a regional tax.

In fact, this is the underlying (and yet, unexpressed) purpose of de jure decentralization. The central government seems to be responding directly

29. I am grateful to Marcia Occomy for bringing this feature of the new budgetary law to my attention. Previously, this right was limited to the central government.

to demands from akims in the five aforementioned "donor" regions (Almaty city, Atyrau, Mangistau, Karaganda, and Pavlodar) for an increase in official levers of control over the economies within their jurisdiction. The reforms provide the first clue, because they are clearly designed to benefit the wealthier regions and, in particular, those regions with a significant amount of foreign investment.[30] The CIT, for example, is generated disproportionately in the donor regions because they are host to a sizeable number of foreign enterprises. The provision on borrowing is also directed at wealthier regions. It is highly unlikely that any regions other than the five donor regions will in fact attract creditors, since the regional government must provide the collateral on all loans. In fact, only Almaty city, Atyrau Oblast, and Mangistau Oblast have issued government bonds since the budgetary law was amended in August 1999.[31] Perhaps the most obvious way in which the new laws are weighted in favor of wealthier regions and against poorer regions, however, is that setting fixed rates for subventions and withdrawals hurts those regions that cannot meet their budgetary needs through their own revenue sources (and, conversely, benefits those that can).

Even more compelling evidence for the contention that de jure decentralization is a deliberate attempt to officially recognize the demands of the wealthier regions for more autonomy is the fact that it is the leaders of these regions who have been demanding greater autonomy in both the economic and political spheres. For several years the central government has ignored de facto decentralization (and even sanctioned it) as a way of gaining these regions' support for privatization (Jones Luong and Weinthal 2001). However, this has led to increasing conflicts with oil and gas investors, who are not only confused about their legal obligations to the central versus regional governments but also frustrated by the frequent and blatant violations of the original terms of their contracts. The akims in these regions want to exercise greater de jure control over the activities and monetary resources of the foreign investors operating in their oblasts to "clear up" this confusion and "address" these contractual inconsistencies.[32]

30. Not surprisingly, the amount of foreign investment is also highly correlated with resource wealth. Almaty was previously Kazakhstan's capital city and continues to be its financial center. Atyrau and Mangistau border the Caspian Sea and possess the largest existing and potential oil and gas reserves in the country. Karaganda has significant mineral wealth, and Pavlodar hosts the country's largest oil refinery.

31. Author's personal communication with Marcia Occomy, op. cit.

32. Author's personal communication with regional administrations in Atyrau and Mangistau, October 1999; Almaty city, November 1999; and Pavlodar, June 2000.

Alternative Explanations

Existing explanations for decentralization in the developing world are based on two sets of arguments. The first concerns the origin of decentralization; that is, whether it was initiated from above or below. In the former case, central authorities themselves either realize the need to devolve more authority or allocate more administrative functions to local government, or are "encouraged" to do so by international lending organizations, such as the World Bank and the United Nations Development Program (UNDP) (see, e.g., Crook and Manor 1998, 1; Agrawal 1999, 12). In the latter, local governments or nongovernmental organizations (NGOs) put pressure on central governments to increase their formal decision-making authority. The second concerns the incentives for decentralization, which are viewed as either primarily economic or political, and is usually focused on the central government rather than local ones. In other words, if the central government initiates decentralization, has centralized control become infeasible for economic or political reasons. Both sets of arguments suggest several possible explanations for the particular pattern of decentralization in Kazakhstan, none of which is fully satisfactory. I briefly consider each in turn below.

Greater Economic Efficiency or Administrative Effectiveness

A common argument across the decentralization literature is that central governments choose to decentralize as a way of achieving greater economic efficiency or administrative effectiveness. In Kazakhstan, then, this would mean that President Nazarbaev and the central ministries delegated more formal responsibilities to regional leaders since 1998 and either ignored or sanctioned their usurpation of informal authority because they wanted to reduce central expenditures and to make regional governments more effective. There are two serious problems with such an argument. First, it rests on the assumption that there is decentralization by Kazakhstan's central government was a conscious and deliberate act, which is clearly not the case here. The central government in Kazakhstan has been placed thus far in the role of choosing whether and how to respond to regional activities, rather than in the role of initiating them. Second, it implies that the government — at least tacitly — supports decentralization as a viable strategy for achieving greater efficiency. Yet, to date, the Kazakhstani government has shown nothing but resistance to decentralization, both privately and publicly, and in fact has attempted to (re-)centralize instead as a way of streamlining and reinvigorating basic governmental functions. It briefly considered implementing some aspects of formal economic decentralization in 1995–96, but rejected this option for fear of inciting regional rivalries and fueling regional separatism (see, e.g., Spanov 1999, 7; and "Economic Separatism," 1998).

Response to "Pressure" from International Organizations

This argument stems from the fact that decentralization, which began to arouse great interest among international development agencies during the 1980s, has recently become a key component of many international organizations' manifestos. In Kazakhstan, to be sure, the UNDP is deeply interested in promoting decentralization. The UNDP office in Kazakhstan, however, has only very recently instituted a program on decentralization, and has encountered a great deal of resistance from all but one governmental agency at the central level — the Agency for Strategic Planning (ASP). Similarly, the World Bank has made some steps toward decentralization as a precondition for its next loan to Kazakhstan. Yet these are only minor, such as clearly defining the central government's structure and authority to avoid administrative overlap and duplication at the local level, and came *after* the ASP's request that the UNDP assist it in designing a program for decentralization.[33]

Desire to Capture Expected Political Gains

Another key motivation for central leaders to decentralize is the indirect political gains they expect to achieve from this policy. These political gains can take several forms in the literature, including an enhancement of central politicians' ability to: (a) "gain a greater share in available resources" (Agrawal 1999, 36); (b) distribute benefits disproportionately to their supporters (Echeverri-Gent 2000, 3); and (c) advance their long-term "career goals," essentially by promoting their short-term electoral success (Eaton 2000). None, however, accurately depicts the calculations of central leaders in Kazakhstan. First, fiscal and budgetary centralization is widely viewed as the most effective strategy for capturing more resources at the center. Second, central parties and party identification are generally weak, and certainly none penetrate the local level to a sufficient degree to build any real partisan support. The only party that might come close to achieving this is OTAN (Fatherland), which was organized in conjunction with the January 1999 presidential elections and supports strong presidential and central power. Finally, legislators have not yet weighed in on the decentralization debate, and so it is difficult to assess their support. This is not to say that there is no link between decentralization

33. Author's personal communication with Gulnara Kurbanova, op. cit.

and national elections. The "electoral connection" here, however, is with presidential elections, which are widely viewed as an opportunity for the local population to approve or disapprove of their regional leaders, who in their estimation represent the president.[34] This undoubtedly gives the center an incentive to allow and even encourage informal influence at the regional level to the extent that it contributes to the socioeconomic well-being of the oblast.

Response to Local Government and NGO Demands

Those explanations that do treat seriously the possibility of decentralization "from below" (rather than "from above") nonetheless focus their analysis on the center's need to give in to local demands, either from local governments or local NGOs, for greater autonomy. In Kazakhstan, this would mean that the central government has allowed greater autonomy in response to regional leaders' demands. Yet, this also fails to capture the dynamics of economic decentralization in Kazakhstan: regional leaders have not demanded *informal* powers but have simply usurped them, and the overt demands for greater *formal* autonomy at the regional level have not been met despite their increasing frequency since 1996. These demands have centered around transferring financial authority to the regional level by formally empowering mayors and governors to determine taxation privileges for investors in their respective regions and to generate their own revenue from local taxation (see, e.g., *Focus Central Asia* 1998; *Jamestown Monitor* 1998). They have also included demands for local elections.

Corruption

Among experts on Central Asia and the local population, perhaps the most popular explanation for both de facto and de jure decentralization in Kazakhstan is that regional officials deliberately abused their authority to enrich themselves at the expense of the population under their jurisdiction. In other words, what we have witnessed from 1995 to the present is not decentralization at all but widespread elite corruption; the codification of decentralization since 1999 is no more than the legalization of corruption. This explanation has some resonance because regional akims are, after all, appointed officials. If President Nazarbaev objected to their usurpation of power, he could simply remove them from office. The fact that he does not do so suggests his complicity.

34. Author's personal communication with candidates to the national legislature, Majilis, names withheld, September 1999.

This is a pervasive explanation because there is a strong popular belief that regional akims, for example, buy their positions or are given these positions as side payments for lending their political support to Nazarbaev. Yet, it is not a satisfying one for several reasons. First, the patterns of expenditure and investment suggest that regional leaders are not merely pocketing money budgeted for social spending. At least two regions, Atyrau Oblast and Pavlodar Oblast, consistently exceed expenditure targets for education (Department of Finance, Atyrau Oblast; Department of Finance, Pavlodar Oblast). Some akims, as mentioned above, are using their extrabudgetary funds to make infrastructural investments in their respective regions. All the akims interviewed expressed a strong sense of obligation to provide the local population with basic social services, including jobs and housing. This is one of the main reasons they cite for their tendency to discourage tax administrators from forcing state enterprises to pay their taxes. Second, even if the president disapproved of a regional akim's behavior, removing him is not necessarily the solution. Technically, regional akims can be replaced by the president at will. But this is not always a viable strategy because there are a limited number of candidates for the position who will be accepted by the local population and have access to the proper social and economic networks in order to be effective at all. In particular, the president relies on akims to get the vote out at election time and this often requires both gaining the trust and respect of the local population as well as maintaining a positive relationship with large industry. As during the Soviet period, enterprise managers have a significant influence on how their workers cast their votes. In the post-Soviet period, managers can also determine whether local governments continue to receive needed goods and services at reduced rates (see, e.g., Woodruff 1999). Finally, the very act of codifying de facto decentralization defies the notion that Nazarbaev somehow consciously benefited from informal power-sharing between the central and regional governments.

Implications for State-Building

The pattern of increasing subnational autonomy over economic policy making and implementation in Kazakhstan demonstrates that decentralization can be initiated informally from below and highlights the potential pitfalls of decentralized economic authority in the context of a weak central state. Thus, the findings presented herein have much broader implications for understanding the state-building process in the former Soviet Union and beyond.

First, they support the growing contention that we gain greater analytical leverage by treating the state as a set of competing actors and institutions rather than as either a unitary, coherent actor or an integral whole. Second, they reveal the conditions under which this competition can occur between governing elites within the state apparatus itself rather than merely between state actors and social forces. Soviet policies and institutions created multiple institutional actors and empowered them over time while at the same time emasculating social forces. In particular, regional leaders were empowered through their unique access to scarce political and economic resources through which they created powerful patronage networks and strong regional identities (Jones Luong 2002, chap. 3). The result is the virtual absence of any independent power centers outside the state apparatus. Instead, as in Uzbekistan (see Ilkhamov, chap. 5), the regional governments have posed the most serious challenge to the central state's authority both under Soviet rule and after independence. The Soviet system is responsible for creating the very local strongmen that the central government must now either co-opt or defeat in order to establish its control over the periphery.[35]

This paints a picture of the state fighting against itself that contrasts starkly with our existing knowledge of other state-building experiences in several fundamental ways. In most developing countries "local strongmen" are depicted as representing social forces and traditional authority that resist the advancement of the modern state (see, e.g., Migdal 1988; Hagopian 1996). The basis for their strength vis-à-vis the state is their hierarchical position within a well-organized society. Yet, as in other Central Asian states, regional leaders in Kazakhstan derive their relative strength from their position within the state, which has both historical and ideological significance, as well as from their position within society (Jones Luong 2002, chap. 3). In this sense, the Soviet legacy has provided a ready-made structure for regional leaders to pick up the slack in the context of a shrinking state since independence. Indeed, owing to the weakness of social forces, they are also in a unique position to do so.

Moreover, regional leaders have a dual source of power vis-à-vis the central government, which limits the scope and effectiveness of available strategies to curb their power. Central authorities cannot develop, for example, a "triangle of accommodation" whereby representatives of the state ("implementers") and local "strongmen agree to exchange political, economic, and social resources" such that "no single group monopolizes

35. Joel S. Migdal (1998) discusses the perennial state-building problem of co-opting or defeating "local strongmen" in the periphery.

power" (Migdal 1988, 247–48, 252). In addition, because these strongmen are actually part of the state apparatus in Kazakhstan and other former Soviet republics, central leaders cannot publicly renounce their legitimacy in the same way that they can in other developing countries such as Egypt, India, and Mexico (Migdal 1988, 249). As a result, they are denied one of the main weapons against these strongmen. The proliferation of foreign investment in Kazakhstan in particular denies them yet another lever to control renegade regional leaders. Whereas during the Soviet period the central government in Moscow could use its monopoly on scarce resources and resource distribution to rein in regional leaders, they have become much more financially independent since independence. Thus, they are not limited in the same way that Migdal's "local strongmen" are by their dependence on the state for resources (Migdal 1988, 253). Nor is their power being expanded by the growth of the central state, as Francis Hagopian (1996) finds in Brazil, but rather by a shrinking central state.

Finally, if de facto economic decentralization is formalized (that is, becomes de jure decentralization) during this formative period it is highly likely to undermine the potentially positive effects of greater subnational autonomy because it will serve to reinforce the position of these "local strongmen." The state is mired in competition among governing elites for spheres of influence rather than engaged in a struggle for control against social forces to establish a monopoly on the legitimate use of force. Intrastate competition is likely to intensify, moreover, when existing resources become scarce, as in Uzbekistan (Ilkhamov, chap. 5), and when new resources are generated — whether through foreign investment, as in Kazakhstan, or through foreign aid more generally (Weinthal, chap. 8). Thus, the expansion of formal subnational control over the economy with limited vertical (upward and downward) accountability is likely to exacerbate this situation by legitimizing these local strongmen and further weakening the prospects for the development of a central state strong enough to regulate their activities and enforce the rule of law. As in Uzbekistan (see Ilkhamov, chap. 5), authoritarian rule has not produced upward accountability and at the same time has greatly limited downward accountability. The potentially negative consequences for society as a whole, which has heretofore been essentially left out of the turf war between central and regional elites, are immense. It will become increasingly dependent on regional authorities, as they grow increasingly independent from the central government. In this regard, the proposed move toward local elections for regional akims would be a step in the right direction. Despite widespread popular support for doing so, however, the central government seems unwilling to fully endorse this form of political decentralization.[36]

Decentralization in the context of a weak state thus turns the problem of taming the predatory state on its head. The primary constraint on economic growth in Kazakhstan and most other postcommunist states is not the arbitrary power of a strong central state but the central state's inability to function as a stable source of public goods provision. Once economic authority has been fully devolved to subnational actors, how does the central government develop such a capacity? More to the point, under what conditions will an increasingly powerful periphery willingly cede back some of its authority to a central governing body? Successful decentralization requires that both central and regional governments possess sufficient infrastructural capacity. This, in turn, requires a conceptualization of power relations that is sum-sum; for example, while the regional governments gain discretion, the central government gains the capacity to regulate, and both gain predictability. Yet, the predominant conceptualization of power relations in Kazakhstan, as in most Central Asia states, is zero sum (Jones Luong, 2002). The central government thus views an expansion of regional governments' discretion as a relative loss rather than a net gain, and power-sharing as an erosion rather than as an expansion of its infrastructural capacity.

36. According to national polls, 78.8 percent of the Kazakhstani population believes oblast akims should be elected. Support for elections is highly correlated with satisfaction with governance, indicating that the population sees a direct connection between accountability and performance. For details, see McGlinchey 2002, 23. Perhaps reflecting this, the platform of the new political party Democratic Choice, founded in November 2001, advocated greater political decentralization and in particular the election of regional akims. The central authorities launched a series of crackdowns on this party and its leaders in 2002.

4

REDEFINING THE STATE

Internal and External Forces

7. The Civic Realm in Kyrgyzstan

SOVIET ECONOMIC LEGACIES AND ACTIVISTS' EXPECTATIONS

KELLY M. MCMANN

When one asks civic leaders in the Kyrgyz Republic (Kyrgyzstan) to characterize the state's relationship to their charity, union, or club, one nearly always hears "*ne meshaet, ne pomogaet*" or "does not bother, does not help."[1] In other words, the government neither interferes with their activities nor provides support for them. The phrase offers a window into the state's behavior, and it also reveals the expectations of societal actors. Namely, government authorities have the means to hamper civic activities, but instead they should be actively supporting them. In fact, civic leaders in Kyrgyzstan desire assistance from the state, even though financial dependence on the government could potentially compromise their missions. A civic group that relies on state resources may choose to adapt its activities to please government officials, or authorities may threaten to revoke assistance if the organization does not comply with their demands. Although civic leaders in Kyrgyzstan desire government help, they do not fear dependence on the state. Why do these attitudes toward the state

The author is grateful to the editor for the invitation to contribute to this book and to the other authors, the anonymous reviewers, and members of the Harvard University Central Asia Working Group for their suggestions. The author also thanks Henry Hale, Marc Howard, and Debra Javeline for their comments and Amanda Gibson for her editorial suggestions and research assistance. Chris Beattie and Gulnora Aminova provided bibliographical support, and Chris Erenburg assisted with formatting. Their help is much appreciated. An earlier version of this chapter was presented at the 33rd National Convention of the American Association for the Advancement of Slavic Studies on November 17, 2001. This material is based on work supported by the National Science Foundation under Grant No. SBR-9729989. Any opinions, findings, and conclusions or recommendations expressed in this material are those of the author and do not necessarily reflect the views of the National Science Foundation. A fellowship from the Institute for the Study of World Politics and numerous grants from the University of Michigan also supported this investigation.

1. Russian is commonly spoken in Kyrgyzstan among elites and nonelites as a result of Soviet language policies.

exist and how do they influence the political and economic development of Kyrgyzstan? Together with the other findings in this book, answers to these questions will help us unravel state-society relations in Central Asia.

Since the demise of the Soviet Union, scholars have suggested that Central Asian "traditions," including deference to authority, respect for elders, kinship-based allegiances, and Islam, would hinder the emergence of a rich civic realm in post-Soviet Central Asia. More recently, scholars, journalists, and policy makers have claimed that nongovernmental organizations (NGOs) in Kyrgyzstan exist only at the initiative and expense of Western groups. Yet, the evidence in this chapter challenges these generalizations. Civic groups in Kyrgyzstan have developed beyond inactive commercial fronts, government-organized groups, quasi NGOs, and "associations" of one person, and many have formed and function without Western advice and funds. Moreover, neither Central Asian traditions nor Western influences but Soviet economic legacies, coupled with economic underdevelopment, have most immediately defined the civic sphere.

The Soviet legacies of party-state ownership of municipal buildings and the minimal production of consumer goods, such as automobiles, force civic activists in Kyrgyzstan to seek office space, facilities, free utilities, and transportation from local authorities. This phenomenon is not unique to Kyrgyzstan but also exists in other post-Communist countries depending on the degree to which formerly state-controlled resources have changed hands and additional resources have been created. Kyrgyzstan's economic underdevelopment has hampered the creation of alternative resources, enabling the state to have a near monopoly on these goods. As a result, even leaders of political organizations in Kyrgyzstan are likely to desire state aid.

Whereas in recent years scholars have emphasized the weakness of post-Soviet states, this chapter highlights a sphere of society in which the state is strong. Although most post-Soviet governments do not manage public life to the extent that the Communist regime did, states continue to shape the expectations of civic activists because governments possess a relative wealth of resources. This observation suggests that we should employ a paradigm of the "strong-weak state," not simply that of the "weak state."

Civic leaders' desire for state assistance largely bodes well for Kyrgyzstan because cooperation between NGOs and governments has been shown to foster political and economic development in Central Asia and other regions of the world. NGOs can promote development by serving as links between people and their government. In Kyrgyzstan, NGOs have reached out to average citizens for development purposes and many citizens are supportive of their work. However, government officials have generally not been receptive to the advances of civic groups. Moreover, the potential for NGOs to become financially dependent on the state means that an unequal partnership may develop, and civic groups may lose their autonomy and, thus, their comparative advantage. A greater diversification of resources for civic activism would enable NGOs to demonstrate their effectiveness to government officials and the general population, facilitating state-society partnerships and protecting NGO autonomy.

The remainder of the chapter introduces the civic groups that form the basis for these conclusions, asks why civic groups desire assistance from the state, considers the impact of this desire on Kyrgyzstan's political and economic development, and explores the relevance of these findings to our understanding of state-building, civil society, and contemporary Central Asia. Throughout the chapter the reader will find similarities to Marianne Kamp's argument (chap. 1) about the Soviet welfare state shaping contemporary expectations and to Pauline Jones Luong's argument (chap. 6) about the importance of resources being shifted and created since the late Soviet era. Some of the chapter's conclusions differ from Erika Weinthal's (chap. 8) because she focuses on one type of NGO — environmental organizations — instead of a variety of groups.

The Civic Groups: Activities and Expectations

The findings in this chapter are based on 252 interviews I conducted with civic groups as well as societal actors,[2] government officials, and representatives of international organizations in the capital cities and provinces of Kyrgyzstan and Russia. Seventeen civic groups in two *oblasts* (regions or provinces) of Kyrgyzstan serve as the centerpiece of the study. One set of sources of information about these groups is their leaders, members, and publications. For corroborating or disconfirming information about these groups, I rely on my interviews with representatives of local governments and international organizations and on printed materials from these institutions. I also gathered socioeconomic statistics and had conversations with "average" citizens while living for extended periods in each location. All the data were collected in 1997 and 1998.

Whereas some scholars exclude political organizations from civil society, I include political parties in my conceptualization of civil society because their impact is often similar (Stepan 1988, 128–36). Even formally

2. Other societal actors included members of the media and candidates for political office.

"nonpolitical" NGOs like charities can have an influence on politics through lobbying and assistance in provision of government services. Consequently, the distinction between "political society" and "civil society" is an unnecessary one for my purposes. I do, however, note in the text where the attitudes and behaviors of "political" and "nonpolitical" NGO representatives differ.

In the Kyrgyzstani oblasts, Osh in the south and Naryn in the center, I interviewed all political groups and randomly selected an additional set of nonpolitical groups of various types until I reached a total of approximately twelve groups in each province.[3] I found civic groups by using lists from government registration specialists, the records of NGO support centers, telephone directories, and my own knowledge of the NGO sector based on living in each region. For a group to be nongovernmental according to my definition, its leadership could not receive salaries from the local, regional, or national authorities, and its funding could not come from any government budget. I initially conducted interviews with twenty-three civic groups, but excluded six associations from the original sample. Five could not be considered NGOs because they were actually government organizations, and one interview was incomplete,[4] thus reaching a total of seventeen.

The in-depth information about seventeen groups of various types enabled me to understand the expectations and activities of civic associations. The additional data corroborate the activists' accounts and provide a picture of how NGOs interact with the state and the rest of society. The focus on activism in the provinces reveals the "typical" civic realm in developing countries where organizers do not have the benefit of the wealth or international access of the capital city. Finally, by comparing civic life in Kyrgyzstan and Russia, we can explore the impact of Central Asian culture and Soviet legacies on activism.

My approach differs from other studies of Central Asian NGOs and offers advantages in generalizing about state-society relationships in Kyrgyzstan and, more broadly, Central Asia. Most studies focus on only one type of NGO, such as environmental organizations (*Capacity Assessment of the NGO Sector in Kyrgyzstan*, 2001; Ikramova and McConnell 1999; Jones Luong and Weinthal 1999; Watters 1999). This limits conclusions about the civic realm as a whole because findings about one type of group do not nec-

3. The same selection procedure was used for civic groups in Russia, which are examined later in the chapter for comparative purposes.

4. The interview was incomplete because the head of a related organization misrepresented himself as the leader, instead of just a member, of the NGO in question. He was not able to answer all the questions about the NGO.

essarily apply to another category of NGO. Other investigations provide only incomplete or indirect accounts of the civic realm because they do not gather information from local NGOs themselves or they interview only those local NGOs that are involved with foreign groups (Abramson 1999a; Abramson 1999b). For example, a study of foreign democracy assistance in Kyrgyzstan and Uzbekistan draws conclusions about local NGOs but almost exclusively uses information from foreign NGOs and foreign NGO support organizations (Adamson 2000, 38–39). Thus, we receive a picture of the local civic realm seen through the eyes of foreign actors, who interact with only a segment of the local NGO population and who have their own biases. In other cases, we hear only from local NGOs tied to the foreign community — groups unlikely to be representative of the entire civic sphere. Another work describes the broad political, economic, regulatory, informational, and cultural environment within which local NGOs operate, but it relies primarily on newspaper articles (J. Anderson 2000, 91–93). Studies of Central Asian NGOs understandably limit their investigations to NGOs in the five Central Asian countries; however, this reduces their ability to reveal whether characteristics of these NGOs are specific to Central Asia or common in other post-Communist regions.

My use of multiple sources to analyze a variety of civic groups in both Kyrgyzstan and Russia enables me to test the conventional wisdom about civic life in Kyrgyzstan. Moreover, with this approach, I can draw some plausible conclusions about state-society relations in Kyrgyzstan, Central Asia, and the entire post-Communist sphere. A larger sample of civic groups from all of Kyrgyzstan would strengthen my findings,[5] but doing in-depth interviews with both a medium-sized sample of NGOs and a broad range of other actors allows me to reveal how civic groups interact with the state and other societal forces.

Activities

There is the perception among local and foreign scholars, journalists, and policy makers that NGOs in Kyrgyzstan and other post-Communist countries are merely fronts for receiving income from naïve international

5. The study could also benefit from a purely random sample of groups. The current sample includes the universe of political groups in the regions and a random sample of non-political groups, meaning that political groups are overrepresented. This overrepresentation of political groups makes the finding that organizations desire state assistance all the more surprising, as we would expect political groups to be more wary of financial dependence on the state. The sample was designed this way for the purpose of a different project on variations in democracy within countries that have undergone democratic transition (McMann 2000).

donors. For example, based on interviews with NGO support organizations, one study concludes that "the majority of local NGOs are inactive or have been set up as a means to acquire Western grant money (so-called BONGOs [business-oriented NGOS])" (Adamson 2000, 17). Of the groups I interviewed, a couple that had registered only months prior to our conversation were still focused on organizational tasks, such as applying for grants and attending foreign-funded training seminars. But, most organizations, both old and new, were engaged in one of six types of small-scale activities: credit lending, consultations with citizens on various topics, resolution of personal and civil problems, charitable giving, cultural promotion, and electoral work, as described below. Government officials, representatives of foreign NGO support organizations, and local citizens confirmed that these groups performed these functions. Certain resources could facilitate these activities, and, as the next subsection demonstrates, civic leaders desire these resources from the state.

Of the six different types of activities, organizing and running credit groups is one of the most popular among local NGOs: it addresses the mission of reducing poverty, outside grants are available for it, and I found that it is one of the more successful means of economic development in present-day Kyrgyzstan. Using a grant from the United Nations Development Programme (UNDP), a charitable organization in Naryn has provided credit to a group that grows wheat and potatoes and to another group that creates handcrafts. With a grant from the Swiss association Helvetas, the organization also provided capital to eight women, each of whom either runs a cafeteria, operates a farm, or makes handcrafts.[6]

Assistance from local NGOs comes not only in the form of credit but also advice. The leader of a farmers' union in Naryn explained, "All we do is so farmers can go farther . . . stand on their feet."[7] Specifically, the union provides farmers with information about agricultural credit, farming techniques, processing, and marketing. Among its approaches for sharing information, the union holds ten to fifteen seminars each year on such topics as how to grow wheat and potatoes, how to create a business plan, and how and where to get credit.[8] To assist in marketing, the union facilitates contracts between farmers and customers in different countries and disseminates data about price variation across regions of Kyrgyzstan.

6. Author's interview with the president of a charity (Organization 11), 10 July 1997, Naryn Oblast, Kyrgyzstan.

7. Author's interviews with the chair of a union (Organization 13), 7 and 11 July 1997, Naryn Oblast, Kyrgyzstan.

8. Ibid.

Some NGOs play a more active role in people's lives than merely providing credit or advice: they attempt to resolve specific problems for individuals. An organization in Naryn tackles employment and family issues. For example, a woman had not received alimony for nine months from her former husband, who worked as a police detective. The NGO leader talked to the man's boss and arranged for alimony to be paid.[9]

A final form of direct assistance to individuals is material aid, most often in the form of donations of money, food, and clothing. A veterans' organization in Osh focuses much of its energy on charity, providing coal and money to veterans and the families of deceased veterans. The organization makes a special effort to give money to the families of deceased veterans on important dates, such as February 15, which marks the withdrawal of Soviet troops from Afghanistan. The organization's construction brigade also builds and repairs homes for the families of deceased veterans as well as for invalid veterans.[10]

Instead of targeting needy individuals, cultural activities concentrate on an entire group of people, such as representatives of a particular ethnicity. An Uzbek cultural organization in Osh holds events in schools and *mahallas* (neighborhoods or communities) for holidays, such as Nooruz (New Year's), and helped found an Uzbek-language newspaper.[11]

During elections political parties are active, even though they are mostly dormant at other times, particularly outside Bishkek, the national capital. As an editor in Osh explained, "Parties mostly exist on paper and that paper is in Bishkek."[12] Nonetheless, parties in Osh have engaged in electoral activities, such as nominating candidates, distributing party literature to citizens, serving on electoral commissions, and working as *dovernnye litsa* (campaign managers) for contenders.[13]

The activities of these groups are not unusual, as the most popular types of NGOs in these Kyrgyzstani provinces are charitable and social-development organizations and professional associations and unions, as the data in table 7.1 indicate.

9. Although part of a national human rights group, this regional organization focuses only on social services for the time being. Author's interview with the coordinator of a human rights organization (Organization 15), 15 July 1997, Naryn Oblast, Kyrgyzstan.

10. Author's interview with the chair of a veterans' organization (Organization 2), 28 May 1998, Osh Oblast, Kyrgyzstan.

11. Author's interview with the chair of an ethnic organization (Organization 1), 11 May 1998, Osh Oblast, Kyrgyzstan.

12. Author's interview with an editor, 6 May 1998, Osh Oblast, Kyrgyzstan.

13. Author's interviews with the chair of a political party (Organization 7), 30 April 1998 and 4 May 1998, Osh Oblast, Kyrgyzstan. Author's interview with the chair of a political party (Organization 9), 7 May 1998, Osh Oblast, Kyrgyzstan.

TABLE 7.1. *Field of Activity of NGOs in Osh and Naryn*[a]

Activity	Number	Percentage
Charity and social development	97	23
Consumer rights	2	<1
Culture and history	12	3
Ecology	14	3
Education	9	2
Ethnic	12	3
Health and illness	32	7
Politics	16	4
Professions and unions	134	31
Religion and spiritual matters	14	3
Science, art and research	2	<1
Soldiers and veterans	15	3
Sports, games and hobbies	19	4
Women	19	4
Youth	11	3
Unclear	19	4
Total	430	

[a]Data in the table are from 1997 and are taken from state registration lists and lists from NGO-support centers and, in some cases, telephone directories. Organizations often fell under more than one category. However, by using the decision rules below, I counted each organization only once. The sign > should be read "takes priority over."

Sports, games, and hobbies > Youth

Politics > Women

Soldiers and veterans, Youth > Charity

Ecology > Culture and history, Politics

"Religion and spiritual matters" does not include places of worship for Osh and Naryn. The category includes only religious organizations.

The numbers in the table reflect the relative popularity of different fields, but not the exact number of active NGOs. I compiled the data from state registration lists, lists from NGO support centers, and telephone directories, and these sources do not necessarily remove defunct groups from their lists. This highlights the importance of not relying only on numbers and secondhand accounts when analyzing the civic realm in post-Communist countries.

TABLE 7.2. *NGO Expectations of the State*[a]

Expectations	
Requested assistance or expressed desire for assistance	76%
Fear dependence on the state	12%

[a]n = 17.

In sum, the activities of the interviewed groups indicate that, contrary to popular perception, NGOs are not merely inactive fronts for receiving money. In fact, as the evidence in the chapter later shows, foreign assistance is neither ubiquitous nor the leading source of support, as many observers of NGOs have assumed.

Expectations of the State

To facilitate their activities, civic leaders desire assistance from the state, meaning from local and regional administrations and legislatures, with which civic groups tend to have the greatest contact. Nearly all NGO leaders I interviewed hoped for aid from the state, yet almost none feared that assistance from the state would compromise their autonomy. Surprisingly, those few groups that were concerned about losing their independence from the state sought government assistance nonetheless.

"If I do not have the strength, [the oblast government] can help," claimed the head of a charitable organization in Naryn.[14] Her counterparts throughout Naryn Oblast and in Osh Oblast tend to agree. Seventy-six percent of the civic leaders interviewed had requested help from government authorities in the past or expressed a desire for state assistance in the course of our conversations. The director of another charity in Naryn explained, "If I need a car or workers, I ask the oblast administration . . . for simple things."[15]

It is "simple things" that activists desire from the state, most often free office space, meeting places for events, utilities, and transportation. For example, the leader of a charity in Naryn planned to ask the oblast administration for an office if the organization secured a grant to open a computer center.[16] Even some of the groups that consider themselves

14. Author's interview with the chair of a charity (Organization 12), 7 July 1997, Naryn Oblast, Kyrgyzstan.

15. Author's interview with the president of a charity (Organization 11), 10 July 1997, Naryn Oblast, Kyrgyzstan.

16. Author's interview with the chair of a charity (Organization 10), 11 July 1997, Naryn Oblast, Kyrgyzstan.

adversaries of the local government desire help. Overall, 29 percent of the groups view themselves as opponents of local authorities, and more than half of the 29 percent have received state aid or hope for it.

Civic activists do not consider state assistance a threat to their autonomy, even though it could potentially encourage or force them to compromise their missions. Only 12 percent of the NGO leaders mentioned the risk of dependence on the state, but these activists also sought government help. For example, the head of a human rights organization in Osh explained that his group would not ask the oblast administration for money because it did not want to lose its independence and be controlled; however, he added that there was no harm in asking for assistance with office space. Similarly, a leader of a charity in Naryn claimed, "We do not want credit from the government. We would be dependent. . . . No one wants to help NGOs. The governor does not want to help . . . but we don't want help . . . [we] would be a government organization." She later revealed that she planned to ask the oblast government for an office, but she ended by reiterating that the oblast government "will help and will interfere. That is the kind of help we would get from it."[17]

Roots of the Relationship: Soviet Economic Legacies

The fact that most of the interviewed civic leaders desire state assistance and do not fear dependency on the state is surprising from a global perspective. We think of NGOs as entities that are separate from the state and that are interested in protecting their autonomy from the government, in part, by maintaining financial independence. In fact, the attitudes and behaviors of NGOs in similar regions of the world meet these expectations. Particularly in poor, nondemocratic, or quasi-democratic countries, government officials may be jealous of NGOs for the funds they have obtained, skeptical of their ability to implement projects, and even fearful that they may pose security threats because of their ties to foreign institutions and local populations (Bratton 1989, 576–78).[18] Consequently, authorities often react by harassing groups, sabotaging their projects, or co-opting the organizations (Azarya 1988; Bratton 1989, 573, 578–79). NGOs respond by avoiding government officials and maintaining a "low profile." For example, some development NGOs in African countries have

17. Ibid.

18. In developed democracies, governments are one of the standard sources of funding, particularly for NGOs that provide welfare services (Salamon, 1995). The wealth of nonstate funding alternatives and the strength of democratic values and institutions enable NGOs in developed democracies to maintain their autonomy.

chosen not to work with their governments for fear of compromising their missions (Bratton 1989, 581–82).

We could expect that civic leaders in Kyrgyzstan would share similar attitudes and behaviors because Kyrgyzstan is also a poor, quasi-democratic country. Moreover, we could posit that Soviet-era memories of government interference in public life would further deter activists in Kyrgyzstan from seeking state assistance. Why then are NGOs in Kyrgyzstan willing to accept risks to their autonomy and interact with the government, and why do they not fear dependence on the state? Accounts of the civic sphere in Kyrgyzstan suggest that Central Asian traditions and Western organizations have the greatest influence, so below I examine the extent to which these factors can account for activists' attitudes toward the state. Finding neither explanation adequate, I suggest that Soviet economic legacies have had a greater impact on activists' attitudes and, in general, the state-society relationship.

Central Asian Traditions

Observers of Kyrgyzstan, and more broadly Central Asia, suggest that the civic sphere has been shaped, and even hampered, by Central Asian "traditions." The chairman of the Human Rights Society of Uzbekistan, Abdummanob Polat, argues that civil society can only successfully be built in Central Asia if traditions, such as respect for authority, are taken into account (Polat 1999, 153). Writing about Kyrgyzstan, Eugene Huskey notes that "amid the strains of the transition from communism, civic traditions have shown little evidence of taking root in a society dominated by a mixture of family, clan, regional, and ethnic loyalties" (Huskey 1997, 267).

Of the characteristics typically labeled Central Asian traditions—including deference to authority, respect for elders, kin-based allegiances, and Islam—deference to authority could most logically explain civic leaders' desire for government assistance and their tendency not to fear dependence on the state. NGO leaders may see themselves as subordinate to government, needing its guidance and help. If this were true, then we would expect that the attitudes of NGO leaders in Russia would be different from Kyrgyzstani activists' outlooks because in Russia these traditions are nonexistent or considerably weaker. Yet, we find that the desire for government help is just as common among leaders of Russian nonpolitical NGOs as it is among leaders of Kyrgyzstani nonpolitical groups.[19]

19. I interviewed twenty-three NGO representatives in Samara Oblast and Ul'ianovsk Oblast, two provinces along the Volga River in European Russia. The selection process was the same as that for the Kyrgyzstani groups, described earlier.

TABLE 7.3. *NGOs Desiring State Assistance*

NGO types	Russia[a]	Kyrgyzstan[b]
Nonpolitical	75%	73%
Political	21%	83%

[a]n = 4 for nonpolitical and 19 for political.
[b]n = 11 for nonpolitical and 6 for political.

(See table 7.3.) In sum, Central Asian traditions cannot explain the tendency of nonpolitical groups in Kyrgyzstan to desire state assistance.

However, among heads of political groups the desire for state assistance is much weaker in Russia than in Kyrgyzstan. This divergence may be attributable to different cultural traditions in the two countries, or it may be the result of economic necessity. The state monopoly of resources in Kyrgyzstan may force even political groups in Kyrgyzstan to seek government aid.

Foreign Influences

Civic development in Kyrgyzstan, as well as in much of the former Eastern bloc, has been attributed to Western organizations (Adamson 2000; McCrann 2001; Mendelson and Glenn 2000; Sperling 1999). "Local groups proliferated in Poland, Hungary, Russia, Kazakhstan, Uzbekistan, and Kyrgyzstan often around issues that Western donors found important, but rarely around issues that locals confronted on a daily basis," according to Sarah Mendelson and John Glenn in their report on the impact of Western democracy assistance. They continue, "All the reports [in the study] note the quandary of aid recipients who become so dependent on international assistance that they become 'ghettoized,' more responsive to international donors than to the local concerns of the groups they claim to represent" (Mendelson and Glenn 2000, 10, 46). If Western NGO support groups have such an influence on the finances and missions of local NGOs, conceivably these Western actors also shape the attitudes of domestic civic groups.

Yet, were these foreign groups to have had an impact on the attitudes of civic leaders we would expect the opposite effect: local activists would not desire state assistance and would fear dependence on the government. Although many Western groups have encouraged local activists to collaborate with government officials on projects, these foreign organizations advocate an autonomous civil society, which would dissuade civic leaders from seeking state assistance. In fact, contact with Western organizations has not discouraged civic groups from hoping for state assistance, although it may account for the few groups that fear dependence on the government. Let us first consider the role Western organizations play in civic development and then their impact on local activists' attitudes.

Some Western organizations assist directly in NGO development, whereas others promote civic activism indirectly.[20] For example, Counterpart International, a U.S.–based NGO committed to civil society development (*Civil Society Programs* 2001) opened an office in Naryn in January 1997 in order to provide support for local NGOs. Counterpart provides training, holds roundtables for NGO leaders, helps NGOs develop connections, and makes a fax machine, telephone, computer, and copy machine available.[21] Seminar topics at Counterpart have included the definition of an NGO, creating a mission, dealing with citizens and the government, and proposal writing.[22] It has assisted approximately twenty NGOS.[23] In contrast, the Poverty Alleviation Project run by the UNDP in Osh has promoted civic development indirectly by working with ten local NGOs to establish credit programs in agricultural areas. The local NGOs review proposals for credit and monitor the work of the borrowers. By 1998, twenty-five groups of ten to twenty people had received credit to grow crops, raise animals, or sew household goods, for example. A portion of the interest — 6 percent of the 40 percent of the interest on loans in 1997 — goes to NGO development.[24]

Contact between local civic groups and Western organizations such as Counterpart and the UNDP has not been as ubiquitous as some observers of Kyrgyzstan have suggested. Based on evidence primarily from Western NGO support organizations, Adamson argues that "local NGOs receive almost 100 percent of their funds from international actors, and can easily become almost 100 percent donor-driven" (Adamson 2000, 19). Yet, only

20. Counterpart International, TACIS, the UN Development Programme/UN Volunteer Program (UNDP/UNV), and the U.S. Peace Corps have assisted directly in NGO development, whereas the work of organizations such as Mercy Corps, the Office of the United Nations High Commissioner for Refugees (UNHCR), the Soros Foundation, and the UNDP's Poverty Alleviation Project promotes civic activism indirectly.

21. Author's interview with an assistant at Counterpart's NGO Support Center, 18 and 19 June 1997, Naryn Oblast, Kyrgyzstan.

22. Author's interview with the chair of a charity (Organization 12), 7 July 1997, Naryn Oblast, Kyrgyzstan.

23. Author's interview with an assistant at Counterpart's NGO Support Center, 18 and 19 June 1997, Naryn Oblast, Kyrgyzstan.

24. Author's interview with a UNDP Poverty Alleviation Project volunteer, 15 May 1998, Osh Oblast, Kyrgyzstan.

TABLE 7.4. *Expectations of NGOs: Western Influence and Relationship with the State*[a]

Expectations	All	Influence	No Influence
Desire assistance from state	76%	86%	70%
Fear dependence on state	12%	29%	0%

[a]n = 17.

59 percent of the NGOs I interviewed in Kyrgyzstan have had any interaction with Western organizations, and only 41 percent have had any substantial contact. Substantial interaction includes participating in NGO development programs run by Western organizations and, in a few cases, being founded at the initiative of Westerners. Other contact included receiving a grant from a Western group, in some instances through the national branch of the domestic NGO.

Even substantial interaction with Western organizations has had little impact on civic groups' attitudes toward the state. Those local NGOs with which they have had substantial contact are just as likely as other groups to desire state assistance. (See table 7.4.) Western influence cannot account for civic groups' attitudes toward assistance from the state. However, it may explain why a small percentage of groups fear losing their autonomy. Of the local activists who fear losing their autonomy, all have interacted with Western organizations. This suggests that either interaction with Western organizations encourages this fear or that Western organizations draw civic groups that already fear dependence.

Soviet Economic Legacies

A more convincing explanation than the influence of Central Asian traditions or Western organizations is the impact of Soviet economic legacies, which in Kyrgyzstan are exacerbated by economic underdevelopment. The need for resources, such as office space, meeting places, utilities, and transportation, forces civic groups in Kyrgyzstan to seek state assistance and overlook possibilities of dependency. State control of these resources is largely a result of Soviet economic legacies of party-state ownership of buildings and the minimal production of consumer goods. The relatively greater poverty and economic underdevelopment in Kyrgyzstan means that alternative sources of these goods have not developed as they have in some other post-Communist countries, such as Russia. As a result, the state in Kyrgyzstan has a de-facto monopoly on certain goods. The limited

TABLE 7.5. *Sources of Material Support for NGOs*[a]

Support	
Leadership's resources	41%
Foreign funds	41%
Local donors	41%
Membership dues	24%
Business ventures	12%

[a]n = 17.

sources of goods leads even those civic groups that see themselves as state adversaries and those groups that fear dependence on the state to seek government assistance.

From whom do civic groups secure resources, and how have Soviet economic legacies and economic conditions in Kyrgyzstan forced them to seek aid from the government? The NGOs I interviewed are mostly funded through their leaderships' personal resources, foreign grants, and local donations. Less common sources of support are membership dues and profits from business ventures. (See table 7.5.) Organizational leaders tend to use their own money to register their groups, because a nascent NGO has little chance of winning a grant or attracting a sponsor. Yet, even after registration, nearly a third of the NGOs rely on the personal resources of their leadership and most dedicated members, in some cases, because they are still relatively new. For example, without the benefit of external funding, members of one charitable organization pool their own used clothes and extra produce and animal products and distribute them to the needy.[25] The use of personal funds for NGO activities indicates that leaders do not seek assistance from the state and other sources for self-enrichment. Instead, they are interested in fulfilling their groups' missions.

Foreign funds come primarily from Western nonprofit groups, such as Counterpart, the UNDP, the European Union's Technical Assistance for the Commonwealth of Independent States (TACIS), and the Soros Foundation–Kyrgyzstan, part of the nonprofit Soros Foundations Network created by American financier George Soros. Interestingly, despite expectations of funding from Islamic groups in the Middle East, the only non-Western institution with which any of these groups have had contact was

25. Author's interview with the president of a charity (Organization 11), 10 July 1997, Naryn Oblast, Kyrgyzstan.

the Russia Duma. The Duma finances the work of Russian diaspora groups. Funds from the Western organizations are used as seed money for local NGOs and also for specific projects, such as credit-lending programs. For example, a farmers' union in Naryn received a grant from the UNDP and distributed credit to four farms and four livestock operations. The borrowers used the money to buy seed and animals in the spring, and then they sold the products in the fall and winter. They returned the loans to the union in January.[26]

This evidence about civic groups' sources of support challenges the perceptions that "almost 100% of their funds are from international actors" (Adamson 2000, 19) and that they cease operations when they cannot get outside funding (Ikramova 1999, 199). Foreign monies are neither ubiquitous nor particularly easy to obtain, nor are they the only source of funding that groups seek. Nearly 60 percent of the groups interviewed had received no foreign money, and many had little prospects of securing any. As the head of a legal organization in Osh complained, foreign donors are typically represented only in Bishkek, and it is difficult to get information about them and maintain contact. Most of the donor money goes to the capital, he lamented.[27] Moreover, half of the organizations that had received foreign funds also relied on another source of support in order to operate.

In regions such as Osh where private commerce is relatively well developed, some local businesspeople, whether members or simply supporters of an organization, provide donations. Businesspeople may serve as long-term sponsors or merely provide periodic donations. A legal organization in Osh found a businessperson to sponsor its consultations with the public and to provide office equipment when the organization began.[28]

Donations from members in the form of dues have been less successful. The population of Kyrgyzstan is so impoverished that little money can be collected. The national affiliate of one party in Osh decided to establish membership dues of one *som*, but the oblast party decided it was not worth collecting the money.[29]

The least common source of funding among the NGOs in Kyrgyzstan is business activities, perhaps because many of the NGO leaders interviewed

26. Author's interviews with the chair of a union (Organization 13), 7 and 11 July 1997, Naryn Oblast, Kyrgyzstan.

27. Author's interview with the president of a legal organization (Organization 6), 7 May 1998, Osh Oblast, Kyrgyzstan.

28. Author's interview with the head of a legal organization (Organization 4), 27 May 1998, Osh Oblast, Kyrgyzstan.

29. Author's interview with the chair of a political party (Organization 9), 7 May 1998, Osh Oblast, Kyrgyzstan.

wrongly claimed that they could not legally engage in business — a right granted by the law on associations.[30] A veterans' organization in Osh does engage in business by cooperating with a Russian union of Afghanistan veterans. The veterans' organizations sell cotton and produce from Osh in Russia and buy metal in Russia. The Osh NGO acts as a middleman, selling the products to other companies.[31]

Considering that NGO leaders can use their personal resources and obtain financial support from foreign organizations and local businesspeople and, in some cases, through membership dues and business ventures, why do they desire state assistance? The problem is that these sources cannot or will not provide all types of goods that NGOs require. Personal resources are too meager to cover the costs of facilities, utilities, and vehicles, and local donations are too sporadic to pay for office rent and utilities and too limited to purchase a vehicle. Whereas foreign NGO support organizations have the means to pay for these goods, they choose not to cover overhead costs such as office space and utilities.[32] They are also less likely to pay for vehicles, which tend to be needed only periodically.

Whereas these other financial sources are either unable or unwilling to cover the costs of facilities, utilities, and transport, the state owns these goods and can conceivably easily provide them for free. Offices and other buildings that are needed for NGO activities, such as conferences or concerts, tend to be owned by local authorities. Not surprisingly, government office buildings and schools are controlled by local officials, but so are cultural institutions and even some apartment complexes. Soviet communism meant that theaters, *doma kultury* (cultural centers), museums, and sta-

30. National affiliates can also be helpful in providing financial support (Skocpol et al. 2000). However, only six of the seventeen groups had national affiliates and of these only two received monetary assistance from them. Typically parties and human rights groups are part of a larger republican organization. None of the parties received funds from Bishkek. A human rights organization in each province received limited funds from the republican level, for the leader's salary, for example; however, the local groups still had to seek additional funds elsewhere. Author's interview with the coordinator of a human rights organization (Organization 15), 15 July 1997, Naryn Oblast, Kyrgyzstan. Author's interview with the chair of a human rights organization (Organization 5), 29 April 1998, Osh Oblast, Kyrgyzstan.

31. Author's interview with the chair of a veterans' organization (Organization 2), 28 May 1998, Osh Oblast, Kyrgyzstan.

32. As Adamson found in her interviews with representatives of foreign NGO support organizations, "many of the local NGOs find it difficult to cover their operating costs, since most grant money available is to support start-up costs or specific projects" (Adamson, 2000, 20).

diums were all owned by the party-state, and private alternatives did not exist. In the post-Soviet era, some of these properties were privatized, but, through the phenomenon of *nomenklatura* privatization, they often became the personal property of local authorities. Cultural institutions and residences that were the property of state enterprises often became the responsibility of local authorities. In an impoverished country like Kyrgyzstan, particularly outside the capital, new cultural institutions have not been built by private businesspeople. Whereas activists can work out of their homes, the desire for a central location and a larger staff may necessitate finding an office in a government building, a school, or an apartment complex. Besides maintaining control of government property such as schools, local officials own many of the centrally located private apartments. People had the opportunity to purchase their state-owned homes, and now most state housing has been privatized (*Investment Guide for the Kyrgyz Republic* 1998, 59; Pomfret 1995, 114). However, Soviet-era leaders, many of whom are still in power, received the homes in the best locations and these homes have appreciated in value at a greater rate than more typical apartments (Pomfret 1995, 115). As a result, the optimal office space is often owned by local leaders and prohibitively expensive.

The accounts of local activists in Osh and Naryn support this argument about how space limitations result in reliance on local authorities. For example, an activist with an ethnic organization in Osh complained that his group faces a perennial problem of finding places for their meetings. They have had to resort to holding meetings in a theater and at schools, with the permission of local authorities.[33] In another case, the head of a charitable organization in Naryn who wanted to begin a laundry service explained that she planned to ask the *raion akim* (district leader) for a room in her apartment building because the apartments are under his authority.[34]

Like buildings, utilities also tend to be under state control, and the combination of state ownership and limited funds forces NGOs to seek free utilities from local authorities. Utilities tend to be government owned, or at least highly regulated, as in many countries of the world. However, because of the meager funds available to NGOs in Kyrgyzstan, activists are required to negotiate with local authorities for discounts on utilities. Because utilities are an operational expense, they are usually not eligible for foreign funds. As a reoccurring and, in some cases, significant

33. Author's interview with the chair of an ethnic organization (Organization 1), 11 May 1998, Osh Oblast, Kyrgyzstan.

34. Author's interview with the president of a charity (Organization 16), 7 May 1998, Osh Oblast, Kyrgyzstan.

expense utilities are also difficult to cover with personal funds or local donations.

Besides state ownership of property, the Soviet economic legacy of limited consumer-good production has forced civic leaders to seek government assistance. In the Soviet era, it was often impossible for the average citizen to obtain a car or else the purchase required a wait of several years. As a result of this legacy only a small portion of the population of Kyrgyzstan owned cars when the Soviet Union disintegrated. Because of the economic underdevelopment of Kyrgyzstan, few people have been able to buy them in the post-Soviet period, despite citizens' newly acquired access to world markets. In fact, car ownership seems to have declined: from 4.4 percent of the population in 1990 to 3.7 percent of the population in 1997 (*2001 World Development Indicators* 2001). Consequently, when a charitable organization wants to distribute goods to outlying villages, for example, it requests a car from local authorities.[35]

This argument about economic legacies and underdevelopment also helps to explain the divergence we saw earlier between the attitudes of political groups in Kyrgyzstan and Russia. Whereas the nonpolitical NGOs interviewed in each country were just as likely to desire government assistance, political groups in Kyrgyzstan were considerably more likely to want state aid than political groups in Russia. The Soviet economic legacies of party-state ownership of property and limited consumer production exist in both Kyrgyzstan and Russia and thus can account for the attitudes of nonpolitical groups in each country. Although these legacies have structured the state-society relationship in both, Kyrgyzstan's relatively greater poverty and economic underdevelopment has exacerbated them in Kyrgyzstan. (See table 7.6.) Even though nomenklatura privatization has also occurred in Russia, greater economic development has meant that businesspeople have built office buildings and cultural institutions, even outside of Moscow. In general, wealthy businesspeople are considerably more common in Russia than in Kyrgyzstan. Greater personal wealth has meant that more residents of Russia have been able to purchase cars. Old resources have not shifted hands in Russia to a greater extent, but new resources have been created. These economic differences between the countries suggest that groups focused on politics — and thus less willing to be dependent on the state — can find and afford nonstate resources in Russia. By contrast, political groups in Kyrgyzstan are forced to rely on local authorities. The comparison highlights the important role of shifting

35. For most of the NGOs' activities a bus is not necessary and a horse would be ineffective. Author's interview with the president of a charity (Organization 11), 10 July 1997, Naryn Oblast, Kyrgyzstan.

TABLE 7.6. *Wealth Indicators for Russia and Kyrgyzstan*

	Russia	Kyrgyzstan[a]
Passenger cars[b] (percentage of population owning, 1997)	12	3
Telephone lines[c] (percentage of population owning, 1997)	19	8
Radios[d] (percentage of population owning, 1997)	42	11
Poverty[e] (percentage of population, 1993–1999)	31	51
Ratio of costs to income[f] (percentage, 1996)	45	100

[a]Comparable data for the two countries are not available in all cases, so I provide a variety of data, the aggregate of which suggests that, on average, people in Kyrgyzstan are poorer than people in Russia.

[b]Calculated and rounded from the 2001 *World Development Indicators*.

[c]A line connecting a customer's phone to the public telephone network. Data originally from the International Telecommunication Union. Calculated and rounded from the 2001 *World Development Indicators*.

[d]A radio receiver used to receive broadcasts by the general public. Calculated and rounded from the 2001 *World Development Indicators*.

[e]The percentage of the population living below the poverty line deemed appropriate for the country by its authorities. Rounded from the 2001 *World Development Indicators*.

[f]The difference between the countries is exaggerated because average monetary income was used for Russia and average salary was used for Kyrgyzstan. Comparable figures are not available (*Average Nominal Salary (Soms)* 2001; McFaul and Petrov 1997; *Minimal Consumer Budget (Soms)* 2001).

and alternative resources in post-Communist politics, as does Pauline Jones Luong in chapter 6.

The accounts of the activists in Kyrgyzstan provide direct evidence about why they seek state assistance, and the statistics on car ownership offer some indirect evidence. However, it would also be useful to have general statistics concerning the availability of office space and facilities not under control of the local authorities. Unfortunately, privatization statistics for specific types of buildings are scant, and when available, they do not indicate whether a piece of property has merely come under the personal control of a local authority. Likewise, statistics on newly built facilities and their true ownership are difficult to obtain. Nonetheless, from living and working in Kyrgyzstan and Russia, I found that newly constructed buildings exist in the Russian provinces and are almost absent in the Kyrgyzstani regions, meaning that NGO leaders in Russia have more opportunities for financial independence from local authorities.

Soviet economic legacies, coupled with economic development, offer a more complete explanation for civic leaders' desire for state aid and tendency not to fear dependence upon it. However, the cultural, political, and international environments also have an impact on civic attitudes. Central Asian culture may, in fact, make it easier for political groups to seek aid from the government in Kyrgyzstan than in Russia. And, in both countries Soviet cultural habits may encourage activists to seek cooperation with the state — just as Marianne Kamp (chap. 1) found that Soviet welfare culture encourages citizens to expect certain benefits from the Uzbekistani state today. Faced with a new environment, such as one of greater political freedoms, activists often resort to tried-and-true repertoires (Skocpol, Ganz, and Munson 2000; Tarrow 1994). As products of the Soviet system, NGO leaders have turned to the inheritor of the party-state, which used to provide funds to "public" groups. Soviet public groups, under party control, relied on funds from the state budget and on membership stamps the party required citizens to purchase (Kasybekov 1999, 71).[36] Although this Soviet cultural pattern likely reinforces the economic necessity of seeking state assistance, it offers a weaker explanation. Groups that view themselves as adversaries of the state and those that fear dependence on the government would not likely desire state aid were there not a critical economic need.

The general political environment in Kyrgyzstan, as well as in Russia, has made it possible for NGOs to hope for state aid. Governments that have a multiparty system, a positive attitude toward foreign development agencies, and weak administrative capacity are most likely to support the work of civic groups, or, at least, not harass them (Bratton 1989, 575). This description is apt for the national governments of Kyrgyzstan and Russia, particularly during much of the 1990s. The fact that only national opposition groups and local political NGOs that have limited economic autonomy from authorities have been severely harassed likely reduces civic leaders' fears of compromising their missions by seeking state assistance (McMann 2000, 2002). Yet, while the political environment may alleviate

36. Interestingly, groups that developed in the independence period are as likely to seek state assistance as those that formed in the Soviet era. The percentages desiring state assistance are 77 percent and 75 percent, respectively.

qualms about dependency, it does not explain why leaders seek state aid rather than other forms of funding. For this we must examine the impact of Soviet economic legacies and levels of development.

The international environment, particularly the fact that Western NGO support organizations rarely cover operating costs, has also shaped civic attitudes and behaviors in Kyrgyzstan and Russia. However, only about half of local NGOs have contact with Western groups, so donor conditions cannot account for the attitudes of all the groups.

In sum, Soviet economic legacies and economic underdevelopment offer the most convincing explanation of why civic leaders in Kyrgyzstan desire state assistance and do not fear dependence on the state. The legacies of party-state ownership and minimal production of consumer goods have given the government access to certain goods valuable to NGO leaders. The relative impoverishment of the population has meant that alternative means to purchase or use these goods have not emerged, as they have in more economically developed post-Communist countries. Consequently, government authorities in Kyrgyzstan have a near monopoly of resources such as facilities, utilities, and transportation.

The Impact of the Relationship on Development: Promising, but Unrealized

Kyrgyzstani civic leaders' interest in state assistance augurs well for the country because state-society collaboration is essential for political and economic development. Yet, in order for these attitudes to be productive, the government must respond favorably, agreeing to work with NGOs. Moreover, the NGOs must use the resources they acquire to actually help the population. After a review of the prevailing wisdom about NGOs and states in development, I explore activists' actual relations with government officials and average citizens in Kyrgyzstan.

NGOs and Development

Development theorists and practitioners have found that state-society collaboration is essential to a country's economic and political development (Ostrom 1997, 107–8; Sanyal 1994). Government and civic groups are each seen as having unique comparative advantages that, when combined, provide "complementarity" (Evans 1997a; Sanyal 1994). This complementarity facilitates the "coproduction" of services for the population (Ostrom 1997). To the partnership a government can offer a legal regime, legitimacy, long-term funding, market creation, and the ability to increase the scale of projects. NGOs can provide links to society, local knowledge, particular skills, and volunteers (Evans 1995; Evans 1997a, 182–83; Fox 1997; Ostrom 1997, 102, 108; Putnam, Leonardi, and Nanetti 1993; Sanyal 1994, 41, 44–47). In terms of political development, scholars emphasize that state-society interactions are not zero sum (Evans 1997b; Flower and Leonard 1996; Migdal, Kohli, and Shue 1994), but "mutually transforming" (Migdal, Kohli, and Shue 1994; Schmitter 1981). Civic groups must have ties to the government so that they can act as watchdogs against state wrongdoings, as counterweights to government, and as mediators between state and society (Buchowski 1996, 82; Cohen and Arato 1992, x, 31; Sanyal 1994, 40–41). In other words, there needs to be "embeddedness" and "connectedness" between the state and societal actors (Bermeo 2000, 244–45; Evans 1995; Evans 1997a, 180, 184, 187).

In advocating state-society interaction, neither the theorists nor the practitioners suggest that civic groups should be incorporated into the state. Instead, civic actors and government institutions should be autonomous so that each can maintain its comparative advantage. This is a particularly important reminder for NGOs in developing, nondemocratic or quasi-democratic countries where financial insecurity or state harassment can undermine groups' missions and activities (Azarya 1988, 5). In a democracy civic groups play the seemingly contradictory role of pressuring states and helping them govern (Buchowski 1996, 82). And, "the institutional arrangement most conducive to democratic development seems to be a combination of civil society's autonomy and its connectedness to other domains of the polity, such as . . . the state . . ." (Kubik 2000, 183).

In addition to theorists and activists in other regions of the world, members of the foreign NGO community in Kyrgyzstan have called for more cooperation between civic groups and the state. These foreign representatives have noted that NGOs in Kyrgyzstan often resolve problems more quickly and less expensively than the government and that civic groups need to engage government officials in order to be more effective (*Capacity Assessment of the NGO Sector in Kyrgyzstan* 2001; Kasybekov 1999, 72; Watters 1999, 100). To what extent has the state-NGO relationship in Kyrgyzstan developed to the point of collaboration?

The Relationship between Civic Leaders and the State in Kyrgyzstan

In saying that the state "does not bother, does not help," the civic groups provide a fairly accurate depiction of state interaction with NGOs on paper and in practice. However, there are two caveats. In some cases, local-government leaders have interfered with the work of civic groups, but only those engaged in political activities. Local authorities have also provided assistance to nearly half of the groups interviewed. Beyond these exchanges civic groups contact government officials to resolve legal problems, and leaders and members of political NGOs interact with authorities during elections.

The state-society relationship outlined by law fell short of civic leaders' expectations because it required little state support. The Kyrgyzstani law "On Public Associations" adopted February 1, 1991, when the country was still a union republic in the Soviet Union, continued to regulate NGOs through most of the 1990s, including the period when I conducted my fieldwork.[37] Whereas in other countries governments offer NGOs grants and generous tax privileges, civic groups in Kyrgyzstan have received few benefits. Although the law gave NGOs a multitude of rights, including the ability to introduce drafts of national legislation, participate in elections, and engage in business to achieve group goals, it provided only one tax privilege — a waiver of income tax on membership dues and donations (*On Social Associations*, 2001). The tax code established a few other privileges, such as an exemption on the Value Added Tax (VAT) (*Capacity Assessment of the NGO Sector in Kyrgyzstan* 2001; Horton and Kazakina 1999, 52). Instead of providing benefits to NGOs, the legal regime has burdened them with numerous obligations and risks, including mandatory registration with the state, potential monitoring by government agencies, and the threat of suspension, dissolution, and even loss of property for acting outside their charters or violating regulations (Horton and Kazakina 1999, 43, 45; *On Social Associations* 2001).

In practice, formal, legal contact with the state is rare beyond registration. Registration itself requires considerable paperwork, a significant sum of money, and patience, but overall it is relatively simple and fair, according to NGO leaders I interviewed and to an analysis by the director of Counterpart International in Kyrgyzstan (Cooper 1999, 215). Refusals have been rare and have tended to follow the letter of the law. For example, all human rights organizations, with the exception of a Uighur organization that aimed to create a Uighur state in northwestern China in violation of Kyrgyzstani law, are believed to have been able to register, and nonpolitical groups have not encountered problems (Horton

37. According to Chapter 1, Article 1, associations include "political parties, popular movements, trade unions, women's and veterans' organizations, organizations of the disabled, youth and children's organizations, scientific, technical, cultural awareness, sport and other voluntary societies, creative unions, fraternities, foundations, associations, and other citizen groups" but do not include cooperatives, organizations with the objective of making a profit, religious organizations, and others.

and Kazakina 1999, 44). None of the groups I interviewed described any experience with government audits, there were no accounts of the government suspending or dissolving groups, and no activists recounted profiting from privileges in the tax code. The tax code benefits tend to be granted on an "ad hoc basis" and foreign NGOs have been more successful in obtaining them. Local NGOs should receive an exemption on the Value Added Tax (VAT), but merchants are wary of granting them and civic leaders do not seek a refund for fear of invoking an audit (Horton and Kazakina 1999, 52).

Although the formal relationship is weak, informal contact between civic activists and government officials is frequent — rarely in the form of harassment and more often in the form of state assistance or unintimidating interaction. For political groups, though, as opposed to civic ones, government harassment is common. When political activists have little opportunity to earn income independent of local authorities, local officials have taken advantage of this situation and punished leaders and members of political groups through job loss, threats of job loss, and sanctions on their businesses (McMann 2002; McMann 2000). This form of state interference is not reflected in the overall sentiments of civic leaders, because the number of political groups is relatively small.[38] Moreover, activists in some regions, such as Osh, have more opportunities to earn a living independent of local officials, so sanctions on their political activities are less effective and thus less likely to be employed by local authorities (McMann 2000).

Cordial relations are more common between civic leaders and government officials. Approximately 44 percent of the groups have received aid from local authorities. In most cases, assistance is in the form of free, long-term office space and utilities. A few groups received a facility free of charge for an event or the use of a car or bus for an activity. NGOs have also interacted with government officials in order to solve problems for people who have requested their assistance and to take part in the electoral process. For example, to help an orphaned girl who ran away from her legal guardian, the leader of a human rights organization in Naryn contacted the chair of the oblast *kenesh* (legislature), the oblast akim, and officials in the raion administration. Political organizations and groups with electoral activities as part of their charters nominate candidates for local and national offices, serve on electoral commissions, and maintain connections with successful nominees — all activities that involve inter-

38. The members of the one political group in Naryn abandoned the organization for fear of sanctions on their livelihoods, and in Osh only six political groups exist.

action with the government.[39] Although the leader of a veterans' organization in Osh claimed, "Politics is not our business. Politics created the war in Afghanistan and we died," his organization nominated a member for the Zhogorku Kenesh (national parliament), campaigned for him, and contentedly watched him win a seat. The group also nominated and campaigned for five candidates to the city kenesh, all of whom won. The organization plans to nominate candidates for all levels of government in the future "because this is not pure politics, but simply for the resolution of social questions."[40] Other, less frequent contact between activists and officials includes NGOs' lobbying for policies, periodic formal meetings with government officials, and assistance to the government, by distributing state charitable goods, for example.

While Kyrgyzstani NGOs are predisposed to involvement with the state and would like to interact more with government officials, they have not crafted and implemented projects with the authorities, as the development theorists advise. The civic groups are incorporated into the state (Azarya 1988), in the sense that they are engaged with it and are dependent on certain resources from local authorities. Yet, they exhibit low levels of "coproduction," "connectedness," and "embeddedness." The paucity of partnerships results from a lack of enthusiasm on the part of the government.

Local authorities acknowledge that NGOs are beginning to have an effect on life in the oblasts and are also playing a role in government by providing advice to officials or helping with implementation.[41] Nonetheless, government officials have not sought out civic groups because of a lack of understanding of the civic sphere, fear of criticism, and weak capacity. Some oblast officials think that *nepravitel'stvennaia organizatsiia* (nongovernmental organization) means "antigovernment organization," a UNDP official in Naryn explained.[42] The head of a legal organization in Osh said that when the group's lawyers visit the prosecutor's office they

39. Author's interview with the chair of a political party (Organization 9), 7 May 1998, Osh Oblast, Kyrgyzstan. Author's interviews with the chair of a political party (Organization 7), 30 April and 4 May 1998, Osh Oblast, Kyrgyzstan. Author's interview with the chair of a political party (Organization 8), 7 May 1998, Osh Oblast, Kyrgyzstan.

40. Author's interview with the chair of a veterans' organization (Organization 2), 28 May 1997, Naryn Oblast, Kyrgyzstan.

41. Author's interview with Oblast Official 1, 19 May 1998, Osh Oblast, Kyrgyzstan. Author's interview with Oblast Official 2, 26 May 1998, Osh Oblast, Kyrgyzstan. Author's interview with Oblast Official 3, 27 May 1998, Osh Oblast, Kyrgyzstan.

42. Author's interview with Adil Duroglu, a community participation specialist with the UNDP, 20 July 1997, Naryn Oblast, Kyrgyzstan.

are greeted with the question "Why did you come? You were not called."[43] Local authorities also try to avoid criticism. "The oblast government likes to be applauded; it does not like it when we pose questions to it. The government created [a similar organization] in order to be applauded," the head of an Uzbek organization in Osh explained.[44] An additional problem with the government is lack of capacity. Government institutions may simply be too overwhelmed to focus on establishing ties to the civic community.

The Relationship between Civic Leaders and Society in Kyrgyzstan

In order for NGOs to further contribute to Kyrgyzstan's economic and political development they must not only seek support from the state but interact with average citizens, serving as links between state and society. NGOs in Kyrgyzstan have contact with their own members and also engage a larger number of citizens through their involvement in the community. Although their impact on society may not be broad, it is qualitatively significant, according to their own accounts and those of government officials, foreign representatives, and average citizens.

A common perception among observers of Kyrgyzstan and other Central Asian countries is that many NGOs have only one member. "Throughout the region it is also generally the case that many of the grandly titled committees, organisations and confederations are little more than a room in an apartment manned by an enthusiastic political entrepreneur," according to one work (Anderson 1997, 93). Yet, in gathering evidence about a variety of groups in Kyrgyzstan, I found no examples of NGOs with only one member. Instead, membership in nonpolitical associations ranged from eleven members in a three-month-old charitable organization in Naryn — all of whom are teachers at one school — to five hundred members of another charitable group in Naryn, many of whom deserted the state Committee for Women because "they did not want to work in the old way."[45] Political parties in Osh each tended to have around three thousand members.[46]

43. Author's interview with the head of a legal organization (Organization 4), 27 May 1998, Osh Oblast, Kyrgyzstan.

44. Author's interview with the chair of an ethnic organization (Organization 1), 11 May 1998, Osh Oblast, Kyrgyzstan.

45. Author's interview with the president of a charity (Organization 11), 10 July 1997, Naryn Oblast, Kyrgyzstan.

46. NGO leaders use different definitions of membership. Political parties enumerate members based on who currently holds a membership card, whereas human rights

In the larger community, civic groups provide welfare, inform citizens, and participate in political processes. The depth of interaction with citizens varies from long-term, in-depth contact through credit programs, to short-term contact by hosting a concert, to momentary contact while passing out campaign literature. Looking just at the nine groups that have successfully provided credit or assisted people in resolving problems, we can estimate that approximately six hundred people have been helped. This estimate is hampered by the organizations' own record keeping and the difficulty of determining how many people have received assistance multiple times or from multiple organizations. Nonetheless, in these cases, NGOs did provide concrete assistance to average citizens, thus promoting economic development. The impact is not wide, considering that 1.7 million people live in these regions.[47] But, when we take into account that NGOs also provide charitable donations, offer consultations and assistance with problems, host cultural events, and engage society in other short-term, less direct ways, we can conclude that NGOs have a meaningful, but perhaps not broad, role in society.

The greatest hindrance to NGOs' promotion of economic and political development results not from their relationship with citizens but from their relationship to the state. Although civic groups interact with the state, they have not collaborated with officials on projects, which, according to theorists and foreign activists in Kyrgyzstan, would benefit development. Civic groups desire greater cooperation with the state, but government officials have not been receptive. Moreover, NGOs' lack of resources and the state monopoly on goods reduces NGO autonomy, thus threatening their comparative advantage.

To increase government receptivity and financial independence, NGOs could recruit more members, but this is an unlikely solution. Larger memberships may make officials more interested in NGOs, and membership

---

organizations and nonpolitical groups use varied definitions of membership. An association of doctors in Naryn counts those who have attended a couple meetings as members, and a charitable group in the region considers people who participate in writing grant proposals members. Author's interviews with the chair of a political party (Organization 7), 30 April 1998, Osh Oblast, Kyrgyzstan. Author's interview with the chair of a political party (Organization 8), 7 May 1998, Osh Oblast, Kyrgyzstan. Author's interview with the chair of a political party (Organization 9), 7 May 1998, Osh Oblast, Kyrgyzstan. Author's interview with the president of a charity (Organization 14), 13 July 1997, Naryn Oblast, Kyrgyzstan. Author's interview with the chair of a charity (Organization 10), 11 July 1997, Naryn Oblast, Kyrgyzstan.

47. Population data are from the National Statistics Committee and are for the beginning of 1997. Osh Oblast has 1,472,100 people and Naryn Oblast has 263,100 people.

dues could reduce the groups' dependence on the state. However, public attitudes and poverty bode poorly for this approach,[48] and expanding membership is not a priority of civic groups. Only one of the seventeen groups mentioned recruitment as one of its activities.[49] Instead, NGOs are focused on finding business sponsors and winning foreign grants. Continuing to rely on a diversity of financial sources, particularly nonstate sources, will help NGOs guard their autonomy from the state. To increase their influence with officials, parties concentrate on nominating and campaigning for candidates,[50] and nonpolitical organizations emphasize assistance to more people in the community.[51] NGO leaders tend to view their work with the general population as helping the government, and they suggest that officials will someday show their gratitude. "If we help people, [government officials] will listen to us, and deputies will come to us."[52]

The State and Civil Society in Kyrgyzstan and Elsewhere

One of the most common claims about post-Soviet states is that they are weak, meaning that they lack the capacity to achieve their goals (Holmes 1997; Linz and Stepan 1996; Sperling 2000; Stavrakis 1993; Volkov 1999). While this statement applies to Kyrgyzstan, it is clear that the Kyrgyzstani state also exhibits strength. In particular, through its monopoly of resources, the state continues to shape the civic sphere, specifically the expectations of civic leaders. This monopoly is a legacy of the Soviet era and a result of the country's underdevelopment. Across the globe, democratic and nondemocratic governments shape NGOs by restructuring or

48. Public attitudes toward NGOs are mixed. In my interviews and conversations with nonactivists, I found both suspicion of NGOs' activities and praise for their work. Some people are skeptical of NGOs because they believe that the NGO leaders are interested in personal gain, not in helping people. Moreover, some citizens are uncomfortable with NGOs because their members do new and unusual things, including traveling abroad for training seminars and receiving foreign grants. On the other hand, a survey of 1,494 adults throughout Kyrgyzstan in 1996 found that 52 percent of people believe NGOs are necessary and 42 percent would give their "time to work for a non-government organization without receiving any pay" (Olds, 1997, pp. iii, 42–44).

49. Author's interviews with the chair of a political party (Organization 7), 30 April 1998 and 4 May 1998, Osh Oblast, Kyrgyzstan.

50. Ibid.

51. Author's interview with the president of a charity (Organization 11), 10 July 1997, Naryn Oblast, Kyrgyzstan.

52. Author's interview with the chair of a charity (Organization 10), 11 July 1997, Naryn Oblast, Kyrgyzstan.

incorporating groups, creating legal regimes, providing or denying political opportunities, and serving as institutional models (Anderson 1996; Azarya 1988; Bermeo 2000, 243; Fish 1995; Fox 1997; Levy 1999; Migdal 1994; Ostrom 1997, 98; Putnam, Leonardi, and Nanetti 1993; Schmitter 1981; Seligman 1992, 7; Skocpol, 1992; Skocpol and Fiorina 1999; Skocpol, Ganz, and Munson 2000; Stepan 1978; Tarrow 1994). Whereas the Soviet government created and directed "public" groups, post-Communist governments are more likely to affect the civic sphere through their continued control of resources. Assuming that post-Communist governments exhibit strengths in other spheres as well, it may be more useful for scholars to use a paradigm of the "strong-weak state" rather than simply the "weak state."

The government monopoly of resources and provision of these resources to civic groups raises the question: Is state assistance to NGOs detrimental to civil society? On the one hand, state assistance is advantageous when it promotes complementarity. For example, the state may provide needed office space to an organization, and an NGO may provide expertise about local community problems to the government, thus creating a mutually beneficial exchange. On the other hand, state assistance is harmful when it undermines the autonomy and thus the comparative advantage of civic groups. Aid that represents a large portion of a group's total support and that comes from a government hostile to pluralism and able to harass is most damaging to NGOs' autonomy. Currently, these detrimental conditions are minimized in Kyrgyzstan. Civic groups rely on resources from multiple sources, although some are most easily obtained from the state. More importantly, the national government and many regional leaders have been supportive of, or at least not interfered with, the development of nonpolitical civic groups. Moreover, government officials often lack the capacity to harass NGOs, particularly when these groups have economic autonomy (McMann 2000).

The fact that state assistance or state behavior, in general, has not harmed the civic sphere in Kyrgyzstan is no guarantee that it will not in the future. Since the data for this chapter were collected in 1997 and 1998, an improved law on civic groups has passed, but the government of Kyrgyzstan has become increasingly hostile to pluralism. The new law on civic groups does not mention risks, such as potential monitoring by government agencies (The Law of the Kyrgyz Republic on Non-Commercial Organizations 1999). However, an attack on pluralism began in 1994 when the government started to criminally prosecute journalists. Through the end of the decade and into the new century this turn away from pluralism has intensified with a further increase in presidential power, laws curbing the right to protest, and criminal investigations of members of parliament. There is little evidence that these events have hindered the ability of nonpolitical civic groups to operate. Nonetheless, the de-facto retreat from pluralism does not bode well. The U.S. "campaign against terrorism," beginning in the fall of 2001, and the accompanying increase in aid to Central Asian military allies have led some journalists and scholars to speculate that U.S. involvement in the region will promote democracy. However, there is no guarantee that the greater U.S. attention to the region will be maintained or that aid will flow to NGOs or in any way bolster the civic sphere.

Ironically, observers of Kyrgyzstan tend to exaggerate the negative influence of the state on civic groups while overlooking the very real impact of state control of resources on NGOs. Western academics and government officials often will casually remark that NGOs in Kyrgyzstan are essentially state organs with a civic veneer, and foreign scholars and activists have documented the presence of government-organized NGOs (GONGOs) and quasi NGOs in Kyrgyzstan and other post-Communist countries (Adamson 2000; Kasybekov 1999, 72; Polat 1999; Sampson 1996, 128; Watters 1999, 93). Yet, I found that most of the organizations calling themselves NGOs do not receive money for their leaders' salaries or their operating expenses from government budgets, and these groups were created by private individuals and groups of citizens, not government authorities. Moreover, the low degree of embeddedness, or informal links between activists and officials, challenges the assumptions about GONGOs and quasi NGOs.

In addition to the prevailing wisdom about GONGOs and quasi NGOs, I also challenge other conclusions about the civic sphere in Kyrgyzstan and other Central Asian countries. First, Western influence has not had the greatest impact on civic groups in Kyrgyzstan: activists have not adopted Western positions on all issues, and they are not enriching themselves with foreign funds. Foreign money is neither ubiquitous nor the only source of NGO funding. Moreover, the foreign money that has reached Kyrgyzstan tends to be from Western development organizations, not from "Eastern" Islamic groups, as some observers expected. Second, Central Asian traditions do not drive the civic sphere, as is indicated by the fact that Kyrgyzstani and Russian activists share some attitudes. Also, the weakness of connections between activists and officials suggests that claims about the influence of clans and patronage on the civic sphere are exaggerated. Third, Kyrgyzstani NGOs are not inactive but are running credit programs, resolving citizens' problems, providing charity, and holding cultural events, among other activities. Fourth, civic groups in Kyrgyzstan are not "couch organizations" with one to three members but, in some cases, even have thousands of members. Finally, civic groups do have ties to average citizens through their charitable work, cultural events, and electoral activities.

Most likely, my findings challenge the conclusions and assumptions made by others because I collected data from multiple sources about a wide variety of civic groups. Not surprisingly, those studies that rely on evidence from foreign NGO support organizations, select groups based on the knowledge of these foreign institutions, or concentrate on groups located in the capital cities are likely to overestimate the influence of foreigners. Claims about the influence of Central Asian traditions often lack empirical evidence to support them and thus can easily be challenged with data from the field. Generalizations about the inactivity, small memberships, and elite character of civic groups have been based either on reports from foreign NGO support organizations, which work with only a limited sector of local groups and which have their own concerns, or data about a specific type of group such as environmental organizations. It is likely that specific types of groups exhibit unique features that do not characterize the civic realm as a whole. For example, environmental groups may have greater access to foreign resources, which, in turn, shapes their activities, memberships, and community outreach, as Erika Weinthal demonstrates in chapter 8.

Although my approach to exploring the civic realm in Central Asia helps fill a void left by other studies, it is also important to consider how generalizable my findings are. A number of aspects of my approach inspire confidence in the generalizability of the findings. First, the data are from multiple regions of the country, instead of just the capital, which is not representative of the civic realm. The two regions, Osh and Naryn, were perhaps the most likely of all the provinces to have confirmed the prevailing wisdom that NGOs in Kyrgyzstan are largely inactive commercial fronts, GONGOs, quasi NGOs, and single-person associations that have formed and function only as a result of Western aid and initiative. Naryn is viewed as backward and Osh as traditional by both residents of Kyrgyzstan and outsiders, and foreign NGO support centers exist in each province. Yet, these two "most difficult" cases challenged the conventional thinking. Second, my selection of all the political groups and a random sample of nonpolitical groups makes it easier to generalize the results. Whereas these two factors suggest that the findings represent the civic realm in Kyrgyzstan, the comparison with Russia helps us generalize outside the borders of Kyrgyzstan.

Both Kyrgyzstan and Russia have more supportive environments for

NGOs than the Central Asian states of Uzbekistan and Turkmenistan. Thus, although state control of resources shapes the civic realm in Kyrgyzstan and Russia, we would expect that both state control of resources and state harassment would influence the civic sphere in these other Central Asian states. The civic spheres in Tajikistan and Kazakhstan more closely resemble that in Kyrgyzstan. Civil war brought extreme poverty and weakened government capacity to Tajikistan. Whereas national leaders in Kyrgyzstan chose to create a more permissible NGO environment, officials in Tajikistan were too busy fighting the war to try to control it. In Kazakhstan national leaders have permitted nonpolitical groups to operate more or less freely, while they have increasingly harassed political NGOs. All the post-Communist countries share the economic legacies that have left states in control of resources. The level of economic development and the political environment for NGOs will interact with these legacies to shape the civic spheres, making them resemble the Kyrgyzstani, Russian, or Uzbekistani and Turkmenistani situations.

Outside the former Eastern bloc we would not expect to find similar state monopolies of resources as we see in Kyrgyzstan. Whereas governments in other regions of the world also control resources, only in Communist countries was there a state monopoly of resources. In economically developed, post-Communist countries, where additional resources have been created, this legacy has begun to erode. This suggests that the civic realm in these countries, such as Russia, is beginning to more closely resemble that of countries outside of the former Eastern bloc. By contrast, the civic realm in economically underdeveloped post-Communist countries such as Kyrgyzstan is still distinguished from the civic sphere in other regions of the world by the state's monopoly on resources.

Despite the continuing post-Communist character of Kyrgyzstan's civic realm and the dire assumptions about civic life in the country, it is clear that civic groups' attention to the state, in addition to their involvement in the community, bodes well for political and economic development. However, civic organizations must convince the government of the importance of cooperation and maintain their independence from the state in order to use and preserve their comparative advantage as societal actors.

8. Beyond the State

TRANSNATIONAL ACTORS, NGOS, AND ENVIRONMENTAL PROTECTION IN CENTRAL ASIA

ERIKA WEINTHAL

Soviet central planning wreaked havoc on the Central Asian natural environment. Although environmental problems are pervasive throughout the world, the Soviet Union's emphasis on quantity and centrally planned targets created several notable regions of ecological stress in Central Asia — in particular, the Aral Sea region and the Semipalatinsk region. Because of poor water management practices and water withdrawals for the expansion of cotton monoculture, the Aral Sea desiccated to half its size between 1960 and 1990, leaving behind an exposed seabed filled with salt and sand (Glantz 1999; Micklin 1992). For decades, the populations living in the near-Aral region have drunk contaminated and saline water, which has led to an increase in the number of waterborne illnesses including typhoid and hepatitis. Because of the 456 nuclear tests that the Soviet Union conducted at the Semipalatinsk polygon in Kazakhstan between 1949 and 1989 (*Bulletin of the Atomic Scientists*, May/June 1998), the radioactive pollution of the environment at this former nuclear test site poses a severe long-term health danger to the residents in the surrounding area. Beyond these major environmental problems, Central Asia is beset by more general problems related to air and water pollution, desertification, threats to biodiversity, and public health issues (Asian Development Bank 1997; Pryde 1995; Feshbach and Friendly 1992; Peterson 1993; Stewart 1992).

Following the Soviet Union's collapse, the newly independent Central Asian states — Kazakhstan, Kyrgyzstan, Tajikistan, Turkmenistan, and Uzbekistan — had to confront a broad array of ecological problems.

The author wishes to thank the other authors in this book, who participated in the Olin Seminar on "Reconceptualizing Central Asia" at the Davis Center, Harvard University, October 2001, organized by Pauline Jones Luong and John Schoeberlein; the participants at the Agrarian Studies Colloquium Series at Yale University, 7 December 2001; and two anonymous reviewers for their comments on an earlier version of this chapter.

Although over a decade has passed since the breakup of the Soviet Union, the Central Asian states are still discovering the magnitude of their ecological situation, largely because many problems were hidden from the average Soviet citizen. For example, the location of a biological weapons facility on Vozrozhdeniye Island in the middle of the Aral Sea was concealed for many years from the local population. If the Aral Sea continues to shrink, a land bridge could form, linking the island with the shore, which could then enable the contaminated wildlife from the island to infect the surrounding human population (Hogan 1999). In addition, independence has created new environmental problems, especially regarding the development of oil and gas reserves in the Caspian region. Scientists and many environmentalists fear that oil and gas exploration will increase the harm to the natural environment and biodiversity in the Caspian region. Since the Soviet Union's collapse, the local sturgeon population in the Caspian has declined dramatically because of overfishing and poaching. Moreover, between March and June 2000, 30,000 dead seals — almost 8 percent of the total population — washed up on the shores of the Caspian (Godunova 2001).[1]

Finding effective solutions to the environmental and health crisis in Central Asia is especially difficult because the Central Asian states are weakly institutionalized and poor. The governments lack the administrative capacity and financial resources even to carry out basic tracking and cataloguing of their environmental problems. Besides the necessary monitoring of environmental problems, the Central Asian governments need to promulgate environmental regulations, negotiate regional environmental treaties, and then implement them. Appropriate solutions require substantial financial and technical resources. The collapse of the Soviet economy and the subsequent decline in economic growth has, however, hampered the Central Asian states' ability to respond to their pressing environmental problems.

The lack of state capacity is one of the main constraints hindering environmental protection in Central Asia. State capacity is generally defined as the ability to implement policies in order to achieve economic, social, or political goals (Barkey and Parikh 1991, 526). Although state capacity is usually equated with institutional capacity, it also includes technical, fiscal, and organizational dimensions. The ability of the Central Asian governments to carry out domestic and regional policies for environmental protection is contingent upon creating new domestic institutions as well as

1. The cause of the seal deaths was unclear and heavily debated among environmentalists, the oil companies, and government officials.

horizontal linkages among the organizations and their staffs. Yet such horizontal linkages were absent during the Soviet period, and decisions were transmitted vertically downward from Moscow. The newly empowered environmental organizations will require substantial financial resources to carry out their tasks and update their infrastructure and equipment. In response to the overall challenge of building state capacity for environmental protection, the Central Asian governments have turned to various transnational actors, particularly international governmental organizations and international nongovernmental organizations (NGOs) to assist them.

In contrast to other chapters in this book that highlight the role of society and domestic actors within the state building process, this chapter — from the vantage point of the environment — will shift attention to transnational actors in order to understand their impact on strengthening state capacity through domestic institution building and shaping state-society relations. The main premise of this chapter is that the extent of state capacity for environmental protection and the nature of state-society relations in Central Asia are directly linked to the way in which transnational actors intervene in the post-Communist state-building process.

In trying to capture the evolving relationship between transnational actors, NGOs, and the state in the realm of environmental protection in post-Soviet Central Asia, I draw upon the two most salient environmental issue-areas in Central Asia — the Aral Sea crisis and Caspian Sea pollution — to elucidate the conditions under which transnational actors enhance or undermine state capacity. In both cases, the Central Asian governments have expressed their willingness to address their environmental problems through participation in multi-lateral programs such as the Aral Sea Basin Program and the Caspian Environment Program. Both these programs have been carried out in conjunction with international donors, primarily the World Bank and the Global Environment Facility.[2] Although transnational actors have attempted to increase state capacity through creating new domestic and international institutions for environmental protection in the Aral basin, I find that many of the newly constituted institutions are merely cosmetic.[3] Transnational actors have, in fact, had

2. The Aral Sea Basin Program involves Kazakhstan, Kyrgyzstan, Tajikistan, Turkmenistan, and Uzbekistan, while the Caspian Environment Program includes Azerbaijan, Iran, Kazakhstan, Russia, and Turkmenistan. On the Aral Sea Basin Program, see Weinthal 2002. On the Caspian Environment Program, see http://www.caspianenvironment.org and Blum 2002.

3. In this chapter, I am using a very broad definition of institutions that includes informal norms, rules, legislation, agreements, and/or organizations. See Haas, Keohane, and Levy 1993, 4–5.

the greatest effect on promoting environmental protection in Central Asia through their support for local NGOs. In the Caspian region, transnational actors have empowered local NGOs by transferring financial resources and diffusing norms concerning the way in which NGOs should behave in the international system and, in fact, helping them serve as environmental watchdogs. At the same time, these linkages between transnational actors and societal actors may actually be having an adverse effect on state-society relations to the extent that they are creating a distinct boundary between state and society that previously did not exist (see, e.g., Gryzmala-Busse and Jones Luong 2002).

Theoretical Perspectives on the Origins of State Capacity and Environmental Protection

The collapse of Communism in Eastern Europe and the Soviet Union has spurred scholars to refocus their attention on the "state" in order to illuminate the linkages between post-Communist transitions and post-Communist state formation (see, e.g., Linz and Stepan 1996; Gryzmala-Busse and Jones Luong 2002). As part of this interest in post-Communist state formation, one of the main questions that has arisen concerns whether the post-Communist states will follow similar paths of state formation as those that took place in Western Europe and hence develop the extractive and redistributive institutions that characterize the modern nation-state (see, e.g., Weinthal 2002, chap. 3; Holmes 1997). Given that one of the main functions of the modern nation-state is the provision of public goods such as education, health care, and a clean environment in exchange for taxation, to what extent have the Central Asian states acquired the institutional capacity to implement policies for environmental protection? Taking into account that different states have different capacities to formulate and carry out social policies such as environmental protection (Haas, Keohane, and Levy 1993; Keohane and Levy 1996), it appears that the newly independent Central Asian states resemble developing countries that lack the institutional capacity to carry out environmental protection, especially in light of the loss of subsidies from Moscow.

In general, the literature in comparative politics finds that a state's capacity is a function of a state's domestic institutions and/or the structure of societal cleavages, and thus, according to Migdal, Kohli, and Shue (1994), states should be analyzed as parts of society and not in opposition to societies. Insofar as states are embedded within societies, their capacities vary depending on their ties to various social forces. The stronger the ties to society the more likely it is that the state can carry out its goals; where the state is autonomous or disconnected from society, it is less likely to be able to implement its goals (as is the case in many developing countries). The type of state-society relations may influence the different types of policy instruments such as, for example, regulatory style available to states in dealing with their environmental problems (O'Neill 2000).

Like states, societies are not homogenous units but are composed of different social forces. One important component of society is its NGOs. The role of NGOs and their relationship to both the state and other societal actors provides insight into a state's capacity to provide public goods such as environmental protection. Typically in the Western advanced industrialized countries, NGOs abet state capacity for environmental protection by placing environmental issues on the policy agenda, by pressuring state leaders to initiate policies to deal with environmental problems, and then by monitoring state activity to ensure government compliance with both domestic and international environmental regulations. Raustiala (1997) argues that states will go so far as to incorporate NGOs into the environmental policy and implementation process because NGO participation benefits states, especially because NGOs can provide information and carry out research concerning different policy options. Overall, NGOs can enhance state capacity by translating environmental concern into policies.

NGO participation should be even more important for increasing the capacity of developing countries, in that they often lack the financial resources and intellectual expertise to perform basic policy evaluations. NGOs can help governments that lack organizational and financial capacity by monitoring whether environmental policies are being implemented. Yet, rather than merely seeking to draw on NGO knowledge and resources, in many developing countries the state has retreated from society to the extent that it has ceded its responsibility for the provision of such public goods to local NGOs (Bratton, 1989). Thus, the rise and autonomy of local NGOs often symbolizes the absence of state capacity to provide public goods.

This emphasis on domestic institutions and the structure of society, however, ignores the role that transnational actors are playing in affecting state capacity for environmental protection through both institutional building programs and strengthening local NGOs.[4] Contrary to the state-society literature in comparative politics, the literature in international

4. A few representative and selective works on transnational actors include Risse-Kappen, 1995; Wapner 1995; Princen and Finger 1994; and Keck and Sikkink 1998.

relations finds that international institutions, organizations, and international NGOs foster state capacity. Specifically, they enhance state capacity for environmental protection by defining the environmental agenda, dispensing financial and material resources, diffusing norms and notions of accepted patterns of environmental protection, and rendering support for local NGOs (Haas, Keohane, and Levy 1993; Keohane and Levy 1996).

With the end of the Cold War, the advanced industrialized countries have sought to build state capacity in former Communist states through the transfer of financial and technical resources. Many international organizations, including the World Bank, have begun to focus on the state (International Bank for Reconstruction and Development 1997) and to recommend the inclusion of capacity-building programs in their environmental assistance packages.[5] In particular, as part of the post-Communist state-building experience, Western countries, through multilateral financial institutions and bilateral aid organizations, have sought to assist the states build new state institutions so that they have the capacity to carry out functions for domestic governance (see, e.g., Mendelson and Glenn 2002; Weinthal 2002; Carothers 1999; Wedel 1998). What distinguishes post-Communist state building from other periods of state building is that states do not just interact with their societies or with each other but, rather, transnational actors are attempting to intentionally design new state institutions that correspond to Western concepts of the nation-state. The ability of international governmental organizations and international NGOs to influence state capacity is shaped by the nature of the state's relationship with transnational actors. Similar to their ceding responsibility to local NGOs, post-Communist states may encourage international involvement to perform what are ostensibly state tasks (for example, the provision of environmental protection and social welfare) because they are weak and poor. While some find (McMann, chap. 7) that local NGOs may still turn to the state for resources such as office space and transport in order to carry out charitable work, the wealth of empirical evidence points to local NGOs in Central Asia turning outward toward the international community for technical and financial assistance to help them deal with pervasive problems of environmental protection, education, farm restructuring, legal reform, and other problems (Adamson 2000; Jones Luong and Weinthal 1999; and Weinthal 2002).

With the end of the Cold War, states are no longer the only major actors in the international system; transnational actors exert both positive and negative influences on state behavior (Barnett and Finnemore 1999).

5. On the need for capacity-building programs, see VanDeveer and Dabelko 2001.

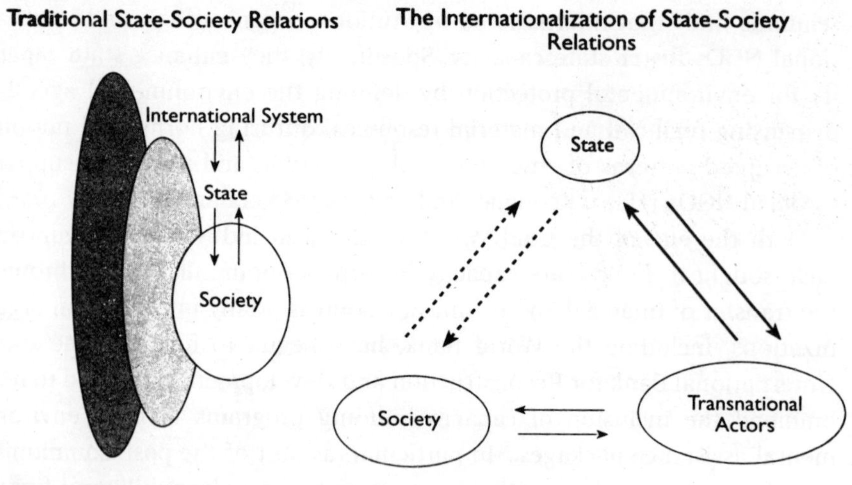

FIGURE 8.1. *State-Society Relations: Traditional versus Internationalization*

Whereas the early literature on the state assumed that the state was Janus-faced, occupying a critical niche between society and the international system (Skocpol 1985), that depiction fails to capture the processes unfolding in post-Soviet Central Asia. States are not mere parts of the international system; transnational actors (that is, international forces) have agency and power to influence both state policy and societal structures. Figure 8.1 captures the changing nature of state-society-transnational relations. The development of state capacity in Central Asia is not only linked to the composition of its society but also directly to the way in which transnational actors intervene in the post-Communist state-building process. In short, the state's ability to carry out and implement policies is not just a function of state-society relations but also a function of state-transnational relations and society-transnational relations.

The Internationalization of Environmental Protection: Diffusion of Norms

As the activities of international governmental organizations and NGOs have expanded in the aftermath of the Cold War, they have intervened in the internal politics of post-Communist states to help them undergo political and economic transitions and, hence, to help them build states (e.g. Mendelson and Glenn 2002; Weinthal 2002). They are, moreover, at the forefront of efforts to help the Central Asian states rectify decades of environmental mismanagement.

The environment is thus a suitable starting point for understanding transnational activity within the Central Asian states after the Soviet Union's collapse, largely because during the late 1980s the environment already served as a focal point for political mobilization throughout the Soviet Union (Dawson 1996). In Kazakhstan, environmental activism—the Nevada-Semipalatinsk movement—succeeded in halting nuclear weapons testing. In Uzbekistan, the Committee for Saving the Aral Sea along with other eco-nationalist movements inspired a campaign that demanded that Moscow lessen the burden on the Central Asian states as the main producers of cotton. At the time of the Soviet Union's collapse there already existed a nascent environmental movement in Central Asia.

As a result, at independence the international community perceived the Aral Sea crisis as ripe for international intervention because of the local and international awareness of the severity of its environmental degradation. On account of a United Nations Environmental Program (UNEP) diagnostic study that was undertaken in 1990, the desiccation of the Aral Sea was the most widely known environmental problem in Central Asia. As the international donor community began to aid the new state economies that are in transition, environmental protection became one part of the donor assistance programs. Because of both domestic and international interest in resolving the Aral Sea crisis, the Central Asian governments developed with the World Bank, the United Nations Development Program (UNDP), and the UNEP a multilateral aid program—the Aral Sea Basin Program—to mitigate the environmental and health consequences in the Aral region, restructure the system of water management (including creating a regional strategy for water management), and foster regional cooperation (for details, see World Bank, UNDP, UNEP, 1994). To ensure implementation of the Aral Sea Basin Program, the donor community devised a separate program devoted to strengthening the capacity of domestic and regional institutions. With the introduction of the Aral Sea Basin Program, capacity building has become a principal feature of most international aid programs in Central Asia.

One of the main ways international organizations build institutional capacity is through the diffusion of norms and values (see, e.g., Boli and Thomas 1999). Regarding the environment generally and the Aral Sea specifically, international organizations spread norms concerning what institutions are necessary for environmental protection and what strategies environmental actors should follow. Through connecting the Central Asian states to a global environmental culture, transnational actors have constructed isomorphic, or similar, environmental structures across the

Central Asian states.[6] Particularly, the influence of global environmental norms has led to a convergence in environmental policy whereby the Central Asian states have created new environmental institutions, taken part in international environmental organizations, promulgated new environmental laws, and signed on to global environmental accords as part of state making (Weinthal 2002). Combined, the intended effect is to help states gain the institutional capacity to formulate and carry out environmental protection, undertake scientific studies, monitor pollution, and implement national and international environmental programs.

The newly independent Central Asian states have learned quickly that in order to attract international environmental assistance and join the international community of nation-states, they needed to adopt international environmental practices. For example, international norms regarding shared water basins manifest themselves through the operational procedures of organizations such as the World Bank, which will not intervene and support development projects until the recipient states demonstrate their intentions to cooperate over a shared resource. As a result, the Central Asian states devised a new institutional framework for water sharing in the Aral Sea basin in order to comply with these international environmental norms. Specifically, the Central Asian states created new interstate organizations in 1993: the Interstate Council for Addressing the Aral Sea Crisis (ICAS) and the International Fund for the Aral Sea (IFAS). Moreover, the Central Asian representatives to the Aral Sea Basin Program adopted the discourse of the donor community when devising a new water strategy. The Central Asian participants agreed that regional requirements for water sharing must conform with the fundamental principles of water law that include: (1) the right of each state in a basin to an equitable and reasonable share; (2) sovereignty of each state over its natural resources; and (3) the principle of no significant harm (Interstate Council for Aral Sea Problems, October 1996, 17).[7]

As part of the broader process of joining this global environmental culture, one of the first steps taken by the newly independent Central Asian states was to reconstitute their environmental ministries and departments.[8] For example, after independence, the Kyrgyzstani government ele-

6. On institutional isomorphism, see DiMaggio and Powell 1991.

7. In contrast, Soviet water law was defined by two properties: (1) water remained the exclusive property of the state; and (2) water was nonalienable.

8. They are the following: Ministry of Environment Protection, Kyrgyzstan; Ministry of Natural Resources and Environment Protection, Kazakhstan; Ministry of Environmental Protection, Tajikistan; Ministry of Natural Resource and Environmental Protection, Turkmenistan; and State Committee for Environmental Protection, Uzbekistan.

vated its previous state environmental agency (Goskompriroda) to the ministerial level in 1996. Yet, it turns out that the Central Asian states did not empower these ministries solely because of functional reasons (that is, to deal with environmental problems), they also did so as a result of the routinization of environmental politics that has taken place since the Stockholm Conference in 1972, whereby states must have environmental ministries in order to take part in the international politics of the environment (Frank et al. 1999). Because only states have the authority to sign international environmental agreements, it has become essential for governments to create environmental agencies in order to assume this role. By signing international environmental agreements, states, moreover, become eligible for international environmental assistance, which is often provided for capacity-building programs so that states can meet their environmental international commitments. In short, the Central Asian states, like other developing countries, are responsive to a world culture in which states have become "environmentalized."

In Central Asia, environmental capacity-building practices are increasingly top-down rather than bottom-up processes. One example of top-down institution building concerns the transfer of techniques and widely accepted practices for environmental protection such as environmental impact assessments and National Environmental Action Plans (NEAPs). When Uzbekistan, Kyrgyzstan, and Kazakhstan joined the Environment for Europe process that aims to assist the former communist countries attain the same level of environmental protection as in the Western democracies, they committed themselves to develop and implement NEAPs. These NEAPs are intended to delineate national environmental policies and to coordinate governmental policy and activities with local NGOs and international organizations in order to attract external funding for environmental programs.[9] By formulating a NEAP, Kyrgyzstan, for example, was able to meet some of the requirements necessary for concessionary credits from the World Bank's International Development Association and to obtain technical assistance (Asian Development Bank 1997, 174).

Following the 1992 Earth Summit in Rio de Janeiro and the 2002 World Summit on Sustainable Development in Johannesburg, the concept of sus-

9. At the Environment for Europe Ministerial Conference in 1993, the environmental ministers from Central and Eastern Europe and the former Soviet Union endorsed the Environmental Action Program for Central and Eastern Europe and established a task force to aid with implementation. For details see http://www.ljudmila.org/retina/eco-forum/ececep49-lhtm. Kazakhstan, Kyrgyzstan, and Uzbekistan joined afterward.

tainable development has become a universal norm in the environmental sphere and is often intimately attached to capacity-building programs. Because many international organizations have incorporated notions of sustainable development into their aid programs, they, in turn, seek to impose their definitions of sustainable development on developing countries. As part of the Aral Sea Basin Program, the Central Asian states constituted the Sustainable Development Commission (SDC) in response to the request of the donor community to address the environmental and health problems in the Aral Sea basin.

One of the main international organizations that funds international environmental programs is the Global Environment Facility (GEF), which was established in 1990 after developed countries asked the World Bank to design an international environmental aid institution to finance action in developing countries on four global environmental problems: biodiversity loss, ozone depletion, global warming, and international waters (Fairman, 1996). As part of their international waters programs, GEF launched a program in September 1998 to stabilize the Central Asian environment and improve the management of the international rivers in the Aral Sea basin.[10] Because donor organizations such as the GEF focus on global environmental problems, it is not surprising that the Central Asian states and their environmental agencies have signed on to many of the major global environmental accords over the last decade (see table 8.1). Moreover, by acceding to the main environmental accords, the Central Asian states are eligible for international environmental investments. Indeed, all the Central Asian states have signed on to the Framework Convention on Climate Change, and Kazakhstan, furthermore, has taken the lead in the international campaign against global warming by calling for voluntary reductions in their greenhouse gas emissions in November 1999.

In short, transnational actors have played a critical role in helping the Central Asian states formulate policies for environmental protection and in providing assistance for capacity-building programs so that they can implement environmental programs related to climate change, sustainable development, and water sharing, among others. Yet, institution building and such aid programs are only the initial step in building capacity to help the Central Asian states protect their environment.

10. This followed the creation of a regional water strategy that had met the World Bank's requirement that to receive international assistance for a transboundary water issue, riparian states must demonstrate a willingness to engage in joint planning. See World Bank 1998.

The Negative Influence of Transnational Activity: Creating Cosmetic Institutions

Despite having committed themselves to environmental protection through signing many of the major global environmental accords, the Central Asian states still lack the organizational and fiscal capacity to meet their international obligations. The establishment of an environmental institution or the accession to a global environmental accord does not automatically endow a state with the capacity for environmental policy making and implementation. The Law and Environment Eurasia Partnership, for example, found that Kazakhstan could not meet many of its international obligations. In particular, Kazakhstan's membership dues were in arrears for the Convention on Biological Diversity and for the Framework Convention on Climate Change. This was illustrative of Kazakhstan's relationship with most international organizations; as of March 2000, Kazakhstan has not paid $21 million it owed in membership dues to about sixty international organizations.[11]

In addition, participation in the multitude of international organizations has rarely led to the formulation of national environmental policies beyond international aid programs and their implementation, largely because environmental treaty making has become a sovereignty-enhancing exercise. In general, the Central Asian states have been busy signing on to treaties and constituting new institutions because this is what states are supposed to do, and, moreover, it is less costly than having to empower domestic actors and these new institutions to implement policies at the domestic level for environmental protection. Thus, linkages to international organizations and environmental regimes have strengthened the Central Asian countries' external sovereignty but not their internal sovereignty. Integration into various international environmental organizations and programs reinforces the state-building process insofar as state building entails building formal institutions.

Given that the Aral Sea Basin Program was one of the largest donor projects in Central Asia, we should expect to see there the most progress in building capacity for environmental protection. Yet, this project has largely been perceived by the Central Asian populations as a disappointment. The new institutions created as part of the Aral Sea Basin Program (ICAS, IFAS, and the SDC) have remained largely dormant and ineffective.[12] Originally,

11. See Law and Environment Eurasia Partnership, *Central Asia Compliance Monitor* no. 3, April 2000, 5, and no. 2, February 2000, 2.

12. For details, see Weinthal 2001. In 1997, the Central Asian leaders merged ICAS and IFAS, ostensibly to increase the effectiveness of the Aral Sea regional institutions.

TABLE 8.1. *International Environmental Treaties*[a]

Treaty	Kazakhstan	Kyrgyzstan	Tajikistan	Turkmenistan	Uzbekistan
Aarhus Convention on Access to Information, Public Participation in Decision-making and Access to Justice in Environmental Matters	Signed 25/06/98 Ratified 11/01/01	Accession 01/05/01	Accession 17/07/01	Accession 25/06/99	
Basel Convention on Transboundary Movements of Hazardous Wastes		Accession 13/08/96		Accession 25/09/96	Accession 07/02/96
Convention on Biological Diversity	Signed 09/06/92 Ratified 06/09/94	Accession 06/08/96	Accession 29/10/97	Accession 18/09/96	Accession 19/07/95
Convention on International Trade in Endangered Species (CITES)	Accession 20/01/2000				Accession 10/07/97
Convention on Migratory Species			Entered into force 01/02/01		Entered into force 01/09/98
Convention to Combat Desertification	Signed 14/10/94 Ratified	Accession 19/09/97	Accession 16/07/97	Signed 27/03/95 Ratified 18/09/96	Signed 07/12/94 Ratified 31/10/95

	09/07/97				
Framework Convention on Climate Change	Ratified 17/05/95	Accession 25/05/00	Accession 07/01/98	Accession 05/06/95	Accession 20/6/93
Kyoto Protocol	Signed 12/3/99			Signed 25/9/98 Ratified 11/01/99	Signed 20/11/98 Ratified 12/10/99
Ramsar Convention on Wetlands of International Importance			Deposited declaration of succession (no sites designated)		Deposited declaration of succession (no sites designated)
Vienna Convention on Ozone Protection	Accession 26/08/98	Accession 31/05/00	Accession 06/05/96	Accession 18/11/93	Accession 18/05/93
Montreal Protocol	Accession 26/08/98	Accession 31/05/00	Accession 07/01/98	Accession 18/11/93	Accession 18/05/93
London Amendments					
Copenhagen Amendments	Accession 26/07/01		Accession 07/01/98	Accession 15/03/94	Accession 10/06/98
Montreal Amendments					Accession 10/06/98
World Heritage Convention	Acceptance 29/04/94	Acceptance 03/07/95	Notification of succession 28/08/92	Notification of succession 30/09/94	Notification of succession 13/01/93

[a]I rely on the official treaty sites to compile this chart. At the same time, the Central Asia Compliance Monitor finds many discrepancies with the specific dates.

the heads of states established IFAS to finance the Aral Sea programs based on contributions from the five states and other donors. However, IFAS was unable to fulfill its primary objective to act as a fund for the Central Asian states, especially since it had failed to collect the money promised to it by the Central Asian states. Despite considerable assistance from the UNDP, the SDC also has "not been active" (United Nations Development Program, 1998). The UNDP (1998) noticed that rather than working on strengthening existing institutions, the Central Asian ministers of the environment were more interested in creating a new regional institution — the Central Asia Regional Ecological Center. Again, the Central Asian governments have been more concerned with creating environmental institutions as part of state making than with empowering these institutions and the actors within them.

More telling is that the environmental and health situation in the Aral Sea basin has not improved since the donors began rendering aid after independence. According to Médecins Sans Frontières, "The water crisis in the region continues on today. Despite countless specialists conducting assessments of the environmental disaster and its ensuing effects, little change has occurred and even less humanitarian assistance has been delivered."[13] One of the main complaints frequently heard was that the new regional institutions for cooperation remained limited and under the control of the previous water *nomenklatura* rather than reaching those most affected by the desiccation of the Aral Sea at the local level. Some consultants in informal discussions have, furthermore, concluded that the World Bank (and other donors) should have refrained from pushing for a new institutional structure, because in the end it was only cosmetic. Instead, they posited that the Central Asian water and environmental specialists already possessed the institutional capacity and know-how to address the Aral Sea crisis and only required financial and technical assistance.

Finally, even if the Central Asian governments were sincere about building new institutions for environmental protection and improving the Aral Sea environment, they were constrained by the importance of the cotton sector as a revenue generator. Related to what Ilkhamov found (chap. 5) about the cotton sector having reinforced regionalism in Uzbekistan, the reliance on cotton exports for foreign revenue has served as a mechanism for social control (Weinthal 2002, chap. 5). Because of the Uzbekistani government's dependence on cotton production, it has failed to take the necessary steps to restructure the agricultural sector by switching to less

13. See http://www.msf.org/aralsea/asa_dis.htm

water-intensive crops that would help mitigate the Aral Sea's desiccation. Moreover, by not linking the environment in the Aral Sea basin to reform in the agricultural sector, the international community undermined its own attempts to strengthen the states' capacities for environmental protection, because different environmental and economic interests have continued to compete with one another for governmental preference (Weinthal 2001).

Internationalization of Environmental Politics: The Growth of NGOs

The dramatic growth in the number of local and international NGOs is indicative of the upsurge in transnational activity throughout the world. The significance of environmental NGOs, in particular, can be seen by their participation in international conferences. For example, at the Earth Summit in Rio de Janeiro, some 22,000 NGO representatives from more than 9,000 NGOs attended (Princen and Finger 1994, 4). Moreover, international lending organizations such as the World Bank have begun to incorporate NGOs into their environmental programs. Whereas between 1973 and 1988, only 6 percent of all World Bank projects included provisions for NGO involvement, by fiscal year 1996 the involvement of NGOs increased to approximately 48 percent of all their projects (Prosser 2000). In response to the growing significance of NGOs in global environmental politics, the donor community has taken concrete steps to encourage their development in Central Asia, because Western donors perceive NGOs as essential for local empowerment and for strengthening civil society in developing countries (Frantz 1987). Yet the new local NGO community has had to deal with the Soviet legacy in which civil society was absent. Prior to glasnost, Moscow had suppressed most forms of individual activism, except for a few instances in which groups focused on conservation issues.[14]

Since the Soviet Union's collapse, a variety of Western NGOs (ISAR, HIVOS, NOVIB, INTRAC) have actively supported the development of environmental NGOs in Central Asia.[15] During the early stage of Western intervention, USAID provided funding to ISAR, Counterpart Consortium, and the American Legal Consortium in order to strengthen the local NGO

14. An early example of Soviet environmentalism was the rise of the student conservation brigades (*druzhiny*). See Weiner 1988 and Deever and Pirigova 2001.

15. They are: Initiative for Social Action and Renewal in Eurasia, Humanist Institute for Co-operation with Developing Countries, Novib is a Dutch development NGO, International NGO Training and Research Centre. For an overview of NGOs in Kazakhstan, see Jones Luong and Weinthal 1999 and Garbutt 1997.

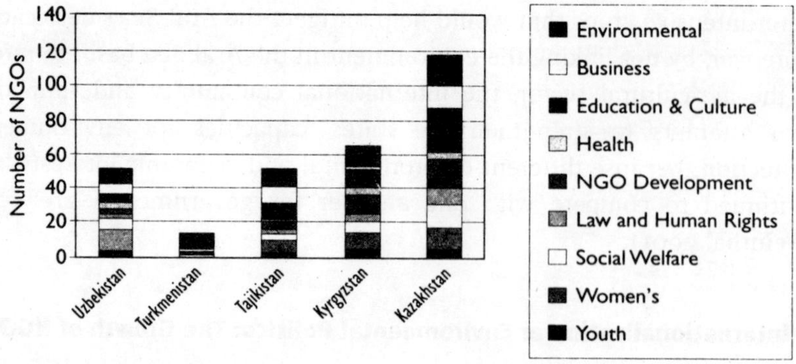

Source: Center for Civil Society International in Seattle. http://www.friends-partners.org/ccsi

FIGURE 8.2. *Distribution of NGOs*

sector. With such funding, between 1994 and 1996 the American Legal Consortium (1996, 1) awarded $1.1 million in small grants to fifty-four NGOs across Central Asia, and ISAR sponsored a "Seeds of Democracy" program between 1993 and 1997 that awarded $480,000 in grants of up to $3,000 to over 360 NGO projects in Central Asia (Watters 1999). Since 2000, ISAR has provided small grants for groups in the more remote areas of Central Asia.[16] Thus, during the first few years after independence foreign aid contributed to the growth of local NGOs. According to the Center for Civil Society, by the late 1990s, 284 NGOs existed in Central Asia, of which 51 worked on environmental issues (see figure 8.2).[17]

This seed money has enabled local NGOs to raise public awareness regarding environmental problems and to put new issues on national and international agendas. A large share of local NGO activity has focused on information collection and dissemination (Jones Luong and Weinthal 1999). For example, CASDIN (Central Asia Sustainable Development Information Network) published a newsletter to coordinate activities among NGOs in Kazakhstan, and it has organized seminars and workshops on NGO management and fund raising. The Law and Environment Eurasia Partnership publishes a periodic report (*Ecostan News*) and a bulletin

16. For projects funded by ISAR, see http://www.isar.org.

17. See the Center for Civil Society International in Seattle, http://www.friends-partners.org/ccse. In contrast, note that Horton and Kazakina (1999) find as of January 1, 1998 that approximately seven hundred nonprofit organizations had been registered in Kyrgyzstan, but only three hundred were considered active. They also point out that in Kazakhstan from 1991 to 1995, 550 NGOs were registered and as of January 9, 1997, 3,050 NGOs had been registered; but again this does not mean all are active or have survived.

(*Central Asia Compliance Monitor*) through the Internet.[18] Many local NGOs have used grants from ISAR to buy computers and establish Internet connections, which has enabled them to remain in contact with one another and with the international community. The Internet has become an important source of communications for Central Asian NGOs, as it has become increasingly difficult to travel within and outside the region because of the expense and visa requirements.

Another way in which Western donors have helped local NGOs attain information is through organizing conferences so that local NGOs can share ideas about environmental issues and the problems with carrying out their activities. Given that at the outset most local NGO activity was concentrated on the Aral Sea crisis, it is not surprising that early attempts to coordinate regional NGO activity focused on NGOs in the Aral Sea basin. Here, NOVIB was instrumental in establishing an association of Aral Sea basin NGOs to lobby national and international organizations on water issues in the Aral Sea basin. The Association of Uzbekistan for Sustainable Water Resources Development (Suvchi) has also held conferences and workshops for Central Asians and foreigners on topics concerning water management issues in the Aral Sea basin.

Because of the collapse of the Soviet system of social services and the governments' lack of financial resources, the Central Asian governments have allowed Western donors to support local NGO activity in order to meet the immediate basic needs of their populations. As most large-scale donor efforts have failed to meet their objectives in the Aral Sea region, NGOs have been left to fill the void. With minimal financial resources, local and international NGOs have struggled to deal with the environmental and health consequences of the Aral Sea crisis. Although a few of these NGOs, such as ECOSAN in Uzbekistan, are directly linked to the government, many other NGOs working on environmental issues in Central Asia operate independently, despite the cumbersome registration process and high registration fees. One of the most prominent NGOs — Perzent (established in 1992) — has carried out numerous programs to improve the status and health of women and children in the Aral Sea region in Karakalpakstan (Ruffin and Waugh 1999). It has conducted research on the negative effect of environmental degradation on reproduction and maternal and child health and has provided education for women and children on health, reproductive, and environmental issues. Similarly, the international NGO Médecins Sans Frontières has been tackling the tuber-

18. See http://www.ecostan.org.index.html. It has received funding from the John D. and Catherine T. MacArthur Foundation.

culosis epidemic in the Aral Sea region; through working with the Ministry of Health in Uzbekistan, it has assisted local health-care workers establish DOTS (Directly Observed Treatment Short Course) treatment facilities in Nukus, Karakalpakstan.[19]

In sum, as in other developing countries with weak state institutional capacity, local and international NGOs in Central Asia are shouldering much of the responsibility for the populations' social and health welfare by either carrying out programs independently of the government or in working with specific government institutions.

The Positive Influence of Transnational Activity: Creating Environmental Watchdogs

In contrast to the cosmetic effect that they have had on building institutional capacity, transnational organizations have substantively bolstered the role of local NGOs as autonomous actors that abet environmental protection in the Central Asian states. Whereas state capacity is often contingent upon effective domestic institutions, the mere process of building institutions is not sufficient for strengthening state capacity; rather, the ability of the Central Asian states to deal with their environmental problems has hinged upon the relationship between societal actors and transnational actors. Through the international transfer of funds and norms to local NGOs, transnational actors build capacity in the environmental arena by assisting local NGOs to carry out environmental monitoring, increasing public awareness, and democratizing the decision-making processes. The participation of NGOs is critical for carrying out independent scientific research, especially given the lack of government financial and technical support for research.

Thus, Western and local NGOs have monitored the Aral Sea Basin Program's activities to make sure that local NGOs have been included in the decision-making process in order to increase the program's effectiveness. Early on, the Aral Sea International Committee pushed for local NGO representation at several workshops sponsored by the World Bank and at the donors' conferences (author's correspondence with Bill Davoren, June 1998). Because the Aral Sea Basin Program has come under attack for excluding local communities in its programs, NGO pressure has increased the number of stakeholders involved in the decision-making processes. NGO participation is considered vital for implementing environmental

19. See http://www.msf.org/projects/asia/uzbekistan/reports/2000/02/pr-dotsnukus.htm.

protection goals in the Aral Sea basin because local NGOs possess a wealth of information about the local health and environmental situation, and, more importantly, their participation is necessary to carry out any program concerning education, sanitation, clean drinking water, and basic hygiene at the local level. Moreover, Médecins Sans Frontières embarked on an international assistance survey in the Aral Sea area to evaluate many of the large donor assistance programs from 1991 to 2001 in order to increase the major donor's accountability to the local populations (author's correspondence with representative from Médecins Sans Frontières).

As the multilateral Aral Sea Basin Program came under NGO scrutiny for its failure to meet its original objectives, the donor community began to shift its focus from the Aral Sea to the Caspian Sea. Although during the Soviet period, the Caspian was facing numerous environmental problems (rising sea levels, diminishing fish stocks, increasing pollution), these environmental problems were considered regional problems, but with the prospects of developing large oil and gas reserves that could threaten further environmental degradation, the Caspian emerged on the international agenda following the Soviet Union's collapse. The entry of foreign oil companies into the Caspian region and the subsequent seismic studies in the northeastern Caspian sparked concern among local and foreign environmentalists that the Caspian's natural environment might be further sacrificed for the sake of oil and gas wealth. In fact, because the northern Caspian was a protected environmental zone during the Soviet period, the Kazakhstani government had to pass a new law to enable the oil and gas companies to carry out their seismic studies in that region.

In response to the foreign oil and gas companies' interest in the Caspian's energy resources, international organizations (United Nations agencies and the World Bank) in coordination with the Caspian littoral states launched the Caspian Environment Program in 1998 to prevent pollution and to encourage monitoring, biodiversity protection, and the management of sea-level fluctuation.[20] Again, this was an internationally driven program that was modeled on other United Nations' regional seas programs such as those in the Mediterranean and Baltic (VanDeveer, 2000; Caspian Environment Program, Concept Paper, 3 May 1998). At the same time, Western NGOs also began to shift the focus of their activities away from the Aral Sea and toward the Caspian basin. In particular, financial support from USAID and UNDP has helped ISAR launch a three-year program to strengthen cooperation among NGOs in the Caspian basin countries — Azerbaijan, Georgia, Iran, Kazakhstan, Russia, and

20. Again see http://www.caspianenvironment.org and Blum 2002.

Turkmenistan (Watters 2000).[21] The program aims at increasing public awareness and participation in the decision-making process regarding oil and gas development. ISAR initiated its Caspian partnership program in April 1999 with a NGO conference in Baku, Azerbaijan that was attended by representatives from approximately fifty environmental NGOs; at this meeting the NGOs identified a list of priority issues in the Caspian region, including the development of a public environmental monitoring system and an examination of alternative export routes. In addition, ISAR established a separate program on environmental and health issues in Atyrau in western Kazakhstan, which is one of the main oil and gas regions in Kazakhstan.

The rapid rise in NGO activity in the Caspian basin is notable, especially given that during the first few years after independence, most local NGOs' activities were concentrated outside the Caspian region, and many local NGOs avoided issues that were politically sensitive.[22] The absence of a Caspian NGO community after independence had its roots in the social and economic context. In Kazakhstan, the government, *akims* (or regional leaders), and the local populations living in the oil and gas regions viewed the entry of foreign oil and gas companies as beneficial for the country's economic development despite the potential harm to the environment.[23] This was because the Kazakhstani government expected the foreign oil and gas companies to cover many of the regions' social costs in the areas where they operated (Jones Luong and Weinthal 1999). As part of their contracts, the oil and gas companies agreed to include a substantial social contribution budget, which usually provided for hospitals, schools, sport facilities, and cultural events (author's interviews with oil and gas representatives, 2000).

In my 1997 interviews with representatives of several oil and gas companies operating in Kazakhstan, they remarked that they did not notice any well-developed environmental NGOs in the oil and gas producing regions. They emphasized that they only dealt with the central and regional governments concerning their operations. This, however, did not prevent the foreign oil and gas companies (including OKIOC — Offshore Kazakhstan International Operating Company) from holding public town meetings to explain the nature of their work and to discuss future pro-

21. See http://www.isar.org/isar/Caspian.html. For a skeptical view see Sievers 2000.

22. Note that the exception was Green Salvation in Almaty, Kazakhstan. See Jones Luong and Weinthal 1999.

23. Because this chapter concerns Central Asia, I do not refer to NGOs in Russia, Azerbaijan, or Iran. Turkmenistan, unlike Kazakhstan, did open up its oil and gas reserves to foreign investors after independence.

jects. In June 2000, one oil company representative remarked that he had noticed an increase in NGO activity in Atyrau, which he attributed to the UNDP program. In his opinion, "Western NGOS are trying to bring environmentalism from abroad to an inhospitable environment."

Similar to the way in which international organizations and NGOs seek to transfer norms concerning a global environmental culture, they are also seeking to diffuse norms concerning the role of environmental NGOs. Bringing NGOs into the decision-making process encourages greater transparency in the important oil and gas sector for countries such as Kazakhstan, especially since the oil and gas sector provides a major share of the government's budget. On the whole, the influx of foreign aid to NGOs has turned them into environmental watchdogs that monitor oil and gas development in the Caspian basin and its effects on the environment. In response to the death of thousands of seals in the first half of 2000, the Regional Caspian Environmental Center based in Astrakhan, Russia and the Atyrau, Kazakhstan-based NGO, Aynalandy Aiyala, have launched a project to save the Caspian seals that are threatened by oil and gas development by encouraging public hearings and the dissemination of articles and films (Godunova 2001).

ISAR has been very instrumental in fostering local NGO development through providing resources and increasing their organizational and networking skills. In March 2000 they sponsored a seminar on "Public Environmental Monitoring in the Caspian Basin" in Baku, Azerbaijan as part of their goal of helping NGOs coordinate their strategies. Such programs have provided opportunities for local NGOs to monitor both the operations of the oil and gas companies and the Kazakhstani government and, in turn, to publicize environmental mishaps and violations.

Many newly formed NGOs in the Caspian basin are assuming the monitoring role of government agencies, which often lack the institutional and human resources to carry out effective monitoring. With the Soviet Union's breakup, the network of experts who monitored environmental issues, such as the system of nature preserves, has collapsed. Because of declining economic conditions and low salaries, scientists have been forced to leave their government positions. International support of local NGOs has enabled many scientists to continue their work on environmental issues outside of government institutions, which have waning monitoring capacity. For example, in Turkmenbashi, Turkmenistan several new NGOs have appeared whose members used to work in the now-closed Krasnovodsk branch of the Caspian Fisheries Institute (Berkeliev 2001). With a diminishing number of experts in government ministries and research institutions, environmental enforcement and monitoring has fallen upon local

NGOs. Thus, when the thousands of Caspian seals washed up dead on the seashore, local NGOs were among the first organizations to bring this catastrophe to the attention of the international media.

Although this linkage of transnational and societal actors is necessary for promoting environmental protection, it is not sufficient for strengthening state capacity. State capacity requires that all three pillars (transnational, societal, and state) are strengthened equally. At present, the weakest pillar is the state's domestic institutions. Despite improving environmental monitoring, increasing public awareness, and democratizing the decision-making processes, NGO influence has been largely restricted to the foreign investor community. For example, Kaspii Tabigati (Caspian Nature, formed in 1998) in Atyrau and Caspian XXI (formed in 2000) have been monitoring OKIOC's operations in Atyrau and have contended that OKIOC is dumping tons of unfiltered sewage and other by-products from its drilling into the Caspian that they say is having a direct impact on the ecosystem around Atyrau.[24]

Because it is easier to target foreign oil and gas companies, international NGOs and international organizations have had a great impact in forcing the oil and gas companies to meet with local NGOs and not only official government representatives. ISAR has been involved in bringing local NGOs in contact with the foreign oil and gas companies. In particular, in September 2000, ISAR organized a seminar on "NGO Interaction with Transnational Corporations" in which approximately forty NGOs and ten representatives from companies that operate in the Caspian region participated in roundtable discussions on ways to enhance cooperation between the companies and NGOs. Then in January 2002, ISAR organized a workshop on corporate responsibility, which sought to address corporate codes of conduct that would improve environmental protection in the Caspian Basin.[25]

In sum, as much as NGO activity has raised environmental awareness in the Caspian region, the pressuring of foreign oil and gas companies should not be confused with increasing state capacity; rather, it reflects an increase in societal capacity. This increased societal capacity, if directed toward government institutions in Central Asia, could, however, lead to an increase in the state's capacity to manage many of the their environmental problems.

24. "Kazakh Ecologists Urge Oil Consortium to Compensate for Damage to Caspian Ecosystem," RFE/RL 23 February 2001.

25. For details, see the proceedings from ISAR, "Public Interest, Corporate Responsibility, and Good Governance: Environmental Protection in the Caspian," Astrakhan, Russia, January 25–27, 2002.

Building State Capacity or Window Dressing?

The parallel but disjointed efforts of transnational actors to build new domestic institutions and to support local NGOs has indeed raised environmental awareness, but it has yet to produce the overall objective of increasing state capacity for environmental protection. The Central Asian governments' support for the linkage between transnational and societal actors prevents the state from having to confront society and also deflects society's criticism of the way the state is managing its environmental resources. As a result, transnational actors are contributing to the formation of a clear division between state and society, whereby the state is not embedded within society or society within the state. Thus, similarly to Ilkhamov (chap. 5) and Jones Luong (chap. 6) who find that society has been left out of the pact between the regions and the center in Uzbekistan and Kazakhstan, respectively, I find that the state's reliance on transnational actors also leaves society out of any pact with the state. This differs from McMann's findings presented in chapter 7 that certain societal groups in Kyrgyzstan desire to form linkages with the state in exchange for economic resources. My findings reinforce those presented by Kamp (chap. 1) that highlight the importance of the Soviet legacy, whereby society still has certain expectations of the state. I have found that when the state cannot, or may choose not to, fulfill expectations for the provision of social welfare and environmental protection, societal groups may turn to actors beyond the state to fill this void.

The development of state institutions for environmental protection in Central Asia is not situated solely within society, but rather it is a function of the internationalization of the Central Asian environment. Transnational actors have been instrumental in constituting new environmental institutions, policies, and legislation in Central Asia. Yet the diffusion of environmental norms concerning the scope and form of institutions has not improved the states' capacity for carrying out policies of environmental protection. At the same time, these transnational actors have enhanced environmental protection through their support of societal forces such as local NGO communities. However, despite their having raised environmental awareness and their monitoring efforts in the Caspian basin, it is still evident that the existence and continued robustness of these NGOs depends on foreign assistance. Indeed, an internal contradiction exists whereby local NGOs are demanding more transparency from the international oil and gas companies, but, because they do not generate funds from the local population, they themselves are not accountable to their local constituencies but rather to foreign donors.

Local NGOs are beholden to the interests of the donor community, depending upon which issue-areas the donors are willing to fund. Many of these new local NGOs did not exist before the influx of transnational actors and foreign aid but were created as part of the state-building process in which the donor community sought to imbue the Central Asian states with the foundations of a civil society that is connected to a larger global civil society.

In general, the rise of Central Asian NGOs symbolizes the inchoate nature of Central Asian state capacity for environmental protection. As has been the case in other developing countries, the Central Asian governments have ceded responsibility to NGOs insofar as they work on nonpolitical issues that do not come into conflict with the governments' political interests. Even though NGO efforts to monitor the environmental situation in the Caspian basin are beginning to influence governmental policy — as with the Kazakhstani parliament's consideration of a law for the Caspian shelf that would establish strict regulations for its development and exploration (Caspinfo Information Service, May 16–31, 2001) — this should not be viewed as NGOs having political clout over government decisions. Indeed, these efforts to tighten environmental restrictions might be another way for the central government to gain more control over the foreign oil and gas companies and to further its own economic interests. Yet, while domestic institutions in Central Asia remain weak and the governments are resisting democratic overtures, Central Asian leaders are still able to deflect pressure coming from societal groups.

In sum, although it is essential for Western NGOs to empower local NGOs to monitor the foreign investor community, these same Western NGOs also need to focus their attention on empowering societal actors to challenge the Central Asian governments to carry out their domestic and international environmental commitments. As long as the governments remain hostile to democracy-building efforts, the proliferation of local NGOs will only enhance societal actors in relation to transnational actors and not in relation to their domestic governments. Moreover, if societal and transnational actors resist challenging state actors, domestic institutions and the state's capacity for environmental protection will remain weak and undeveloped.

Conclusion

CENTRAL ASIA'S CONTRIBUTION TO THEORIES OF THE STATE

PAULINE JONES LUONG

The scholarship on Central Asia that has emerged over the past decade in general and the chapters in this book in particular provide a strong empirical basis for reconsidering the predominant views of this region and an opportunity to reassess its broader contribution to social science theory. Like their counterparts throughout the post-Communist world, the countries that comprise Central Asia are undergoing a process of state-building. At the core of this process lies the interaction between elites who are competing "over the authority to create the structural framework through which policies are made and enforced" (Grzymala-Busse and Jones Luong 2002, 531) and the societies that will ultimately be subjected to these policies. As many other scholars have argued, the state's ability to formulate and implement coherent policies is constrained by its relationship with society, which in turn, is a function of how (and how well) society is organized (Levi 1988; Migdal 1988; Migdal, Kohli, and Shue 1994)[1] as well as the perceived legitimacy of state action in the periphery (see, e.g., Jackman, 1993; Poggi, 1978; Weber, translated and edited in Roth and Wittich, 1978).

In sum, our collective findings both substantiate and build on key insights gleaned from this rich literature on the state and state-societal relations. On the one hand, they confirm the need to disaggregate states and societies as well as the importance of institutional and policy legacies

The author is grateful to Anna Grzymala-Busse and Erika Weinthal for their thoughtful commentary and useful suggestions.

1. Joel Migdal (1988, chap. 1) argues that societies are more capable of resisting the state when they are organized into autonomous groups, whether these groups are diffuse or hierarchical, because the leaders of such groups exercise a high degree of social control. In the same spirit, Margaret Levi (1988) argues that a ruler's ability to extract revenue depends on his bargaining power relative to private economic actors.

in creating multiple centers of state authority and shaping elites' "perceptions concerning how to maintain order and to promote economic development" (Kohli 2002, 104). They also acknowledge the danger of overestimating the power of the state vis-à-vis society (see, e.g., Migdal, Kohli, and Shue 1994, esp. chap. 1). On the other hand, our collective findings suggest generalizable microcausal explanations for the emergence and persistence of multiple state actors as well as their relative strength vis-à-vis societal actors. Moreover, they specify the conditions under which struggles among actors within the state are likely to be more intense than those between the state and social forces as well as how international actors influence this struggle.

Multiple Centers of State Authority

Although scholars of the developing world have increasingly moved away from treating the state as a unitary and coherent actor (see, e.g., L. Anderson 1986; Migdal 1988; Migdal, Kohli, and Shue 1994; Waldner 1999), this assumption once pervaded the literature on the state. This book provides support for the alternative view that the state consists of multiple actors, and that actors at lower levels are as important as central ones in determining the shape of the state as well as its effectiveness — the ability to implement policies and achieve its goals — in several ways.

First, it deliberately encompasses state actors at multiple levels — central, regional (*oblast*), local (*raion*), and rural or village — and demonstrates their influence on state policy. Laura Adams (chap. 3) examines the role of cultural elites within a central bureaucracy and finds that even within a single ministry, the Ministry of Culture, in which they share ideological goals, these elites often clash over the allocation of resources and matters of interpretation or how best to convey state ideology to the public. Alisher Ilkhamov (chap. 5) and Pauline Jones Luong (chap. 6) both demonstrate the ability of regional leaders to thwart the goals of central authorities by refusing to implement economic policies. Marianne Kamp (chap. 1) shows that the local, rural and urban *mahalla* committees in Uzbekistan enable the state to continue to provide its citizens with basic social services, albeit in a form that is greatly reduced and more discriminatory than its Soviet predecessor.

Second, several chapters provide evidence that these actors are part of the institutional and policy legacy of the preceding state. Similar to other developing countries in which the previous ruling apparatus, often colonialism, left behind multiple centers of authority, the key state actors operating in Central Asia today are direct descendants and beneficiaries of

Soviet rule.[2] All five of the region's presidents from independence through the late 1990s were high-ranking Communists. Four out of five were Communist Party officials at the time of independence — three as first secretaries of their respective republic's Communist Party (Nazarbaev, Niyazov, and Karimov) and one as the first secretary of an oblast party committee (Rakhmonov). Regional leaders in Central Asia were also created and empowered under the Soviet system, wherein they served a crucial role in overseeing the production of raw materials in exchange for access to scarce resources, amassing powerful patronage networks in the process (Jones Luong 2002, chap. 3; Weinthal 2002, chap. 5).

In addition, this book contributes to previous studies by explicitly linking the origin of multiple state actors to control over scarce resources and their persistence to the continuation of this privileged access. It thus offers a more satisfactory explanation for which elites dominate the state-building process — not only because it is more generalizable beyond a single country or group of countries but also because it is more dynamic. State actors exercise authority in post-Soviet Central Asia not merely because they did so under Soviet rule, but because they were able to either maintain or expand their power base after independence through their privileged access to scarce resources and control over distribution networks. This is manifested in the persistence of personalistic politics and patronage networks at both the central and regional levels of government. President Nazarbaev of Kazakhstan, for example, skillfully dispenses political patronage in order to enrich his relatives, maintain the support of close allies, and to co-opt potential opposition (see, e.g., Dave 2000; Olcott 2002). For regional leaders, these networks fostered strong political identities that have also endured after Soviet rule (Jones Luong 2002). Regional leaders were able to preserve these networks after independence in Turkmenistan and Uzbekistan, for example, because the cotton sector continued to play the dominant role in the state's economy (Jones Luong and Weinthal 2001). They augmented these networks after independence in Kazakhstan and Kyrgyzstan by appropriating resources that had belonged to the Communist Party (McMann, chap. 7) or from the influx of foreign investment and international aid (Jones Luong, chap. 6; Weinthal, chap. 8).

Blurred Boundaries and Societal Weakness

The experience of the Soviet Central Asian republics-turned-independent states also provides an important corrective to the literature that seeks to

2. This applies to other Soviet successor states as well, particularly Russia (see Solnick 1998).

assess the strength of societies in developing countries. As Joel Migdal demonstrates in his seminal work *Strong Societies and Weak States*, states are often unable to achieve social control because they encounter strong resistance from societies that are organized into diffuse social structures, such as clans, tribes, and farming communities (Migdal 1988, chap. 1). The Soviet state thus stands out for achieving its goal of state predominance, in large part because it actively reorganized society along multiple dimensions — political, economic, and sociocultural — and hence blurred the boundary between state and societal actors. The absence of an autonomous sphere in which societal actors could develop precluded their rebellion against the state. In contrast, where Communist regimes were unable to erase the preexisting distinction between states and societies in most of Eastern Europe (including the Baltic states), and instead reinforced this distinction, they faced mobilized opposition before their collapse (Grzymala-Busse and Jones Luong 2002).

Indeed, the weakness of social forces vis-à-vis the state in post-Soviet Central Asia can best be understood as the result of the degree to which these two Soviet legacies — blurred boundaries and societal weakness — have persisted. Central Asia societies not only remain dependent on the state for their basic needs, they continue to believe that the state's primary role is to provide for them (Kamp, chap. 1). This situation is reinforced by the fact that the boundary between the state and society remains blurred. When the state can control or manipulate sources of personal income, for example, citizens are reticent to engage in political activity (McMann 2000, 2002). As Kelly McMann finds in Kyrgyzstan, the extent to which political and economic elites remain the same and "public" property remains under these elites' control impedes the development of a truly independent sphere of social activity (McMann, chap. 7). At the same time, the co-optation of the very elites that might have served as the leadership for emergent social forces after independence — or what Laura Adams refers to as "cultural elites" — prevented them from serving this role. Rather, she argues in chapter 3 that in Uzbekistan such elites, who are an artifact of the Soviet state, considered themselves a part of the post-Soviet state and thus chose to closely align themselves with the Karimov regime. Because cultural elites lack access to alternative discourses, moreover, they are severely limited in their ability to develop anything other than a single, monolithic alternative to Communist ideology — that is, the limited form of Uzbek nationalism prescribed by governing elites.

This points to one of the fundamental ways in which the post-Soviet Central Asian states are distinct from their counterparts in the developing world. They enjoy a distinct advantage vis-à-vis society concerning both the relative degree of autonomy and of capacity.[3] In addition to interventionist attitudes concerning the proper role of the state, Central Asian elites inherited an elaborate institutional infrastructure that successfully penetrated society across political, economic, and cultural spheres and an extensive surveillance apparatus with which to regulate and monitor societal forces. Not all state elites have attempted to maintain this boundary to the same degree since independence. Compare, for example, Kazakhstan's passive withdrawal from the cultural sphere, reflected in both its policies toward bride kidnapping (Werner, chap. 2) and implementing Kazakh as the state language (Dave, chap. 4), with Uzbekistan's deliberate attempts to (re-)construct social relations (Kamp, chap. 1) and an Uzbek national identity (Adams, chap. 3) from above. Nonetheless, their ability to maintain the blurred boundary between state and society should be viewed not only as the result of concerted efforts to control and co-opt society at all levels but as yet another enduring legacy of Soviet rule.

"Strongmen" and Struggles within the State

Given the relative weakness of society compared to the state in the post-Soviet context described above, it is perhaps not surprising that the main obstacles to establishing hegemonic control over the periphery come from within the state itself. Several chapters in this book highlight the conflict between state actors, who are ostensibly engaged in the same enterprise — namely, achieving state predominance over society. Yet, these actors make demands on the state, compete with the state, and challenge its authority. Laura Adams (chap. 3) describes the degree to which cultural elites and bureaucrats in Uzbekistan's Ministry of Culture compete among themselves over institutional resources and the presentation of new cultural symbols, such as Amir Timur. They are less concerned, however, with how successfully their message is conveyed to the general public. Similarly, Bhavna Dave (chap. 4) argues that the success of language policy and implementation in Kazakhstan relative to Kyrgyzstan can best be explained by the greater degree of consensus among cultural elites in

3. As noted in the introduction, state "strength" or "capacity" is the ability of the state to formulate and implement policy throughout the territory under its control through coercive or infrastructural means (Mann, 1993). In his award-winning book, Nicolas Van de Walle attributes Africa's persistent failure to develop economically to the fact that "African states combine high levels of autonomy with extremely low capacity" because, although power is centralized, they do not have a bureaucratic apparatus that is either willing or able to penetrate the periphery because of rampant clientelism (2001, 16).

Kazakhstan. Intraelite competition for control over scarce political and economic resources is particularly acute. Presidents have routinely eliminated potential challengers at the central and regional level by accusing them of corruption in order to maintain their privileged position.[4] Alisher Ilkhamov (chap. 5) and Pauline Jones Luong (chap. 6) demonstrate the degree to which regional and central leaders in Uzbekistan and Kazakhstan struggle over the key sources of revenue — cotton and oil and gas, respectively.

The finding that the state tends to struggle against itself in post-Soviet Central Asia diverges from the existing literature, which focuses instead on the struggle between state and society, or between state actors and social forces. Although the need to disaggregate the state, as mentioned above, has been widely recognized in recent years, the greatest obstacle to building effective states in developing countries is still depicted as the struggle for domination between those actors that make up the state and those that constitute social forces (see Migdal 1988; Migdal, Shue and Kohli 1994).[5]

Moreover, this volume sheds light on the conditions under which competition between state actors is likely to be more salient than competition between the state and social forces. Just as social actors and their relative influence vis-à-vis state actors can be shaped by the previous state or ruling apparatus, so too can the mode of competition. By distributing control over scarce resources among a finite set of state leaders, the Soviet system not only created multiple centers of authority but also laid the foundation for the competitive relationship between these actors. Republican governments competed with one another for resource transfers from Moscow while, within each republic, regional governments competed for production inputs and budgetary allocations from their respective republican governments via Moscow (see, e.g., Hough 1969). The state's continued hold on the resources of former republican (and now national) as well as regional governments following independence, coupled with the exit of Moscow as the key player in resource distribution, thus perpetuated competition along these lines. In addition, by greatly constraining the development of countervailing social forces, the Soviet legacy in Central Asia privileged conflict among state elites for their own interests — or "self-contained" competition — over conflict among societal elites for the interests of their constituencies — or "representative" competition (Grzymala-Busse and Jones Luong 2002).

4. Examples include Shukrullo Mirsaidov in Uzbekistan, Feliks Kulov in Kyrgyzstan, and Akezhan Kazhegeldin and Galymzhan Zhakianov in Kazakhstan. See, e.g., Dave 2000, Ilkhamov (chap. 5), and Olcott 2002 for details.

5. An important exception in this regard is Hagopian's (1996) study of Brazil.

Thus, in contrast to other developing countries, local "strongmen" in Central Asia developed within, not outside, the state apparatus; they are a core part of the state rather than representatives of autonomous societal organizations.[6] This has several important implications. First and foremost, it is much more difficult to defeat these strongmen. The fact that regional leaders are part of the state — and indeed, monopolize state power in the periphery — reduces the strategies available to central state leaders. Central authorities cannot simply renounce the legitimacy of regional strongmen, as they did, for example, in Nasser's Egypt (Migdal 1988, 249), because this would call into question the legitimacy of the state as a whole. The president in each country depends on regional leaders to get out the vote at election time, but these leaders must have some local legitimacy and experience to be effective in doing so (Jones Luong, chap. 6). Thus, there is a limited pool of cadre from which a president can select new regional leaders to replace those who have disappointed him.

Second, there is also no potential for a "triangle of accommodation" to develop among state actors and social forces, as it has elsewhere, because the same actors who act as local "strongmen" in Central Asia are also those that are supposed to be "implementers" on behalf of the state (Migdal 1988, chap. 7). In other words, there is no middleman between central state authorities and local strongmen; they must negotiate and seek accommodation with one another. If this accommodation fails to take place, moreover, it can impair the state's ability to develop effective institutions and even lead to an anarchical situation analogous to the scenario of weak states and weak societies in Migdal (1998, 35).

Finally, this struggle has a direct effect on the form and success of economic reform. As chapters 5 and 6 demonstrate, regional elites can challenge the authority of central officials to formulate economic policies without their consent by ignoring or undermining central directives. This is a common feature across the Central Asian states. The precise effect, negative or positive, on economic reform, however, has varied considerably both across and within these states. For example, in those states in which the central government has been the most receptive to economic reform, regional leaders have both supported and obstructed large-scale privatization of natural resources (Kazakhstan), state enterprises (Kyrgyzstan), and land-use rights (Tajikistan). Whereas regional leaders supported privatization of the energy sector in Kazakhstan in exchange for guarantees that the local economy would benefit from foreign invest-

6. The term "strongmen" comes from Migdal 1988. See chapter 1 for details.

ment (Jones Luong and Weinthal 2001), many regional leaders continue to subsidize private industry in order to maintain full employment in Kyrgyzstan[7] and to ignore the rights of farmers to decide what to grow in the traditional cotton-producing regions in Tajikistan.[8]

International Actors and the State-Society Struggle

The experience of the Central Asian states, which were granted independence in the post-Cold War era, also illuminates the direct and indirect ways in which the international community is influencing the relative power of different domestic actors. As in previous periods of new state emergence, international actors have played a crucial role in providing the legal framework and official recognition for statehood. In the current international system, however, "institutional requirements for statehood are embodied in the charters of multiple supranational organizations, which can deny . . . membership to countries that fail to meet these formal requirements" (Grzymala-Busse and Jones Luong 2002, 547). Moreover, international actors have the ability to directly affect state capacity — not only by recognizing state sovereignty but also by shifting the balance of power within states, both among state actors and between state and societal actors.

In short, they achieve this by serving as new social or economic actors who provide an alternative to existing resources, and thus to resource distribution networks. For example, transnational environmental actors offered attractive side payments to state leaders in Central Asia who were willing to comply with international norms (at least on paper) in the form of financial and material resources to key domestic constituencies during

7. Kyrgyzstan has undergone the most extensive economic reform in the region, at least on paper. Beginning in mid-1993, the central government launched a broad reform package that included macroeconomic stabilization, an open trade regime and WTO membership, price liberalization, and an extensive privatization program, resulting in the transfer of 97 percent of all enterprises and over 50 percent of all land from state control to private ownership. (For more detail, see Jones Luong 2003.)

8. Tajikistan officially ended the state monopsony in cotton in 1996 and dissolved the official government purchasing and export agency for cotton, Glavkhlopkoprom, in 1998. Nonetheless, regional monopolies have emerged in its place. Local officials use their authority to enforce de facto production quotas and artificially low prices by withholding inputs from farmers who refuse to grow cotton, blocking farmers' access to external markets, and allocating the best land to cotton while leaving the worst land for growing food. Cotton production is concentrated in two regions: Sughd Oblast (formerly Leninabad) in the north contains about 30 percent of the total area under cultivation for cotton; Khatlon Oblast in the southwest (formerly divided into two oblasts, Kurgan Tyube and Koulab) contains about 60 percent. (For more detail, see Jones Luong 2003.)

the transition period (Weinthal 2002). These new resources provided a sharp boost to government officials at the national (former republican) and regional levels as well as to chairmen of former state farms (kolkhozes), all of whom had lost important subsidies with the fall of the Soviet Union and the end of Moscow's direct involvement in their affairs. As a result, these officials could continue many of their functions and, more importantly, maintain the patronage networks that undergird their power (Weinthal 2002).[9] In addition, international organizations have used financial and normative transfers to empower local environmental NGOs in Central Asia to pressure governments and multinational corporations to meet their environmental commitments (Weinthal, chap. 8). Similarly, foreign direct investment has provided a new source of domestic capital and extrabudgetary revenue for regional leaders, which they have used to directly challenge central authorities. In Kazakhstan, this has shifted the balance of power toward regions that are rich in oil, gas, and minerals or process them (Jones Luong, chap. 6).

At the same time, owing to the nature of their economic resource base and regional (inter-state) pressures,[10] Central Asian states have tended to be much more "resistant" to international pressures for both political and economic reform, particularly in comparison to the post-Communist states in East Central Europe (Grzymala-Busse and Jones Luong 2002, 547). Kazakhstan, Turkmenistan, and Uzbekistan are more insulated from the international community as well as from their own populations because they rely primarily on external rents for revenue, derived from different combinations of their natural resource wealth and agricultural production.[11] Although the desire for foreign investment has helped drive economic liberalization in Kazakhstan, for example, the scope of this reform has been limited and, some might argue, has had the reverse effect on political reform because investors prefer authoritarian systems.[12] In Kyrgyzstan and Tajikistan, whose economies are much more dependent on interstate trade, regional pressures have trumped international ones, leading to the erosion of economic and especially political liberalization.

9. Foreign aid has had a similar effect on clientelism in Africa. See Van de Walle 2001, esp. chap. 5.

10. "Regional" in this section refers to the Central Asian region rather than to subnational units within the Central Asian states.

11. Kazakhstan and Turkmenistan rely more heavily on revenue from oil and gas reserves, while Uzbekistan relies primarily on the export of cotton and gold.

12. Tax reform, for example, has been stalled because of the classic "obsolescing bargain," whereby over time foreign investors lose their bargaining power vis-à-vis the state (Weinthal and Jones Luong 2002).

Although this regional convergence toward authoritarian regimes and closed economies began in the mid-1990s, it has accelerated since the incursion of armed Islamic militants into the region beginning in 1999. Moreover, by most accounts, this trend is likely to continue as long as these states remain a central component of the global "war on terrorism."[13] The overwhelming result has been to circumscribe the legitimate channels through which societal actors can challenge the state.

The Limitations of State Power

Finally, the chapters in this volume also support the notion that we should not "overestimat[e] state power and autonomy" (Migdal, Kohli, and Shue 1994, 14), even in the post-Communist setting wherein the state once appeared to be omnipotent. Although the empirical evidence presented throughout this book verifies the Soviet state's profound effect on both Central Asian states and societies, it also reveals the limitations of state power. Many post-Soviet Central Asian leaders have clung to the institutional and policy legacies of Soviet rule out of a desire to maintain centralized control and avoid challenges to their rule. Yet, they do not appear capable of turning the societies they govern into either fully acquiescent subjects or "quasi-voluntary" compliant citizens.[14] The Soviet Union's relative success in this regard depended not only on a combination of infrastructural and coercive power (Mann 1993), on which it relied extensively, but also on a certain degree of legitimacy across a diverse population based on a broad social contract that started to break down under Gorbachev (Hauslohner 1987). In contrast, Laura Adams and Bhavna Dave (chaps. 3–4) demonstrate that Central Asian leaders have little interest in legitimating their authority beyond a small group of elites.

State power in Central Asia thus hinges entirely on its infrastructural and coercive capabilities. To enhance these capabilities, Central Asian leaders have sought to maintain their control over resource distribution networks and to limit democratization. This has left the state in Central Asia both strong and weak — the "paradoxically strong-weak state," as Kelly McMann (chap. 7) refers to it. States are strong in terms of their ability to shape citizens' expectations and opportunities by limiting their access to scarce resources (Kamp, chap. 1; McMann, chap. 7), and to

13. Military bases were established in Uzbekistan and Kyrgyzstan in the fall of 2001 from which to launch military strikes into and provide humanitarian aid to Afghanistan. In exchange, these two countries have received unconditional financial assistance. See, e.g., Jones Luong and Weinthal 2002.

14. On quasi-voluntary compliance, see Levi 1988, 52–53.

harass, imprison, and torture their political opponents. Yet, they are also weak in that they cannot formulate coherent goals and implement policies consistently across the respective territories they govern, despite efforts at greater centralization (Ilkhamov, chap. 5; Jones Luong, chap. 6).

The convergence toward authoritarianism across Central Asia since 1995, then, is a testament to the declining rather than the rising power of these states. Waning legitimacy in the face of declining standards of living and rampant official corruption has important political as well as economic consequences for these states. Quasi-voluntary compliance is a much more "cost-effective" way to govern yet more difficult to achieve because it "requires a trustworthy government" (Levi 2002). This produces a vicious cycle: as these states fail to bolster their legitimacy to rule, they also jeopardize their capacity to govern (Jackman 1993). Not surprisingly, then, the rise of authoritarian regimes has coincided with the inability of these states to enforce their laws and directives, protect their environment, guard their borders, and engage their population.

Foreign Words and Terms

Adabiyot va Sa"nat. (Uzbek: Literature and Art) A newspaper published in Tashkent

Adolat. (Uzbek) justice

Aka. (Uzbek) literally, older brother; title used to address an older male

Akim. (Kyrgyz and Kazakh) local (regional, city, district) administrative head, governor, mayor, and so forth

Aksakals. (Kyrgyz) white beards; respected male elders in the community

Alyp Qashu. (Kazakh) kidnap marriage; literally "to take and run"

Amir Timur. Fourteenth-century ruler based in Samarkand; new national hero of Uzbekistan

Asaba. (Kyrgyz) Kyrgyz nationalist movement founded in Kyrgyzstan in 1990

Atlas. (Uzbek) a type of ikat silk fabric commonly used in women's dresses in Uzbekistan

Aul. (Kazakh) encampment for nomadic group

Betashar. (Kazakh) "face-opening" ceremony; a marriage ritual during which a new bride is formally presented to her husband's family

Bi. (plural *bilar*) (Kazakh) traditional judge

Birlik. (Uzbek) unity; a banned political party active in Uzbekistan in the early 1990s

Bosmachi. (Uzbek) the name of the rebellious movement that fought against the Bolsheviks in Turkestan in the 1920s

Doma kultury. cultural centers

Dombyra. (Kazakh) a guitar-like musical instrument with two strings

Druzhiny. (Russian) student conservation brigades

Doverennye litsa. (Russian) election campaign managers

ECOLOT. state-sponsored lottery in Uzbekistan used to fund social and cultural projects

Emir. ruler of the Bukharan Khanate; also used to designate a military chieftain in Muslim countries

Erk. (Uzbek) freedom; a banned political party active in Uzbekistan in the early 1990s

Fidokorlar. (Uzbek) Self-sacrificers; political party established in Uzbekistan in January 1999

Goskompriroda. state environmental agency

Guberniya. (Russian) governorate-generals; administrative-territorial unit in the Russian Empire

Hizb-ut-Tahrir. (Arabic) international Islamic political party that seeks the return of the Caliphate

Hokim. (Uzbek) local (regional, city, district) administrative head, governor, mayor, and so forth

Hokimiat. (Uzbek) local (regional, city, district) administrative office headed by hokim

Ishans. Sufi clerics

Kelin. (Kazakh) daughter-in-law

Kelisimmen alyp qashu. (Kazakh) consensual kidnap marriage

Kelisimsiz alyp qashu. (Kazakh) nonconsensual kidnap marriage

Kenesh. (Kyrgyz) council or legislative body

Keshirim. (Kazakh) "apology"; used to describe the informal delegation of relatives who are sent to a bride's family after a kidnapping and to describe the money that is sent as bridewealth in the case of a kidnap marriage

Kiit. (Kazakh) gifts presented to in-laws

Korenizatsiia. (Russian) nativization; refers to Soviet policies toward titular nationalities in the 1920s and early 1930s

Kyrgyz Til. NGO in Kyrgyzstan that wants the Kyrgyz language to be made the official language

Mahalla. (Uzbek) neighborhood or community

Milliy Tiklanish. (Uzbek) National Rebirth; political party established in Uzbekistan in the mid 1990s

Navroz. (Persian; *Nooruz* in Uzbek) New Year; a holiday celebrated in Uzbekistan on March 21

"*Ne meshaet, ne pomogaet.*" (Russian) "does not bother, does not help"

Nepravitel'stvennaia organizatsiia. (Russian) nongovernmental organization

Nomenklatura. (Russian) the system of cadre control and promotion adopted by Communist Party of the Soviet Union

Nyet iazyka, nyet natsii. (Russian) "There is no nation without a language."

Oblasts. (Russian) regions or provinces; administrative-territorial unit created in the Soviet Union but still used in many former Soviet republics

Obkom. (Russian) regional committee of the Communist Party of the Soviet Union

Oq soqols. (Uzbek) local elders; literally, white-beards

Olii Majlis. (Uzbek) Supreme Assembly; Uzbekistan's national parliament established in 1993

Opa. (Uzbek) literally, older sister; title used to address an older female

Oramal. (Kazakh) small kerchief or head scarf that married women wear in rural Kazakhstan; it covers most of the hair and is tied in a knot behind the head

Patir. (Uzbek) flaky Uzbek flat bread

Piyola. (Uzbek) teacup shaped like a small bowl

Qazaq tili. NGO in Kazakhstan advocating for the elevation of the Kazakh language

Qalynmal. (Kazakh) bridewealth; transfer of livestock and/or money from groom's family to bride's family

Quda tusu. (Kazakh) arranged marriage

Qughynshy. (Kazakh) the "pursuers"; the members of the bride's family who visit her shortly after a kidnapping has taken place

Raion. (Russian) district

Shangyraq. (Kazakh) name for the wooden cover of a yurt; a symbol of hearth and home

Shirkat. (Uzbek) cooperative farm

Uezd. (Russian) administrative-territorial unit in the Russian Empire; subordinated to *guberniya*

Vatan Tarakkiyoti. (Uzbek) Progress of the Homeland; pro-presidential political party established in Uzbekistan in the early 1990s

Volost. (old Russian) administrative-territorial unit in the Russian Empire; subordinated to *uezdy*

Zhogorku Kenesh. (Kyrgyz) Supreme Council; national parliament in Kyrgyzstan established in 1994

Zhuz. (Kazakh) tribe; name of the three Kazakh hordes, lesser, middle, and greater

Bibliography

Abdurazakova, Sh., ed. 1986. *Deiatel'nost'Kompartii Uzbekistana po usileniiu sotsial'noi aktivnosti zhenshchin: sbornik dokumentov i materialov (1959–1975)*. Tashkent, Uzbekistan.

Abramson, David. 1998. "From Soviet to Mahalla: Community and Transition in Post-Soviet Uzbekistan." Ph.D. diss., Indiana University.

———. 1999a. "Civil Society and the Politics of Foreign Aid in Uzbekistan." *Central Asia Monitor* 6: 1–12.

———. 1999b. "A Critical Look at NGOs and Civil Society as Means to an End in Uzbekistan." *Human Organization* 58, 3: 240–50.

———. 2001. "Engendering Citizenship in Post-Communist Uzbekistan." Paper presented at the Kennan Institute Workshop on the Role of Women in Post-Communist Transitions. Washington, D.C., November 1–3.

Abu-Lughod, Lila, ed. 1998. *Remaking Women: Feminism and Modernity in the Middle East*. Princeton: Princeton University Press.

Adam, Jan. 1991. *Economic Reforms and Welfare Systems in the USSR, Poland, and Hungary: Social Contract in Transformation*. New York: St. Martin's Press.

Adams, Laura L. 1999a. "Invention, Institutionalization, and Renewal in Uzbekistan's National Culture." *European Journal of Cultural Studies* 2: 355–73.

———. 1999b. "The Mascot Researcher: Identity, Power, and Knowledge in Fieldwork." *Journal of Contemporary Ethnography* 28: 331–63.

———. 2000. "Who's Afraid of the Market? Cultural Policy in Post-Soviet Uzbekistan." *Journal of Arts Management, Law, and Society* 30: 29–41.

Adamson, Fiona B. 2000. "Building Civil Society from the Outside: An Evaluation of Democracy Assistance Strategies in Uzbekistan and Kyrgyzstan." Carnegie Endowment for International Peace, 2000. Accessed November 1. http://www.ceip.org/files/pdf/Adamson.pdf.

Agrawal, Arun. 1999. *Decentralization in Nepal: A Comparative Analysis*. Oakland, Calif.: Institute for Contemporary Studies.

Agrawal, Arun, and Jesse Ribot. 1999. "Accountability in Decentralization: A Framework with South Asian and West African Cases." *Journal of Developing Areas 33* (Summer): 473–502.

Akaev, Askar. 1995. *Izbrannie vystupleniia i rechi*. Bishkek, Kyrgyzstan.

Akbarzadeh, Shahram. 1996. "Nation-building in Uzbekistan." *Central Asian Studies* 15, 1: 23–32.

Akin, John, Paul Hutchinson, and Koleman Strumpf. 2001. "Decentralization and Government: Provision of Public Goods Measure Evaluation." http://www.dec.org/pdf_docs/PNACM175.pdf.

Akiner, Shirin. 1995a. *The Formation of Kazakh National Identity: From Tribe to Nation-State*. London: Royal Institute of International Affairs.

———. 1995b. "The Struggle for Identity." In *After Empire: The Emerging Geopolitics of Central Asia,* edited by Jed C. Snyder. Washington, D.C.: National Defense University Press.

———. 1997. "Between Tradition and Modernity: The Dilemma Facing Contemporary Central Asian Women." In *Post-Soviet Women: From the Baltic to Central Asia*, edited by Mary Buckley. New York: Cambridge University Press, 261–304.

Aldamzharov, Zulkharnai. 1995. "Kontseptsia 'russkoiazychnogo naselenia' formiruet faktor rusofobii." *Sovety Kazakhstan* (28 February): 2–3.

Alimova, D. A. 1991. *Zhenskii Vopros v Srednei Azii*. Tashkent, Uzbekistan: Fan.

Allworth, Edward A. 1989. "The Focus of Literature." In *Central Asia: 120 Years of Russian Rule, edited by* Edward Allworth. Durham, N.C.: Duke University Press, 397–433.

———. 1989a. *Central Asia: 120 Years of Russian Rule*. Durham, N.C.: Duke University Press.

———. 1990. *The Modern Uzbeks from the Fourteenth Century to the Present: A Cultural History*. Stanford: Hoover Institution Press.

American Legal Consortium. 1996. "Innovations and Impacts: Success Stories of Central Asian NGOs." Almaty, Kazakhstan: American Legal Consortium.

Aminova, Rahima. 1977. *The October Revolution and Women's Liberation in Uzbekistan*. Translated by B. M. Meerovich Moscow: Nauka.

Amsler, Sarah, and Russ Kleinbach. 1999. "Bride Kidnapping in the Kyrgyz Republic." *International Journal of Central Asian Studies* 4: 185–216.

Anderson, David G. 1996. "Bringing Civil Society to an Uncivilised Place." In *Civil Society: Challenging Western Models, edited by* C. .M. Hann and Elizabeth Dunn. New York: Routledge, 97–120.

Anderson, John. 1997. *The International Politics of Central Asia*. Manchester, England: Manchester University Press.

———. 1999. *Kyrgyzstan: Central Asia's Island of Democracy?* Amsterdam: Harwood Academic Publishers.

———. 2000. "Creating a Framework for Civil Society in Kyrgyzstan." *Europe-Asia Studies* 52, 1: 77–93.

Anderson, Lisa. 1986. *The State and Social Transformation in Tunisia and Libya, 1830–1980*. Princeton: Princeton University Press.

Argynbaev, Khalel. 1978. "Marriage and Marriage Rites among the Kazakhs in the 19th and Early 20th Centuries." In *The Nomadic Alternative: Modes and Models of Interaction in the African-Asian Deserts and Steppes*, edited by Wolfgang Weissleder, 331–41.

———. 1996. *Qazaq otbasy*. Almaty, Kazakhstan: Kainar Press.

Arora, Vivek B., and John Norregaard. 1997. "Intergovernmental Fiscal Relations: The Chinese System in Perspective." Fiscal Affairs Department Series: Working Paper WP/97/129. Washington, D.C.: International Monetary Fund.

Asian Development Bank. 1997. *Central Asian Environments in Transition*. Manila.

Atkin, Muriel. 1989. *The Subtlest Battle: Islam in Soviet Tajikistan*. Philadelphia: Foreign Policy Research Institute.

Ayres, Barbara. 1974. "Bride Theft and Raiding for Wives in Cross-Cultural Perspective." *Anthropological Quarterly* 47, 3: 238–52.

Azarya, Victor. 1988. "Reordering State-Society Relations: Incorporation and Disengagement." In *The Precarious Balance: State and Society in Africa*, edited by Donald S. Rothchild and Naomi Chazan, 3–21. Boulder, Colo.: Westview.

Badran, Margot. 1995. *Feminists, Islam, and Nation: Gender and the Making of Modern Egypt*. Princeton: Princeton University Press.

Bahry, Donna. 1987. *Outside Moscow: Power, Politics, and Budgetary Policy in the Soviet Republics*. New York: Columbia University Press.

Barkey, Karen, and Sunita Parikh. 1991. "Comparative Perspectives on the State." *Annual Review of Sociology* 17: 523–49.

Barnett, Michael, and Martha Finnemore. 1999. "The Politics, Power, and Pathologies of International Organizations." *International Organization* 53: 699–732.

Bates, Daniel G. 1974. "Normative and Alternative Systems of Marriage among the Yoruk of Southeastern Turkey." *Anthropological Quarterly* 47, 3: 270–87.

Bates, Robert H. 1984. *Market and States in Tropical Africa*. Berkeley: University of California Press.

Baudrillard, Jean. 1983. *Simulations*. New York: Semiotext[e].

Bauer, Armin, Nina Boschmann, and David Green. 1997. *Women and Gender Relations in Kazakhstan: The Social Cost*. Manila, Philippines: Asian Development Bank.

Beissinger, Mark R. 1992. "Elites and Ethnic Identities in Soviet and Post-Soviet Politics." In *The Post-Soviet Nations: Perspectives on the Demise of the USSR*, edited by Alexander J. Motyl. New York: Columbia University Press.

———. 2002. *Nationalist Mobilization and the Collapse of the Soviet State: A Tidal Approach to the Study of Nationalism*. New York: Cambridge University Press.

Bennigsen, Alexandre, and Marie Broxup. 1983. *The Islamic Threat to the Soviet State*. London: Croom Helm.

Bennigsen, Alexandre, and S. Enders Wimbush. 1985. *Muslims of the Soviet Empire*. London: C. Hurst.

Berg, Andrea. 2001. "Old Wine in New Bottles? Uzbekistani Women and Non-Governmental Organizations." Paper presented at the Kennan Institute Workshop on the Role of Women in Post-Communist Transitions. Washington, D.C., 1–3 November.

Berkeliev, Timur. 2001. "Turkmenistan Environmental NGOs Turn Attention to Caspian Coast." *Give and Take* 3 (winter): 18–19.

Bermeo, Nancy Gina. 2000. "Civil Society after Democracy: Some Conclusions." In *Civil Society before Democracy: Lessons from Nineteenth-Century Europe*, edited by Nancy Gina Bermeo and Philip G. Nord, 237–60. Lanham, Md.: Rowman and Littlefield.

"Beseda po kruglom stolom: put′, ukrepliayushii nezavisimost′." 1993. *Narodnoe Slovo* (31 August): 1–2.

Biddison, J. Michael. 1999. "The Current Status of the Oil and Gas Legal and Regulatory Environment in the Republic of Kazakhstan." Presentation at the 7th annual Kazakhstan International Oil and Gas Conference, Almaty, Kazakhstan, 6–7 October.

Blum, Douglas W. 2002. "Beyond Reciprocity: Governance and Cooperation in the Caspian Sea." In *Environmental Peacemaking*, edited by Ken Conca and Geoffrey D. Dabelko. Washington: Woodrow Wilson Center Press; Baltimore: Johns Hopkins University Press.

Bock, Gisela, and Pat Thane, eds. 1991. *Maternity and Gender Policies: Women and the Rise of the European Welfare States, 1880s–1950s*. New York: Routledge.

Boli, John, and George M. Thomas. 1999. *Constructing World Culture: International Nongovernmental Organizations since 1875*. Stanford: Stanford University Press.

Brass, Paul. 1992. "Language and National Identity: Soviet Union and India." In *Thinking Theoretically about Soviet Nationalities*, edited by Alexander Motyl. New York: Columbia University Press.

Bratton, Michael. 1989. "The Politics of Government-NGO Relations in Africa." *World Development* 17, 4: 569–87.

Bremmer, Ian, and Ray Taras, eds. 1997. *New States, New Politics: Building the Post-Soviet Nations*. New York: Cambridge University Press.

Bremmer, Ian, and Cory Welt. 1996. "The Trouble with Democracy in Kazakhstan." *Central Asian Survey* 15, 2: 179–99.

Breslauer, George. 1992. "In Defense of Sovietology." *Post-Soviet Affairs* 8, 3: 197–238.

Browning, Genia. 1987. *Women and Politics in the USSR: Consciousness Raising and Soviet Women's Groups*. New York: St. Martin's.

Brubaker, Rogers. 1994. "Nationhood and the Nationality Question in the Soviet Union and Post-Soviet Eurasia." *Theory and Society* 23: 47–78.

———. 1995. "National Minorities, Nationalizing States, and External National Homelands in the New Europe." *Daedalus* 124, 2 (spring): 107–32.

Brukman, Jan. 1974. "Stealing Women among the Koya of South India." *Anthropological Quarterly* 47, 3: 304–13.

Bryson, Phillip J., and Gary C. Cornia. 2000. "Fiscal Decentralization in Economic Transformation: The Czech and Slovak Cases." *Europe-Asia Studies* 52, 3: 507–23.

Brzezinski, Zbigniew K. 1967. *Ideology and Power in Soviet Politics*. New York: Praeger.

Buchowski, Michal. 1996. "The Shifting Meanings of Civil and Civic Society in Poland." In *Civil Society: Challenging Western Models*, edited by C. M. Hann and Elizabeth Dunn, 79–98. New York: Routledge.

Buckley, Cynthia. 1998. "Rural/urban Differentials in Demographic Processes: The Central Asian States." Population Research and Policy Review 17: 71–89.

Buckley, Mary. 1989. *Women and Ideology in the Soviet Union*. Ann Arbor: University of Michigan Press.

———. 1997. *Post-Soviet Women: From the Baltic to Central Asia*. New York: Cambridge University Press.

Burg, Steven L. 1986. "Central Asian Elite Mobility and Political Change in the Soviet Union." *Central Asian Survey* 5, 3/4: 77–89.

Carlisle, Donald S. 1991. "Power and Politics in Soviet Uzbekistan." In *Soviet Central Asia, edited by William* K. Fierman, 93–130. Boulder, Colo.: Westview.

———. 1995. "Islam Karimov and Uzbekistan: Back to the Future?" In *Patterns in Post-Communist Leadership*, edited by Timothy Colton. Boulder, Colo.: Westview.

Carothers, Thomas. 1999. "Aiding Democracy Abroad: The Learning Curve." Caspian Environment Program, Concept Paper, 3 May 1998. Washington, D.C.: Carnegie Endowment for International Peace. Carrere d'Encausse, Helene. 1981. *Decline of an Empire: The Soviet Socialist Republics in Revolt*. New York: Harper and Row.

———. 1993. *The End of the Soviet Empire: The Triumph of the Nations*. New York: Basic Books.

Caspian Environment Program, *Concept Paper*, 3 May 1998.

Caspinfo Information Service, May 16–31, 2001, ISAR's Caspian Program.

Cavanaugh, Cassandra. 2001. "Backwardness and Biology: Medicine and Power in Russian and Soviet Central Asia, 1868–1934." Ph.D. diss., Columbia University.

Chapman, Jane. 1991. "Drastic Changes in the Soviet Social Contract." In *Economic Reforms and Welfare Systems in the USSR, Poland, and Hungary: Social Contract in the Transition*, edited by Jan Adam. New York: St. Martin's.

Chukhovich, Boris. 1998. "Kul'turniy Mir Molodykh Khudozhnikov Uzbekistana 80-x–90-x Godov: Opyt Sotsiologicheskogo Issledovaniia." *Ijtimoiy Fikr/Obshchestvennoe Mnenie/Public Opinion* 1: 139–54.

Cirtautas, Arista Maria. 1995. "The Post-Leninist State: A Conceptual and Empirical Examination." *Communist and Post-Communist Studies* 28: 379–92.

Clawson, Patrick. 1995. "The Former Soviet South and the Muslim World." In *After Empire: The Emerging Geopolitics of Central Asia*, edited by Jed C. Snyder. Washington, D.C.: National Defense University Press.

Clements, Barbara Evans. 1997. *Bolshevik Women*. New York: Cambridge University Press.

Cohen, Jean L., and Andrew Arato. 1992. *Civil Society and Political Theory*. Cambridge: MIT Press.

Collins, Kathleen 2003. The Political Role of Clans and Conflict in Central Asia. *Comparative Politics* 35, 2: 171–90.

Conant, Francis P. 1974. "Frustration, Marriage Alternatives, and Subsistence Risks among the Pokot of East Africa: Impressions of Co-Variance." *Anthropological Quarterly* 47, 3: 314–27.

Conquest, Robert. 1970. *The Nation-Killers: The Soviet Deportation of Nationalities*. London: Macmillan.

Constantine, Elizabeth. 2001. "Public Discourse and Private Lives: Uzbek Women under Soviet Rule, 1917–1991." Ph.D. diss., Indiana University.

Constitution of the Republic of Uzbekistan. 1992. English version of the text is found at http://www.umid.uz/Main/Uzbekistan/Constitution/constitution.html.

Cooper, Jay. 1999. "The Real Work: Sustaining NGO Growth in Central Asia." In *Civil Society in Central Asia*, edited by M. Holt Ruffin and Daniel Clarke Waugh, 214–31. Seattle: University of Washington Press.

Counterpart International. 2001. "Civil Society Programs." 2001 (accessed October 1). Available from http://www.counterpart.org/programs.civisoc/.

Critchlow, Jim. 1988. "Corruption, Nationalism, and the Native Elites in Soviet Central Asia." *Journal of Communist Studies* 4, 2: 143–61.

———. 1991. "Prelude to Independence: How the Uzbek Party Apparatus Broke Moscow's Grip on Elite Recruitment." In *Soviet Central Asia*, edited by William K. Fierman, 131–56. Boulder, Colo.: Westview.

Crook, Richard C., and James Manor. 1998. *Democracy and Decentralization in South Asia and West Africa: Participation, Accountability, and Performance*. New York: Cambridge University Press.

Cummings, Sally N. 2000. *Kazakhstan: Centre-Periphery Relations*. London: Royal Institute of International Affairs and the Brookings Institution.

Darden, Keith A. 2000. "The Origins of Economic Interests: Explaining Variation in Support for Regional Institutions among the Post-Soviet States." Ph.D. diss., University of California, Berkeley.

Dave, Bhavna. 1996a. "A New Parliament Consolidates Presidential Authority." *Transition* 2, 6 (22 March): 33–37.

———. 1996b. "Language Revival in Kazakhstan: Language Shift and Identity Change." *Post-Soviet Affairs* 12, 1 (January–March): 51–72.

———. 2000. "Democracy Activism in Kazakhstan: Patronage, Opposition, and International Linkages." Paper presented at the fifth annual convention of the Association for the Study of Nationalities, Columbia University, New York, 13–15 April.

———. 2003. "Entitlement through Numbers: Nationality and Language Categories in the First Post-Soviet Census of Kazakhstan." Forthcoming in *Nations and Nationalism*.

Dawisha, Karen, and Bruce Parrott, eds. 1997. *Conflict, Cleavage, and Change in Central Asia and the Caucasus*. New York: Cambridge University Press.

Dawson, Jane. 1996. *Eco-Nationalism: Anti-Nuclear Activism and National Identity in Russia, Lithuania, and Ukraine*. Durham, N.C.: Duke University Press.

Debord, Guy. 1995 [1967]. *The Society of the Spectacle*. New York: Zone Books.

Deever, John, and Irina Pirigova. 2001. "The *Druzhina* Movement: Forty Years of Youth Activism." *Give and Take* 4: 13–15.

Devereux, John, and Bryan Roberts. 1997. "Direct Foreign Investment and Welfare in the Transforming Economies: The Case of Central Asia." *Journal of Comparative Economics* 24: 297–312.

DiMaggio, Paul J., and Walter W. Powell. 1991. "The Iron Cage Revisited: Institutional Isomorphism and Collective Rationality in Organizational Fields." In *The New Institutionalism in Organizational Analysis*, edited by Walter W. Powell and Paul J. DiMaggio, 63–82. Chicago: University of Chicago Press.

Djalili, Mohammad-Reza, Frederic Grare, and Shirin Akiner, eds. 1997. *Tajikistan: The Trials of Independence*. New York: St. Martin's.

Doi, Mary Masayo. 2002. *Gesture, Gender, Nation: Dance and Social Change in Uzbekistan*. Westport, Conn.: Bergin and Garvey.

Durkheim, Emile. 1915. *The Elementary Forms of the Religious Life*. New York: Free Press.

Eaton, Kent. "2000 Fiscal Decentralization in Developing Democracies: What's at Stake for Legislators?" Paper prepared for the Yale Colloquium on Decentralization and Development. http://www.yale.edu/ycias/events/decentralization/.

Echeverri-Gent, John. 2000. "Globalization and Decentralization: Lessons for Good Governance from China and India." Paper prepared for the Yale Colloquium on Decentralization & Development. http://www.yale.edu/ycias/events/decentralization.

"Economic Separatism Could Become a Threat in Kazakhstan." 1998. *Focus Central Asia Annual Report 1998*, 77–78.

Edgar, Adrienne. 1997. "Nationality Policy and National Identity: The Turkmen Soviet Socialist Republic, 1924–29." *Journal of Central Asian Studies* 1, 2 (spring/summer): 2–20.

Ellner, Andrea. 1997. "Whither Transition — Development and Security in the Former Soviet Central Asia." *Journal of International Development* 9, 4: 549–61.

Esman, Milton J. 1992. "The State and Language Policy." *International Political Science Review* 13 (4): 381–96.

Eurasianet. 2001. "Musicians Are Struggling to Adjust to the New Working Environment since the Collapse of the Soviet Union." http://www.eurasianet.org/departments/qanda/articles/eav012601.shtml.

European Bank for Reconstruction and Development. *Transition Report*. 1999. London.

Evans, Peter B. 1995. *Embedded Autonomy: States and Industrial Transformation*. Princeton: Princeton University Press.

———. 1997a. "Government Action, Social Capital, and Development: Reviewing the Evidence on Synergy." In *State-Society Synergy: Government and Social Capital in Development*, edited by Peter B. Evans, 178–209. Berkeley: International and Area Studies, University of California at Berkeley.

———. 1997b. "Introduction: Development Strategies across the Public-Private Divide." In *State-Society Synergy*, edited by Peter B. Evans, 1–10.

Fainsod, Merle. 1970. *How Russia Is Ruled*. 1953. Revised ed. Cambridge: Harvard University Press.

Fairman, David 1996. "The Global Environment Facility: Haunted by the Shadow of the Future." In *Institutions for Environmental Aid*, edited by Robert O. Keohane and Marc A. Levy. Cambridge: MIT Press.

Falkingham, Jane. 1999. *Welfare in Transition: Trends in Poverty and Well-being in Central Asia*. CASE paper 20. London: Centre for Analysis of Social Exclusion.

Falkingham, Jane, Jeni Klugman, and Sheila Marnie, eds. 1997. *Household Welfare in Central Asia*. London: Macmillan.

Feng, Yi, Ismene Gizelis, and Jeili Li. 1999. "Political, Economic, and Social Rationale of Welfare and Social Security: A Comparative Analysis of Malaysia and China." *International Journal of Economic Development* 1, 4: 369–97.

Fernea, Elizabeth, and Basima Bezirgan. 1977. *Middle Eastern Muslim Women Speak*. Austin: University of Texas Press.

Feshbach, Murray, and Alfred Friendly, Jr. 1992. *Ecocide in the USSR*. New York: Basic Books.

Fierman, William K. 1991a. Language Planning and National Development: The Uzbek Experience. New York: Mouton de Gruyter.

———. 1995. "Independence and Declining Priority of Language Law in Uzbekistan." In *Muslim Eurasia: Conflicting Legacies*, edited by Yaacov Ro'i, 205–30. Portland: Frank Cass.

———. 1997. "Political Development in Uzbekistan: Democratization?" In *Conflict, Cleavage, and Change in Central Asia and the Caucasus*, edited by Karen Dawisha and Bruce Parrot, 360–408. New York: Cambridge University Press.

———, ed. 1991b. Soviet Central Asia: The Failed Transformation. Boulder, Colo.: Westview.

Firth, Raymond. 1957 [1936]. *We, the Tikopia: A Sociological Study of Kinship in Primitive Polynesia*. Boston: Beacon Press.

Fish, M. Steven. 1995. *Democracy from Scratch: Opposition and Regime in the New Russian Revolution*. Princeton: Princeton University Press.

Flower, John, and Pamela Leonard. 1996. "Community Values and State Co-optation: Civil Society in the Sichuan Countryside." In *Civil Society: Challenging Western Models*, edited by C. M. Hann and Elizabeth Dunn, 199–221. New York: Routledge.

Focus Central Asia. 1998. 28–29 June. Almaty.

Foucault, Michel. 2000. *Power. Essential Works of Foucault 1954–1984. Vol. 3*. Edited by James D. Faubion. New York: New Press.

Fox, Jonathan. 1997. "How Does Civil Society Thicken? The Political Construction of Social Capital in Rural Mexico." In *State-Society Synergy*, edited by Peter B. Evans, 119–49.

Frank, David John, et al. 1999. "The Rationalization and Organization of Nature in World Culture." In *Constructing World Culture: International*

Nongovernmental Organizations since 1875, edited by John Boli and George M. Thomas. Stanford: Stanford University Press.

Frantz, Telmo Rudi. 1987. "The Role of NGOs in the Strengthening of Civil Society." *World Development* 15: 121–27.

Frazer, Glenda. 1987. "Basmachi — I." *Central Asian Survey* 6, 1: 1–73.

Friedgut, Theodore. 1979. *Political Participation in the USSR*. Princeton: Princeton University Press.

Friedrich, Carl J., and Zbigniew K. Brzezinski. 1956. *Totalitarian Dictatorship and Autocracy*. Cambridge: Harvard University Press.

G'ulomova, Dilbar. 1999. *Xotin-Qizlar Entsiklopediiasi*. Tashkent, Uzbekistan: Millii entsiklopediiasi.

Garbutt, Anne. 1997. "NGO Support Organizations in Central Asia." Discussion paper prepared for INTRAC.

Gellner, Ernest. 1983. *Nations and Nationalism*. Oxford: Blackwell.

George, Aleksandra. 2001. *Journey into Kazakhstan: The True Face of the Nazarbayev Regime*. Lanham, MD: University Press of America.

Glantz, Michael H., ed. 1999. *Creeping Environmental Problems and Sustainable Development in the Aral Sea Basin*. New York: Cambridge University Press.

Gleason, Gregory. 1990a. "Marketization and Migration: The Politics of Cotton in Central Asia." *Journal of Soviet Nationalities* 1.

———. 1990b. "Nationalism or Organized Crime? The Case of the 'Cotton Scandal' in the USSR." *Corruption and Reform* 5: 87–108.

———. 1997. *The Central Asian States: Discovering Independence*. Boulder, Colo.: Westview.

———. 2002. *Nations in Transit: Uzbekistan 2001*. New York, NY: Freedom House. http://216.119.117.183/research/nitransit/2001/country/26_uzbekistan.htm.

Godunova, Galina. 2001. "Massive Die-off of Caspian Seals — A Warning Sign for Human Beings." *Give and Take* 3 (winter): 12–14.

Goldfarb, Jeffrey C. 1980. *The Persistence of Freedom: The Sociological Implications of Polish Student Theater*. Boulder, Colo.: Westview.

———. 1991. *Beyond Glasnost: The Post-Totalitarian Mind.* Chicago: University of Chicago Press.

Goldman, Wendy Z. 1993. *Women, the State, and Revolution: Soviet Family Policy and Social Life, 1917–1936*. New York: Cambridge University Press.

Gorenburg, Dmitry. 1999. "Regional Separatism in Russia: Ethnic Mobilization or Power Grab?" *Europe-Asia Studies* 51, 2: 245–74.

Gould, Arthur. 1993. *Capitalist Welfare Systems: A Comparison of Japan, Britain, and Sweden*. Essex, England: Longman.

Graney, Katherine. 1999. "Projecting Sovereignty: Statehood and Nationness in Post-Soviet Tatarstan." Ph.D. diss., University of Wisconsin, Madison.

Gray, Laurel Victoria. 1998. "Uzbekistan." In *The World Encyclopedia of Contemporary Theater*, edited by Don Rubin, Ravi Chaturvedi, Ramendu Majumdar, Chua Soo Pong, and Minoru Tanokura. New York: Routledge.

Grzymala-Busse, Anna, and Pauline Jones Luong. 2002. "Reconceptualizing the State: Lessons from Post-Communism." *Politics and Society* 30, 4 (December): 529–54.

Haas, Peter M., Robert O. Keohane, and Marc A. Levy, eds. 1993. *Institutions for the Earth: Sources of Effective International Environmental Protection*. Cambridge: MIT Press.

Haddad, Yvonne, and John Esposito, eds. 1999. *Islam, Gender, and Social Change*. Oxford: Oxford University Press.

Haghayegdi, Mehrdad. 1994. "Islam and Democratic Politics in Central Asia." *World Affairs* 156, 3: 186–98.

Hagopian, Francis. 1996. *Traditional Politics and Regime Change in Brazil*. New York: Cambridge University Press.

Hale, Henry E. 1998. "Statehood at Stake: Democratization, Secession, and the Collapse of the Union of Soviet Socialist Republics." Ph.D. diss., Harvard University.

Haney, Lynne. 1996. "Homeboys, Babies, Men in Suits: the State and the Reproduction of Male Dominance." *American Sociological Review* 61: 759–78.

———. 1998. "Engendering the Welfare State." *Comparative Studies in Society and History* 40: 748–67.

Hauslohner, Peter. 1987. "Gorbachev's Social Contract." *Soviet Economy* 3, 1: 54–89.

Hayit, Baymirza. 1987. *Islam and Turkestan under Russian Rule*. Istanbul: Can Matbaa.

Hiro, Dilip. 1994. *Between Marx and Muhammad: The Changing Face of Central Asia*. London: Harper Collins.

Hirsch, Francine. 2000. "Toward an Empire of Nations: Border-Making and the Formation of Soviet National Identities." *Russian Review* 59 (April): 201–26.

Hogan, Beatrice. 19 August 1999. "Uzbekistan: U.S. Begins Survey of Chemical Weapons Plant." Radio Free Europe/Radio Liberty. http://www.rferl.org/newsline/1999/08/190899.asp.

Holmes, Stephen. 1997. "What Russia Teaches Us Now: How Weak States Threaten Freedom." *American Prospect* 33: 30–39.

Horowitz, Donald. 1985. *Ethnic Groups in Conflict*. Berkeley: University of California Press.

Horton, Scott, and Alla Kazakina. 1999. "The Legal Regulation of NGOs: Central Asia at a Crossroads." In *Civil Society in Central Asia*, edited by M. Holt Ruffin and Daniel Clarke Waugh, 34–56. Seattle: University of Washington Press.

Hough, Jerry. 1969. *The Soviet Prefects*. Cambridge: Harvard University Press.

———. 1977. *The Soviet Union and Social Science Theory*. Cambridge: Harvard University Press.

Human Rights Watch. May 1998. "Crackdown in the Fergana Valley: Arbitrary Arrests and Religious Discrimination." http://www.hrw.org/reports98/uzbekistan/.

———. October 1999. "Kazakhstan: Freedom of the Media and Political Freedoms in the Prelude to the 1999 Elections." http://www.hrw.org/reports/1999/kazakhstan/.

———. 1999. "Uzbekistan. Human Rights Developments." *Human Rights Watch World Report*. http://www.hrw.org/hrw/worldreport99/europe/uzbekistan.html.

———. July 2001. "Sacrificing Women to Save the Family? Domestic Violence in Uzbekistan." *HRW Publications* 13, 4. http://www.hrw.org/reports/2001/Uzbekistan/.

Hunter, Shireen T. 2000. "Iran, Central Asia, and the Opening of the Islamic Iron Curtain." In *Islam and Central Asia*, edited by Roald Sagdeev and Susan Eisenhower. Washington, D.C.: Center for Strategic and Political Studies.

Huskey, Eugene. 1995. "The Politics of Language in Kyrgyzstan." *Nationalities Papers* 3: 549–72.

———. 1997. "Kyrgyzstan: The Fate of Political Liberalization." In *Conflict, Cleavage, and Change in Central Asia and the Caucasus*, edited by Karen Dawisha and Bruce Parrott. New York: Cambridge University Press.

Hyman, Anthony. 1997. "Power and Politics in Central Asia's New Republics." In *Beyond the Soviet Union: The Fragmentation of Power*, edited by Mark Beloff. Aldershot, England: Ashgate.

Ikramova, Ula, and Kathryn McConnell. 1999. "Women's NGOs in Central Asia's Evolving Societies." In *Civil Society in Central Asia, edited by* M. Holt Ruffin and Daniel Clarke Waugh, 198–213. Seattle: University of Washington.

Ilkhamov, Alisher. 1998. "Shirkats, Dekhqon Farmers, and Others: Farm Restructuring in Uzbekistan." *Central Asian Survey* 17, 4: 539–60.

———. 2000a. "Divided Economy: Kolkhozes versus Peasant Subsistence Farms in Uzbekistan." *Central Asian Monitor* 4: 5–14.

———. 2000b. "A Bicameral Parliament for Uzbekistan?" *Eurasia Insight*. http://www.eurasianet.org/departments/insight/articles/eav-2200.shtml. Posted June 22, 2000.

Instruktsiia: o poriadke provedennia perepisi naseleniia 1999 goda i zapolneniia perepisnoi dokumentatsii. 1998. Almaty: Natsional'noe statisticheskoe agentstvo Respubliki Kazakhstana.

International Bank for Reconstruction and Development. 1997. *World Development Report 1997: The State in a Changing World*. Oxford: Oxford University Press.

International Crisis Management Group (ICG). March 2001. "Central Asia: Islamist Mobilization and Regional Security." *ICG Asia Report No. 14*. Osh, Uzbekistan, and Brussels.

———. August 2001. "Uzbekistan at Ten: Repression and Stability." *ICG Asia Report No. 21*. Osh and Brussels.

———. August 2002. "Kyrgyzstan's Political Crisis: An Exit Strategy." Osh/Brussels, *http://www.crisisweb.org*.

International Monetary Fund. 1992. *Economic Review Uzbekistan*. Washington D.C.: IMF.

International Women's Rights Action Watch (IWRAW). January 2001. Report, Uzbekistan, Section 5, Sex Roles and Stereotyping. http://www.igc.org/iwraw/publications/countries/uzbekistan.html.

Interstate Council for Aral Sea Problems developed with the Assistance of the World Bank for Kazakhstan, Kyrgyz Republic, Tajikistan, Turkmenistan, and Uzbekistan. 1996. "Fundamental Provisions of Water Management Strategy in the Aral Sea Basin: Common Strategy of Water Allocation, Rational Water Use and Protection of Water Resources." October. Tashkent, Uzbekistan.

Jackson, Robert, and Carl Rosberg. 1992. "Why Africa's Weak States Persist: The Empirical and the Juridical in Statehood." *World Politics* 35, 1: 1–24.

Jackman, Robert. 1993. *Power without Force: The Political Capacity of Nation-States*. Ann Arbor: University of Michigan Press.

Jalilov, Shuhrat. 1994. *Davlat hokimiiati mahallii organlari islohoti: tajriba wa muammolar*. Tashkent, Uzbekistan.

Jamestown Monitor. 1998. "President says no to regional financial autonomy." 4, 128 (July 6). http://www.jamestown.org/pubs/view/mon_004_128_000.htm#014.

Jones Luong, Pauline. 1998. *Ethnopolitics and Institutional Design: Explaining the Establishment of Electoral Systems in Post-Soviet Central Asia*. Ph.D. diss., Harvard University.

———. 1999. "The Future of Central Asian Statehood." *Central Asian Monitor* 1: 1–10.

———. 2002. *Institutional Change and Political Continuity in Post-Soviet Central Asia: Power, Perceptions, and Pacts*. New York: Cambridge University Press.

———. 2003. "Political Obstacles to Economic Reform in Uzbekistan, Kyrgyzstan, and Tajikistan: Strategies to Move Ahead." Paper prepared for the World Bank Lucerne Conference of the CIS-7 Initiative, January 20–22.

Jones Luong, Pauline, and Lucan Way. 2001. "Getting a Second Opinion: Is Market-Preserving Federalism the Right Diagnosis for What Ails the Post-Soviet Economy?" Paper presented at the annual meeting of the American Political Science Association, San Francisco, 1–4 September.

Jones Luong, Pauline, and Erika Weinthal. 1999. "The NGO Paradox: Democratic Goals and Non-Democratic Outcomes in Kazakhstan." *Europe-Asia Studies* 51, 7: 1267–84.

———. 2001. "Prelude to the Resource Curse: Explaining Energy Development Strategies in the Soviet Successor States and Beyond." *Comparative Political Studies* 34, 4: 367–99.

———. 2002. "New Friends, New Fear in Central Asia." *Foreign Affairs* 81, 2 (March–April): 61–70.

Joseph, Suad, ed. 2000. *Gender and Citizenship in the Middle East*. Syracuse, N.Y.: University of Syracuse Press.

Jowitt, Kenneth. 1992. *New World Disorder: The Leninist Legacy*. Berkeley: University of California Press.

Kaiser, Robert J. 1994. *The Geography of Nationalism in Russia and the USSR*. Princeton: Princeton University Press.

Kamp, Marianne. 1998. "Unveiling Uzbek Women." Ph.D. diss., University of Chicago.

Kandiyoti, Deniz. 1991. *Women, Islam and the State*. Philadelphia: Temple University Press.

———. 1996. "Modernization without the Market? The Case of the 'Soviet East.'" *Economy and Society* 25, 4: 529–42.

———. 1999. "Poverty in Transition: An Ethnographic Critique of Household Surveys in Post-Soviet Central Asia." *Development and Change* 30: 499–524.

Karabel, Jerome. 1996. "Towards a Theory of Intellectuals and Politics." *Theory and Society* 25: 205–33.

Karmysheva, Dzh. Kh. 1967. "Sem'ia i semeinyi byt'" (Family and Family Life.) In *Kul'tura i byt Kazakhskogo kolkhoznogo aula*, edited by A. Kh. Margulan and V. V. Vostrov. Almaty, Kazakhstan: Nauka Publishers.

Karpat, Kemal. 1983. "Moscow and the Muslim Question." *Problems of Communism* 32: 71–79.

Kasybekov, Erkinbek. 1999. "Government and Nonprofit Sector Relations in the Kyrgyz Republic." In *Civil Society in Central Asia*, edited by M. Holt Ruffin and Daniel Clarke Waugh, 71–84. Seattle: University of Washington Press.

Keck, Margaret E., and Kathryn Sikkink. 1998. *Activists beyond Borders: Advocacy Networks in International Politics*. Ithaca: Cornell University Press.

"Kelazhagimiz parlament: siosii donishmandlik va professionalism." 2000. *Milly Tiklanish*, 13 June. Tashkent, Uzbekistan.

Keohane, Robert, and Marc Levy, eds. 1996. *Institutions for Environmental Aid.* Cambridge: MIT Press.

Khalid, Adeeb. 1998. *The Politics of Muslim Cultural Reform: Jadidism in Central Asia*. Berkeley: University of California Press.

Khamidov, Bakhtiyar. 1999. "Social Stability and Social Protection in Uzbekistan." Manila Social Forum, The New Social Agenda for Central, East, and Southeast Asia, 9–12 November. http://aric.adb.org/conference/msf/papers/UZB-Pl_2.htm.

Khliupin, Vitaly N. 1998. *Bol'shaia sem'ia' Nursultana Nazarbaeva: Politicheskaia elita sovremennogo Kazakhstana*. Moscow: Institut aktual'nykh politicheskikh issledovanii.

Kinzer, Stephen. 13 October 1999. "Kazakhstan: New Premier Picked." *New York Times*.

Klugman, Jeni. 1998. "A Survey of Health Reform in Central Asia." World Bank Technical Paper no. 344. Social Challenges of Transition series. Washington, D.C.

Klugman, Jeni, Sheila Marnie, John Micklewright, and Philip O'Keefe. 1997. "The Impact of Kindergarten Divestiture on Household Welfare in Central Asia." In *Household Welfare in Central Asia*, edited by Jane Falkingham, Jeni Klugman, Sheila Marnie, and John Micklewright, 183–201. New York: St. Martin's.

Kohli, Atul. 1986. *The State and Development in the Third World*. Princeton: Princeton University Press.

———. 2002. "State, Society and Development." In *Political Science: The State of the Discipline*, edited by Ira Katznelson and Helen Milner, 84–117. New York: W. W. Norton.

Kolstø, Pål. 1998. "Anticipating Demographic Superiority: Kazakh Thinking on Integration and Nation-Building." *Europe-Asia Studies* 50: 51–69.

———. 1999. "Territorializing Diasporas: The Case of Russians in the Former Soviet Republics." *Millennium: Journal of International Studies* 28, 3: 607–31

Konstitutsiia Respubliki Uzbekistan. 1992. Tashkent, Uzbekistan.

Koroteyeva, V., and E. Makarova. 1998. "The Assertion of Uzbek National Identity: Nativization or State-Building Process?" In *Post-Soviet Central Asia*, edited by T. Atabaki and J. O'Kane. New York: I. B. Tauris.

Korth, Britta. 2001. "The Limits of Language Revival: The Kyrgyz Case." Paper presented at the sixth annual Association for the Study of Nationalities (ASN) Convention, New York, 5–7 April 2001.

Kosmarskaia, Natalia. 2000. "'Ethnic Relations in Central Asia'—A Sensitive Issue?" *Central Asia and the Caucasus* 1: 65–73.

Kotkin, Stephen. 2001. "Modern Times: The Soviet Union and the Interwar Conjuncture." *Kritika: Explorations in Russian and Eurasian History* 2, 1: 111–64.

Koven, Seth, and Sonya Michel, eds. 1993. *Mothers of a New World: Maternalist Politics and the Origins of Welfare States*. New York: Routledge.

Kreindler, Isabelle. 1991. "Forging a Soviet People." In *Soviet Central Asia: A Failed Transformation*, edited by William K. Fierman. Boulder, Colo.: Westview.

Kubicek, Paul. 1997. "Regionalism, Nationalism, and Realpolitik in Central Asia." *Europe-Asia Studies* 49, 4 (June): 637–55.

Kubik, Jan. 2000. "Between the State and Networks of 'Cousins': The Role of Civil Society and Noncivil Associations in the Democratization of Poland." In *Civil Society before Democracy*, edited by Nancy Gina Bermeo and Philip Nord. 181–207. Lanham, Md.: Rowman and Littlefield.

Kudat, Ayse. 1974. "Institutional Rigidity and Individual Initiative in Marriages of Turkish Peasants." *Anthropological Quarterly* 47, 3: 288–303.

Kudat, Ayse, Stan Peabody, and Cağlar Keyder, eds. 2000. "Social Assessment and Agricultural Reform in Central Asia and Turkey." Europe and Central Asia Environmentally and Socially Sustainable Development Series, Technical Paper No. 461. Washington, D.C.: *The World Bank*.

Kuehnast, Kathleen. 1998. "From Pioneers to Entrepreneurs: Young Women, Consumerism, and the 'World Picture' in Kyrgyzstan." *Central Asian Survey* 17, 4: 639–54.

Kul'chik, Yuri, Andrei Fadin, and Viktor Sergeev. 1996. *Central Asia after the Empire*. London: Pluto Press.

Kunzel, Regina. 1993. *Fallen Women, Problem Girls*. New Haven: Yale University Press.

Kuru, Ahmet T. 2002. "Between the State and Cultural Zones: Nation-Building in Turkmenistan." *Central Asian Survey* 21, 1: 71–90.

Kuznetsova, Sofia. 1999. "Polozhenie russkikh v Kazakhstane." *Rossiia i Musalmanskii mir* 80: 23–26.

Laitin, David D. 1992. *Language Repertoires and State Construction in Africa*. Cambridge: Cambridge University Press.

Landau, Jacob, and Barbara Kellner-Heinkele. 2001. *Politics of Language in the Ex-Soviet Muslim States*. London: Hurst and Company.

Lapidus, Gail. 1978. *Women in Soviet Society: Equality, Development, and Social Change*. Berkeley: University of California Press.

"Law of the Kyrgyz Republic on Non-Commercial Organizations." 1999. International Center for Non-Profit Law. http://www.icnl.org/library/nis/laws/kyrkawNCOs.htm.

Lawyer's Committee for Human Rights. 1994. "Karimov's Way: Freedom of Association in Uzbekistan." *Freedom of Association Project Briefing Paper* 1: 1–32.

Lazreg, Marnia, ed. 2000. "Making the Transition Work for Women in Europe and Central Asia." Europe and Central Asia Gender and Development Series, Discussion paper No. 411. Washington, D.C.: The World Bank.

Levi, Margaret. 1988. *Of Rule and Revenue*. Berkeley: University of California Press.

———. 2002. "The Study of the State of the State." In *Political Science: The State of the Discipline*, edited by Ira Katznelson and Helen Milner, 33–55. New York: W. W. Norton.

Lévi-Strauss, Claude. 1969 [1949]. *The Elementary Structures of Kinship*. Boston: Beacon Press.

Levin, Theodore. 1996. *The Hundred Thousand Fools of God: Musical Travels in Central Asia (and Queens, New York)*. Bloomington: Indiana University Press.

Levshin, A. I. 1832. *Opisaniia Kirgiz-Kaisachikh, ili, kirgiz-kazakhikh, ord i step'i*. St. Petersburg.

Levy, Jonah D. 1999. *Tocqueville's Revenge: State, Society, and Economy in Contemporary France*. Cambridge: Harvard University Press.

Linz, Juan J., and Alfred C. Stepan. 1996. *Problems of Democratic Transition and Consolidation: Southern Europe, South America, and Post-Communist Europe*. Baltimore: Johns Hopkins University Press.

Lipovsky, Igor. 1995. "The Central Asian Cotton Epic." *Central Asian Survey* 14, 4: 529–42.

Liu, Morgan. 2000. "Articulating Locality and State without Thinking Nationality: Authority and Political Imagination among Uzbeks in Osh, Kyrgyzstan." Paper presented at the fifth annual Association for the Study of Nationalities (ASN) Convention, New York, 13–15 April 2000.

Liushkevich, F. D. 1989. "Traditsii mezhsemeinykh sviazei Uzbeksko-Tadzhikskogo naseleniia Srednei Azii: k probleme bytovaniia kalyma i drugikh patriarkhal'nykh obychaev." *Sovetskaia etnografiia* 4: 58–68.

Lockwood, William. 1974. "Bride Theft and Social Maneuverability in Western Bosnia." *Anthropological Quarterly* 47, 3: 253–69.

Lubin, Nancy. 1984. *Labor and Nationality in Soviet Central Asia: An Uneasy Compromise*. Princeton: Princeton University Press.

Madison, Bernice. 1968. *Social Welfare in the Soviet Union*. Stanford: Stanford University Press.

Makarova, Ekaterina. 1999. "The Mahalla, Civil Society, and the Domestication of the State in Soviet and Post-Soviet Uzbekistan." Paper presented at the workshop on Home-grown Models of Civil Society in the Muslim World, Brown University.

Mann, Michael. 1993. *The Sources of Social Power*. Vol. 2. New York: Cambridge University Press.

Massell, Gregory. 1974. *The Surrogate Proletariat: Moslem Women and Revolutionary Strategies in Soviet Central Asia, 1919–1929*. Princeton: Princeton University Press.

Margolin, Leslie. 1997. *Under the Cover of Kindness: The Invention of Social Work*. Charlottesville: University Press of Virginia.

Marshall, Gordon, ed. 1998. *A Dictionary of Sociology*. New York: Oxford University Press.

Martin, Terry. 2001. *An Affirmative Action Empire: Nations and Nationalism in the Soviet Union, 1923–1939*. Ithaca: Cornell University Press.

Martin, Virginia. 2001. *Law and Custom in the Steppe: The Kazakhs of the Middle Horde and Russian Colonialism in the Nineteenth Century*. London: Curzon Press.

McAuley, Alastair. 1995. "The Economies of Central Asia: The Socialist Legacy." In *Muslim Eurasia: Conflicting Legacies*, edited by Yaacov Ro'i. Portland: Frank Cass.

McCrann, Patrick J. 2001. *Building Civil Society: Annual Needs Assessment of the Local NGO Sector in Azerbaijan*. ISAR-Azerbaijan.

McFaul, Michael, and Nikolai Petrov, eds. 1997. *Politicheskii Al'manakh Rossii 1997: Sotsial'no-Politicheskie Portrety Regionov*. Vol. 2. Moscow: Tsentr Karnegi.

McGlinchey, Eric. 2002. "Paying for Patronage: Regime Change in Post-Soviet Central Asia." Ph.D. diss., Princeton University.

McLennan, John F. 1970 [1865]. *Primitive Marriage: An Inquiry into the Origin of the Form of Capture in Marriage Ceremonies*. Chicago: University of Chicago Press.

McMann, Kelly. 2000. "Symbiotic Transitions: Democratic Development and Economic Independence in Post-Soviet Provinces." Ph.D. diss., University of Michigan.

———. 2002. "The Personal Risks of Party Development." In *Dilemmas of Transition in Post-Soviet Countries*, edited by Joel C. Moses. Chicago: Burnham Inc. Publishers.

Megoran, Nick. 2000. "Remembering Batken: Militarism and Pop Concerts." *Eurasianet*. http://www.eurasianet.org/departments/culture/articles/eav112100.shtml.

Melvin, Neil. 2001. "Patterns of Centre-Regional Relations in Central Asia: The Cases of Kazakhstan, the Kyrgyz Republic, and Uzbekistan." *Journal of Regional and Federal Studies*: 165–93.

Mendelson, Sarah Elizabeth, and John K. Glenn. 2000. *Democracy Assistance and NGO Strategies in Post-Communist Societies*. Washington, D.C.: Carnegie Endowment for International Peace.

Michaels, Paula. 1998. "Kazak Women: Living the Heritage of a Unique Past." In *Women in Muslim Societies: Diversity within Unity*, edited by Herbert L. Bodman and Nayereh Tohidi, 187–202. Boulder, Colo.: Lynne Rienner.

Migdal, Joel S. 1988. *Strong States and Weak Societies: State-Society Relations and State Capabilities in the Third World*. Princeton: Princeton University Press.

———. 1994. "The State in Society: An Approach to Struggles for Domination." In *State Power and Social Forces*, edited by Joel S. Migdal, Atul Kohli, and Vivienne Shue, 7–34. New York: Cambridge University Press.

Migdal, Joel S., Atul Kohli, and Vivienne Shue, eds. 1994. *State Power and Social Forces: Domination and Transformation in the Third World*. New York: Cambridge University Press.

Micklin, Philip P. 1992. "The Aral Crisis: Introduction to the Special Issue." *Post-Soviet Geography* 33: 269–82.

Mitchell, Timothy. 1991. "The Limits of the State: Beyond Statist Approaches and Their Critics." *American Political Science Review* 85: 77–96.

Moaddel, Mansoor. 2001. "Conditions for Ideological Production: The Origins of Islamic Modernism in India, Egypt, and Iran." *Theory and Society* 30: 669–731.

Montinola, Gabriella, Yingyi Qian, and Barry R. Weingast. 1996. "Federalism Chinese Style: The Political Basis for Economic Success." *World Politics* 48, 1: 50–81.

Moser, Keith R. 2002. "Internal 'Stability' versus Democracy in Kazakhstan and Uzbekistan." Paper presented at the U.S. Naval Academy Foreign Affairs Conference, Marquette University.

Najmabadi, Afsaneh. 1998. "Crafting an Educated Housewife in Iran." In *Remaking Women, Feminism and Modernity in the Middle East*, edited by Lila Abu-Lughod, 91–125. Princeton: Princeton University Press.

National Human Development Report. 2000. Tashkent, Uzbekistan: CER. http://www.cer.uz/nhdr/2000/ch-3.htm Accessed 6 January 2002.

Naumkin, Vitaly V. 1994. *Central Asia and Transcaucasia: Ethnicity and Conflict*. Westport, Conn.: Greenwood Press.

"NGOs Face Off with Corporations and Find Potential for Cooperation." 2001. *Give and Take* 3 (winter): 22–27.

Normativnye akty Kyrgyzskoi Respubliki. 1998. Vol. 3 (February): 10–14.

Norris, Era-Dabla, Jorge Martinez-Vasquez, and John Norregaard. 2000. "Making Decentralization Work: The Case of Russia, Ukraine, and Kazakhstan." Paper presented at the Conference on Fiscal Decentralization, IMF Headquarters, Washington, D.C., 20–21 November.

"Nuclear Notebook: Soviet Nuclear Testing, August 29, 1949–October 24, 1990." 1998. *Bulletin of the Atomic Scientists* (May/June): http://www.thebulletin.org/issues/nukenotes/mj98nukenote.html.

O'Neill, Kate. 2000. *Waste Trading among Rich Nations*. Cambridge, Mass.: MIT Press.

Oates, Wallace. 1972. *Fiscal Federalism*. New York: Harcourt Brace Jovanovich.

Odgaard, Karen, and Jens Simonsen. 1999. "The New Kazak Elite." In *Contemporary Kazaks: Cultural and Social Perspectives*, edited by Ingvar Svanberg, 17–45. New York: St. Martin's.

Odom, William, and Robert Dujarric. 1995. *Commonwealth or Empire? Russia, Central, and the Transcaucasus*. Indianapolis: Hudson Institute.

OECD Economic Surveys: The Russian Federation. 1997. Paris: Organization for Economic Cooperation and Development.

OECD Investment Guide for the Kyrgyz Republic. 1998. Paris: Organization for Economic Cooperation and Development.

OECD Economic Surveys: Mexico. 2000a. Paris: Organization for Economic Cooperation and Development.

OECD Economic Surveys: The Russian Federation. 2000b. Paris: Organization for Economic Cooperation and Development. Olcott, Martha Brill. 1987. *The Kazakhs*. Stanford: Hoover Institution Press.

———. 1991. "Women and Society." In *Soviet Central Asia*, edited by William K. Fierman, 235–54. Boulder, Colo.: Westview.

———. 1993. "Central Asia on Its Own." *Journal of Democracy* 4, 1: 92–103.

———. 1994. "Central Asia's Islamic Awakening." *Current History* 93, 582: 150–54.

———. 1996. *Central Asia's New States: Independence, Foreign Policy, and Regional Security*. Washington, D.C.: United States Institute of Peace Press.

———. 2002. *Kazakhstan: Unfulfilled Promise*. Washington, D.C.: Carnegie Endowment for International Peace.

Olds, Hugh W., Jr. April 1997. *Public Opinion in Kyrgyzstan, 1996*. Washington, D.C.: International Foundation for Election Systems.

Olimova, Saodat. 2000. "Islam and the Tajik Conflict." In *Islam and Central Asia*, edited by Roald Sagdeev and Susan Eisenhower. Washington, D.C.: Center for Strategic and Political Studies.

"On Social Associations." 2001. Ecostan. [cited November 1]. http://www/ecostan.org/Laws/kyr/kyrngo.html.

Orloff, Ann. 1993. "Gender and the Social Rights of Citizenship: The Comparative Analysis of State Policies and Gender Relations." *American Sociological Review* 58: 303–28.

Ostrom, Elinor. 1997. "Crossing the Great Divide: Coproduction, Synergy, and Development." In *State-Society Synergy*, edited by Peter B. Evans, 85–118.

Palenom, Konstantin K. 1910. "Otchet po razvitiyu Turkestanskogo kraia, proizvedennoi po vysochaishemu poveleniyu senatorom gofmeisterom grafom." In *Uyezdnoe upravlenie*, edited by K. K. Palenom, Saint Petersburg: Senatskaia tip.

Payne, Matthew J. 2001. "The Forge of the Kazakh Proletariat? The Turksib, Nativization and Industrialization during Stalin's First Five Year Plan." In *A State of Nations Empire and Nation-Making in the Age of Lenin and Stalin*, edited by Ronald Grigor Suny and Terry Martin, 223–52. New York: Oxford University Press.

Peterson, D. J. 1993. *Troubled Lands: The Legacy of Soviet Environmental Destruction*. Boulder, Colo.: Westview.

Poggi, Gianfranco. 1978. *The Development of the Modern State: A Sociological Introduction*. Stanford: Stanford University Press.

Polat, Abdumannob. 1998. "Trying to Understand Uzbekistan's Dilemma." *Central Asia Monitor*: 13–20.

———. 1999. "Can Uzbekistan Build Democracy and Civil Society?" In *Civil Society in Central Asia*, edited by M. Holt Ruffin and Daniel Clarke Waugh, 135–57. Seattle: University of Washington Press.

Polsky, Andrew. 1991. *The Rise of the Therapeutic State*. Princeton: Princeton University Press.

Pomfret, Richard W. T. 1995. *The Economies of Central Asia*. Princeton: Princeton University Press.

———. 1996. *Asian Economies in Transition: Reforming Centrally Planned Economies*. Cheltenham, England: E. Elgar.

Porkhomovskii, Victor Ia. 1994. "Historical Origins of Interethnic Conflicts in Central Asia and Transcaucasia." In *Central Asia and Transcaucasia: Ethnicity and Conflict*, edited by Vitaly V. Naumkin. Westport, Conn.: Greenwood Press.

Princen, Thomas, and Matthias Finger, eds. 1994. *Environmental NGOs in World Politics: Linking the Local and the Global*. New York: Routledge.

Prosser, Sarah. 2000. "Reform within and without the Law: Further Challenges for Central Asian NGOs." *Harvard Asia Quarterly* 4: 4–16.

Pryde, Philip R. 1995. *Environmental Resources and Constraints in the Former Soviet Republics*. Boulder, Colo.: Westview.

Pukhova, Z. P. 1988. "Ayolni uyga qaytarish kerakmi?" *Saodat* 10: 2–9.

Putnam, Robert D., Robert Leonardi, and Raffaella Nanetti. 1993. *Making Democracy Work: Civic Traditions in Modern Italy*. Princeton: Princeton University Press.

Rakowska-Harmstone, Teresa. 1970. *Russia and Nationalism in Central Asia: The Case of Tadzhikistan*. Baltimore: John Hopkins University Press.

———. 1994. "Soviet Legacies." *Central Asian Monitor* 3: 1–23.

Rashid, Ahmed. 1994. *The Resurgence of Central Asia: Islam or Nationalism?* London: Zed Books.

Raustiala, Kal. 1997. "States, NGOs, and International Environmental Institutions." *International Studies Quarterly* 41: 719–40.

Red, T. I., S. P. Tolstov, et. al. 1962. *Narody Srednei Azii i Kazakhstana*. Moscow: Izdatelstvo Akademii nauk SSSR.

Read, Benjamin. 2000. "Revitalizing the State's Urban Nerve Tips." *China Quarterly* 163: 806–20.

Rener, Tanja, and Mirjana Ule. 1998. "Back to the Future: Nationalism and Gender in Post-Socialist States." In *Women, Ethnicity, and Nationalism: The Politics of Transition*, edited by Rick Wilford and Robert L. Miller, 120–32. New York: Routledge.

Report on the Status of Women in Uzbekistan. 1999. New York: Regional Programme in Support to Gender in Development of RBEC/UNDP. http://www.cer.uz/Gender/index-e.hm. Accessed March 1, 2001.

"Republic of Kazakhstan: Selected Issues and Statistical Appendix." 1999. *IMF Country Staff Report no. 99/95*. Washington, D.C.: International Monetary Fund.

Radio Free Europe Central Asia and Caucasus Report, 27 July 2001, 1.

Rigby, T. H. 1978. "The Soviet Regional Leadership: The Brezhnev Generation." *Slavic Review* 37, 1: 1–24.

Risse-Kappen, Thomas, ed. 1995. *Bringing Transnational Relations Back In: Non-State Actors, Domestic Structures, and International Relations*. New York: Cambridge University Press.

Ritzer, George. 1999. *Enchanting a Disenchanted World: Revolutionizing the Means of Consumption*. Thousand Oaks, Calif.: Pine Forge Press.

Ro'i, Yaacov. 2000. *Islam in the Soviet Union: From the Second World War to Gorbachev*. London: Hurst and Company.

Rodden, Jonathon, and Susan Rose-Ackerman. 1997. "Does Federalism Preserve Markets?" *Virginia Law Review* 83: 1521–1615.

Roeder, Philip G. 1991. "Soviet Federalism and Ethnic Mobilization." *World Politics* 43, 2: 196–233.

Roth, Guenther, and Claus Wittich. 1978. *Max Weber: Economy and Society*. Vol. 2. Berkeley: University of California Press.

Roy, Olivier. 2000. *The New Central Asia: The Creation of Nations*. London: I. B. Tauris.

Rubin, Barnett R. 1993. "The Fragmentation of Tajikistan." *Survival* 35, 4: 71–91.

Ruffin, M. Holt, and Daniel Waugh, eds. 1999. *Civil Society in Central Asia*. Seattle: University of Washington Press.

Rumer, Boris. 1989. *Soviet Central Asia: A Tragic Experiment*. Boston: Unwin Hyman.

Rumer, Boris, and Eugene Rumer. 1992. "Who will stop the Next Yugoslavia?" *World Monitor* 5, 11: 37–44.

Rumer, Boris, and Stanislav Zhukov. 1998. *Central Asia: The Challenges of Independence*. Armonk, N.Y.: M. E. Sharpe.

Rumer, Eugene. 1995. "Russia and Central Asia after the Soviet Collapse." In *After Empire: The Emerging Geopolitics of Central Asia*, edited by Jed C. Snyder. Washington, D.C.: National Defense University Press.

Rywkin, Michael. *Russia in Central Asia*. 1963. New York: Collier Books.

———. 1982. *Moscow's Muslim Challenge*. Armonk, N.Y.: M. E. Sharpe.

Saidov, Akmal. 1993. *Mustakillik Komysi*. Tashkent, Uzbekistan.

Sainsbury, Diane. 1999. *Gender and Welfare State Regimes*. Oxford: Oxford University Press.

———, ed. 1996. *Gender, Equality, and Welfare States*. New York: Cambridge University Press.

———, ed. 1994. *Gendering Welfare States*. London: Sage Publications.

Saktanber, Ayşe and Asli Özataş-Baykal. 2000. "Homeland within Homeland: Women and the Formation of Uzbek National Identity." In *Gender and Identity Construction: Women of Central Asia, the Caucasus, and Turkey*, edited by Feride Acar and Ayşe Güneş-Ayata. Leiden: Brill.

Salamon, Lester M. 1995. *Partners in Public Service: Government-Nonprofit Relations in the Modern Welfare State*. Baltimore: Johns Hopkins University Press.

Sampson, Steven. 1996. "The Social Life of Projects." In *Civil Society: Challenging Western Models*, edited by C. M. Hann and Elizabeth Dunn, 121–42. New York: Routledge.

Sanyal, Bishwapriya. 1994. *Cooperative Autonomy: The Dialectic of State-NGOs Relationship in Developing Countries*. Geneva: International Institute for Labour Studies.
Saroyan, Mark. 1997. "Rethinking Islam in the Soviet Union." In *Minorities, Mullahs, and Modernity: Reshaping Community in the Late Soviet Union*, edited by Edward Walker. International and Area Studies Research Series No. 94. Berkeley: University of California Press.
Schatz, Edward. 2000. "Tribes and Clans in Modern Power: The Sta e-led Production of Subethnic Politics in Kazakhstan." Ph.D. diss., University of Wisconsin, Madison.
Schmitter, Philippe C. 1981. "Interest Intermediation and Regime Governability in Contemporary Western Europe and North America." In *Organizing Interests in Western Europe: Pluralism, Corporatism, and the Transformation of Politics*, edited by Suzanne Berger, 285–327. New York: Cambridge University Press.
Schoeberlein, John. 1994. "Conflict in Tajikistan and Central Asia: The Myth of Ethnic Animosity." *Harvard Middle Eastern and Islamic Review* 1, 2: 1–55.
———. 2001. "Cultural Nationalism and State Ideology in Central Asia." Paper presented at the 2001 Olin Critical Issues Lecture Series, Davis Center for Russian Studies, Harvard University.
Scott, James. 1998. *Seeing Like a State: How Certain Schemes to Improve the Human Condition Have Failed*. New Haven: Yale University Press.
Sedaitis, Judith B., and Jim Butterfield, eds. 1991. *Perestroika from Below: Social Movements in the Soviet Union*. Boulder, Colo.: Westview.
Seligman, A. 1992. *The Idea of Civil Society*. New York: Free Press.
Shapiro, Leonard. 1972. *Totalitarianism* New York, NY: Praeger.
Shomonsurova, Rahima. 1998. *Er Eplamoq oson, lekin. . . .* Tashkent: O'zbekiston millii entsiklopediiasi.
Sievers, Eric W. 2000. "How NGOs Abandoned Governance in the Caspian Region." In *The Caspian Sea: A Quest for Environmental Security*, edited by William Ascher and Natalia Mirovitskaya. Dordrecht: Kluwer.
———. 2002. "Uzbekistan's Mahalla: From Soviet to Absolutist Residential Community Associations." *Journal of International and Comparative Law at Chicago-Kent* 2: 91–158.
Silver, Brian D. 1976. "Bilingualism and Maintenance of the Mother Tongue in Soviet Central Asia." *Slavic Review* 35, 3 (fall): 406–24.
Skocpol, Theda. 1985. "Bringing the State Back In: Strategies of Analysis in Current Research." In *Bringing the State Back*, edited by Peter B. Evans, Dietrich Rueschemeyer, and Theda Skocpol. New York: Cambridge University Press.
———. 1992. *Protecting Soldiers and Mothers: The Political Origins of Social Policy in the United States*. Cambridge: Harvard University Press.
Skocpol, Theda, and Morris P. Fiorina. 1999. *Civic Engagement in American Democracy*. Washington, D.C.: Brookings Institution Press.
Skocpol, Theda, Marshall Ganz, and Ziad Munson. 2000. "A Nation of Organizers: The Institutional Origins of Civic Volunteerism in the United States." *American Political Science Review* 94, 3: 527–46.

Slider, Darrell. 1997. "Regional and Local Politics." In *Developments in Russian Politics*, edited by Stephen White, Alex Pravda, and Zvi Gitelman. Durham, N.C.: Duke University Press.

Slezkine, Yuri. 1994. "The USSR as a Communal Apartment, or How a Socialist State Promoted Ethnic Particularism." *Slavic Review* 53, 2: 414–52.

Smith, Graham, Vivien Law, Andrew Wilson, Annette Bohr, and Edward Allworth. 1998. *Nation-Building in the Post-Soviet Borderlands: The Politics of National Identities*. New York: Cambridge University Press.

Solnick, Steven L. 1998. *Stealing the State: Control and Collapse in Soviet Institutions*. Cambridge: Harvard University Press.

———. 1999. "Federalism and State-Building: Post-Communist and Postcolonial Perspectives." Paper presented at Constitutional Design 2000 conference, University of Notre Dame, Notre Dame, Indiana.

Solomon, Susan Gross, Editor. 1983. *Pluralism in the Soviet Union*. London: Macmillan Press.

Spanov, Magbat U. 1999. "Diskussionnyi stol: Naskol'ko effecktivna regional'naya politika v Kazakhstane?" *Sayasat* (August): 9–13.

Sperling, Valerie. 1999. *Organizing Women in Contemporary Russia: Engendering Transition*. New York: Cambridge University Press.

———, ed. 2000. "Introduction: The Domestic and International Obstacles to State-Building in Russia." In *Building the Russian State: Institutional Crisis and the Quest for Democratic Governance*, 1–23. Boulder, Colo.: Westview.

Spoor, Max. 1995. "Agrarian Transition in Former Soviet Central Asia: A Comparative Study of Uzbekistan and Kyrgyzstan." *Journal of Peasant Studies* 23, 1: 46–63.

———. 1997. "Upheaval Along the Silk Route: The Dynamics of Economic Transition in Central Asia." *Journal of International Development* 9, 4: 479–587.

Srednaia Aziia i Kazakhstan: Politicheskii Spektr. 1992. Moscow: PAN.

Stark, David, and László Bruszt. 1998. *Postsocialist Pathways: Transforming Politics and Property in East Central Europe*. New York: Cambridge University Press.

Stavrakis, Peter. 1993. *State-Building in Post-Soviet Russia: The Chicago Boys and the Decline of Administrative Capacity*. Washington, D.C.: Kennan Institute.

Stepan, Alfred C. 1978. *The State and Society: Peru in Comparative Perspective*. Princeton: Princeton University Press.

———. 1988. *Rethinking Military Politics: Brazil and the Southern Cone*. Princeton: Princeton University Press.

Stewart, John Massey, ed. 1992. *The Soviet Environment: Problems, Policies, and Politics*. New York: Cambridge University Press.

Stites, Richard. 1990. *The Women's Liberation Movement in Russia: Feminism, Nihilism, and Bolshevism, 1860–1930*. 1978. Reprint. Princeton: Princeton University Press.

Stoner-Weiss, Kathryn. 1999. "Central Weakness and Provincial Autonomy: Observations on the Devolution Process in Russia." *Post-Soviet Affairs* 15, 1: 87–106.

———. 2001. "W(h)ither the Central State? The Regional Sources of Russia's Stalled Reforms." Unpublished manuscript, Princeton University.

Stross, Brian. 1974. "Tzeltal Marriage by Capture." *Anthropological Quarterly* 47, 3: 328–46.

Suny, Ronald. 1993. *The Revenge of the Past: Nationalism, Revolution, and the Collapse of the Soviet Union*. Stanford: Stanford University Press.

Sydykova, Zamira. 1997. *Za kulisami demokratii po-kirgizskii*. Bishkek, Kyrgyzstan.

Tadjbakhsh, Shahrbanou. 1998. "Between Lenin and Allah: Women and Ideology in Tajikistan." In *Women in Muslim Societies: Diversity within Unity*, edited by Herbert L. Bodman and Nayereh Tohidi, 163–85. Boulder: Lynne Reiner.

Taizhanov, G. E. 1995. *Kazakhi: Istorikho-etnograficheskoe issledovanie*. Almaty, Kazakhstan: Kazakhstan Publishers.

Takahashi, Mutsuko, and Raija Hashimoto. 1997. "*Minsei i'in* — between Public and Private: A Local Network for Community Care in Japan." *International Social Work* 40: 303–13.

Tanzi, Vito. 1995. "Fiscal Federalism and Decentralization: A Review of Some Efficiency and Macroeconomic Aspects." Annual World Bank Conference on Development Economics.

Tarrow, Sidney G. 1994. *Power in Movement: Social Movements, Collective Action, and Politics*. New York: Cambridge University Press.

Tatimov, Makash. 1993. "Qanshamiz qazaqsha bilmeimiz?" *Ana tili* (15 March).

Tett, Gillian. 1994. "'Guardians of the Faith?': Gender and Religion in an (ex)Soviet Tajik Village." In *Muslim Women's Choices: Religious Belief and Social Reality*, edited by Camillia Fawzi El-Solh and Judy Mabro, 128–51. Oxford: Berg Publishers.

Tilly, Charles. 1993. "Contentious Repertoires in Great Britain, 1758–1843." *Social Science History* 17: 253–80.

Tishkov, Valery. 1995. "'Don't Kill Me, I'm a Kyrgyz!' Anthropological Analysis of Violence in the Osh Ethnic Conflict." *Journal of Peace Research* 32, 2: 133–49.

———. 1997. *Ethnicity, Nationalism, and Conflict in and after the Soviet Union: The Mind Aflame*. London: Sage Publications.

Tohidi, Nayereh. 1998. "Guardians of the Nation: Women, Islam, and the Soviet Legacy of Modernization in Azerbaijan." In *Women in Muslim Societies: Diversity within Unity*, edited by Herbert L. Bodman and Nayereh Tohidi, 137–61. Boulder, Colo.: Lynne Reiner.

———. 2001. "Gender, Citizenship, and Rights in the Muslim Republics of the Former Soviet Union." Paper presented at the Kennan Institute Workshop on The Role of Women in Post-Communist Societies, Washington, D.C., 1–3 November.

Tokhtakhodjaeva, Marfua. 1992. *Between the Slogans of Communism and the Laws of Islam*. Translated by Sufian Alsam. Lahore, Pakistan: Shirkat Gah Women's Resource Centre.

———. "Traditional Stereotypes and Women's Problems over the Period of Transition." http://www.undp.uz/GID/eng/UZBEKISTAN/NGO/uzneg_res.html. Accessed 5 March 2001.

Treisman, Daniel S. 1997. "Russia's Ethnic Revival: The Separatist Activism of Regional Leaders in a Post-communist Order." *World Politics* 49, 2 (January): 212–49.

———. 1999. "Russia's Tax Crisis: Explaining Falling Revenues in a Transitional Economy." *Economic and Politics* 11, 2: 145–69.

———. 2000. "The Causes of Corruption." *Journal of Public Economics* 76: 399–457.

Trivedi, Harish. 2002. "The 'Postcolonial' and 'South Asia': A Confusion of Categories?" Public Lecture at School of Oriental and African Studies (SOAS), University of London, April 25, 2002.

Tursunov, Khabib. 1962. *Vosstanie 1916 goda v Srednei Azii I Kazakhstane*. Gos.izdatelstvo Uzbekskoi SSR.

United Nations Development Program. 1998. *Final Report of the Evaluation Mission. Aral Sea Basin Capacity Development Project (Phase II)*. REF/98/005/B/01/31.

———. 2001. "Capacity Assessment of the NGO Sector in Kyrgyzstan, 2001." United Nations Development Program in Kyrgyzstan. http://www/undp.kg/english/publications/ngo/.

United States Energy Information Administration (USEIA). Caspian Sea Region. July 2001. http://www.eia.doe.gov/emeu/cabs/caspian.html.

Van de Walle, Nicolas. 2001. *African Economies and the Politics of Permanent Crisis, 1979–1999*. New York: Cambridge University Press.

VanDeveer, Stacy D. 2000. "Protecting Europe's Seas: Lessons from the Last Twenty-five Years." *Environment* 42 (July/August): 10–26.

VanDeveer, Stacy D., and Geoff Dabelko. 2001. "It's Capacity, Stupid: International Assistance and National Implementation." *Global Environmental Politics* 1, 2: 18–28.

Volkov, Vadim. 1999. "Violent Entrepreneurship in Post-Communist Russia." *Europe-Asia Studies* 51, 5: 741–54.

Waite, Mark. 1997. "The Role of the Voluntary Sector in Supporting Living Standards in Central Asia." In *Household Welfare in Central Asia*, edited by Jane Falkingham, Jeni Klugman, and Sheila Marnie, 221–36. London: Macmillan.

Waldner, David. 1999. *State Building and Late Development*. Ithaca: Cornell University Press.

Wallerstein, Immanuel. 1974. *The Modern World-System*. New York: Academic Press.

Wapner, Paul. 1995. "Politics beyond the State: Environmental Activism and World Civic Politics." *World Politics* 47: 311–40.

Watters, Kate. 1999. "Environmental NGOs and the Development of Civil Society in Central Asia." In *Civil Society in Central Asia*, edited by M. Holt Ruffin and Daniel Clarke Waugh, 85–108. Seattle: University of Washington Press.

———. 2000. "Environment and the Development of Civil Society in the Caspian Region: The Role of NGOs." In *The Caspian Sea: A Quest for Environmental Security* edited by William Ascher and Natalia Mirovitskaya. Dordrecht: Kluwer.

Way, Lucan. 2000. "Weak States and the Pitfalls of Decentralization: Subnational Revenues in Post-Soviet Ukraine." Paper presented at the annual meeting of the American Political Science Association, Washington, D.C., 31 August–3 September.

———. 2001. "Weak Formal Institutions and Reform: The Case of Post-Soviet Fiscal Decentralization." Unpublished manuscript, Harvard University.

Weatherford, Jack. 2000. "Blood on the Steppes: Ethnicity, Power, and Conflict." In *Conformity and Conflict: Readings in Cultural Anthropology, edited by* James Spradley and David W. McCurdy. 10th ed. Boston: Allyn and Bacon.

Weber, Eugen. 1976. *Peasants into Frenchmen: The Modernization of Rural France.* Stanford: Stanford University Press.

Weber, Max. 1953. *From Max Weber: Essays in Sociology*. Edited by H. H. Gerth and C. Wright Mills. New York: Oxford University Press.

Wedel, Janine R. 1998. *Collision and Collusion: The Strange Case of Western Aid to Eastern Europe, 1989–1998*. New York: St. Martin's.

Weiner, Douglas R. 1988. "The Changing Face of Soviet Conservation." In *The Ends of the Earth: Perspectives on Modern Environmental History*, edited by Donald Worster. New York: Cambridge University Press.

Weingast, Barry R. 1993. "Constitutions as Governance Structures: The Political Foundations of Secure Markets." *Journal of Institutional and Theoretical Economics* 149, 1: 286–311.

———. 1995. "The Economic Role of Political Institutions: Market-Preserving Federalism and Economic Development." *Journal of Law, Economics, and Organization* 11, 1: 1–29.

Weinthal, Erika. 2001. "Sins of Omission: Constructing Negotiating Sets in the Aral Sea Basin." *Journal of Environment and Development* 10, 1: 50–79.

———. 2002. *State-Making and Environmental Cooperation: Linking Domestic Politics and International Politics in Central Asia*. Cambridge: MIT Press.

Weinthal, Erika, and Pauline Jones Luong. 2000. "Weak State in Formation?: Energy Wealth and Tax Reform in Kazakhstan." Paper presented at the annual meeting of the American Political Science Association, Washington, D.C.

———. 2002. "Energy Wealth and Tax Reform in Russia and Kazakhstan." *Resources Policy* 27, 4 (September): 1–9.

Werner, Cynthia. 1997. "Marriage, Markets, and Merchants: Changes in Wedding Feasts and Household Consumption Patterns in Rural Kazakstan." *Culture and Agriculture* 1, 2: 6–13.

———. 1999. "The Dynamics of Feasting and Gift Exchange in Rural Kazakstan." In *Contemporary Kazaks: Cultural and Social Perspectives*, edited by Ingvar Svanberg, 47–72. London: Curzon Press.

———. 2000a. "Consuming Modernity, Imagining Tradition: Transnational Processes, National Identity Formation, and Wedding Feasts in Post-Soviet Kazakhstan." *Anthropology of East Europe Review: Central Europe, Eastern Europe, and Eurasia* 18, 2: 125–34.

———. 2000b. "Gifts, Bribes, and Development in Post-Soviet Kazakhstan." *Human Organization* 59, 1: 11–22.

———. 2001. "Feminizing the New Silk Road: Women Traders in Rural Kazakhstan." Paper presented at the Kennan Institute Workshop on The Role of Women in Post-Communist Transitions, Washington, D.C., Nov. 1–3.

Wood, Elizabeth. 1997. *The Baba and the Comrade: Gender and Politics in Revolutionary Russia*. Bloomington: Indiana University Press.

Woodruff, David. 1999. *Money Unmade: Barter and the Fate of Russian Capitalism*. Ithaca: Cornell University Press.

World Bank. 1993. *Kazakhstan: Transition to a Market Economy*. Washington, D.C.

———. 1993. *Uzbekistan: An Agenda for Economic Reform*. Washington, D.C.

———. 1998. Aral Sea Basin Program — Water and Environmental Management Project. Project Document. Volume 1 — Main Report. Report No. 17587-UZ. May.

———. 2001 World Development Indicators. On CD-ROM.

———. "Average Nominal Salary (Soms)." 2001. Kyrgyzstan Development Gateway. [accessed November 1]. http://wbweb13.worldbank.org/kyrgyz/en/economy/average_nominal_salary.

———Minimal Consumer Budget (Soms). 2001. Kyrgyzstan Development Gateway, 2001 (accessed November 1). http://wbweb13.worldbank.org/kyrgyz/en/economy/minimal_consumer_budget.htm.

World Bank, United Nations Development Program, United Nations Environmental Program. 1994. Aral Sea Program — Phase 1, Briefing Paper for the Proposed Donors Meeting to be Held on June 23–24, 1994 in Paris. May.

Xolmatova, M. 1999. "Gender muammosi va uni O'zbekiston hal etishning o'ziga xosligi." In *O'zbekistonda oila, davlat va jamiyat qurilishida ayollarning roli va gender muammolari*, edited by Dilarom Alimova, 23–28. Tashkent, Uzbekistan: Fan Nashriyoti. *Zakon Respubliki Kazakhstan "O brake i sem'ye."* 1999. Almaty: Ayan Adet Publishers.

"Zakon o mestnom upravleniye Respublika Uzbekistan." 1995. *Novye Zakony Uzbekistana*. Tashkent: Adolat.

Zaslavsky, Victor. 1992. "The Evolution of Separatism in Soviet Society under Gorbachev." In *From Union to Commonwealth: Nationalism and Separatism in the Soviet Republics*, edited by Gail Lapidus, Victor Zaslavsky, and Philip Goldman. New York: Cambridge University Press.

Zhenshchiny Tsentral'noi Azii, Sbornik Statei No. 8. 2001. Tashkent, Uzbekistan: Tashkentskii Zhenskii Resursnyi Tsentr.

Zhuravskaya, Ekaterina V. 2000. "Incentives to Provide Local Public Goods: Fiscal Federalism Russian Style." *Journal of Public Economics* 76: 337–68.

Zhurzhenko, Tatiana. 2001. "Women and Reproduction in Post-Soviet Ukraine: Nationalism, State-Building and Family Politics." Paper presented at the Kennan Institute Workshop on the Role of Women in Post-Communist Transitions. Washington, D.C., 1–3 November.

Contributors

LAURA ADAMS
is a postdoctoral fellow at Georgetown University's Center for Eurasian, Russian and East European Studies.

BHAVNA DAVE
is a lecturer in the Department of Political Studies, School of Oriental and African Studies, University of London.

ALISHER ILKHAMOV
is the executive director of the Open Society Institute Assistance Foundation — Uzbekistan.

PAULINE JONES LUONG
is an assistant professor in the Department of Political Science at Yale University.

MARIANNE KAMP
is an assistant professor in the Department of History at the University of Wyoming.

KELLY M. MCMANN
is an assistant professor of political science at Case Western Reserve University.

ERIKA WEINTHAL
is an assistant professor of political science at Tel Aviv University.

CYNTHIA WERNER
is an assistant professor in the Department of Anthropology at Texas A&M University.

Index